If you are looking for a comprehensive, accessible and thought-provoking overview of current research trends in political violence, this is the book to turn to.

Nils Weidmann, Professor of Political Science, University of Konstanz (Germany)

Peace and Conflict 2016, as with its predecessors, proves to be an invaluable source of up-to-date information on conflicts around the world. Various facets of political violence and their respective recent trends are documented in detail. New trends and challenges in conflict research are admirably discussed, as are traditional and more recent attempts in mitigating conflicts, from peacekeeping missions to criminal justice. Combining chapters on these themes written by the leading scholars in the field makes this volume a must-have for scholars and practitioners alike.

Simon Hug, Professor of Political Science, University of Geneva (Switzerland)

Peace and Conflict 2016

Edited by David A. Backer, Ravi Bhavnani and Paul K. Huth

CIDCM
CENTER FOR INTERNATIONAL
DEVELOPMENT & CONFLICT MANAGEMENT

THE
GRADUATE
INSTITUTE
GENEVA

INSTITUT DE HAUTES
ÉTUDES INTERNATIONALES
ET DU DÉVELOPPEMENT

GRADUATE INSTITUTE
OF INTERNATIONAL AND
DEVELOPMENT STUDIES

Routledge
Taylor & Francis Group

NEW YORK AND LONDON

First published 2016
by Routledge
711 Third Avenue, New York, NY 10017

and by Routledge
2 Park Square, Milton Park, Abingdon, Oxon OX14 4RN

Routledge is an imprint of the Taylor & Francis Group, an informa business

British Library Cataloguing in Publication Data
A catalogue record for this book is available from the British Library

Library of Congress Cataloging in Publication Data
A catalog record for this book has been requested

ISBN: 978-1-857-43829-1 (hbk)
ISBN: 978-1-857-43843-7 (pbk)
ISBN: 978-1-315-62561-4 (ebk)

Typeset in Bembo
by Taylor & Francis Books
Printed in Great Britain by
Ashford Colour Press Ltd, Gosport, Hants

 Terms

 Important / Names

 Research

Contents

Contents

List of Illustrations

Figures

Tables

Boxes

List of Contributors

David A. Backer is an Associate Research Professor and Assistant Director of the Center for International Development and Conflict Management, as well as Director of the Minor in International Development and Conflict Management, at the University of Maryland. His research focuses on conflict dynamics and post-conflict processes. He is Co-Director of the West Africa Transitional Justice Project and the Constituency-Level Elections Archive.

Ravi Bhavnani is a Professor and Head of the Department of Political Science and International Relations at the Graduate Institute of International and Development Studies (Switzerland). His research explores the micro-foundations of violence, examining the endogenous relationships among the characteristics, beliefs, and interests of relevant actors, as well as social mechanisms and emergent structures that shape attitudes, decision making, and behavior. He has published articles in the *American Journal of Political Science, Journal of Politics, Journal of Conflict Resolution* and *Comparative Politics*. He received his PhD from the University of Michigan.

Paul K. Huth is a Professor of Government and Politics at the University of Maryland and Director of the Center for International Development and Conflict Management. He is also editor of the *Journal of Conflict Resolution*. He has published books and widely in journals on subjects related to the study of international conflict and war, including deterrence behavior, crisis decision making, territorial disputes, the democratic peace, international law and dispute resolution, and the civilian consequences of war.

Caroline Bergeron is the Partnerships Associate at AidData and a mediator, certified by the Commonwealth of Virginia. Her academic interests include conflict analysis, conflict resolution methods, conflict prevention, negotiation and transitional justice in the international system. She holds a BA in Psychology from the University of Virginia.

Nils-Christian Bormann is a Lecturer at the University of Exeter. Research interests include ethnic coalitions, horizontal inequality, and civil wars. His work has been published with or is forthcoming in the *Journal of Conflict Resolution*, the *Journal of Peace Research*, and *Electoral Studies*. He received his PhD from ETH Zürich in 2014.

Tilman Brück is Professor and Team Leader – Development Economics at IGZ – Leibniz Institute for Vegetable and Horticultural Crops near Berlin. He is also the Founder and Director of the ISDC – International Security and Development Center in Berlin, Visiting Professor at the London School of Economics and Political Science (LSE), and the Co-Founder and Co-Director of the Households in Conflict Network (HiCN), a global research network. His research interests focus on the economics of household behavior and well-being in conflict-affected and fragile economies, including the measurement of violence and conflict in household surveys and the impact evaluation of peace-building programs in conflict-affected areas and of humanitarian assistance. He studied economics at Glasgow University and Oxford University and obtained his PhD in economics from Oxford University.

Halvard Buhaug is Research Professor at the Peace Research Institute Oslo (PRIO); Professor of Political Science at the Norwegian University of Science and Technology (NTNU); and Associate Editor of the *Journal of Peace Research* and *Political Geography*. He leads and has directed research projects on security dimensions of climate change and geographic aspects of armed conflict. Recent publications include the co-authored *Inequality, Grievances, and Civil War* (Cambridge University Press, 2013) and journal articles in *Global Environmental Change, International Security, Journal of Conflict Resolution, Political Geography*, and *PNAS*.

Lars-Erik Cederman is Professor of International Conflict Research, ETH Zürich. His interests include nationalism, ethnic conflict, democratization, and state formation. He is the (co-)author of *Emergent Actors in World Politics: How States Develop and Dissolve* (Princeton University Press, 1997), *Inequality, Grievances and Civil War* (Cambridge University Press, 2013), and recent articles in the *American Political Science Review, International Organization, Journal of Conflict Resolution, Journal of Peace Research*, and *World Politics*.

Deniz Cil is a PhD candidate in Government and Politics at the University of Maryland and a Research Assistant for the Aiding Resilience Project, funded by the Minerva Initiative of the US Department of Defense, studying the effect of foreign aid on different phases of civil conflict. Her main research focuses on the implementation of peace agreements following civil wars, and explores variation in the degree of implementation and the factors that incentivize parties to continue implementation. She also works on peace process outcomes, peace duration, and civilian organization in wartime.

David E. Cunningham is an Associate Professor in the Department of Government and Politics at the University of Maryland and a Research Associate at the Peace Research Institute Oslo. His research focuses on civil war, conflict bargaining, conflict management and international security. He is the author of *Barriers to Peace in Civil Wars* (Cambridge University Press, 2011), as well as articles in the *American Journal of Political Science*, the *British Journal of Political Science, International Organization*, and the *Journal of Conflict Resolution*.

Karsten Donnay is a Postdoctoral Researcher at the Graduate Institute of International and Development Studies, Geneva. His research uses detailed, disaggregated data on empirical violence and a range of statistical and computational modeling techniques to study micro-level conflict processes. Focusing mainly on asymmetric intrastate conflict, he has worked on the Israeli-Palestinian conflict – Jerusalem in particular – and the conflict in Iraq.

Laura Dugan is a Professor in the Department of Criminology and Criminal Justice at the University of Maryland. She is a Co-Principal Investigator for the Global Terrorism Database (GTD) and the Government Actions in Terrorist Environments (GATE) dataset. Her research examines the consequences of violence and the efficacy of violence prevention/intervention policy and practice. She received an MS/PhD in Public Policy and Management and an MS in Statistics from Carnegie Mellon University.

Hanne Fjelde is an Associate Professor at the Department of Peace and Conflict Research at Uppsala University. Her research focuses on the relationship between political institutions and organized violence, civil war dynamics, and violence against civilians. Her recent publications include articles in *Journal of Conflict Resolution, Journal of Peace Research, British Journal of Political Science*, and *Political Geography*.

Aude-Emmanuelle Fleurant is Director of the Arms and Military Expenditure (AMEX) Programme at the Stockholm International Peace Research Institute (SIPRI) in Sweden. Before joining SIPRI in 2014, she directed the Arms and Defense Economics research group at Paris-based Military Academy Strategic Research Institute. Previously, she headed the market intelligence brand on defense and security issues for Technopole Défense & Sécurité. She has authored several articles on the arms industry and military expenditure and taught undergraduate and graduate classes in international relations and global defense political economy. She received her PhD in Political Science from the Université du Québec à Montréal.

Mark Gibney is the Carol Belk Distinguished Professor at the University of North Carolina-Asheville and the inaugural Raoul Wallenberg Visiting Chair at the Faculty of Law at Lund University (Sweden) and the Raoul Wallenberg Institute. Recent book projects include *International Human Rights Law: Returning to Universal Principles* (2015); *The SAGE Handbook of Human Rights* (2014); *Litigating Transnational Human Rights Obligations* (2014); and *Watching Human Rights: The 101 Best Films* (2013).

Kristian Skrede Gleditsch is Professor in the Department of Government at the University of Essex and a Research Associate at the Peace Research Institute Oslo (PRIO). His research interests include conflict and cooperation, democratization, and spatial dimensions of social and political processes. Recent publications include *Inequality, Grievances, and Civil War* (Cambridge University Press, 2013, with Lars-Erik Cederman and Halvard Buhaug) and articles in the *American Political Science Review, International Organization, International Studies Quarterly, Journal of Peace Research*, and *World Politics*.

Peter Haschke is an Assistant Professor of Political Science at the University of North Carolina–Asheville and a principal investigator with the Political Terror Scale project. His current research explores mechanisms of state perpetrated violence in democracies. He teaches courses in comparative politics, electoral systems, conflict, violence, and human rights, as well as political methodology. He received his PhD from the University of Rochester.

Lisa Hultman is an Associate Professor at the Department of Peace and Conflict Research at Uppsala University. Her research focuses in particular on the protection of civilians by international actors and her broader interests include topics related to peacekeeping and violence against civilians. Her recent publications include articles in *American Political Science Review*, *American Journal of Political Science*, *Journal of Conflict Resolution*, and *Journal of Peace Research*.

Madhav Joshi is a Research Assistant Professor and Associate Director of the Peace Accords Matrix Project at the Joan B. Kroc Institute for International Peace Studies at the University of Notre Dame. His current research explores peace processes, peace agreement design and implementation in civil wars, quality peace, and the Maoist insurgency in Nepal. He has published articles in journals such as the *British Journal of Political Science*, *Journal of Peace Research*, *Journal of Conflict Resolution*, *International Studies Quarterly*, and *Social Science Quarterly*. He received his PhD from University of North Texas.

Patricia Justino is a Professional Fellow at the Institute of Development Studies (UK), where she directs the Conflict and Violence cluster. She is co-founder and co-director of the Households in Conflict Network (www.hicn.org) and was the Director of MICROCON (www.microconflict.eu). She is a development economist specializing in applied microeconomics. Her current research work focuses on the impact of violence and conflict on household welfare and local institutional structures, the microfoundations of violent conflict and the implications of violence for economic development.

Roudabeh Kishi is a Post-Doctoral Fellow at the University of Sussex, affiliated with the Armed Conflict Location and Event Data project as well as the Geographies of Political Violence Across African States project. In addition, she is currently a Visiting Researcher at the Robert S. Strauss Center for International Security and Law at the University of Texas at Austin. She is also an associated researcher with the Aiding Resilience project at the University of Maryland. Her work focuses on conflict patterns in Africa and the impact of foreign aid on conflict dynamics.

Anupma L. Kulkarni is a Fellow at the Stanford Center for International Conflict and Negotiation. Her research focuses on the impact of truth commissions, international and national war crimes prosecutions, and reconciliation policies in Africa. She co-directs the West African Transitional Justice Project and the Liberia Reconciliation Barometer Initiative. She is currently working on two book projects: *The Arc of Transitional Justice: Violent Conflict, Its Victims & Redress in Ghana, Liberia, Nigeria and Sierra Leone* (with David Backer) and *Demons and Demos: Truth, Accountability and Democracy in Post-Apartheid South Africa*. She received her PhD in Political Science from Stanford University.

Gary LaFree is Director of the National Consortium for the Study of Terrorism and Responses to Terrorism (START) and a Distinguished Scholar and Professor of Criminology and Criminal Justice at the University of Maryland. He is currently a Fellow of the American Society of Criminology (ASC) and a member of the National Academy of Science's Crime, Law and Justice Committee. He has served as President of the ASC and of the ASC's Division on International Criminology. Much of his ongoing research is on the causes and consequences of violent crime and terrorism.

Andrew M. Linke is a faculty member in the Department of Geography at the University of Utah. His research investigates violent conflict, political geography, and the effects of environmental change in Kenya using GIS and spatial analysis, large population surveys, and qualitative fieldwork. His recent articles have been published in *Global Environmental Change*, *Political Geography*, *International Interactions*, *International Studies Review*, and other peer-reviewed academic journals. He completed his PhD in Geography at the University of Colorado Boulder in 2013.

Bradley Parks is the Co-Executive Director of AidData and Research Faculty at the College of William and Mary's Institute for the Theory and Practice of International Relations. His research is focused on aid allocation and impact, development policy and practice, and the design and implementation of policy and institutional reforms in low income and lower-middle income countries. His publications include *Greening Aid? Understanding the Environmental Impact of Development Assistance* (Oxford University Press) and *A Climate of Injustice: Global Inequality, North-South Politics, and Climate Policy* (MIT Press). Brad holds a PhD in International Relations and an M Sc in Development Management from the London School of Economics and Political Science.

Yannick Quéau is executive director of OSINTPOL, a think tank based in Paris. He is a senior researcher on armaments, his fields of interest covering conventional arms production, acquisition processes, transfers and control and nuclear deterrence. He is an associate researcher with the Research and Information Group on Peace and Security (Groupe de recherche et d'information sur la paix et la sécurité – GRIP) based in Brussels. Previously, he taught international relations, defense policies and military history at the Canadian Defence Academy. He holds diplomas from the University of Québec in Montréal (Canada) and the University of Bradford (UK).

Jason Michael Quinn (PhD, Comparative Politics, North Texas, 2010) is a Research Assistant Professor at the Kroc Institute for International Peace Studies at the University of Notre Dame. Quinn is a researcher for the Peace Accords Matrix Project and his research and teaching centers on civil conflict management, peace agreement implementation, and the duration of peace after civil wars. He has published research on these topics in the *British Journal of Political Science*, *Journal of Conflict Resolution*, *Journal of Peace Research*, *Negotiation Journal*, *Defense and Peace Economics*, *International Studies Perspectives* and *International Interactions*.

Clionadh Raleigh is a Professor of Political Geography and Conflict at the University of Sussex. She is the creator and Director of the Armed Conflict Location and Event Dataset project, an affiliate of the International Peace Research Institute in Oslo (PRIO), and an associated researcher with the Minerva CCAPS project at the University of Texas. Her work focuses on African conflict patterns, the social and political consequences of climate change, and the political geography of developing states. She currently manages a European Research Council project on "Conflict Landscapes and Life Cycles," which tracks, models, and predicts local political violence patterns across Africa.

Idean Salehyan is an Associate Professor of Political Science at the University of Texas – Dallas and Co-Director of the Social Conflict Analysis Database. His research interests include civil and international conflict, refugee migration, and environmental security. He is the author of *Rebels without Borders: Transnational Insurgencies in World Politics* (Cornell University Press, 2009) and his articles appear in journals such as the *American Journal of Political Science*, *World Politics*, and *International Organization*. He received his PhD from the University of California, San Diego.

Margareta Sollenberg is an Assistant Professor at the Department of Peace and Conflict Research at Uppsala University. Her research has focused on the relationship between foreign aid and armed conflict and various topics relating to conflict data collection. She has been involved in the Uppsala Conflict Data Program (UCDP) for the past two decades and has published on UCDP data in the *Journal of Peace Research* and *SIPRI Yearbook* among a range of venues.

Håvard Strand is an Associate Professor of Political Science at the University of Oslo and Senior Researcher at the Peace Research Institute Oslo (PRIO). His research topics include the relationship between political institutions and armed conflict, conceptual problems in the study of armed conflict, and consequences of civil wars. His research is published in the *American Journal of Political Science*, *Journal of Conflict Resolution*, *Journal of Peace Research*, *Journal of Development Studies*, *Security Dialogue*, and *World Development*.

Michael J. Tierney is the George and Mary Hylton Professor of Government and the Director of the Institute for the Theory and Practice of International Relations at the College of William and Mary. He teaches courses on international relations, international development, and international organizations. Dr. Tierney has published two books and over 25 journal articles. His current research focuses on public support for the use of military force, subnational effects of development finance, the rise of new donors, such as China, Russia, and Brazil, and the conditions under which research in international relations shapes the real world of international relations. He completed his PhD from the University of California at San Diego.

Philip Verwimp holds the Marie and Alain Philippson Chair in Sustainable Human Development at the Solvay Brussels School of Economics and Management, Université Libre de Bruxelles, where he is also a fellow of ECARES. He specializes in studying economic causes and consequences of conflict at the micro level. He is currently engaged in longitudinal studies of health, schooling and nutrition in Burundi, where he is the lead researcher in a partnership between his university and UNICEF-Burundi, involving impact evaluation. He has also done quantitative work on the death toll of the genocide and on the demography of post-genocide Rwanda. He obtained his PhD in Economics from the University of Leuven.

Manuel Vogt is a visiting post-doctoral research associate at Princeton University (2015–2016). He is the executive manager of the *Ethnic Power Relations* (EPR) Core dataset. His research interests include ethnic conflict, mobilization, and inequality in multi-ethnic societies, (post-conflict) democratization, and Latin American and African politics. He has conducted field research in Ecuador, Gabon, Guatemala, and Ivory Coast. His academic publications have appeared or are forthcoming in the *Journal of Conflict Resolution* and *Latin American Politics and Society*. He received his PhD from ETH Zürich.

Reed M. Wood is an Assistant Professor of Political Science at Arizona State University. He is also co-manager of the Political Terror Scale (PTS), an index of state violations of physical integrity rights. Among his areas of specialization are human rights, state repression, civil conflict, and conflict management. His current research focuses primarily on the dynamics of violence during internal armed conflict, including female recruitment into insurgent movements and their roles within these groups. He received his PhD from the University of North Carolina-Chapel Hill.

Introduction to
Peace and Conflict 2016

David A. Backer, Ravi Bhavnani and Paul K. Huth

The Center for International Development and Conflict Management (CIDCM) at the University of Maryland has produced *Peace and Conflict* since 2001. To date, seven editions have been released – the most recent in 2014 – on a biennial cycle. The current edition, *Peace and Conflict 2016*, marks a number of major, exciting changes designed to invigorate this already well-established publication.

CIDCM has initiated a new partnership with the Graduate Institute of International and Development Studies in Geneva, Switzerland, to produce *Peace and Conflict*. This partnership links two significant hubs of high-quality, policy-relevant research on contemporary issues of importance to the international community. Production of *Peace and Conflict* will be bolstered by the capable assistance of the staff of the Graduate Institute's Publication Services. In conjunction, Ravi Bhavnani – head of the Graduate Institute's Department of International Relations/Political Science – has joined the editorial team. He replaces Jonathan Wilkenfeld, who was involved with *Peace and Conflict* since the 2008 edition.

Also, *Peace and Conflict* has shifted to a new publisher. Paradigm Publishers was responsible for the past four editions. Routledge – with which Paradigm Publishers merged in early 2015 – has now assumed this role. Recognized worldwide as one of the top outlets of research on international relations, Routledge affords services and support that will enhance the accessibility and depth of *Peace and Conflict*. For the first time, the book will be made available in an ebook format; in fact, Routledge has committed to the digital release of the back catalog, acquired via the merger of Paradigm Publishers. In addition, *Peace and Conflict* will capitalize on Routledge's more extensive global marketing reach and online presence to engage with a wider, larger readership.

Our pending plans include the launch of a companion website that we envision will be populated with fresh, complementary material alongside and in the interim between the releases of each edition. In particular, regular and invited contributors will author short analytical posts that illuminate current events. This online material will maintain the defining features of *Peace and Conflict*, including a broad comparative perspective on patterns, trends and relationships, rigorous scholarship using cutting-edge data and methods, and the distillation of key insights in ways that are comprehensible to diverse audiences, capitalizing on tools of data visualization. Looking ahead, *Peace and Conflict* will move to an annual schedule of publication, to keep more current with ongoing developments in ways that enhance the value, especially to those who rely on the material in regular cycles of planning, teaching, research, and reporting.

Finally, *Peace and Conflict 2016* exhibits considerable expansion in content, with many new contributors covering topics not addressed in previous editions. A total of 16 substantive chapters are organized into three sections, a framework that is expected to be maintained for future editions. The first section, "Global Patterns and Trends" (Chapters 2–13), examines core topics that are likely to appear in each edition. The range of topics has grown in comparison to *Peace and Conflict 2014*. The second section, "Special Feature" (Chapter 14), spotlights novel research related to a select topic, which will vary from edition to edition. The third section, "Profiles" (Chapters 15–17), has been enlarged to survey developments in instances of civil wars, peacekeeping missions, and international criminal justice proceedings that were active around the world during 2014. The remainder of this introduction offers an overview of the individual chapters, highlighting the new additions.

In Chapter 2, Karsten Donnay and Ravi Bhavnani give a thorough review and assessment of recent advances in scholarly research on various aspects of conflict and peace. They focus on important developments in available datasets and analytic methods, as well as findings that address enduring theoretical debates in the field.

In Chapter 3, Håvard Strand and Halvard Buhaug analyze patterns in international and intrastate armed conflict from 1946–2014 (taking over a topic covered by David Backer and Paul Huth in *Peace and Conflict 2014*). Their analysis relies on information compiled by the Uppsala Conflict Data Program (UCDP). One of their main observations is that 2014 was unusually violent relative to trends during the preceding decade.

Chapter 4 is a new contribution by Roudabeh Kishi, Clionadh Raleigh, and Andrew Linke, which exemplifies the evolution in research toward the disaggregation of conflict, engaging the dimension of geography. Drawing on an emergent information resource, the Armed Conflict Location and Event Data (ACLED) Project, the authors summarize the trends in armed conflict across Africa from 1997–2014, accompanied by plentiful maps. They report a steady increase in conflict events since 2011. A notable aspect of their analysis is the presentation of micromorts, which gauge the relative risk of fatalities from political conflict averaged over the populations of individual countries.

Chapter 5 is another new contribution by Hanne Fjelde, Lisa Hultman, and Margareta Sollenberg, which spotlights global trends in armed attacks against civilian populations by government and rebel armed forces from 1989–2013. Their analysis also relies on information compiled by UCDP. They show that the number of civilians killed annually has declined since peaking in 1996 and that one-sided violence is consistently concentrated in Africa.

Continuing the new contributions, Chapter 6, by David Cunningham, Kristian Gleditsch, and Idean Salehyan, examines non-state actors operating in intrastate armed conflicts. Their analysis relies on the latest update of a dataset they have compiled. The authors point out that although the number of civil wars has declined recently, the wars are increasingly becoming more complex, involving multiple rebel groups and greater external military and economic support channeled to governments.

In Chapter 7, Manuel Vogt, Nils-Christian Bormann, and Lars-Erik Cederman review global patterns in ethnic exclusion and discrimination from 1946–2013, based on the Ethnic Power Relations family of datasets. They train specific attention on the continuing high levels of ethnic exclusion in the Middle East and Northern Africa in the wake of the Arab Spring.

In Chapter 8, Gary LaFree and Laura Dugan employ the Global Terrorism Database (GTD) to analyze more than 125,000 terrorist attacks around the world from 1970–2013. One of the patterns they examine is the surge in activity by violent Islamic extremist groups, since 9/11, which helps explain the global upsurge in terrorist events since 2011, reaching unprecedented levels.

Chapter 9 is a new contribution by Aude-Emmanuelle Fleurant and Yannick Quéau, who provide a careful analysis of global trends in defense spending and the production and export of military armaments from 1988–2014. One of their main conclusions is that a recent decrease in global military spending may be coming to an end, as many countries recover from the great recession and face more threatening security environments.

Chapter 10 is a new contribution by Jason Quinn and Madhav Joshi, who evaluate the implementation of 34 post-civil war peace agreements from 1989–2014. Their analysis is based on the latest version of the Peace Accords Matrix dataset, which they are responsible for compiling. An interesting pattern they identify is substantial variation in the rates of implementation of provisions of accords when the responsibility is left solely to governments, compared to uniformly high rates when external third-party actors have mandates to implement provisions.

Chapter 11 is a new contribution by Reed Wood, Mark Gibney, and Peter Haschke, which examines global trends in physical integrity abuses by governments from 1976–2014. Their analysis utilizes the Political Terror Scale dataset, for which they serve as co-directors. Among their central findings is that domestic political and social conflicts, including protests, riots, and other challenges to state authority, are likely to provoke repressive state responses, particularly by non-democratic regimes.

Chapter 12, by Bradley Parks, Michael Tierney, and Caroline Bergeron, is the final new contribution in the first section of the book. The authors provide an excellent overview and discussion of recent scholarship on the relationship between foreign development aid and conflict. One of their primary observations is that the latest research increasingly emphasizes micro-level analyses utilizing disaggregated data.

In Chapter 13, which concludes the first section, David Backer and Paul Huth present the latest findings from the Peace and Conflict Instability Ledger – a worldwide ranking of the risk of countries experiencing large-scale political instability during the years 2014–2016. Particular attention is paid to the 25 countries at the greatest risk of instability, as well as countries that have experienced the largest changes in risk scores over the past five years. Not surprisingly, countries such as Somalia, Afghanistan, and Nigeria rank among the most at risk, while Africa is the region with the largest concentration of countries ranked at high or highest risk of instability.

The "Special Feature" contribution for *Peace and Conflict 2016* is authored by Tilman Brück, Patricia Justino, and Philip Verwimp. In Chapter 14, they review and assess recent scholarship about measuring the economic and welfare consequences of armed conflict. They make the case for a new survey instrument, the Conflict Exposure Module, in order to collect more systematic and comprehensive information on conflict processes and their welfare consequences at the individual and household level.

Chapter 15, the first in the "Profiles" section, reprises a basic topic that has appeared in every edition of *Peace and Conflict* to date. A new contributor, Margareta Sollenberg, provides a summary of all ongoing armed conflicts that reached the level of war in 2014, or had escalated to war in prior years. Her analysis covers 23 major active armed conflicts in 21 countries.

Chapter 16 is a new contribution to the section authored by Deniz Cil, which digests details about the 16 international peacekeeping missions that were active during 2014. Some date back to the early years of the United Nations, while others commenced recently. The profiles of the missions supply information on mandates, personnel, and budgetary support, together with brief chronologies.

Chapter 17 is another new contribution to the section authored by Anupma Kulkarni, which gives a synopsis of legal activities taking place around the world during 2014 that confront possible crimes by individuals under various international conventions pertaining to situations of armed conflict and other forms of turmoil. She discusses domestic court proceedings in 16 countries where armed conflict took place, ICC-based proceedings that relate to armed conflicts in another 14 countries, and 13 cases where legal proceedings are underway in countries that were not involved in armed conflicts, but seek prosecutions of alleged criminal acts committed elsewhere based on the principle of universal jurisdiction.

Once again, we are pleased to bring together such rich content from a roster of researchers who are leading specialists in the field. The content has grown in meaningful ways, while staying true to and reinforcing the traditional hallmarks of *Peace and Conflict*. As usual, this publication stresses comparative analysis, often global in scope, of patterns, trends, and relationships that are integral to understanding peace and conflict as empirical phenomena and as essential challenges for the international community to address. A common thread to all the work is pushing the boundaries of knowledge with analysis and reference material that has both theoretical and applied relevance, in the process using and improving the latest resources and methodology that are made available to advance research. Our aim remains to target and welcome a diverse readership, spanning the domains of academia, policymaking, practice, and media. With those goals in mind, we continue to do our utmost to ensure that the presentation is universally intelligible, avoiding being overly technical, while still remaining rigorous and incisive. Frequent graphical visualizations bring the data analysis to life and amplify crucial developments and findings in research. These hallmarks will be preserved as strong anchors of future editions of *Peace and Conflict*. We appreciate your interest in the subject matter and this collection of material and look forward to serving your needs by offering constructive perspective and insight for years to come.

The Cutting Edge of Research on Peace and Conflict

Karsten Donnay and Ravi Bhavnani

Introduction

This chapter provides an overview of cutting-edge research about peace and conflict, focusing on studies from the last five years and especially those published in 2014 and thus far in 2015.[1] Our review pays particular attention to recent developments in data and methods that are driven by and also influence theoretical innovation. We consider vibrant and unsettled debates in the field, as well as instances of progress and novelty – research that offers fresh takes or goes in original directions. In conducting this review, our aim is not to be comprehensive. Instead, we seek to highlight types of theoretical innovation that are observed and their connections to major advances in data and methods that are moving analysis and understanding forward in a constructive fashion.

Among the key aspects of this evolution is a renewed focus on the systematic study of transitions to peace and the role of peacekeeping, examination of the impact of humanitarian and development assistance on conflict, and the growing share of conflict in urban areas. On the data front, we discuss improvements to more established conflict datasets, the greater availability of detailed geocoded data on conflict covariates, and the marked rise in independent initiatives to collect micro-level data for particular settings. Under the rubric of "new" data, we detect a turn towards the use of detailed historical and archival data, data gathered by means of remote-sensing technologies, and data typically subsumed under the heading of "Big Data." With respect to methods, we comment on the challenges associated with merging conflict and covariate data, the use of quasi-experimental research designs, and the implementation of bottom-up computational models.

Theoretical Innovation

Recent scholarship demonstrates a richer appreciation for the complexity associated with conflict and peace. For instance, scholars more readily acknowledge the existence of multiple overlapping causes of the initiation, intensification, persistence, and termination of violence in a given context. Recognition of the complexity associated with individual and group identities – the increasingly intricate dynamics of group formation and fragmentation – is also growing, beyond the lip service paid to key constructivist insights. Working with fine-grained spatiotemporal data, scholars are hard-pressed to ignore intricacies in the incidence, spread, and scale of conflict. In addition, the latest research is more inclined and better able to specify underlying mechanisms associated with various forms and aspects of conflict.

Leadership and Conflict

Three studies on leadership by McCauley (2014), DeJuan and Bank (2015) and Tiernay (2015) demonstrate these trends in innovation. Studying the elite mobilization of public support, with its attendant implications for conflict, McCauley suggests that group members primed along ethnic lines prioritize club goods (i.e., items that are subject to exclusion of non-members, but not rivalry among members), whereas identical individuals primed along religious lines prioritize behavioral policies and moral probity. The argument, tested with empirical data from a framing experiment in Côte d'Ivoire and Ghana, underscores the proclivity and ability of elites to mobilize supporters along different identity dimensions. Recognizing such distinctions in political preferences that can emerge at the individual level represents important progress over a conventional preference for lumping religious, linguistic, racial, caste, and other identity-driven forms of competition under the rubric of ethnicity. De Juan and Bank conclude that violent opposition is less likely to occur in subnational regions bound to the ruling elite through patron–client networks. Their findings are based on a combination of crowd-sourced data on the number and geospatial locations of fatalities in the Syrian civil war, together with satellite images of nighttime lights, which are used as a proxy for the public distribution of electricity during power shortages. These data sources help to overcome certain of the serious challenges of collecting detailed empirical data in the midst of an active conflict. Tiernay argues that leadership changes in state or rebel groups, especially the capture or death of a founding leader of a rebel group or of a state leader who presided over the start of a conflict, affect the probability that a civil war will end. His analysis relies on an original (though more conventional in source and content) dataset on the leaders of rebel groups, in conjunction with existing data on state leaders. All three of these studies exemplify the constructive use of different types of data, encompassing a mix of traditional and novel, obtained through various sources and techniques, to tackle important questions that can be hard to study through ordinary means.

The Spread of Conflict

Research on the location, contagion, and diffusion of conflict also demonstrates theoretical innovation. Butcher (2015) asks why some civil wars are fought in the periphery, while others devastate capital cities. The inventive suggestion is that bargaining theory, quite apart from its standard applications, can be put to good use in explaining spatial patterns of violent conflict. Fighting provides information on the relative capability of adversaries, and fighting in the capital depends on the number of and the balance of power between contending groups: asymmetric conflicts are fought furthest away from, bipolar conflicts fought marginally closer to, and multipolar conflicts the closest to capital cities. With a comparable focus on relative military capacity, Holtermann (2014) examines the emergence and spread of the Maoist insurgency in Nepal. The argument suggests that key correlates – inaccessible terrain, pre-existing rebel networks, and proximity to insurgent areas – vary in their salience and as a function of shifts in the relative military capacity of belligerents, rather than having a constant effect throughout a conflict. Braithwaite and Johnson (2014) draw an analogy between the clustering of insurgent attacks in Iraq and the dynamics of disease transmission, as well as rely on a set of approaches common to the scientific study of criminal activities, to explain the incidence and contagion of insurgent attacks. Using a geographical model of Baghdad that disaggregates the city into more than 3,000 grid cell locations, they find that violence clusters in connection with elevated population levels, road density, and military presence. These several studies depart from the longstanding practices of country-year analyses, in which covariates were assumed to remain constant across the territory of individual states, if not static for the duration of a given conflict. Instead, the studies epitomize a recent shift in research toward more careful, fine-grained measurement of both covariates and outcome variables, with higher levels of spatial and temporal resolution.

In addition, advances on the theoretical front are accompanied by helpful reflection. Reviewing the literature on diffusion in civil wars, Forsberg (2014) cautions about the difficulties inherent in studying unobservable processes that pose problems for empirical modeling. Her review raises the bar for future research, tasking scholars with identifying the agents of diffusion, distinguishing between mechanisms such as direct and indirect diffusion, and examining diffusion in different types of conflict. In addition, she points to the problems associated with selecting units of observation and analysis and the risks of over- and under-estimating cases of diffusion.

Combatant Characteristics

Innovation on the theoretical front is also bolstered by an emergent historical turn in the literature. Two notable recent studies in this vein focus on the characteristics of combatants. Using data from the *Archivo General de la Guerra Civil* for the period from January to August 1937, McLauchlin (2014) finds that combatants in the Spanish Civil War from the hill country, which is characterized by rough terrain, were considerably more likely to desert than combatants from hometowns located on flat ground. The article breathes fresh life into a standard correlate of conflict, rough terrain, and aptly demonstrates how micro-level research can make a good case for the use of structural variables that would typically be discarded in favor of individual-level data – here, the two effectively overlap. Asal et al. (2015b) likewise resort to historical data: 5,461 improvised explosive device (IED) events and all fatal shootings involving the Provisional Irish Republican Army (PIRA), as well as information on the socio-demographic and operational behavior of 1,240 PIRA members, for the 1970–1998 period. The study finds that multiple parameters, such as the level of technical expertise, cadre age, exposures to counter-terrorism policies, brigade size, and IED components and delivery methods, affect the incidence and nature of attacks. These examples of turning to historical data demonstrate that theoretical innovation does not require studying the very latest events. Research of this sort suggests that the field should not be entirely preoccupied with collecting new data on the here and now, when a lot of good data on the past is available to analyze. These data may actually be more accessible, with the necessary legwork to track down archives and distill the information they contain.[2]

Peacekeeping

Positive vs. negative peace.

Existing research on conflict is complemented by a growing focus on peace as a phenomenon to be studied in its own right – as opposed to just being thought of as the mere absence of conflict. The recent literature on peacekeeping contributes a more nuanced understanding of the effectiveness of missions, in addition to shedding light on why nations contribute to peacekeeping efforts in the first place. Studies confirm that while peacekeepers are typically deployed to areas most affected by violence (Costalli 2014; Powers et al. 2015), mission effectiveness depends critically on the nature of the peacekeeping intervention. Costalli (2014) finds that the United Nations Protection Force mission in Bosnia-Herzegovina from 1992–1995 was largely ineffective in decreasing violence in the absence of a more systematic tactical approach and sufficient military strength. Similarly, Beardsley and Gleditsch (2015) show that peacekeeping operations in Africa tend to decrease the scope of violence when robust forces are deployed and rebel groups have strong ethnic ties. Uzonyi (2015) establishes that troop commitments, a critical prerequisite for success in UN peacekeeping missions since 1990, are influenced by refugee inflows. Countries faced with hosting large numbers of refugees are prompted to contribute to peacekeeping missions by a desire to avoid incurring potential burdens: a strain on economic resources, an increase in domestic tensions and grievances, and the diffusion of conflict across borders. The analysis goes on to identify the states most likely to send support, the size of their contribution, and the conflict-affected areas to which specific assistance will likely be sent.

Emerging Topics

A number of research topics continue to gain prominence, driven by developments in theory, data, and the need for more effective policy and practice. We highlight work in three specific domains.

The first domain is the relationship between humanitarian assistance and conflict, which researchers are lately reassessing by analyzing causal mechanisms not previously considered. Steinwand (2015) underscores the ability of donors to actively manage, but not eliminate, the risk of aid-induced conflict. Nunn and Qian (2014) find that food aid has little effect on conflict onset, but significantly increases duration, which they suggest could be a by-product of appropriation of aid, especially by armed groups. In a reanalysis using Nunn and Qian's dataset, but adding in standard covariates that were omitted from their analysis, Huth, Aronson, and Backer (2014) show that the results do not hold up – instead, the relationship conforms with conventional expectations (aid at least does not exacerbate conflict). Narang (2015) provides evidence of another unintended effect of aid: increasing combatants' uncertainty about the relative strength of opponents. The research in this domain has particular significance in an environment of greater restrictions on budgets of donors of development aid (including governments and intergovernmental organizations), increased attention to evaluation of the effectiveness of this aid, and the move toward norms of evidence-based analysis of cost-benefit trade-offs.

The second domain is the dynamics of urban violence, which exhibits an expanding volume of research that increasingly involves detailed analysis. Raleigh (2015) probes the shift from rural to urban conflict and accounts for the multiple, low-intensity forms of urban violence that are observed. Her research suggests that the variegated forms of urban violence – militia attacks, communal contests, riots, and protests – illustrate the growing heterogeneity in the identities of participants, and the resulting absence of more coherent, collective and sustained movements. Work on urban violence by Cunningham and Gregory (2014) considers the ethnic complexity of segregated cities like Belfast, distinguishing between "sanctuaries" (highly segregated Catholic and Protestant communities) and "interfaces" (zones characterized by peace lines) in an analysis that seeks to account for evident spatial variation in patterns of fatalities. Their novel, counter-intuitive finding is that fatalities were higher within the sanctuaries relative to the interfaces. Research of this sort illuminates that violence is not found to be homogenous, let alone uniform, once one conducts analysis at a greater degree of resolution, within specific contexts, using improved types of data. The research also amplifies the need for careful formulation of urban policies, which appropriately reflect the complex dynamics of urban violence.

A third emerging area is not new, but takes existing work in a different direction, extending and refining the growing body of work on climate change and conflict by highlighting the importance of seasonal variability of climates. Landis (2014) examines the relationship between monthly temperature changes and conflict onset. He finds that longer spells of warm weather generate greater resources and more predictability for rebel movements, thereby increasing conflict risk. The finding is particularly germane to areas affected by strong seasonality and where atypical spells of warm weather increase the opportunity to engage in violence. By contrast, Carter and Veale (2015) evaluate the "hydraulic argument," which suggests that inclement weather, like rain, alters the timing of conflict events within a calendar year, rather than resulting in an increase or decrease in the overall extent of conflict. The argument is tested with georeferenced data on events from the Ugandan civil war. The findings indicate that inclement weather actually has multiple effects, both restraining conflict overall and shifting the timing of conflict activity. These contributions to the literature are vital to understanding specific dimensions of the vulnerability of countries and communities to conflict, as well as in assisting the strategic decision-making and operational planning of those with direct roles in conflict avoidance, mitigation, and resolution.

The small sets of studies surveyed above point to a vibrant interplay between advances on the theoretical, methodological, and data fronts. Taken together, this research demonstrates a growing awareness and attention to the simultaneity of multiple forms of conflict, an ongoing shift in the epicenter of civil conflict from rural to urban areas, a diverse array of underlying causes including multiple intersecting mechanisms, and the complexity of identity and its endogenous relationship to violence. The studies also show how current research on peace and conflict continues to be engaged with advancing knowledge of empirical phenomena in ways that have clear, meaningful applications to real-world events, policy and practice.

Advances in Data

Over the past year in particular, the availability, breadth and coverage of data on conflict, peace and relevant covariates has increased markedly. Among the prominent additions are extensions and other improvements to established datasets and data collection programs – some featured elsewhere in this book – on conflict, peace accords, peacekeeping and power-sharing. Specific micro-level data collection efforts have also multiplied, enabling researchers to study the complex, often endogenous relationships between conflict and the local contexts and conditions. In this section, we review evolutionary developments in data, highlighting the utility of this progress for the study of intrastate conflict and peace processes.

Large-Scale Datasets on Conflict

Quantitative studies of violent conflict have benefited substantially from the increasing availability of detailed event data. Several initiatives referenced elsewhere in this book have contributed importantly to significant progress in the coverage, depth, and precision of these conflict event data.[3] In particular, Chapters 3, 5, 6, 13 and 15 draw on work of the Uppsala Conflict Data Program (UCDP); Chapter 4 on the Armed Conflict Location and Event Data Project (ACLED); and Chapter 8 on the Global Terrorism Database (GTD). Of note, these initiatives are based in three different countries: UCDP at Uppsala University in Sweden, ACLED at the University of Sussex in the United Kingdom, and GTD at the National Consortium for the Study of Terrorism and Responses to Terrorism (START) at the University of Maryland in the United States. Thus, multiple major hubs of conflict data collection are active, forming foundations of a vibrant, international research community.

All three of these data initiatives provide detailed geocoded information on the date, type, scale, and perpetrators/targets of individual events of violence. Just as important, they have established new standards for the coverage, collection and coding of event data. These standards appear robust to variation in reporting environments and conditions. ACLED, for example, identified attempts by governments to distort the reporting of conflict events in only a few cases (Wigmore-Shepherd 2015).[4] While no coding or coverage is flawless, the major data collection initiatives champion the use of transparent procedures (START 2013; UCDP 2014; Raleigh and Dowd 2015), which has markedly improved data reliability and quality (Salhyan 2015). By being up front about possible limitations of their data, these initiatives help to set high standards for the entire field and especially the analysis that can be conducted in a rigorous, reliable manner (Sundberg and Melander 2013; Wigmore-Shepherd 2015; LaFree et al. 2015).

In terms of coverage, the georeferenced data that has been available from UCDP and ACLED was largely limited to Africa until recently.[5] Both initiatives are in the midst of ongoing expansions of data coverage to Asia,[6] which are a crucial step toward the long-term goal of global coverage of conflict events – akin to that provided by GTD for terrorist incidents.[7] At present, the most recent update of UCDP Georeferenced Event Dataset (GED) has greater geographic coverage than does ACLED.[8] Eck (2012) suggests that beyond the differences in country-year coverage, discrepancies between UCDP GED and ACLED also exist in the coding of individual events. In practice, differences across these two datasets – geographic and temporal coverage, data structure, type of event, etc. – imply that one dataset may be more suitable for a specific analysis than the other. This observation holds true with reference to the wider pool of conflict event datasets: no two are identical. Thus, researchers have choices to make of whether to favor one dataset or patch together relevant information from multiple sources.

The fact that neither UCDP GED nor ACLED currently offers global coverage has immediate implications for the feasible designs of research, even placing constraints on whether and how countries can be studied in conflict analyses.

Fortunately, alternative sources exist that permit the examination of countries not yet covered by UCDP GED or ACLED.

Some of these sources are country specific. Perhaps the most (in)famous example is the Significant Action (SIGACT) data on Afghanistan and Iraq. Logs of activity involving or observed by the US-led coalition forces in these countries were compiled by the US military, then acquired and controversially released by WikiLeaks, after which the contents were ultimately converted into a dataset. Another prominent example is the Iraq Body Count (IBC) data on Iraq, collected by an NGO. In line with the institutional initiatives described above, IBC relies primarily on media reports, is transparent with respect to data coding, and evaluates the quality of its data.[9] Comprehensive conflict event data also exists for other select countries such as Colombia, Israel, and Syria, drawing on official records, NGO initiatives, and crowdsourcing.

A further alternative that has recently appeared on the scene is event datasets that rely on machine-coding techniques to automate the processing of sources of raw information such as media reports. Major examples include the Global Database of Events, Language and Tone (GDELT), the Integrated Conflict Early Warning System (ICEWS), the Open Event Data Alliance, and the Social, Political, and Economic Event Database (SPEED). The advantages of these datasets include global coverage, often in near-real time, with a breadth of information about a wide variety of event types encompassing violent conflict, potential covariates and many other things. At this time, however, data quality and precision appear to be a major issue.[10] We discuss the merits and current limitations of machine-coded data in further detail later in the chapter.

The Social Conflict Analysis Database (SCAD) complements existing data collection efforts by coding protests, riots, strikes, inter-communal conflict, government violence against civilians, and other forms of social conflict not systematically covered by conflict datasets (Salehyan et al. 2012). SCAD's key innovation is to extend the coverage of violent and non-violent conflict beyond the criteria for coding an armed conflict by UCDP. SCAD codes social conflicts from 1990–2013 in all of Africa, as well as Mexico, Central America, and the Caribbean.

Similarly, the Nonviolent and Violent Campaigns and Outcomes Dataset (NAVCO) (Chenoweth and Lewis 2013) provides global coverage of major resistance campaigns from 1900–2006 (NAVCO 1.1), annual data on campaign behavior from 1945–2006 (NAVCO 2.0), and event data on tactical selection during campaigns from 1987–2011 (NAVCO 3.0). The explicit focus is the interaction between political movements/insurgent groups and governments, and how this interaction affects the outcomes of organized resistance campaigns. The data draw attention to the endogenous link between government and insurgent actions, permitting researchers to study reciprocal dynamics, such as reactive violence.

The current generation of conflict datasets is designed with detailed temporal and/or geographical coverage in mind – often in the foreground – and standardized reporting of actor and event types.[11] The data allow researchers to observe conflict dynamics at the more granular time and distance scales at which they actually unfold in practice,[12] enabling the study of endogenous conflict dynamics in realistic ways. Disaggregating geographically can help to avoid the problem of lumping together otherwise unrelated conflict dynamics – urban vs. rural conflict, for example. The coding of actor types facilitates research on who is doing what to whom, while the coding of event types permits a distinction between different forms of violence, including their characteristics (e.g., selective vs. indiscriminate) and motivations (e.g., capture territory vs. control natural resources).

Quantitative research on the micro-level dynamics of civil conflict typically focuses on recent or contemporary conflicts – often within the last 25 years. Yet an important segment of the literature involves the use of detailed historical data on earlier episodes of conflict, as we noted previously. Other examples published in the last couple of years have focused on conflicts in pre-colonial Africa between 1400 and 1700 (Besley and Reynal-Querol 2014), the role of combatant hometowns in facilitating desertion during the Spanish Civil War (McLauchlin 2014), and the effect of native governing authorities on resistance against the Nazi occupation of France during World War II (Ferwerda and Miller 2014).

Data on Peace

The longstanding and emergent data collection efforts focusing on conflict are complemented by a recent flourishing of datasets on peace. Historically, peace was treated as the absence of conflict, which effectively precluded the need for separate data collection devoted to measuring peace. Scholars and practitioners have increasingly come to recognize peace as a phenomenon to be measured in its own right – an outcome with tangible positive dimensions.[13] Part of the impetus is the understanding that cases falling below the threshold of active conflict at a given point, which may be labeled as post-conflict, are not all the same. In fact, these cases can be quite different, in terms of ongoing violence, instability, quality of life and other parameters. Those disparities, in conjunction with how countries make transitions to situations where conflict has diminished or been eliminated, are vital to study. This attention is reflected in an assortment of new datasets, which cover specific topics such as conflict mediation, peace agreements and their implementation, peacekeeping operations, and economic and military sanctions.[14] As such, they encompass a mixture of inputs and outcomes. These data are coded at the level of individual instances, providing information on type, location, timing, duration and impact.

Information on duration and impact not only captures the implementation of specific measures, but also supplies a basis for assessing the nature and magnitude of the effect of those measures on attaining or maintaining peace.

Multiple new datasets on conflict mediation and the implementation of peace agreements have emerged over the past five years. The Civil War Mediation (CWM) dataset covers diplomatic conflict mediation initiatives worldwide for the 1946–2004 period (DeRouen et al. 2011). The data are disaggregated by conflict episode, with detailed information on mediators and mediation outcomes. The UCDP Peace Agreement Dataset covers peace agreements signed between two or more opposing parties in an armed conflict in the 1975–2011 period (Högbladh 2011). This dataset contains detailed information on the provisions of each agreement and the termination of violence. The observations are coded to be compatible with the coding of conflict dyads reflected in other UCDP datasets. The Implementation of Pacts (IMPACT) dataset, also released by UCDP, contains detailed information on the implementation of political, military and territorial pacts found in peace agreements for the period 1989–2004 (Jarstad et al. 2012). In a similar vein, the Peace Accords Matrix Implementation Dataset (PAM_ID) provides post-1989 data on the implementation of provisions in negotiated peace agreements for subsequent ten-year windows (Joshi et al. 2015; see also Chapter 10).[15] The Power-Sharing Event Dataset (PSED) codes instances of power-sharing (or the promise thereof) for the government-rebel dyad in peace agreements signed after the end of a civil conflict during the 1989–2006 period, with coverage extended to a five-year window following an agreement to evaluate the success of the agreements (Ottmann and Vüllers 2015). Together, these datasets make several important contributions to research. One is that several relevant resources are available, with certain aspects that overlap, but others that are distinct, which improves the scope of analysis. The datasets also have impressive geographic and temporal coverage, which again ensures that the scope of research can be expansive. The datasets are on par with and even directly paired to existing conflict datasets, which facilitates studies that integrate analysis of both conflict and peace – and the transitions back and forth between the two conditions. This potential is especially important given the legacies of recurring conflict, interrupted by periods of peace, in many affected countries. In addition, the datasets about peace are valuable for evaluation purposes.

Newer and better datasets on peacekeeping operations have also come into existence, with the data typically provided by international organizations and coded by individual researchers. For example, the Stockholm International Peace Research Institute (SIPRI) maintains the Multilateral Peace Operations Database, supplying comprehensive information on nearly 600 peace operations for the period 2000–2010. The International Military Interventions (IMI) dataset covers a broad range of forceful external interventions into states – including peacekeeping operations – between 1946 and 2005 (Pickering and Kisangani 2009). Beardsley (2011) used the IMI dataset to derive a list of peacekeeping interventions that distinguishes between robust missions, in which at least 1,000 military personnel were deployed, and observational missions. Similarly, Kathman (2013) relies on data coded from detailed reports of peacekeeping missions and the personnel commitments of member states, released by the United Nations Department of Peacekeeping Operations (UNDPKO). The International Peace Institute's Peacekeeping Database summarizes total uniformed personnel contributions of each contributing country, by type (troop, police, or expert/observer) and by mission, on a monthly basis from November 1990 to present. The Peacekeeping Operations Locations and Event Dataset (PKOLED) codes disaggregated information on UN peacekeeping operations in intrastate conflicts for the period 1989–2005, based on reports on peacekeeping missions prepared by the UN Secretary-General for the UN Security Council (Dorussen and Ruggeri 2007). The dataset includes the exact location of troop deployments and information about individual events associated with the peacekeeping operations, as well as aggregate monthly information on peacekeeping operations at the level of provinces. Meanwhile, Chapter 16 provides descriptive profiles of and data on all the UN peacekeeping missions that were active in 2014.

Another topic of data that is pertinent to peace (and conflict) is sanctions, which can be designed to serve as means to thwart conflict or to pressure conflicting parties to end violent confrontations. The Threat and Imposition of Economic Sanctions (TIES) dataset provides detailed information for the period 1945–2005 on instances in which one or more states threatened or imposed economic sanctions on a single country (Morgan et al. 2014). SIPRI's Arms Embargoes Database codes data on weapons embargoes from 1998 until the present. Linking data on sanctions to data on peace and conflict allows us to study the conditions under which sanctions can serve to mitigate violence or maintain the peace, as well as to identify situations where sanctions are ineffective or even detrimental. With sanctions playing a visible role in the arena of international politics, data that permits a critical evaluation of their effectiveness is of immediate policy interest.

Covariate Data

To be rigorous and effective, quantitative studies of peace and conflict require detailed data – ideally geocoded – on covariates such as population density, GDP, education and elevation. Data of this sort are now available at greater spatial and temporal resolution than ever before.

In developed countries, accessing information on standard geographic, population and economic covariates at smaller units of analysis is relatively straightforward. In conflict-affected contexts, however, official statistics released by government agencies tend to be unavailable or outdated, especially when conflict coincides with low levels of development.[16]

Several existing datasets provide information on relevant covariates at the subnational level, some of which rely on remote sensing technologies. NASA's Shuttle Radar Topographic Mission (SRTM) provides comprehensive data, with global coverage, on elevation for grid cells at a resolution of less than 100 meters (Jarvis et al. 2008). The Gridded Population of the World (GPW) dataset uses detailed, local census data to construct a gridded population dataset with global coverage at a resolution of about 4 km (CIESIN 2005). The LandScan population dataset has an even higher grid resolution of about 1 km. In addition to local census data, a range of auxiliary data sources, including road networks, land cover and nighttime lights, are used to improve data quality and resolution. While their spatial coverage is excellent, these datasets are limited with respect to their temporal resolution. In many cases, data are only available at five-year intervals and the most recent release is from the mid-2000s. These limitations may not necessarily pose problems for all types of analyses, especially if the expectation is that the values of particular indicators remain stable over time (e.g., elevation). The limitations may, however, pose a serious impediment to quantitative analysis in which contemporaneous and/or current values are essential, particularly when actual quantities fluctuate over time in significant and unpredictable ways. For example, conflict can cause dramatic shifts in variables like population (Czaika and Kis-Katos 2009) and economic activity (Witmer 2015). In this case, an outdated ten-year-old dataset might serve as a rough, suggestive baseline, beyond which its utility is likely to be undermined by known dynamics.

More recently, progress has also been made using remote sensing techniques to infer local economic conditions, especially GDP (Weidmann and Schutte 2016; see Section 3 for details). The clear advantage is that nighttime lights data exist at a high spatial resolution with comprehensive and up-to-date coverage. Another recent development is datasets specifically dedicated to coding relevant information about identity groups and armed actors. GeoEPR provides detailed geo-coded data, updated most recently in 2014, on settlement patterns of politically active ethnic groups around the world and their access to executive government power from 1946–2013 (Vogt et al. 2015; see also Chapter 7). The GeoEPR data are accessible via the GROW[up] online platform, which is maintained by the International Conflict Research group at ETH Zürich, together with data on federal administrative units, physical elevation, nighttime lights, population and GDP by area – making it the most comprehensive collection of conflict covariate data to date (Girardin et al. 2015). Meanwhile, the Minorities at Risk (MAR) project just released AMAR, a dataset of socially relevant ethnic groups and their component structure worldwide (Birnir et al. 2015). The revised coding addresses a number of key concerns with the original MAR data, defining socially relevant groups more broadly rather than concentrating on at-risk groups alone. Other datasets specifically focus on actor groups covered in the UCDP dataset family. The UCDP actor dataset contains information on all actors included in UCDP's datasets on organized violence (UCDP 2014). The Non-State Actors (NSA) dataset contains detailed information on state–rebel group dyads (Cunningham et al. 2013), covering the entire set included in the UCDP Dyadic Dataset (Pettersson and Wallensteen 2015).

Other institutional data collection initiatives focus on coding particular covariates that have both theoretical and policy relevance. For example, the Natural Resources and Armed Conflict project, which is based at the University of North Carolina at Charlotte and funded by the Minerva Initiative of the US Department of Defense, aims to develop a comprehensive dataset of natural resources worldwide, including whether and how rebels exploit those resources (Asal et al. 2015a). The Climate Change and African Political Stability (CCAPS) project, based at the University of Texas at Austin and also funded by the Minerva Initiative, has been investigating how climate change affects African and international security, in the process assembling a variety of geocoded data that allow researchers to map and quantitatively study the relationships among climate, conflict and climate aid. The AidData initiative – a partnership between the College of William and Mary, Brigham Young University, and Development Gateway – focuses on generating comprehensive datasets of development finance at the project level. A number of geocoded country datasets are already available with more countries currently being coded (see also Chapter 12). These datasets are being extended and used to explore the relationship between foreign assistance and intrastate conflict as part of a collaborative Minerva-funded project based at the University of Maryland.

All the aforementioned data on covariates shares – with data on peace and conflict – an emphasis on disaggregation, geocoding, quality and transparency. The parallel development of datasets in these respects is helping to establish the foundations for groundbreaking types of analysis that are far more granular and intricate than what has traditionally been the case. In addition, one can examine spatial and temporal proximity of conflict events and causal mechanisms, as well as consider important dimensions such as diffusion and spillover, in a more precise manner. An essential ambition is comprehensive and seamless integration of conflict and covariate data, with particular attention to data specified at different levels of granularity – a considerable challenge for matching, subsequent analysis and inference (see the discussion below). A few data initiatives are making headway on those fronts, including GROW[up], CCAPS and the UCDP actor datasets.

Additional progress is needed to advance toward complete and standardized integration, encompassing a wider range of conflict- and peace-related data.

Innovative Sources of New Data

Research on conflict and peace has exhibited a turn towards new, innovative sources of data, as a deliberate response to major shortcomings in existing data sources. A particular focus of many of these innovations is to efficiently – without extensive human coding efforts or fieldwork – address problems of geographical coverage, temporal resolution and near real-time availability of data on conflict and peace and their covariates. Moreover, the data innovations are intended to provide novel, fine-grained renderings of human interactions that go beyond the kind of dynamics typically captured by existing datasets.

Earlier, we mentioned data gathered by means of remote-sensing technologies, specifically satellite imagery. These data capture detailed features of physical (e.g., elevation) and human (e.g., settlements) geography. Such factors are increasingly used to examine both the short- and long-term mechanisms and effects of conflict, especially in regions like Sudan where fieldwork is too difficult or dangerous to conduct (Witmer 2015). Analyses have used the data derived from satellite imagery to detect specific dimensions of conflict, including troop movements, damage to communities and property (through bombings, arson, bulldozing, etc.), one-sided violence, mass atrocities, population displacement, or humanitarian crises.[17] All these topics are challenging to study absent remote-sensing data, since the events of interest are hard to observe, especially on a large scale while also gauging relevant variation at a high enough resolution. Remote-sensing data has considerable potential to alleviate those hurdles.

Remote-sensing technologies, while fruitful and promising for research on conflict and peace, are hardly a panacea; impediments remain to their broader use. High-resolution imagery is costly and may actually not be reliably accessed during conflicts (Campbell 2001). Acquiring the necessary technical expertise to process remote-sensing imagery is another challenge, especially for researchers not associated with specialized institutions (Witmer 2015). Combining automatic image processing and detection with easy-to-use human coding interfaces is one feasible solution. Recent applications of this approach include the crisis-mapping tool CrisisMappers, which relies on crowd-sourced inputs of both images and processing.

Another key application that has emerged in recent years, which we mentioned earlier, is the use of satellite data on nighttime lights (National Geophysical Data Center 2014). Past research conducted at both a national and subnational level demonstrates a strong correlation between nighttime lights and economic activity in developing countries (Elvidge et al. 1997; Henderson et al. 2011; Sutton et al. 2007; Chen and Nordhaus 2011), for which data on local economic conditions are often of low quality or simply non-existent.[18] Recent work by Weidmann and Schutte (2016) uses comprehensive data from the Demographic and Health Surveys (DHS) to examine this relationship in 39 developing countries. The study confirms that nighttime lights are indeed accurate predictors of economic wealth, in terms of both identifying new locations in a known country and generating predictions for previously unstudied countries.

Major innovations have also occurred in the category of "Big Data" that are pushing the potential of analysis of conflict and peace. Whereas traditional approaches to data collection tend to be more focused and selective, because of resources (time, personnel, funding, etc.) and processing capacity, the Big Data approach is distinguished by its reliance on vacuuming up, in an expansive manner, online digital records generated each day at a rapidly increasing pace. These records include social media traffic, as well as archives of news media reports, economic data and various other primary and secondary sources. Big Data therefore involves vast amounts of machine-readable material that, in principle, enable detailed renderings of human interactions at a fine-grained resolution. In the case of Twitter, for example, data is available at the level of individual users and their social networks. This richness comes at the cost of requiring technical capacity, in order to process the vast quantities of data, and also poses new methodological challenges. Perhaps for these reasons, the applications of Big Data to study conflict and peace have been relatively modest thus far. One standout example is a study that found news media has significant value in predicting the onset of interstate conflict (Chadefaux 2014).

Another key area of progress pertains to machine-coded datasets such as ICEWS, GDELT or SPEED. These initiatives are generating data on conflict and conflict-related events around the world, making them publicly accessible in close to real time. The timeliness and rapid release schedule represents a clear advantage over other datasets that rely on conventional methods of collection and processing. The closest competitor, ACLED, publishes weekly updates, with significantly less geographic coverage. The near-real-time schedule and global coverage is especially attractive to producers and consumers of forecasts of international crises. ICEWS, for instance, is the product of a program to advance the state of the art in conflict early warning, undertaken on behalf of the US military.

A fundamental question concerns whether such machine-coded data collection and release in near real time can match the precision of the slower, methodical data collection using human coders. No published work currently exists that performs a systematic comparison of ICEWS and/or GDELT to datasets such as ACLED or UCDP.[19] That said, researchers working with machine-coded data have voiced serious concerns regarding accuracy and reliability.[20] Pending further confirmation of the validity of machine-coded data relative to established and more thoroughly tested datasets, researchers should be wary when using the machine-coded datasets for substantive and policy-relevant analyses.

At the same time, we should emphasize that these concerns are not restricted to machine-coded data. Researchers have raised issues of systematic reporting biases in regards to different types of conflict datasets, including those compiled through conventional means. The main reason is that many datasets rely on news media as the primary source of information about numerous parameters of conflict (events, actors, interactions, connections, etc.). The use of media sources can introduce biases in datasets, given the assortment of documented inconsistencies in the coverage and reporting of conflict events (Davenport and Ball 2002; Davenport 2010; Eck 2012; Chojnacki et al. 2012; Raleigh 2012; Weidmann 2013; Weidmann 2015).

Social media is a fresh source of data, which has both significant merits and notable limitations. On the plus side, social media provides a continuous stream and unprecedented depth of information on the sentiments, actions, and interactions of individuals, groups, organizations and institutions around the world. This information is accessible in near real time. It is also highly granular. The information relies on the agency and discretion of users, rather than the conceptualization of a specific research design by a scholar or other data collector. As such, the information provides a potential lens into a rich diversity of micro-level activity as it unfolds. Previously, this sort of information was unavailable and unrealistic to compile, especially at scale and on a timely basis. Yet the exciting new possibilities for analysis are not without drawbacks.

The challenge is that Twitter is neither a comprehensive nor a randomly generated data source. The coverage is strongly influenced by wealth, demographics, and political constraints (Ulfelder 2015), as well as technology, especially Internet access and speed, access to smartphones, etc. In addition, extracting "meaning" from the short messages posted on Twitter, beyond identification of simple keywords, is difficult, despite the significant improvements in natural language processing. The most promising approaches rely on machine-learning techniques, but they also extract relatively high-level information such as the "mood" of a given message (Golder and Macy 2011). Most important, to fully exploit the potential of social media data and extract information on conflict or conflict-related events, one would have to geolocate messages with some degree of reliability and ensure that the author of the message reports on events in her own geographic vicinity.[21] Unfortunately, the rate of geolocated tweets is low (~1 percent). In addition, the reliability of self-declared location information contained in the user profile is presumed to be low. Twitter users have strong incentives to mask their locations for multiple reasons, including out of fear of persecution, which is all the more pronounced in conflict settings and under autocratic regimes – precisely where the spatial resolution of data is most essential for purposes of analysis.

Advances in Methods

The use of geocoded or georeferenced data with fine-grained temporal resolution has become the new standard in the analysis of intrastate conflict, which is embraced by most established data collection programs as well as by a growing number of individual researchers. While these data hold enormous promise (Gleditsch and Weidmann 2012), they also present methodological challenges. Here, we highlight a few of the key challenges before turning to discuss new methods developed specifically for the analysis of spatiotemporal data.

New Challenges

Data on conflict and peace are increasingly arrayed in the form of event-level data, i.e., geographic point data that codes the location and timing of an incident (up to a given extent of coding uncertainty). An alternative is polygons, which capture of affected areas – these need not be precise or regular or have the same resolution – in a given time period. The specific format of the data is driven by a combination of research questions and the degree of empirical granularity at which the data can be reliably coded. Meanwhile, disaggregated data on covariates are available either for polygons, including those corresponding to geographic areas with administrative or other boundaries, or in raster form with finite resolution; the former data may be coded at the level of the polygons, whereas the latter data are often interpolated to the raster unit.

For purposes of analysis, all these data should ideally be compatible, in the sense of accommodating matching or merging using the same unit of observation. Yet this is not always possible, since the units of observation tend to differ across datasets and even types of data within the same dataset. This basic incompatibility is a longstanding issue known in the geographical literature as the "change of support" problem (Gehlke and Biehl 1934).

Differences in temporal and spatial granularity pose fundamental challenges to merging data on conflict, peace and covariates. In datasets like ACLED and UCDP GED, conflict is coded at the level of events, often with information on specific dates and locations. Standard covariates such as population density, elevation or group-specific properties are coded at higher levels of aggregation both spatially (polygons or spatial grids) and temporally (years or longer intervals of time, rather than days or even months). To be amenable to standard spatial econometric analysis, conflict event data must therefore be aggregated to grid cells. This yields event count variables per spatial unit (for example, a 1x1 km cell) and per time unit (typically, month or year). Data on covariates coded as spatial polygons can similarly be projected on a spatial grid by intersecting grid cells and polygons.

The process of aggregation proves to be complex for several reasons. Intersecting covariate data coded as polygons (or grids) with a specific spatial grid is not straightforward, given that grid cells may span more than one polygon. Established methods to scale data to comparable units, such as spatial interpolation, may negatively affect quantitative inferences given that observations in adjacent cells, by construction, tend to be highly correlated (Runfola et al. 2015). This is especially true for the small cell sizes favored in disaggregated analyses.[22] The typically large number of grid-cell-years (or -months) may then render even the smallest signals statistically significant. In addition, the specific grid cell onto which an event is coded varies with the dimension and position of the grid, thereby driving the results of spatial econometric inference – a problem commonly known as the modifiable areal unit problem (MAUP) (Cressie 1996; Dark and Bram 2007; Openshaw 1984).

These issues go beyond potential problems associated with spatial econometric inference, given systematic bias in the process of spatial (and temporal) aggregation prior to estimation. To our knowledge, no standard solutions to these issues exist, though research is under way to develop new and more robust methods. A straightforward but computationally intensive way to estimate the impact of aggregation on the results of quantitative inference is Monte Carlo analysis, in which spatial econometric inferences are repeated for a large range of grid sizes and positions using different techniques of spatial interpolation. By systematically exploring all the possible ways in which aggregation may affect inference, researchers can begin to discern whether their findings are sensitive to these initial choices.

New Methods

Two notable developments have been observed recently on the methodological front that are influencing research on conflict and peace, among other topics, in important ways. These developments have particular utility in studying conflict-affected settings, which tend to be relatively data poor and are not as conducive to optimal forms of data collection, including those involving experimental techniques.

One methodological development is an increased interest in quasi-experimental research designs, which approximate natural experimental settings in observational data. This interest is prompted in significant measure by the high spatial and temporal resolution of data, as well as the characterization of incidents by perpetrators, victims, and type of events, all of which enhance the identification of specific incidents. A typical quasi-experimental setup includes one type of incident (treatment) hypothesized to have a strong effect on the subsequent levels of violence, as compared to another type of incident (control) that does not. Quasi-experimental methods, utilized in conjunction with spatiotemporal contextual data, address some of the fundamental challenges to inference discussed above and are often more feasible than conducting actual field experiments.[23] Quasi-experimental methods constitute a next-best solution for studying causal relationships in environments where elaborate, on-the-ground data collection and complex research designs are infeasible.

For example, Schutte and Donnay (2014) developed a method labeled Matched Wake Analysis (MWA), a new causal inference design specifically suited for spatiotemporal event data. This methodology analyzes how different types of interventions affect subsequent levels of reactive events. MWA uses sliding spatiotemporal windows to address the MAUP, as well as statistical matching to counter selection bias. Covariates are assigned to each event using nearest neighbor mapping, i.e., the conditions under which events occurred are characterized by the covariate values most closely related to their location (and timing).[24]

Quasi-experimental methods have also been applied to fixed geographical units of analysis, e.g., administrative divisions and other types of regions. For example, Linke et al. (2015) pair Afrobarometer survey data with aggregated ACLED conflict events to test the effect of population attitudes on the spread of political violence in 16 African countries. Working with natural spatial units of analysis – information on the administrative divisions where the 18,500 Afrobarometer respondents are located is available in the dataset – shields the analysis against the MAUP. The causal inference design addresses potential problems associated with spatially correlated observations by explicitly accounting for the possible interdependence of levels of violence, as well as population attitudes in adjacent districts.

A second methodological development is the growth of "bottom-up" agent-based modeling (ABM). This method is similarly well suited to study micro-level causal hypotheses. Recent studies have demonstrated that these models – when seeded with empirical data on the physical, demographic, economic or social topology and optimized to correspond to observed patterns of violence – exhibit a high degree of validity (Weidmann and Salehyan 2013; Bhavnani et al. 2014). Moreover, they are particularly suited to accommodate data of varying granularity, since observations can be matched at their respective level of reporting without the need to aggregate to arbitrary units of analysis. By construction, the dynamics and interdependencies in bottom-up models vary continuously across space, thereby accounting intrinsically for the interdependence of neighboring spatial units. Once validated with empirical data, these frameworks also enable counterfactual analysis to answer "what-if" types of questions, supplying a powerful, versatile tool for policy design and evaluation.

Conclusion

In this chapter, we have reviewed a selection of new research on peace and conflict, highlighting the interplay between theoretical developments, advances in data and innovation in methods.

On the theoretical front, we noted a richer appreciation for the complexity associated with conflict and peace: the simultaneity of multiple forms of violence and instability; an ongoing shift in the epicenter of civil conflict from rural to urban areas; greater attention to a diverse set of potential underlying mechanisms that has identified the existence of multiple overlapping causes; and increasing awareness of identity complexity, its endogenous relationship to violence, and the implications for the dynamics of group formation and fragmentation.

On the data front, we observed notable progress in the availability, quality and granularity of data on peace and conflict, especially the large-N resources generated by established institutional initiatives. Fine-grained micro-level data still remains hard to locate and access and suffers from a lack of standardization, making comparisons of richly detailed cases more difficult. Nonetheless, both established and emergent data collection initiatives have begun addressing concerns about bias, to the extent possible. Full transparency about coding procedures and possible limitations of data are rapidly becoming the new industry standard. As improvements in data granularity continue, awareness of the methodological challenges associated with the use of disaggregate data is growing (see also Gleditsch and Weidmann 2012).

With respect to new data sources, the aspiration for social media data to significantly improve quantitative analysis of peace and conflict remains strong, despite our observation that its application has been rather limited to date – and may face a ceiling of utility for a long time to come.[25] Comprehensive exploration of the broader applicability of these data, as well as machine-coded data, is an essential next step, which is likely to hinge on the progress of large-scale research projects that incorporate those data.[26]

Innovations on the methodological front have been instrumental in enabling research into the characteristics and dynamics of conflict and peace processes. These innovations are driven in large measure by the need to develop appropriate methods to analyze and exploit the full potential of the richer, more disaggregated data that are now available. Key innovations include quasi-experimental methods and bottom-up computational modeling techniques. Both methods enable robust analysis of causal relationships in complex, dynamical settings, while affording a high degree of empirical validity. They represent a turn towards the use of methods better suited for the analysis of complex, dynamic systems, recognizing the problems associated with the application of standard statistical approaches to disaggregated spatio-temporal data.

Research on peace and conflict has advanced significantly over the past years, thanks to substantial progress in data and methods that both drive and are driven by theoretical development. Emerging, innovative research is by no means immune to the challenges associated with conducting disaggregated, micro-level research. Our emphasis on advances and associated challenges throughout this overview is intended to provide useful guidance to researchers, policymakers and practitioners who are attentive to where the field has been heading, what the cutting-edge data, methods, studies and findings contribute to understanding, and how this work can be employed and fostered in the future.

Notes

1 We are indebted to Umut Yüksel for research assistance with this chapter.
2 See also Loyle, Davenport and Sullivan (2014), which uses a disaggregated events-based dataset for the period of the Troubles in Northern Ireland (1968–1998), as well as work by Sullivan (2015) that relies on archival records of the Guatemalan National Police.
3 Other examples of conflict event datasets were among the topics of *Peace and Conflict 2014*: Chapter 7 discussed what was then called the Social Conflict in Africa Database (now called the Social Conflict Analysis Database), while Chapter 11 examined the crowdsourcing of event data on conflict, other humanitarian crises, and responses.
4 Wigmore-Shepherd (2015) demonstrates that reliance on a diverse assortment of primary news media sources – from local to global – helps avoid issues of reporting bias highlighted in the literature. Different media sources exhibit different preferences for covering certain types or locations of events. "Averaging" across multiple media sources is one strategy to ensure more unbiased coverage. In addition, ACLED data coding relies on sources such as NGO reports, truth commissions, etc. As more and more

reliable information becomes available following a conflict, the coding of already published conflict event datasets routinely undergoes systematic revision.

5 ACLED recently released version 5 of its Africa dataset, which is updated weekly.

6 Version 1.9 of UCDP's Georeferenced Event Dataset (GED), released in June 2015, covers countries in South, Southeast and East Asia during years of active armed conflict. As of February 2015, ACLED has been releasing near real-time data for eleven countries in Asia on a monthly basis.

7 The latest GTD release for 2014 is underway at the time of writing. While GTD's coverage is global and very extensive, it remains partially incomplete.

8 The broader universe of UCDP's data generally affords more country-year coverage relative to ACLED, given that the latter exclusively covers conflict events.

9 A recent study finds significant discrepancies in the "on the ground" reported SIGACT data (Donnay and Filimonov 2014). Whether these arise from the media-based coding of conflict events in IBC or a biased reporting by US troops cannot be conclusively determined, but the observed differences are consistent with the relative strengths and weaknesses of both types of reporting.

10 The GDELT project has also faced major legal challenges, which have complicated its use by scholars.

11 Reporting within major datasets tends to be standardized. So while variation in coding across datasets exists, coding rules for major institutional initiatives – UCDP and ACLED, for example – tend not to differ fundamentally.

12 The manner in which dynamic and spatial dimensions are operationalized tends to vary across datasets, as does precision of measurement, largely as a function of specific information sources used (see, for example, Eck 2012).

13 The Everyday Peace Indicator project investigates alternative, bottom-up indicators of peace. It builds on the premise that local communities are better at identifying positive changes in their own circumstances and corresponding indicators than external experts.

14 We include economic and military sanctions in this section, recognizing their role in leveraging actors to maintain peace. They may, however, also be directly related to or be issued in response to conflict.

15 The dataset is current even despite its coverage of events until the mid-2000s, given that evaluation and coding for a subsequent ten-year window necessitates a significant temporal lag.

16 The database of Global Administrative Areas (GADM) provides basic information on a country's geography and its administrative subdivisions. It is an invaluable tool for any researcher concerned with subnational units of analysis, since information on boundaries is a critical prerequisite for subsequent, disaggregate analysis. The coverage of GADM's GIS database is global, providing the names and locations of administrative areas from ADM0 typically down to ADM2 level.

17 See, for example, the Satellite Sentinel Project, the Signal Project of the Harvard Humanitarian Initiative, Amnesty International's Remote Sensing for Human Rights, the Geospatial Technologies Project of AAAS and work by Human Rights Watch.

18 The approach has limitations for developed countries (Mellander et al. 2013).

19 While ICEWS, SPEED and GDELT rely on the CAMEO coding framework, their relative precision and coverage vary significantly. For a detailed comparison of GDELT and ICEWS, see Ward et al. (2013).

20 See, for example, Hanna (2014), Weller and McCubbins (2014) or Kishi (2015).

21 Researchers are currently developing techniques to more reliably infer the most likely location of Twitter users from their message history.

22 The problem is all the more pronounced if conflict data are coded as spatial polygons, rather than point data, since this effectively renders completely identical the observations in a large number of adjacent grid cells.

23 Field experiments in conflict-affected settings are possible. See, for example, the work of Callen and Long (2015) on monitoring election fraud in Afghanistan and Blattman and Annan (2015) on employment incentives in Liberia.

24 In this setup, uncertainty in the assignment of covariate values stems from coding the location and timing of events and the coding of covariates as polygon or grid data.

25 See, for example, Zeitzoff (2011).

26 See, for example, http://geog.umd.edu/project/computational-modeling-grievances-and-political-instability-through-global-media.

References

Asal, Victor, Michael Findley, James A. Piazza, and James I. Walsh. 2015a. "Political Exclusion, Oil, and Ethnic Armed Conflict." *Journal of Conflict Resolution*.

Asal, Victor, Paul Gill, R. Karl Rethemeyer, and John Horgan. 2015b. "Killing Range: Explaining Lethality Variance within a Terrorist Organization." *Journal of Conflict Resolution* 59(3): 401–427.

Bhavnani, Ravi, Karsten Donnay, Dan Miodownik, Maayan Mor, and Dirk Helbing. 2014. "Group Segregation and Urban Violence." *American Journal of Political Science* 58(1): 226–245.

Beardsley, Kyle. 2011. "Peacekeeping and the Contagion of Armed Conflict." *Journal of Politics* 73(4): 1051–1064.

Beardsley, Kyle, and Kristian S. Gleditsch. 2015. "Peacekeeping as Conflict Containment." *International Studies Review* 17(1): 67–89.

Besley, Timothy, and Marta Reynal-Querol. 2014. "The Legacy of Historical Conflict: Evidence from Africa." *American Political Science Review* 108(2): 319–336.

Birnir, Johanna K., Jonathan Wilkenfeld, James D. Fearon, David Laitin, Ted Robert Gurr, Dawn Brancati, Stephen Saideman, Amy Pate, and Agatha S. Hultquist. 2015. "Socially Relevant Ethnic Groups, Ethnic Structure and AMAR." *Journal of Peace Research* 52(1): 110–115.

Blattman, Christopher, and Jeannie Annan. 2015. "Can Employment Reduce Lawlessness and Rebellion? A Field Experiment with High-Risk Men in a Fragile State." Available from SSRN, http://papers.ssrn.com/sol3/papers.cfm?abstract_id=2621343.

Braithwaite, Alex, and Shane D. Johnson. 2014. "The Battle for Baghdad: Testing Hypotheses about Insurgency from Risk Heterogeneity, Repeat Victimization, and Denial Policing Approaches." *Terrorism and Political Violence* 27(1): 112–132.

Butcher, Charles. 2015. "'Capital Punishment': Bargaining and the Geography of Civil War." *Journal of Peace Research* 52(2): 171–186.

Callen, Michael, and James D. Long. 2015. "Institutional Corruption and Election Fraud: Evidence from a Field Experiment in Afghanistan." *American Economic Review* 105(1): 354–381.

Campbell, Duncan. 2001. "US Buys Up All Satellite War Images." *The Guardian*, October 17. http://www.theguardian.com/world/2001/oct/17/physicalsciences.afghanistan.

Carter, Timothy A., and Daniel J. Veale. 2015. "The Timing of Conflict Violence: Hydraulic Behavior in the Ugandan Civil War." *Conflict Management and Peace Science* 32(4): 370–394.

Chadefaux, Thomas. 2014. "Early Warning Signals for War in the News." *Journal of Peace Research* 51(1): 5–18.

Chen, Xi, and William D. Nordhaus. 2011. "Using Luminosity Data as a Proxy for Economic Statistics." *Proceedings of the National Academy of Sciences* 108(21): 8589–8594.

Chenoweth, Erica, and Orion A. Lewis. 2013. "Unpacking Nonviolent Campaigns: Introducing the NAVCO 2.0 Dataset." *Journal of Peace Research* 50(3): 415–423.

Chojnacki, Sven, Christian Ickler, Michael Spies, and John Wiesel. 2012. "Event Data on Armed Conflict and Security: New Perspectives, Old Challenges, and Some Solutions." *International Interactions* 38(4): 382–401.

CIESIN (Center for International Earth Science Network), Columbia University and Centro Internacional de Agricultura Tropical (CIAT). 2005. *Gridded Population of the World Version 3 (GPWv3): Population Grids*. Palisades, NY: Socioeconomic Data and Applications Center (SEDAC), Columbia University. Available at http://sedac.ciesin.columbia.edu/gpw.

Costalli, Stefano. 2014. "Does Peacekeeping Work? A Disaggregated Analysis of Deployment and Violence Reduction in the Bosnian War." *British Journal of Political Science* 44(2): 357–380.

Cressie, Noel. 1996. "Change of Support and the Modifiable Areal Unit Problem." *Geographical Systems* 3(2–3): 159–180.

Cunningham, David E., Kristian S. Gleditsch, and Idean Salehyan. 2013. "Non-state Actors in Civil Wars: A New Dataset." *Conflict Management and Peace Science* 30(5): 516–531.

Cunningham, Niall, and Ian Gregory. 2014. "Hard to Miss, Easy to Blame? Peacelines, Interfaces and Political Deaths in Belfast during the Troubles." *Political Geography* 40: 64–78.

Czaika, Mathias, and Krisztina Kis-Katos. 2009. "Civil Conflict and Displacement: Village-Level Determinants of Forced Migration in Aceh." *Journal of Peace Research* 46(3): 399–418.

Dark, Shawna J., and Danielle Bram. 2007. "The Modifiable Areal Unit Problem (MAUP) in Physical Geography." *Progress in Physical Geography* 31(5): 471–479.

Davenport, Christian. 2010. *Media Bias, Perspective and State Repression: The Black Panther Party*. Cambridge: Cambridge University Press.

Davenport, Christian, and Patrick Ball. 2002. "Views to a Kill: Exploring the Implications of Source Selection in the Case of Guatemalan State Terror, 1977–1995." *Journal of Conflict Resolution* 46(3): 427–450.

De Juan, Alexander, and André Bank. 2015. "The Ba'athist Blackout? Selective Goods Provision and Political Violence in the Syrian Civil War." *Journal of Peace Research* 52(1): 91–104.

DeRouen, Karl, Mark J. Ferguson, Samuel Norton, Young Hwan Park, Jenna Lea, and Ashley Streat-Bartlett. 2010. "Civil War Peace Agreement Implementation and State Capacity." *Journal of Peace Research* 47(3): 333–346.

Donnay, Karsten, and Vladimir Filimonov. 2014. "Views to a War: Systematic Differences in Media and Military Reporting of the War in Iraq." *EPJ Data Science* 3(1): 1–29.

Dorussen, Han, and Andrea Ruggeri. 2007. "Introducing PKOLED: A Peacekeeping Operations Location and Event Dataset." Paper presented at the Disaggregating the Study of Civil War and Transnational Violence Conference, University of Essex, November.

Eck, Kristine. 2012. "In Data we Trust? A Comparison of UCDP GED and ACLED Conflict Events Datasets." *Cooperation and Conflict* 47(1): 124–141.

Elvidge, Christopher D., Kimberley E. Baugh, Eric A. Kihn, Herbert W. Kroehl, Ethan R. Davis, and Chris W. Davis. 1997. "Relation between Satellite Observed Visible-Near Infrared Emissions, Population, Economic Activity and Electric Power Consumption." *International Journal of Remote Sensing* 18(6): 1373–1379.

Ferwerda, Jeremy, and Nicholas L. Miller. 2014. "Political Devolution and Resistance to Foreign Rule: A Natural Experiment." *American Political Science Review* 108(3): 642–660.

Forsberg, Erika. 2014. "Diffusion in the Study of Civil Wars: A Cautionary Tale." *International Studies Review* 16(2): 188–198.

Gehlke, C.E., and Katherine Biehl. 1934. "Certain Effects of Grouping upon the Size of the Correlation Coefficient in Census Tract Material." *Journal of the American Statistical Association* 29: 169–170.

Girardin, Luc, Philipp Hunziker, Lars-Erik Cederman, Nils-Christian Bormann, and Manuel Vogt. 2015. GROW^{up} – Geographical Research on War, Unified Platform. ETH Zurich. http://growup.ethz.ch/.

Gleditsch, Kristian S., and Nils B. Weidmann. 2012. "Richardson in the Information Age: Geographic Information Systems and Spatial Data in International Studies." *Annual Review of Political Science* 15: 461–481.

Golder, Scott A., and Michael W. Macy. 2011. "Diurnal and Seasonal Mood Vary with Work, Sleep, and Daylength across Diverse Cultures." *Science* 333(6051): 1878–1881.

Hanna, Alex. 2014. "The Current State of Protest Event Data." Blog post. https://mobilizingideas.wordpress.com/2014/06/05/the-current-state-of-protest-event-data/.

Henderson, Vernon, Adam Storeygard, and David N. Weil. 2011. "A Bright Idea for Measuring Economic Growth." *American Economic Review* 101(3): 194–199.

Högbladh, Stina. 2011. "Peace Agreements 1975–2011: Updating the UCDP Peace Agreement Dataset", in Thérése Pettersson and Lotta Themnér (eds), 2012, *States in Armed Conflict 2011*. Department of Peace and Conflict Research Report no. 99. Uppsala: Uppsala University. 39–56.

Holtermann, Helge. 2014. "Relative Capacity and the Spread of Rebellion: Insights from Nepal." *Journal of Conflict Resolution*, doi: 10.1177/0022002714540470.

Humanitarian Tracker. 2015. Syria Tracker: Crowdsourced Mapping of the Syrian Conflict. Accessible at https://syriatracker.crowdmap.com/.

Huth, Paul, Jacob Aronson, and David Backer. 2014. "(Re)assessing the Relationship between Food Aid and Armed Conflict." USAID Technical Brief. http://www.usaid.gov/sites/default/files/documents/1866/USAID%20food%20aid%20technical%20brief.pdf.

Jarstad, Anna, Desirée Nilsson, and Ralph Sundberg. 2012. "The IMPACT (Implementation of Pacts) Dataset Codebook." Version 2.0, Department of Peace and Conflict Research, Uppsala University. Available at http://www.pcr.uu.se/data/.

Jarvis, Andy, Hannes I. Reuter, Andrew Nelson, and Edward Guevara. 2008. "Hole-Filled SRTM for the Globe Version 4." Available from the CGIAR-CSI SRTM 90m Database, http://srtm.csi.cgiar.org.

Joshi, Madhav, Jason M. Quinn, and Patrick M. Regan. 2015. "Annualized Implementation Data on Comprehensive Intrastate Peace Accords, 1989–2012." *Journal of Peace Research* 52(4): 551–562.

Kathman, Jacob D. 2013. "United Nations Peacekeeping Personnel Commitments, 1990–2011." *Conflict Management and Peace Science* 30(5): 532–549.

Kishi, Roudabeh. 2015. "Conflict Data Collection Practices: ACLED versus Others." Blog post. http://www.crisis.acleddata.com/conflict-data-collection-practices-acled-versus-others/.

LaFree, Gary, Laura Dugan, and Erin Miller. 2015. *Putting Terrorism in Context: Lessons from the Global Terrorism Database.* London: Routledge.

Landis, Steven T. 2014. "Temperature Seasonality and Violent Conflict: The Inconsistencies of a Warming Planet." *Journal of Peace Research* 51(5): 603–618.

Linke, Andrew M., Sebastian Schutte, and Halvard Buhaug. 2015. "Population Attitudes and the Spread of Political Violence in Sub-Saharan Africa." *International Studies Review* 17(1): 26–45.

Loyle, Cyanne, Christian Davenport, and Christopher Sullivan. 2014. "The Northern Ireland Research Initiative: Data on the Troubles from 1968–1998." *Conflict Management and Peace Science* 31(1): 94–106.

McCauley, John F. 2014. "The Political Mobilization of Ethnic and Religious Identities in Africa." *American Political Science Review* 108(4): 801–816.

McLauchlin, Theodore. 2014. "Desertion, Terrain, and Control of the Home Front in Civil Wars." *Journal of Conflict Resolution* 58(8): 1419–1444.

Mellander, Charlotta, Kevin Stolarick, Zara Matheson, and José Lobo. 2013. "Night-Time Light Data: A Good Proxy Measure for Economic Activity?" CESIS Electronic Working Paper Series no. 315. Stockholm: Royal Institute of Technology.

Morgan, T. Clifton, Navin Bapat, and Yoshiharo Kobayashi. 2014. "Threat and Imposition of Economic Sanctions 1945–2005: Updating the TIES Dataset." *Conflict Management and Peace Science* 31(5): 541–558.

Narang, Neil. 2015. "Assisting Uncertainty: How Humanitarian Aid Can Inadvertently Prolong Civil War." *International Studies Quarterly* 59(1): 184–195.

National Geophysical Data Center. 2014. "Version 4 DMSP-OLS Nighttime Lights Time Series." Electronic resource. http://ngdc.noaa.gov/eog/dmsp/downloadV4composites.html.

Nunn, Nathan, and Nancy Qian. 2014. "US Food Aid and Civil Conflict." *American Economic Review* 104(6): 1630–1666.

Openshaw, Stan. 1984. *The Modifiable Areal Unit Problem.* Norwich: Geo Books.

Ottmann, Martin, and Johannes Vüllers. 2015. "The Power-Sharing Event Dataset (PSED): A New Dataset on the Promises and Practices of Power-Sharing in Post-Conflict Countries." *Conflict Management and Peace Science* 32(3): 327–350.

Pettersson, Thérèse, and Peter Wallensteen. 2015. "Armed Conflicts, 1946–2014." *Journal of Peace Research* 52(4): 536–550.

Pickering, Jeffrey, and Emizet F. Kisangani. 2009. "The International Military Intervention Dataset: An Updated Resource for Conflict Scholars." *Journal of Peace Research* 46(4): 589–599.

Powers, Matthew, Bryce W. Reeder, and Ashly A. Townsen. 2015. "Hot Spot Peacekeeping." *International Studies Review* 17(1): 46–66.

Raleigh, Clionadh. 2012. "Violence against Civilians: A Disaggregated Analysis." *International Interactions* 38(4): 462–481.

Raleigh, Clionadh. 2015. "Urban Violence Patterns across African States." *International Studies Review* 17(1): 90–106.

Raleigh, Clionadh, and Caitriona Dowd. 2015. "Armed Conflict Location and Event Data Project (ACLED) Codebook." Retrieved from http://www.acleddata.com/wp-content/uploads/2015/01/ACLED_Codebook_2015.pdf.

Runfola, Daniel M., Thomas Hamill, Robert G. Pontius, John Rogan, Colin Polsky, Albert Decatur, and Samuel Ratick. 2015. "Exploring Hybrid Remote Sensing and Interpolative Approaches for Rapidly Mapping Discrete Units of Interest." Forthcoming in *International Journal of Geospatial and Environmental Research.*

Salehyan, Idean. 2015. "Best Practices in the Collection of Conflict Data." *Journal of Peace Research* 52(1): 105–109.

Salehyan, Idean, Cullen S. Hendrix, Jesse Hamner, Christina Case, Christopher Linebarger, Emily Stull, and Jennifer Williams. 2012. "Social Conflict in Africa: A New Database." *International Interactions* 38(4): 503–511.

Schutte, Sebastian, and Karsten Donnay. 2014. "Matched Wake Analysis: Finding Causal Relationships in Spatiotemporal Event Data." *Political Geography* 41: 1–10.

START (National Consortium for the Study of Terrorism and Responses to Terrorism). 2013. "Global Terrorism Database: Codebook: Inclusion Criteria and Variables." Retrieved from http://www.start.umd.edu/gtd/downloads/Codebook.pdf.

Steinwand, Martin C. 2015. "Foreign Aid and Political Stability." *Conflict Management and Peace Science* 32(4): 395–424.

Sullivan, Christopher. 2015. "Undermining Resistance: Mobilization, Repression, and the Enforcement of Political Order." *Journal of Conflict Resolution*, doi: 10.1177/0022002714567951.

Sundberg, Ralph, and Erik Melander. 2013. "Introducing the UCDP Georeferenced Event Dataset." *Journal of Peace Research* 50(4): 523–532.

Sutton, Paul C., Christopher D. Elvidge and Tilottama Ghosh. 2007. "Estimation of Gross Domestic Product at Sub-national Scales Using Nighttime Satellite Imagery." *International Journal of Ecological Economics and Statistics* 8(S07): 5–21.

Syriahr. 2015. Syrian Observatory for Human Rights. Accessible at http://www.syriahr.com/en/.

Tiernay, Michael. 2015. "Killing Kony: Leadership Change and Civil War Termination." *Journal of Conflict Resolution* 59(2): 175–206.

UCDP (Uppsala Conflict Data Program). 2014. "UCDP Actor Dataset 2.2–2014." Uppsala University. http://www.pcr.uu.se/research/ucdp/datasets/ucdp_actor_dataset/.

Ulfelder, Jay. 2015. "The Myth of Comprehensive Data." Blog post. https://dartthrowingchimp.wordpress.com/2015/05/07/the-myth-of-comprehensive-data/.

Uzonyi, Gary. 2015. "Refugee Flows and State Contributions to Post–Cold War UN Peacekeeping Missions." *Journal of Peace Research*, doi: 10.1177/0022343315574353.

Vogt, Manuel, Nils-Christian Bormann, Seraina Rüegger, Lars-Erik Cederman, Philipp Hunziker, and Luc Girardin. 2015. "Integrating Data on Ethnicity, Geography, and Conflict: The Ethnic Power Relations Dataset Family." *Journal of Conflict Resolution* 59(7): 1327–1342.

Ward, Michael D., Brian Greenhill, and Kristin Bakke. 2010. "The Perils of Policy by p-Value." *Journal of Peace Research* 47(4): 363–375.

Weidmann, Nils B. 2013. "The Higher the Better? The Limits of Analytical Resolution in Conflict Event Datasets." *Cooperation and Conflict* 48(4): 567–576.

Weidmann, Nils B. 2015. "On the Accuracy of Media-Based Conflict Event Data." *Journal of Conflict Resolution* 59(6): 1129–1149.

Weidmann, Nils B., and Idean Salehyan. 2013. "Violence and Ethnic Segregation: A Computational Model Applied to Baghdad." *International Studies Quarterly* 57(1): 52–64.

Weidmann, Nils B., and Sebastian Schutte. 2016. "Using Night Lights for the Prediction of Local Wealth." Forthcoming in *Journal of Peace*.

Weller, Nicholas, and Kenneth McCubbins. 2014. "Raining on the Parade: Some Cautions regarding the Global Database of Events, Language and Tone Dataset." Blog post. http://politicalviolenceataglance.org/2014/02/20/ /raining-on-the-parade-some-cautions-regarding-the-global-database-of-events-language-and-tone-dataset/.

Wigmore-Shepherd, Daniel. 2015. "Reporting Sources." ACLED Working Paper no. 5. Armed Conflict Location and Event Data Project.

Witmer, Frank D. W. 2015. "Remote Sensing of Violent Conflict: Eyes from Above." *International Journal of Remote Sensing* 36(9): 2326–2352.

Zeitzoff, Thomas. 2011. "Using Social Media to Measure Conflict Dynamics: An Application to the 2008–2009 Gaza Conflict." *Journal of Conflict Resolution* 55(6): 938–969.

3

Armed Conflict, 1946–2014

Håvard Strand and Halvard Buhaug

Introduction

After a steady and pronounced drop in armed conflict from the end of the Cold War era into the early 2000s, the global rate of conflict has fluctuated over the past decade, with no apparent underlying trend. At the same time, recent events in countries such as Syria, Libya, Nigeria, and Ukraine, which are making headlines, give the impression that the world is becoming ever more violent. Fortunately, such a conclusion is not warranted. Despite the seeming stagnation of the decline of war and the fact that 2014 was unusually violent in comparison with preceding years, the seventy years that have passed since the end of World War II may well constitute the most peaceful period in human history (Goldstein 2011; Pinker 2011). Indeed, measured in terms of the number of people killed on the battlefield, the first fifteen years of the 21th century have been especially peaceful.

The main reason for the long-term decline in conflict-related casualties is that war between countries is almost extinct. While civil wars certainly can be destructive, they rarely produce catastrophes at the level of interstate wars. The major human disasters of the 20th century involved repugnant ideologies like fascism, communism and, to a lesser degree, imperialism, which are largely buried. Totalitarian tendencies within political Islam are a cause for concern, but they are yet to produce mayhem at the same level as conventional wars.

Overall Trends

The Uppsala Conflict Data Program (UCDP), the leading provider of statistics on political violence, has identified 259 distinct armed conflicts since 1946. This includes all organized military conflict over control of government or territory involving one or more state government(s) and causing at least 25 battle-related fatalities in a calendar year. The dataset distinguishes between three main forms of armed conflict: extrasystemic conflict, which is defined as conflict between a state and a non-state actor outside the state's territory (such as colonies); interstate conflict, which captures fighting between independent states; and internal (or civil) conflict, which is understood as conflict between a state and a non-state actor within the state's territory. Internal conflicts where one or both sides receive military support from other states are sometimes referred to as internationalized internal conflict.

Figure 3.1 (see next page) displays the number of conflicts around the world by type and year since 1946. Two trends over the long term are immediately detectable.

The first trend is that extrasystemic and interstate conflicts, which accounted for half of all armed conflict early in the period, have largely waned. The liberation of Angola and Mozambique from Portuguese rule in 1975 marked the end of the colonial era, and military confrontations between states have become increasingly rare, too. Today, the predominant form of conflict is internal to a state, although quite often involving external state actors, as exemplified by Russia supporting separatist rebels in Eastern Ukraine, and Cameroon, Chad, and Niger joining Nigeria's fight against the *Jama'atu Ahlis Sunna Lidda'awati wal-Jihad* (also known as *Boko Haram*).

The second trend is the distinct "inverted U-shaped" surrounding a peak in conflict frequency in 1991. During the first two decades of the data series, the number of conflicts in the world hovered at a comparatively low rate of 15 to 20 per year. Despite the low number of conflicts, this period contained some of the most deadly wars in the post–World War II era, notably the Chinese Civil War (1946–1949) and the Korean War (1950–1953). About a fourth of the cases were

Number of
Active Conflicts

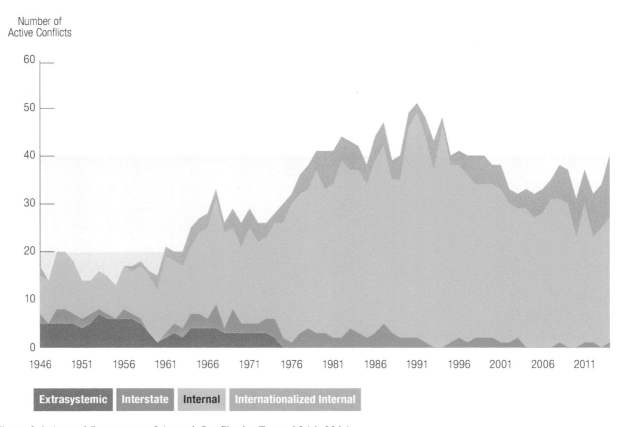

Figure 3.1 Annual Frequency of Armed Conflict by Type, 1946–2014

extrasystemic conflicts, predominantly in Asia, and all of them eventually resulted in successful independence for the separatist territories. Moreover, several of the internal conflicts during the period were remnants of World War II, such as Greece (1946–1949), the Soviet Union (Baltic region and Ukraine, 1946–1952), and Iran (South Azerbaijan, 1946).

Beginning in the early 1960s, the number of conflicts per annum increased fairly steadily for three decades. The main reason was that conflicts became more lasting. Consequently, more conflicts started than ended. This pattern is illustrated in Figure 3.2 (see next page). Many of these conflicts were so-called proxy wars, where the Cold War antagonists supported each side in the conflict with money, weapons, intelligence, and expertise, and sometimes boots on the ground. The civil wars in Angola, Cambodia, El Salvador, and Ethiopia during the 1970s and 1980s are examples of such indirect major power contestation. Waging large-scale war is very costly, and external financial support was crucial to sustaining violence in many of these cases.

The imminent collapse of the Soviet Union and the seeming global victory of liberal democracy and free markets around 1990 were accompanied by extensive – and largely unforeseen – eruption of violence. The transformation from totalitarian despotism to liberal democracy was highly successful in select countries such as Poland, but many other countries were less fortunate. The Burmese communists were replaced by a military junta, the Chinese regime vehemently struck down on peaceful pro-democracy activists, and the violent breakups of the Soviet Union and Yugoslavia also contributed to a global peak in armed conflict. The war in Bosnia (1992–1995) was especially atrocious, and the country remains in a fragile situation even today. Furthermore, the disappearance of a communist threat meant that Western powers were much less willing to condone dictators in the third world. As a by-product, a series of violent transitions engulfed Africa. Some were largely successful in establishing law and order (e.g., South Africa, Kenya), whereas others failed miserably (e.g., Zimbabwe, Somalia, Rwanda). The absence of third-party support also meant that rebels had to find their income elsewhere. Often, the solution was looting of precious natural resources, pillaging of the local population, and extensive drug trafficking.

A more benign consequence of the demise of major power rivalry was that it allowed the United Nations Security Council to emerge as a potent force for peace. The number of peacekeeping and peace-enforcing missions organized by either the UN or regional organizations spiked during the 1990s. This increased international activism, accompanied by an increasing acceptance for "liberal" values such as democracy and respect for human rights, contributed to an unprecedented drop in the number of armed conflicts (Gleditsch 2008). For the first time since 1945, the rate of conflict

Number of New Conflicts

Average Duration of Active Conflicts (years)

Figure 3.2 Annual Frequency of New Conflict Outbreaks and Average Conflict Duration, 1946–2014

resolutions exceeded the number of conflict outbreaks for several consecutive years. This positive development has since lost momentum, however, and 2014 set the record for the highest number of active conflicts (40) in this century.

Figure 3.2 gives a more systematic portrayal of the dynamics of conflict outbreak and duration. The red trend line represents the average duration (in years) for all active conflicts. The orange bars represent the number of conflicts that either appear for the first time or return from some period of inactivity. Following the general increase in conflict frequency, the average duration of conflicts rose during the Cold War period. In 1960, the average conflict had been active for just five years, whereas in 1988 – a year with no new outbreaks of conflict – the average duration had nearly tripled, to 14 years. This figure has since dropped somewhat, partly due to the end of the long-lasting proxy wars. Nonetheless, the average conflict today remains considerably longer in duration than what was observed during most of the Cold War era. Aside from the escalation of violence in the wake of the Soviet collapse, the rate of outbreaks has remained fairly stable over the past half century at around four to seven new conflicts per year.

In this regard, 2014 stands out as well, with 13 conflicts that either started or restarted – more than in any other year since 1997. Four of these conflicts were clustered in Ukraine. They appeared in succession; only one was still ongoing at the end of the year. The remaining cases were renewed conflicts in India, Mali, Nagorno-Karabakh, Kashmir, Gaza, Lebanon, Egypt, Myanmar, and Libya. Several of these cases can be directly linked to the aftermath of the Arab spring. Whether 2014 will turn out to be a new 1989 is too early to tell.

Simple statistics of the incidence of conflict provide useful information on the state of security in the world, but they also can be misleading. The 259 armed conflicts since 1946 vary enormously, in terms of the number of warring parties, geographic scope, the duration of hostilities, and the extent of casualties. Some conflicts, like the Korean War, are relatively short, yet very violent. Indeed, very intense conflicts usually do not last for more than a decade. At the other end of the spectrum, more than one in ten conflicts lasted less than a year with less than 1,000 casualties, while one in five never totaled 1,000 casualties during their entire span.

If we seek information on whether the world is becoming more or less violent, the number of fatalities is a better indicator. Figure 3.3 (see next page) shows the estimated number of battle-related deaths in armed conflicts by year since 1946, expressed as a proportion of the contemporaneous global population. The trend, when compared to Figure 3.1 above, is striking. Overall, there is a remarkable downward trend over time. To culminate the trend, the rate of conflict fatalities in the 21st century is only a fraction of what it was during the Cold War. The trend of battle-related fatalities is not smooth over time. Figure 3.3 is dominated by a limited number of very severe conflicts, such as the Chinese Civil War (1946–1949), Korea (1950–1953), Vietnam (1955–1975), Algeria (1950s and 1990s), Iran-Iraq (1980–1988), and the Soviet Union's involvement in Afghanistan (1980–1989).[1] The civil war in the Democratic Republic of the Congo at the turn of the 21st century, sometimes referred to as Africa's World War, also caused a visible bump in the graph. It is worth

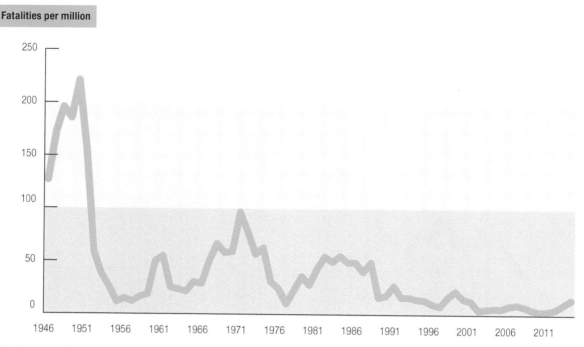

Fatalities per million

Figure 3.3 Annual Rate of Battle-Related Deaths in Armed Conflict, 1946–2014

noting, however, that every new spike throughout the post-World War II period is lower than the previous one. The same is true if we consider the absolute fatality figures, instead of fatalities relative to the global population.[2]

A typical characteristic of long-lasting conflicts is that they tend to be maintained at relatively low levels of intensity. Indeed, some of the oldest ongoing conflicts, such as those found in peripheral parts of India and Myanmar where indigenous groups have been fighting for generations, periodically fail to meet the UCDP dataset's threshold criterion of 25 battle-related deaths per annum and thus are not considered "active" in every year. Similarly, both the increasingly drug-oriented conflict in Colombia and the Palestinian insurgency in Israel have persisted for over half a century, but violence has been at a relatively low level of severity for most of this time.

Understanding the Decline

The trends portrayed above imply that the average conflict is claiming fewer lives over time. An important explanation for the decline of war is major shifts in the world order. The final stages of World War II gave hope to many former colonies. The Atlantic Charter outlined a process of independence for existing colonies, but the post-war animosity between the former allies as well as the death of President Roosevelt put these promises on hold (Tønneson 2009). The resulting gap between promises and realities led to a string of nationalist uprisings. Many of these conflicts became aligned with the Cold War. Since the dominant colonial powers were largely western states, rebel organizations draped a communist ideology in exchange for military support from the Soviet bloc.

The East-West rivalry maintained its grip on many conflicts beyond the decolonization era. East Asia – the center of gravity for political violence from the 1950s through 1970s – managed to escape the conflict trap after the fall of Pol Pot in 1979. By contrast, Latin America and Sub-Saharan Africa continued to be fueled by the competing ideologies. With the demise of the Cold War, funding and military supplies dried up. In some cases, rebels managed to convert to new sources of funding, such as trade in diamonds and illicit drugs. This transition was observed most notably across Western and Central Africa, as well as in Afghanistan, Colombia, and Myanmar. Many other conflicts in Latin America and elsewhere lacked the means to sustain themselves under the new geopolitical order at the end of the 1980s.

In an increasingly interdependent world, war becomes costlier. At the same time, the spread of democracy, growing membership of countries in intergovernmental organizations (IGOs), and a more active United Nations have created new norms, fora, and mechanisms fostering dialogue and mediation that have paved the way for peaceful resolution of disputes between states. Economic interdependence and prosperity may also contribute to the decline in the severity of conflict within states. Low level of economic development and poor economic performance are robustly associated with higher conflict risk, because unemployed and poor people are comparatively cheap to recruit and weak states are less able to deliver public goods such as education, health, and security (Blattman and Miguel 2010). More capable governments not

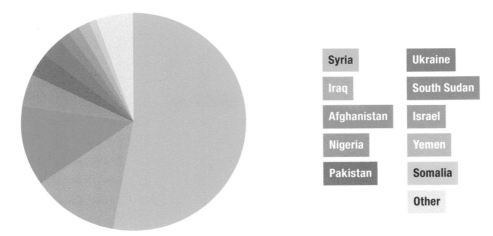

Syria   Ukraine

Iraq   South Sudan

Afghanistan   Israel

Nigeria   Yemen

Pakistan   Somalia

Other

Figure 3.4 Distribution of Battle-Related Deaths among Armed Conflicts in 2014, by Country

only tend to reduce social grievances and motives for protest, they are generally better able to curb emerging violence and limit uprisings to peripheral, less densely populated areas. This combination of factors may help explain why the fatality levels of recent conflicts have remained far below the levels of the revolutionary civil wars of the 1960s and 1970s.

Improvements in technology and changing military doctrines may also have contributed to the decline of conflict fatalities.[3] The major wars of the 1950s and 1960s saw large-scale military battles between huge conventional forces, involving heavy artillery and aerial bombardment. The conflicts (including counter-insurgencies) of the 21st century are more often characterized by highly asymmetric battles involving improvised explosive devices (IEDs), small arms and light weapons, and drones and other smart weapons technology. This general trend is not without exceptions, however, as exemplified by the ongoing war zones of Syria, Libya, and Eastern Ukraine.

Islam's Internal Conflict

Although much of the world is considerably more peaceful today than 15–20 years ago, the Middle East and North Africa (MENA) region has evolved in the opposite direction. Likewise, predominantly Muslim countries outside the Middle East have either experienced a deteriorating security situation or have failed to put a lasting end to enduring violent unrest.[4] In addition, several countries with heterogeneous populations are sites of insurgencies involving Islamist groups. As a result, an increasing share of the world's armed conflicts occurs in Muslim countries or involves Islamist non-state actors.

The increasing concentration of armed conflicts in the Muslim world is especially notable for the most severe internal conflicts, namely civil wars (commonly defined as causing at least 1,000 fatalities per year). Since the initial wave of uprisings across the Arab world in 2011, more than 95% of all battle-related deaths in armed conflict occurred in Muslim countries. Not surprisingly, the civil war in Syria and the battles involving ISIS in Syria and Iraq account for a large fraction of these casualties. Figure 3.4 displays the distribution of conflict fatalities in 2014. The wars in Syria, Iraq, and Afghanistan together generated nearly 79,000 deaths (UCDP conservative estimate), which is more than three-quarters of all recorded fatalities in 2014. Ukraine is the only country in the top-10 list that did not involve a conflict actor with an Islamist ideology.

Does this imply that Samuel P. Huntington's (1991) 25-year-old thesis of a clash of civilizations is coming true? Certainly not in the strictest sense. The fact that the large majority of victims as well as perpetrators of violence in these conflicts are Muslims is incompatible with both the notion of "the West against the rest" and "Islam's bloody borders." Rather, most of these conflicts are the result of incompatible views within the Muslim population on the organization of the state and the extent to which Islamic codes and law, such as *Sharia*, should play a formal role in politics and society.

At the same time, the US-led "war on terror" since 2001, with military interventions and strikes in Afghanistan, Iraq, Libya, Pakistan, Somalia, Yemen, and elsewhere, has served as a motivation for widespread radicalization in many Muslim countries and growing support for Islamist movements and ideology. In turn, radicalized, disgruntled youths have risen up against oppressive, semi-secular dictators, many of whom were originally instated or remained in power with Western blessing and support. Moreover, the liberal popular movements shaping the initial stages of the "Arab spring" uprisings of 2011 have since been replaced largely by militant Islamism.

2014 and the Future

The facts about conflict show that 2014 was a particularly troublesome year. The civil war in Syria and the crisis in the Ukraine occupied much of the attention, but large-scale conflict also unfolded in a widely dispersed list of countries such as Afghanistan, Iraq, Nigeria, Pakistan, Somalia, and Yemen, as well as in Gaza.

Our starting place was the count of conflicts as defined by UCDP. If nothing else changes, we expect a reduction in the number of conflicts from 2014 to 2015. The reason is that UCDP has defined four different conflicts in Ukraine in 2014, only one of which is currently active (Novorossiya). Hence, the three other Ukrainian conflicts coded in 2014 are not expected to remain part of the count for 2015. This does not make the situation on the ground any better as such. Rather, it underscores that all statistics must be read with some caution.

What is less subject to interpretation is the fact that more than 100,000 people died as a direct consequence of conflict in 2014, for the first time since 1989. This is proper cause for concern. The civil war in Syria is responsible for more than half of this number, but several other conflicts escalated in intensity from 2013 to 2014.

That said, it is important to put things in perspective. The current situation is not as bad as it was during the 1980s, when Cold War politics were fueling numerous proxy conflicts and the massive Iran-Iraq war was underway. Massive warfare in East Asia – conflicts on an entirely different scale – has ceased to exist for the last generation.

In sum, 2014 was a horrible year for conflict viewed in the context of the last 25 years, but not as severe in the context of the last 70 years since World War II.

Notes

1 These wars account for about 50% of all casualties in the post-Word War II period.
2 These figures reflect battle-related casualties. Estimating the total number of casualties associated with conflict, including indirect effects (e.g., civilian collateral damage, starvation/malnutrition, disease, displacement), is notoriously difficult. See the Human Security Report (2009:101ff) for a very good discussion of these issues.
3 Fazal (2014) argues that the corresponding technological improvement in the art of saving lives is responsible for the decline of war casualties. Countering this argument, one might ask whether these improvements are readily available in the more war-prone regions of the world.
4 For simplicity, we consider a country to be Muslim if Islam constitutes the majority religion.

References

Blattman, Christopher, and Edward Miguel. 2010. "Civil War." *Journal of Economic Literature* 48(1): 3–57.
Fazal, Tanisha. 2014. "Dead Wrong? Battle Deaths, Military Medicine, and Exaggerated Reports of War's Demise." *International Security* 39(1): 95–125.
Gleditsch, Nils Petter. 2008. "The Liberal Moment Fifteen Years On." *International Studies Quarterly* 52(4): 691–712.
Goldstein, Joshua S. 2011. *Winning the War on War: The Decline of Armed Conflict Worldwide.* New York: Dutton.
Human Security Report. 2009. "The Causes of Peace and the Shrinking Cost of War." http://www.hsrgroup.org/human-security-reports/20092010/text.aspx.
Huntington, Samuel P. 1993. "The Clash of Civilizations?" *Foreign Affairs* 72(3): 22–49.
Pinker, Steven. 2011. *The Better Angels of Our Nature.* New York: Viking.
Tønnesson, Stein. 2009. *Vietnam 1946: How the War Began.* Berkeley: University of California Press.

4

Patterns and Trends of the Geography of Conflict

Roudabeh Kishi, Clionadh Raleigh and Andrew M. Linke

Introduction

Recent scholarly work suggests a decline in violence rates generally (Pinker 2011), as well as in Sub-Saharan Africa specifically (Straus 2012). Such conclusions are reinforced by evidence that violent interstate conflict and civil wars have become less frequent (Gleditsch and Pickering 2014). Yet, when considering multiple forms of political violence, the rate of conflict occurrence in Africa remains staggeringly high (see Figure 4.1, displaying the reported numbers of conflict events by type [left axis] and fatalities [right axis, yellow line] between 1997 and 2014).[1] The Armed Conflict Location and Event Data (ACLED) Project (Raleigh, Linke, Hegre, and Karlsen 2010) recorded a reported total of 10,174 organized, armed conflict events in Africa for 2014.[2] This represents a 21.4 percent increase from the 8,379 reported organized, armed conflict events that were recorded by ACLED for 2013.[3]

In this chapter, we discuss the agents, multiple types, geography, and dynamics of political violence and protest. An underlying aim is to address a fundamental question: how are conflict patterns and dynamics changing over time?

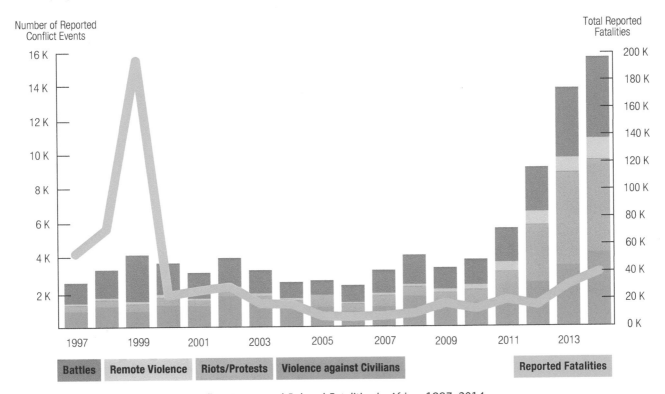

Figure 4.1 Annual Prevalence of Conflict Events and Related Fatalities in Africa, 1997–2014

Our analyses present descriptive accounts of recent trends in violence, relying on Version 5 of the ACLED dataset, released in 2015 (Version 6 was released in 2016, after this book went to press). By using this source, we more fully account for incidents of violence (e.g., civilian targeting; battles between groups that do not meet specific fatality thresholds; social unrest, such as riots and protests) that do not necessarily constitute war as defined by other datasets. As a result, our findings deviate from studies that use more traditional understandings of conflict, especially that which involves fighting among states and non-state armed actors.

We concentrate on the extensive data collected for Africa from 1997–2014 (see Figure 4.2 for a map of all political conflict and protests across Africa in 2014).[4] As ACLED-Africa covers North Africa in addition to all Sub-Saharan states, we capture some of the relevant dynamics of the current crisis in the Middle East and North Africa region, which has been ongoing since the Arab Spring. The rising number of reported violent incidents across the continent over the last several years is largely driven by violence in Nigeria (especially Boko Haram conflict activity), Libya (increased use of remote violence tactics), and Somalia (where Al Shabaab violence persists).[5] In select cases, reported conflict has become more deadly on average (with conflict events typically resulting in a greater number of fatalities): the ratio of reported fatalities to events has nearly doubled in Nigeria and more than doubled in Libya. More often, conflict is becoming less deadly: the ratio of reported fatalities to events has even decreased for several especially violent countries, including South Sudan, Somalia, Sudan, the Central African Republic (CAR), and the Democratic Republic of the Congo (DRC). Our focus on Africa is supplemented with data recently collected for South and Southeast Asia. ACLED-Asia is collecting information on political conflict and protests that extends back to 1997 for most countries, and to 2010 for India and Pakistan. To facilitate comparison with our present sample, we compare African and Asian contexts using the concept of a *micromort*, or a "unit of risk" over the coverage period. These micromorts are examined in further detail at the end of the chapter.

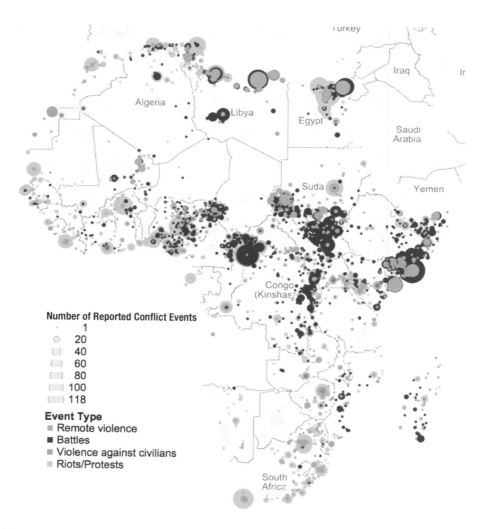

Figure 4.2 Conflict in Africa during 2014, by Event Type

Types of Violence

Figure 4.3 displays the proportions of reported conflict events by type (top) and the corresponding proportions of reported fatalities by event type (bottom). In 2014, riots and protests comprised the largest share of reported social unrest events in Africa (34 percent), followed closely by political violence including battles between armed groups (30 percent), and violence against civilians (27 percent), with remote violence (8 percent) a distant last among the measured types.

Violence against Civilians

In 2014, over 4,200 reported instances of civilian targeting were observed in Africa. This figure represents an increase of 737 events from 2013 and is the highest since ACLED records began in 1997. The intensity of these attacks increased as well, accounting for 34 percent of all reported conflict-related fatalities (over 13,500 deaths). Over 4,000 more civilian fatalities were reported in 2014 relative to 2013.[6]

Civilians are most at risk in Somalia, Sudan, Nigeria, the CAR, and the DRC; each country experienced over 350 reported instances of violence against civilians in 2014. In the CAR, Sudan, and Nigeria, civilian targeting comprised more than half of the reported organized, armed conflict events in 2014 (66.9 percent, 60.7 percent, and 60.5 percent, respectively). Violence against civilians was also responsible for significant shares of reported organized, armed violence in the DRC (49.9 percent) and Somalia (24 percent).

This ominous trend is driven by the growing role of political militias in targeting civilians. Militias have been attracting increased attention as a conflict actor, especially within the relevant literature (for example, see the August 2015 special issue of the *Journal of Conflict Resolution* on militias in civil wars). Political militias are militant groups that use violence as a means to shape and influence the existing political system, but do not seek to overthrow national regimes. These groups often operate as armed gangs for different political elites, including politicians, governments, and opposition groups (Raleigh 2016). Political militias are distinct from communal militias – local, community-based armed units that are involved in conflict as a result of power vacuums, livelihood competition, and persistent localized contests, as opposed to power dynamics within the political system.

Figure 4.4 (see next page) depicts the proportions of reported events involving various conflict agents (top), as well as the proportion of reported fatalities associated with each agent (bottom). In 2009, political militias were responsible for only about 9 percent of reported civilian fatalities (476 deaths). In 2014, militias accounted for 58 percent of reported civilian fatalities (over 7,900 deaths) – the highest level in the 18 years covered by ACLED. Meanwhile, the proportions

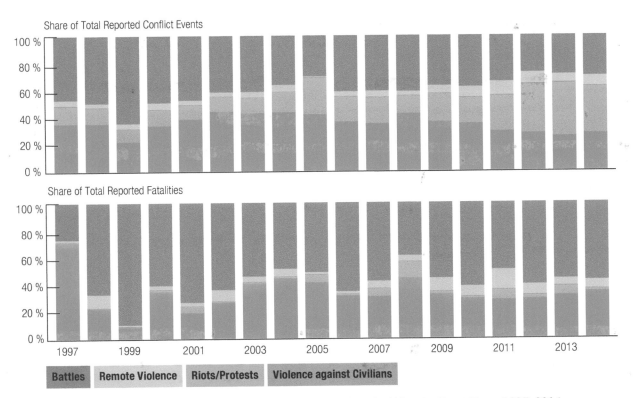

Figure 4.3 Annual Distributions of Conflict Events and Related Fatalities in Africa, by Event Type, 1997–2014

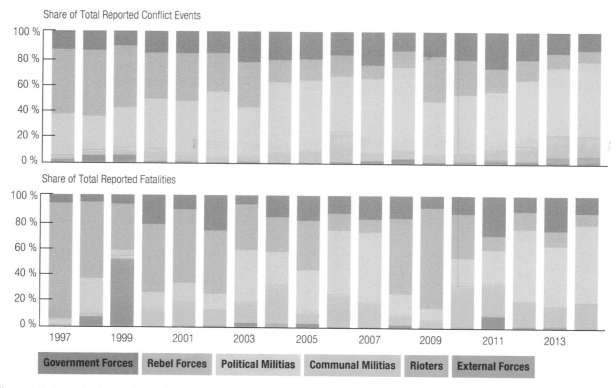

Share of Total Reported Conflict Events

Share of Total Reported Fatalities

Government Forces | Rebel Forces | Political Militias | Communal Militias | Rioters | External Forces

Figure 4.4 Annual Distributions of Conflict Events and Related Fatalities in Africa, by Perpetrator, 1997–2014

of reported civilian targeting decreased from 2013 to 2014 for government forces (16 percent to 13 percent), rebel groups (10 percent to 8 percent), and communal militias (16 percent to 15 percent).

Some of the deadliest non-state actors are responsible for the majority of violence against civilians. The deadliest of all conflict actors across Africa in 2014, Boko Haram, single-handedly accounted for 31 percent of reported civilian fatalities. This statistic is especially remarkable considering the group's relatively limited zone of activity. Operating primarily in northeastern Nigeria, Boko Haram (in navy) was responsible for 3,428 reported civilian fatalities in 2014, compared to 1,009 (15 percent of reported civilian fatalities across Africa) in 2013 (see Figure 4.5 on next page).

In 2014, the Anti-Balaka and Séléka militias, operating in the western part of the CAR, were each responsible for around 800 reported civilian fatalities (1,599 deaths in total; 14 percent of all reported civilian fatalities across Africa). This level of involvement in civilian targeting represents a dramatic increase: in 2013, the two groups together were responsible for around 800 reported civilian deaths (11 percent of all reported civilian fatalities across Africa). Meanwhile, the Rapid Support Forces (RSF) was responsible for 270 reported civilian fatalities (2.4 percent of all reported civilian fatalities across Africa) in western Sudan in 2014.

Of government forces in Africa, the militaries of Nigeria and South Sudan were the most violent toward civilians in 2014. Each of these militaries was attributed responsibility for over 600 reported civilian deaths (5 percent of all reported civilian fatalities across Africa apiece). The high level of deaths from civilian targeting by the Nigerian military is notable (see Figure 4.5 on next page, in orange, comparing the severity of such cases of targeting killings in 2013 [left map] and 2014 [right map]), given that they were responsible for just 54 reported civilian deaths (less than 1 percent of all reported civilian fatalities across Africa) in 2013. By contrast, the military forces of South Sudan had been responsible for 939 reported civilian deaths (12 percent of all reported civilian fatalities across Africa) in 2013. The reduction is largely attributable to the mutiny of the military forces of South Sudan and the subsequent formation of the rebel group SPLA/M-In Opposition (SPLA/M-IO). In 2014, the SPLA/M-IO killed 485 civilians (4 percent of all reported civilian deaths across Africa) in northeastern South Sudan, making it the deadliest rebel group in Africa.

Another rebel force active in civilian targeting was Al Shabaab, responsible for killing a reported 345 civilians (3 percent of all reported civilian fatalities in Africa), primarily in southern Somalia and eastern Kenya, during 2014. Among communal militias, the Fulani ethnic militia of Nigeria was the most deadly in targeting civilians, responsible for over 1,300 reported killings (over 12 percent of all reported civilian fatalities across Africa) in central Nigeria during 2014. This figure is over three times the number perpetrated by Fulani fighters against civilians in 2013, when the group was responsible for

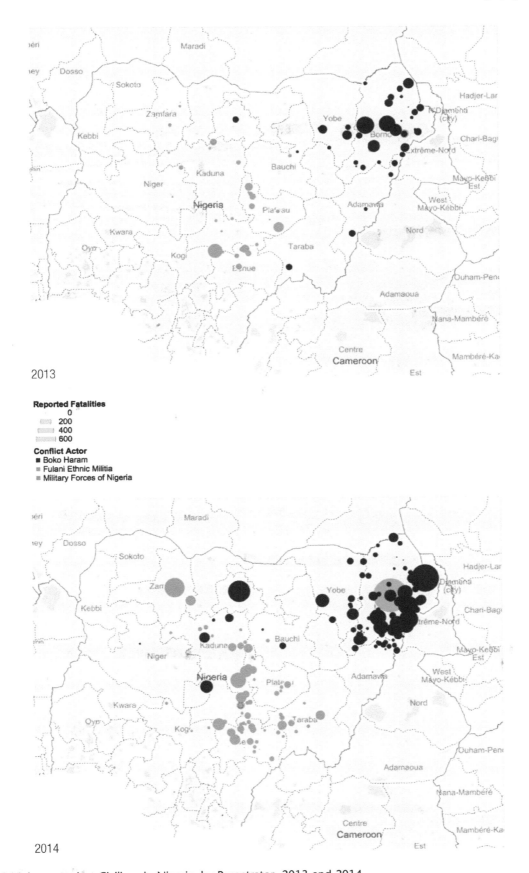

2013

Reported Fatalities
- 0
- 200
- 400
- 600

Conflict Actor
- Boko Haram
- Fulani Ethnic Militia
- Military Forces of Nigeria

2014

Figure 4.5 Violence against Civilians in Nigeria, by Perpetrator, 2013 and 2014

417 reported deaths (5 percent of all reported civilian fatalities across Africa). Figure 4.5 shows the geographic distribution of these events (in blue) relative to those perpetrated by Boko Haram and the Nigerian military, clearly depicting the increase between 2013 (left map) and 2014 (right map).

Remote Violence

Scholars argue that tools of remote violence are symbolic weapons, which can be used to demonstrate a regime's vulnerability to violence or a government's inability to protect its citizens (McCormick and Giordano 2007). By targeting agents of the state, civilians, or popular locations and monuments, conflict actors can use these weapons to undermine confidence in the government and influence public opinion and government policies (Merari 1993). For non-state actors such as political militias that are weaker than government forces, remote violence is an ideal tactic to either damage state forces with minimal risk or to coerce the state without controlling it. This tactic also fits into a strategy of groups resorting to so-called "weapons of the weak" after losing territory and influence, which has been observed in numerous settings, including Afghanistan (Denselow 2010).

The use of remote violence is becoming more common and deadlier in conflict zones around the world, with Africa mirroring this trend (ACLED 2015b). Remote violence is defined as a violent event where a spatially removed group determines the time, place, and victims of the attack using an explosive device. In these types of events, including bombings, improvised explosive device (IED) attacks, and missile attacks, conflict engagement does not require the physical presence of the perpetrator. As governments consolidate more control over their territory and as credible attempts to usurp state power decrease, remote violence may become a more frequent fixture of African conflicts.

During 2014, over 1,200 remote violence events were reported – the highest number during the period that ACLED covers. Remote violence events also comprised 8 percent of all reported conflict events in 2014, up from 6 percent in 2013. Also, 7 percent of all reported conflict-related fatalities in 2014 were attributed to remote violence, compared to the average of 5 percent for the period that ACLED covers. The proportion of reported conflict-related fatalities attributed to remote violence increased by about 20 percent, from 5.6 percent in 2013 to 6.7 percent in 2014, while the total number of reported fatalities was up 56 percent from 1,677 in 2013 to 2,621 in 2014. More developed states (e.g., Libya) have been increasingly involved in conflict. As a result, the tools of violence have become more advanced. Examples of remote violence attacks include bombings and other armed campaigns against Islamist militants in Nigeria (by government forces).

Figure 4.6 (see next page) displays the locations and prevalence of reported remote violence events across Africa from 1997–2002 (left map), 2003–2008 (middle map), and 2009–2014 (right map) to 2014. An immediate observation is that remote violence takes place across nearly all geographical regions of Africa. Yet some stark spatial patterns emerge. The largest share (32 percent) of reported remote violence events during 2014 occurred in Somalia, which was also the deadliest country for remote violence (35 percent of reported fatalities across Africa) in 2014 (see Figure 4.7 on p. 32, which compares remote violence in Somalia during 2013 [left map] and 2014 [right map]). These findings are largely attributable to the increasing use of such tactics by Al Shabaab – as well as unidentified armed groups, which may be acting on behalf of other conflict actors (ACLED 2015c) – in lieu of relying on more conventional heavy armaments. Remote violence is also carried out by government forces and their allies in Somalia.

The next-most deadly country for remote violence in 2014 was Nigeria (27 percent of reported fatalities across Africa). These events primarily involved political militias attacking civilians through the use of bombs and explosives. Libya (14 percent) and Sudan (9 percent) follow on the list of countries responsible for the deadliest use of remote violence in 2014.

The use of remote violence has grown throughout much of North Africa, in the wake of increased instability following the Arab Spring. In particular, high concentrations of remote violence were observed during 2014 in Libya (22 percent of the 1,247 reported remote violence events across Africa) and Egypt (15 percent). Sudan exhibits a contrasting trend. In the mid-2000s, Sudan was responsible for the majority of reported remote violence events across Africa, primarily involving bombs used by the Sudanese military against civilians. In 2014, about 72 percent of reported remote violence events in Sudan were attributable to this type of activity. Yet Sudan's share of reported remote violence events in Africa (11 percent), though still substantial, is significantly lower than in previous years.

Riots and Protests

Many scholars are interested in riots and protests as manifestations of unrest that have the potential to further destabilize a political system and ultimately lead to physical insecurity and overt conflict. Of course, riots themselves can be deadly, and events that begin as protests can evolve into riots and even battles, or result in violence against civilians.[7]

Over the last several years, riots and protests as a share of the total social unrest events in Africa has risen compared to earlier years, especially those prior to 2005 (see top panel of Figure 4.3 on p. 27). During 2014, riots and protests

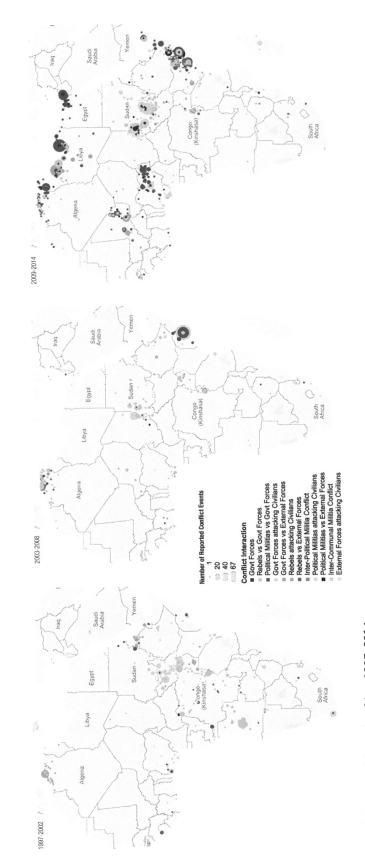

Number of Reported Conflict Events

- 1
- 20
- 40
- 67

Conflict Interaction

- Govt Forces
- Rebels vs Govt Forces
- Political Militias vs Govt Forces
- Govt Forces attacking Civilians
- Govt Forces vs External Forces
- Rebels attacking Civilians
- Rebels vs External Forces
- Inter-Political Militia Conflict
- Political Militias attacking Civilians
- Political Militias vs External Forces
- Inter-Communal Militia Conflict
- External Forces attacking Civilians

1997-2002

2003-2008

2009-2014

Figure 4.6 Remote Violence in Africa, 1997–2014

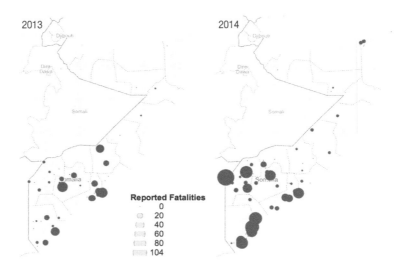

Figure 4.7 Remote Violence in Somalia, 2013 and 2014

comprised 34 percent of all reported political conflict and social unrest events in Africa. The number of reported riots and protests decreased slightly from 5,359 events in 2013 to 5,339 events in 2014 (see Figure 4.8), depicting the number of riots and protests each year [left axis, purple bars], as well as the number of fatalities associated with these events [right axis, orange line]). Yet these figures remain well above the average prevalence for the time period covered by ACLED (blue horizontal line). The number of fatalities associated with these events also decreased between 2013 and 2014, though again remaining above the historical average (red horizontal line).

Nearly half of the reported riots and protests observed across Africa during 2014 were concentrated in three countries: Egypt (18 percent), South Africa (17 percent), and Nigeria (11 percent) (see Figure 4.9 on next page). In Egypt, these events were driven largely by the continued fallout from the Arab Spring, including the Egyptian protest law (see Amnesty International, 2013). In South Africa, the riots and protests were associated primarily with competition surrounding the general elections and mobilization around national issues such as corruption and service delivery (see Paton 2014; Hartley 2014). In Nigeria, the main impulses for riots and protests included Boko Haram and the oil industry.

Agents of Violence

Since 1997, the profile of the major perpetrators of political violence on the African continent has exhibited distinct changes. While every type of violent actor is observed to have engaged in increasing numbers of reported events over recent years, political militias and the armed forces of governments are now responsible for the largest shares of political conflict. Figure 4.10 (see next page) turns the attention to the actors perpetrating events. The results total show a slow rise over time in the number of reported incidents attributed to political militias (in turquoise) from 1997–2008; the number of people reported as killed in these attacks by political militias jumped dramatically from 2009 (3,190 fatalities) to 2014 (21,154 fatalities), accompanying a similarly significant jump in the number of incidents.

Figure 4.11 (see next page) depicts the proportion of involvement in conflict activities by each type of actor. Political militias (in turquoise) were the most active armed group over the last two years, accounting for over 36 percent of all reported political violence in 2013 and 38 percent in 2014. Their level of activity first surpassed rebel forces (in blue) in 2004 and government forces (in purple) in 2005.

In 2013, political militia activity largely involved targeting civilians and battles with government forces. In 2014, civilian targeting increased, comprising almost half (45 percent) of reported political militia activity, resulting in over 8,800 reported fatalities – almost double the figure from 2013. Meanwhile, reported political militia actions against government forces decreased from 40 percent of activity in 2014 to 32 percent in 2014.

Figure 4.12 (see page 35) is a representation of all non-state groups that participated in violent events in Africa during 2014, reflecting the total number of reported fatalities in the reported events with which these groups were associated. The groups are color coded by type of actor. A number of the top participants are also labeled by name. Of note, Islamist groups were heavily active in several countries. Boko Haram participated in events during 2014 with the largest number of fatalities, in total, by a substantial margin. These events resulted in over 9,000 deaths, more than three times the number reported in events with which the group was associated in 2013. The activities of Boko Haram are the principal

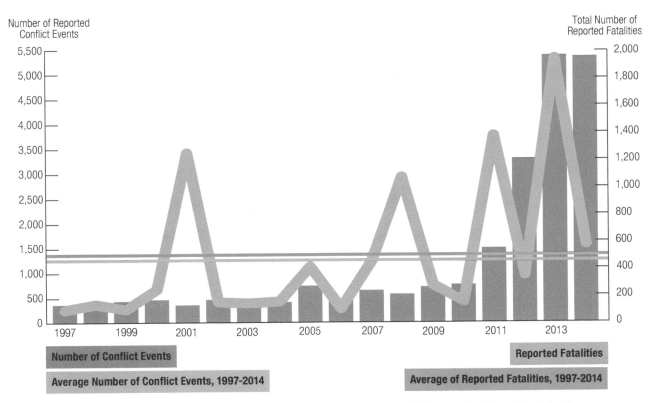

Figure 4.8 Annual Prevalence of Conflict and Related Fatalities due to Riots and Protests in Africa, 1997–2014

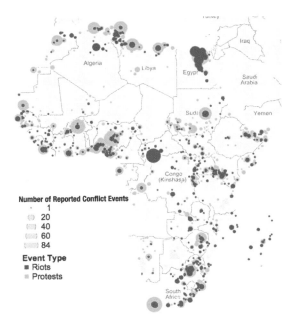

Figure 4.9 Riots and Protests in Africa, 2014

reason why Nigeria is rated the deadliest country for political violence in Africa, with over 29 percent (11,529 deaths) of all reported conflict-related fatalities in 2014, almost twice the share for the second deadliest country (South Sudan).

    Second on the list of non-state participants in deadly violence during 2014 is the Sudan People's Liberation Army/Movement-In Opposition (SPLA/M-IO). The events in which SPLA/M-IO participated resulted in 3,317 reported fatalities in South Sudan. Proportionate to population, more people reportedly died in the events in which SPLA/M-IO participated (South Sudan has a population of 11 million) than those in which Boko Haram participated (Nigeria has a population of 174 million). The non-state actor involved in the largest number of conflict events in 2014 was Al Shabaab

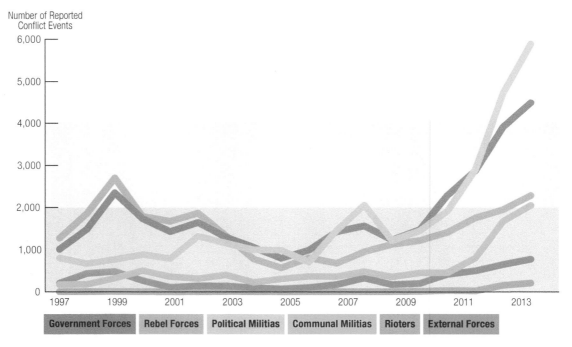

Figure 4.10 Annual Prevalence of Conflict Involvement in Africa, by Type of Actor, 1997–2014

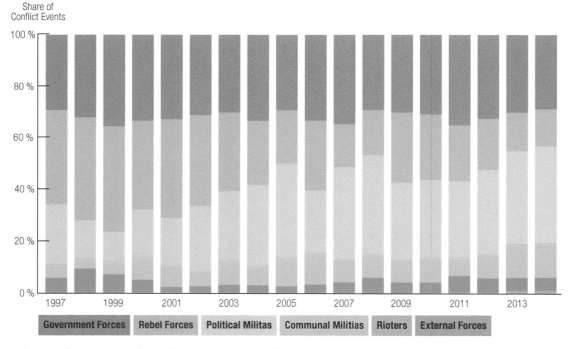

Figure 4.11 Annual Proportion of Conflict Involvement in Africa, by Type of Actor, 1997–2014

(1,277). These events resulted in 3,269 reported fatalities, as a result of which Al Shabaab ranks third in terms of overall participation in deadly violence in Africa during 2014. Al Shabaab was involved in over three times as many conflict events as the SPLA/M-IO, yet the conflicts involving the latter group resulted in more reported fatalities.

The Anti-Balaka and Séléka militias operating in CAR complete the list of the top five non-state participants in deadly violence in Africa during 2014. The role of these militias, each of which participated in events that resulted in over 1,600 reported fatalities in CAR, point to the precarious situation in the country, which has been described as "the worst crisis people have never heard of" by Samantha Power (2013), the US Ambassador to the UN. The prevalence and regional proportion of violent events in CAR nearly doubled from 2013 to 2014, largely a result of the doubling of both the

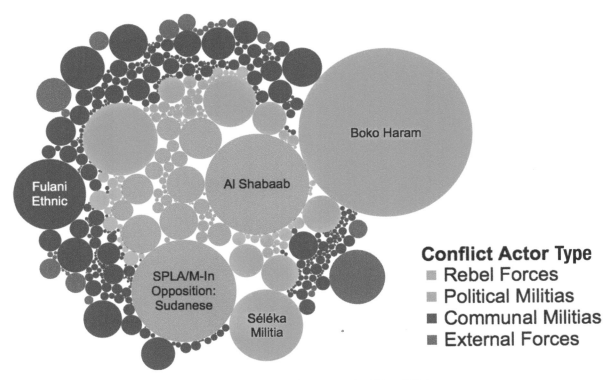

Figure 4.12 Participation of Non-State Actors in Deadly Conflict Events in Africa, 2014

Note: The size of each graduated circle reflects the number of reported fatalities in the conflict events in which an actor participated.

number of battles in the western portion of the country (over 260 battles in 2014) and civilian targeting led by the Anti-Balaka and Séléka militias (over 530 instances of violence against civilians in 2014).

Major Cases of Violence

The top-five deadliest countries for political violence in Africa during 2014 were Nigeria, South Sudan, Sudan, Somalia, and the Central African Republic. Several of these cases have already been discussed in depth. One that we have not featured is Sudan, which faces multiple ongoing crises, some of which overlap, others of which are discrete.

Figure 4.13 (see next page) shows the conflict activity due to these crises that was reported in 2013 (left map) and 2014 (right map). In particular, violence increased in the Darfur region (in the west), which exhibited the highest number of reported conflict events in 2014 of any subnational administrative division among all African countries. This is reflected by the dense cluster of events observed in this region on the map. Violence in Darfur has been a perpetual problem since a decade ago, when the Sudan Liberation Movement/Army (SLM/A) and the Justice and Equality Movement (JEM) rebelled against the state, citing accusations of discrimination, and the state responded with a counter-insurgency campaign (Reuters 2014). According to estimates, hundreds of thousands of people have died in fighting and millions have been displaced (Tran 2014). Another prominent crisis in Sudan involved a campaign of violence against opposition groups in the south of the country, with increased activity by pro-government militias and the Rapid Support Forces (RSF), a paramilitary force operated by the Sudanese government. A third crisis has been simmering tensions between Sudan and South Sudan, which has persisted since the latter gained independence in 2011.

As Figure 4.14 (see p. 37) shows, South Sudan also experienced a major upsurge of communal violence in 2014 (right map), relative to 2013 (left map). This increase in violence was associated with a breakdown among the leadership coalition that led to a civil war between government forces of President Salva Kiir and rebel forces of his former deputy Riek Machar. Large clusters of battles were observed in several parts of the country, whereas violence against civilians had predominated in 2013.

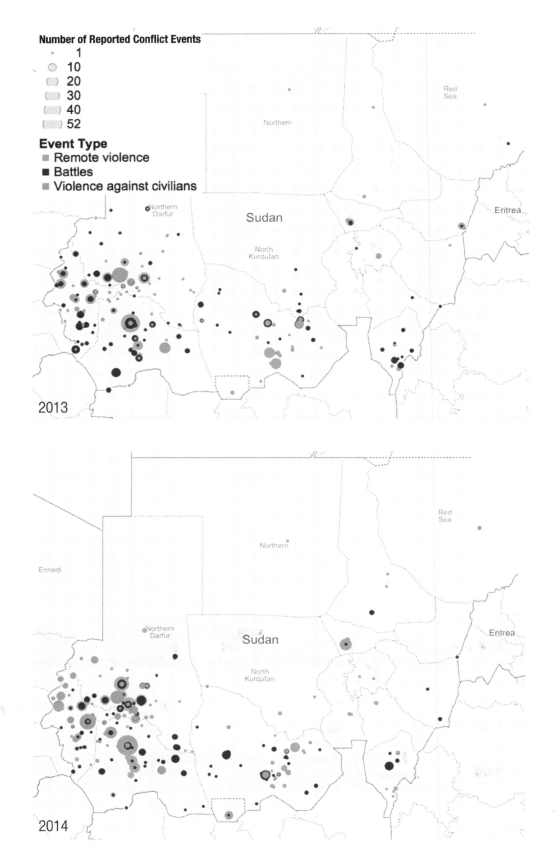

Figure 4.13 Conflict in Sudan, by Event Type, 2013 and 2014

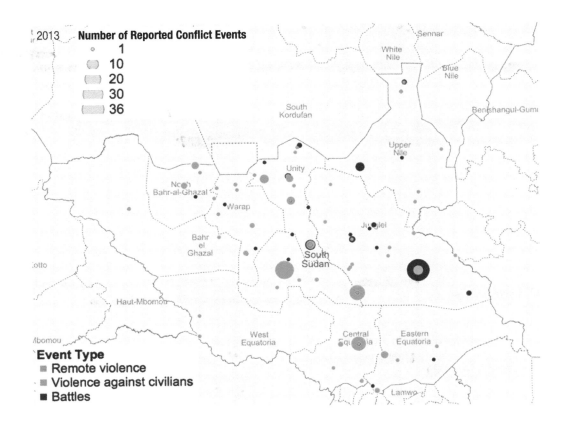

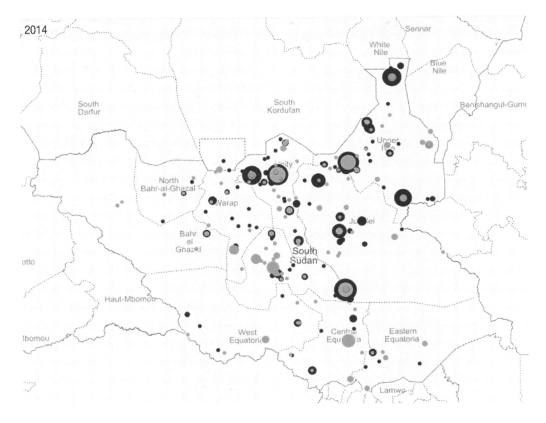

Figure 4.14 Conflict in South Sudan, by Event Type, 2013 and 2014

Dynamics of Violence

Conflict dynamics are not always consistent, even when comparing similar political-economic contexts. Across South and Southeast Asia, for example, the modes of conflict are predominantly riots and protests (see Figure 4.15). Research has shown that violent rioting in unstable contexts tends to be directed towards similar goals as deadly political militia violence in Africa, e.g., political party competition near elections (Wilkinson 2006). The varying forms of conflict in such a cross-regional comparison may also be a function of the stability of underlying regimes. The most serious and deadliest forms of conflict, including armed confrontations between actors, are most likely in the poorest (Fearon and Laitin 2003) and least representative (Reiter and Stam 2002; Collier and Hoeffler 2004) political settings. Thus, the fact that India – a generations-old functioning democracy – should experience rioting instead of deadly recurring and targeted battles, such as those that occur in South Sudan, Somalia, northern Nigeria, or Afghanistan, is not a surprise.

The Risk of Conflict-Related Mortality and Micromorts

One important consideration in the cross-national analysis of conflict is that countries vary considerably in terms of scale, including with respect to population size. These differences affect the relative extent of exposure to violence. Consider Figure 4.16 (see next page), which maps the populations of African countries along with the locations of conflict-related fatalities in each country in 2014. The vast majority of these conflict-related fatalities occurred in Nigeria (11,529 deaths). The next-deadliest country, South Sudan (6,388 deaths), experienced about half as many fatalities. Yet Nigeria has over six times the population of South Sudan. Consequently, the relative risk of conflict-related mortality at the individual level is higher for a South Sudanese person than it is for a Nigerian. This example demonstrates that a measure of relative risk is necessary to draw appropriate comparisons of exposures of civilians to violence or even death from political conflict.

For this purpose, we opt for the micromort, an indicator often used within decision analysis to determine the riskiness of various activities (Howard 1980). In general terms, a micromort represents the "microprobability" of death, gauging the risk of this outcome being experienced at the individual level. Here, we apply the micromort concept to determine the risks to civilians from political conflict across Africa in 2014. We base the analysis on fatality data, to generate a rough estimate of the average risk of death from political conflict that individuals in various countries experienced on a daily basis. Micromort values can be calculated for a given geographic unit (country, region, etc.) in three steps: (1) divide the number of conflict-related fatalities in that unit by the 365 days in the year, (2) divide the resulting number by the population of the unit, and (3) multiply the resulting value by one million in order to determine the average daily risk per million persons.

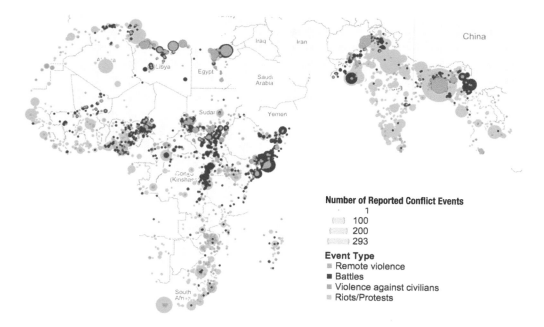

Figure 4.15 Conflict in Africa and South and Southeast Asia, by Event Type, January–June 2015

Note: ACLED began collecting real-time data for 11 Asian countries in 2015. Data for six of these countries is available selectively from 1996–2010.

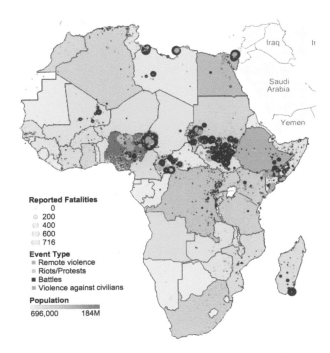

Figure 4.16 Conflict-Related Fatalities, by Event Type, and Populations in Africa, 2014

To emphasize, this risk reflects the *average relative risk over a population, not the risk to a specific individual*, or even the risk to a person drawn randomly from the population. It is plausible that certain individuals within countries experience a higher or lower risk relative to their peers, as a result of differences in their locations of residence, the surrounding conditions, their group affiliations and affinities, their personal characteristics, etc. For example, individuals living in Darfur face a higher risk of lethal violence from political conflict relative to others within Sudan, as much of the political conflict within Sudan is located in that region. Micromorts can also be determined sub-nationally, but for this exercise we compare countries.

Figure 4.17 (see next page) maps micromorts for each country across Africa in 2014. Micromorts are highest (lowest) for countries with relatively smaller (larger) populations and a higher (lower) number of reported fatalities. It happens that the same six countries atop the list of deadliest countries for political conflict across Africa in 2014 – Nigeria, South Sudan, Somalia, Sudan, the CAR, and Libya – also exhibit the highest average risks of mortality to their citizens. The order of micromorts, however, differs: the CAR leads the rankings, with an average daily risk of nearly two conflict-related deaths per million people, followed by South Sudan, Libya, Somalia, Sudan, and Nigeria. This analysis emphasizes the importance of not just focusing on absolute numbers of casualties observed as a result of conflict in various geographic units (or other groupings). Instead, the relative risks, taking into account the population of these geographic units (and other groupings), ought to be examined.

Conclusion

The distinctive evidence from the ACLED dataset demonstrates that political violence and protest in Africa increased from 2013 to 2014. This conclusion is based on the consideration of *several forms* of political violence and social upheaval, not just interstate or civil wars. Civilian targeting has become more prevalent, largely a result of violence perpetrated by political militias – a conflict actor not included in most conflict datasets. Usage of tactics of remote violence, a type of event not specifically coded by most conflict datasets, has become more prevalent and lethal and is now at the highest reported levels to date. Meanwhile, every type of conflict actor has increased its frequency of violence in recent years.

Countries across Africa exhibit variation in the levels and types of violence – and therefore a diversity of security challenges. The list of the most violent and deadliest states is led by Somalia, Libya, Sudan, Nigeria, South Sudan, and the CAR. Analyses using absolute figures and micromorts reinforce these findings, differing only in terms of the order of rankings. Among non-state actors, Boko Haram (operating largely in northern Nigeria) is involved in the deadliest events, while Al Shabaab (operating in Somalia and Kenya) is responsible for initiating the largest number of conflict events. The disparities in conflict patterns across high-activity areas underscores how political violence is closely associated with the capacity of the state and political relationships between regimes and political elites (Raleigh 2014).

Figure 4.17 Micromorts for Africa, 2014

Note: This map represents each country in terms of a micromort, which is a measure of the average daily risk of the number of conflict-related fatalities per 1 million people

Notes

1 The highest number of conflict-related fatalities was reported in 1999, largely due to violence in Angola, the DRC, and Sierra Leone.
2 ACLED recorded a total of 16,709 reported events in 2013, of which 1,196 are nonviolent events and 5,339 are riots and protests.
3 Organized, armed conflict events include battles between armed groups, remote violence, and instances of violence against civilians. Riots and protests are not accounted for in these totals.
4 While we focus in this chapter on African conflict data from 1997 to 2014 (per ACLED's Version 5 data release), ACLED offers real-time conflict data, updated weekly, to the present day.
5 Whether increases in conflict event numbers are a function of reporting is taken into account. Any disaggregated conflict data project should be clear about sourcing, levels of change in source materials, scales of sourcing, and reliability. ACLED has produced two working papers on this subject (ACLED 2012; ACLED 2015a), which conclude that the number of available local and national sources has increased, but this alone cannot account for the increases in events. The trend is driven largely by the increase in riots and protests that have been reported in recent years. Figure 4.3 shows that while the proportion of reported organized, violent conflict has not fluctuated greatly, the proportions of reported riots and protests has been steadily increasing.
6 Fatality figures represent the total number of deaths suffered by both sides of a violent event. A caveat concerns instances of violence against civilians. By ACLED's definition, civilians do not exhibit aggression. Therefore, the only fatalities associated with these events are experienced by civilians. Fatality figures are often difficult to obtain, verify, and crosscheck; they are also subject to higher levels of reporting bias than overall conflict events. As a result, ACLED codes the lower end of reported ranges. In instances when only a total number of fatalities is given for multiple events taking place across more than one day and/or in more than one place, the number of fatalities is divided evenly among the events.
7 A riot is defined as a violent disturbance of the public peace by three or more persons assembled for a common purpose, and can be either spontaneous or organized. Protests are defined as nonviolent, spontaneous organizations of civilians for a political purpose. If violence occurs during a protest as a result of protesters' actions, it is categorized as a riot and not a protest. If violence is committed against protesters, without any violence by protesters in return, the event is deemed an instance of violence against civilians.

References

ACLED. 2012. "ACLED Data Sources." ACLED Working Paper Series no. 1, July 2012. http://www.acleddata.com/wp-content/up loads/2014/12/ACLED_Sources-Working-Paper_July-2012_updated.pdf.
ACLED. 2015a. "Reporting Sources." ACLED Working Paper Series no. 5, April 2015. http://www.acleddata.com/wp-content/uploa ds/2015/04/ACLED_Reporting-Sources-Working-Paper-No.-5_2015.pdf.
ACLED. 2015b. "Remote-Violence, Bombings and Conflict Part 3: Overall Trends in the Use of Improvised Explosive Devices." *ACLED Crisis Blog,* November 6, 2014. http://www.crisis.acleddata.com/remote-violence-bombings-and-conflict-part-3-overa ll-trends-in-the-use-of-improvised-explosive-devices/.

ACLED. 2015c. "The Strategic Use of Unidentified Armed Groups in Conflict Zones." *ACLED Crisis Blog*, April 9. http://www.crisis.acleddata.com/the-strategic-use-of-unidentified-armed-groups-in-conflict-zones/.

Amnesty International. 2013. "Egypt: New Protest Law Gives Security Forces Free Rein." November 25. https://www.amnesty.org/en/latest/news/2013/11/egypt-new-protest-law-gives-security-forces-free-rein/.

Collier, Paul, and Anke Hoeffler. 2004. "Greed and Grievance in Civil War." *Oxford Economic Papers* 56(4): 563–595.

Denselow, James. 2010. "Roadside Bombs: Weapons of the Weak." *The Guardian*, June 18. http://www.theguardian.com/commentisfree/2010/jun/18/roadside-bombs-afghanistan.

Fearon, James D., and David D. Laitin. 2003. "Ethnicity, Insurgency, and Civil War." *American Political Science Review* 97(1): 75–90.

Gleditsch, Kristian Skrede, and Steve Pickering. 2014. "Wars Are Becoming Less Frequent: A Response to Harrison and Wolf." *The Economic History Review* 67(1): 214–230.

Hartley, Wyndham. 2014. "Funds Needed to Control Protests." *Business Day Live*, September 8. http://www.bdlive.co.za/national/2014/09/08/funds-needed-to-control-protests.

Howard, Ronald A. 1980. "On Making Life and Death Decisions." In Richard C. Schwing and Walter A. Albers, Jr. (eds). *Societal Risk Assessment*. New York: Plenum Press. 89–113.

Journal of Conflict Resolution. 2015. "Militias in Civil Wars." *Journal of Conflict Resolution* 59(5): 755–946.

McCormick, Gordon H., and Frank Giordano. 2007. "Things Come Together: Symbolic Violence and Guerrilla Mobilisation." *Third World Quarterly* 28(2): 295–320.

Merari, Ariel. 1993."Terrorism as a Strategy of Insurgency." *Terrorism and Political Violence* 5(4): 213–251.

Paton, Carol. 2014. "Service Delivery Protests: Why Now?" *Business Day Live*, February 17. http://www.bdlive.co.za/national/2014/02/17/service-delivery-protests-why-now.

Pinker, Steven. 2011. *The Better Angels of Our Nature*. New York: Viking.

Power, Samantha. 2013. "Remarks at the EU/OCHA Ministerial Breakfast on the Central African Republic." September 25. http://usun.state.gov/briefing/statements/214763.htm.

Raleigh, Clionadh. 2014. "Political Hierarchies and Landscapes of Conflict across Africa." *Political Geography* 42 (September): 92–103.

Raleigh, Clionadh. 2016. "Pragmatic and Promiscuous: Explaining the Rise of Competitive Political Militias across Africa." *Journal of Conflict Resolution* 60(2): 283–310.

Raleigh, Clionadh, Andrew Linke, Håvard Hegre, and Joakim Karlsen. 2010. "Introducing ACLED: An Armed Conflict Location and Event Dataset: Special Data Feature." *Journal of Peace Research* 47(5): 651–660.

Reiter, Dan, and Allan C. Stam. 2002. *Democracies at War*. Princeton, NJ: Princeton University Press.

Reuters. 2014. "Darfur Conflict." Thomson Reuters Foundation, updated July 31. http://www.trust.org/spotlight/Darfur-conflict.

Straus, Scott. 2012."Wars Do End! Changing Patterns of Political Violence in Sub-Saharan Africa." *African Affairs* 111(443): 179–201.

Tran, Mark. 2014. "Darfur Conflict: Civilians Deliberately Targeted as Tribal Violence Escalates." *The Guardian*, March 14. http://www.theguardian.com/global-development/2014/mar/14/darfur-conflict-sudan-civilians-deliberately-targeted.

Wilkinson, Steven I. 2006. *Votes and Violence*. Cambridge: Cambridge University Press.

5

Violence against Civilians during Civil War

Hanne Fjelde, Lisa Hultman and Margareta Sollenberg

Introduction

In December 2013, government-affiliated militias in the Central African Republic, called ex-Séléka, massacred at least 800 civilians in Bangui in the course of two days. After Séléka forces had overthrown President Bozizé in March 2013 and taken power, violence spiraled along religious lines, pitting the predominantly Muslim de facto government of ex-Séléka against the mainly Christian anti-Balaka militias comprised of forces that had been affiliated with Bozizé. Both sides have since been responsible for large-scale atrocities against the civilian population.

Unfortunately, the Bangui massacre is hardly an extraordinary event in the context of civil war. Not all actors involved in armed conflicts attack civilian populations. Yet such atrocities are an all-too-common practice. Governments, rebel groups, and militia groups alike are responsible for perpetrating violence against civilians, which is observed across different types of armed conflicts. These incidents are observed despite the fact that International Humanitarian Law strictly prohibits the killings of people not actively participating in armed conflict, and protecting civilians and guaranteeing fundamental human security has recently become a top priority for the United Nations (Bellamy 2009; Wills 2009).

In this chapter, we describe the patterns of *one-sided violence*, which captures direct, deliberate lethal violence against civilians by organized armed actors, in clear violation of the laws of armed conflict. While this violence against civilians often coincides with armed conflict, the two can be distinguished conceptually from each other. Armed conflicts are typically defined by military confrontations between armed units – so-called battle-related violence, which also encompasses civilians directly caught in crossfire and civilian casualties caused by attacks against military targets (referred to as collateral damage in military jargon). One-sided violence refers instead to civilian fatalities caused by actions deliberately directed against the civilian population, which are distinct in pitting an organized, armed actor against an unorganized, unarmed civilian population.

We begin by describing some general trends in one-sided violence over time and across regions, covering the period from 1989 to 2013. We then discuss patterns in the specific links between one-sided violence and armed conflict. These trends and patterns are based on data on one-sided violence provided by the Uppsala Conflict Data Program (UCDP).[1] These data are collected using secondary written sources, including news reports and human rights reports, and cover violence against civilians by governments or non-state organizations where at least 25 people are killed over the course of a year. The fatality estimates included in the UCDP data are conservative, in the sense that we can be fairly confident that the deaths reported indeed occurred. Yet these data do not always exhaustively capture all one-sided violence that occurred in a conflict. In many cases, this violence either goes unreported or the perpetrators remain unknown.

Throughout this chapter, we have chosen to exclude the genocide in Rwanda in 1994 from the analysis. This event stands out as the most extreme manifestation of one-sided violence in the period that we analyze, resulting in an estimated 500,000 civilian deaths over the span of only a few months. This number is roughly twice as large as the total number of deaths from one-sided violence committed by all other actors globally for the entire time period that is covered by the data and analysis. Given the extreme level of violence, the genocide in Rwanda overshadows trends and patterns that are otherwise discernible in the data. Acknowledging the exceptional level of atrocities in the Rwandan genocide, we have decided to leave out this case in the interest of focusing on more general global patterns reflected in the rest of the observed cases.

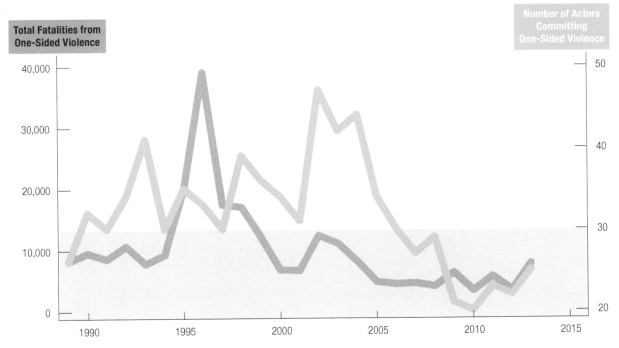

Figure 5.1 Overall Trends in One-Sided Violence, 1989–2013

Trends in One-Sided Violence

One-sided violence is a frequent phenomenon, but the number of civilians killed varies quite considerably from year to year. Figure 5.1 shows the trends in annual fatalities from one-sided violence in the period from 1989 to 2013. The green line (labeled on the left y-axis) shows the total number of civilians killed in attacks by state or non-state actors by year. Again, we remind the reader that the exceptional case of the Rwandan genocide is not included in the graph. Had this case been included, we would have observed a dramatic spike in 1994, with a total number of deaths 50 times higher than that currently reflected by the graph. Instead, the graph reveals a spike in 1996, with close to 40,000 victims of one-sided violence worldwide. Most of those civilians were killed by the Alliance of Democratic Forces for the Liberation of Congo (AFDL) rebel group in the Democratic Republic of Congo (DRC). Whereas those deaths occurred within the domestic context of the DRC and were perpetrated by an alliance of rebel actors opposing the central government, these dynamics cannot be understood without considering the Rwandan events in 1994. Of note, the ADFL was strongly supported by the new Rwandan government that took control in the wake of the genocide and many of the civilians who were killed in the DRC were Hutu refugees from Rwanda, who had allegedly participated in the 1994 genocide.

After the peak in 1996, the extent of one-sided violence worldwide has followed a downward trend. This trend may reflect the overall decline of violence, described by Pinker (2011). At the same time, spikes in violence such as the Rwandan genocide in 1994 or the massacres in the DRC in 1996 occur at irregular intervals. The current levels of civilian killings in Syria by the Syrian government and rebel groups, notably the Islamic State (IS), point to a new spike in 2014–2015. Thus, saying anything definitive about a clear, robust downward trend, based on this relatively short time period, is likely premature.

The blue line in Figure 5.1 (labeled on the right y-axis) shows the number of actors that reached the 25-casualty threshold for inclusion into the one-sided violence category in each year. Although the overall number of fatalities decreased after 1996, the number of actors who committed one-sided violence actually increased around this time and proliferated especially around 2002–2003. Since then, the number of armed actors engaged in civilian targeting has decline markedly, reaching a low point in 2010.

Figure 5.2 (see next page) shows the annual number of fatalities from one-sided violence, disaggregated by state and non-state perpetrators. In total, 795 cases where an actor killed more than 25 civilians in a calendar year were observed over the entire time period. Of these cases, 526 involved non-state actors (including rebel groups fighting a civil war and other organized armed groups such as militias), while 269 involved state actors (i.e., governments and their security forces). Hence, non-state actors were responsible for almost twice as many observations (i.e., actor-years) as state actors. The imbalance is even more pronounced when we examine the number of unique actors: 175 different rebel groups killed civilians, compared to 58 different governments. A similar pattern is evident in the fatality numbers: 159,140 civilians were killed by non-state actors, whereas 87,169 civilians were killed by state actors. Considering the rate of fatalities,

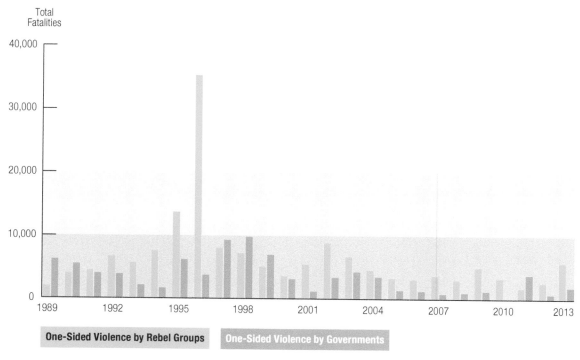

Figure 5.2 Annual Fatalities Due to One-Sided Violence, by Type of Actor, 1989–2013

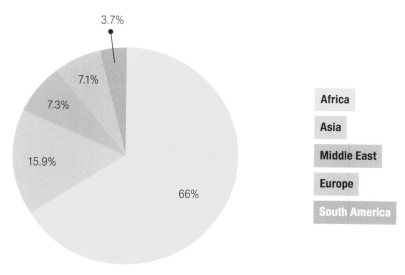

Figure 5.3 Fatalities Due to One-Sided Violence, by Region, 1989–2013

by actor-year, governments actually engage in more intense one-sided violence. The average number of civilians killed for each observation of government violence is 324, whereas the corresponding number for rebel groups is 302.

One-sided violence tends to cluster geographically. These spatial patterns are evident in Figure 5.3. A clear majority (66 percent) of victims of one-sided violence was located in Africa. The most likely reason is the disproportionately high prevalence of internal armed conflict in this region. Rwanda obviously stands out as the most extreme example of civilian targeting in the context of civil war. Other intense civil wars, including those in the DRC, Sudan, Uganda, Burundi, Liberia and Sierra Leone, have been accompanied by extreme levels of violence against civilians. Below, we describe in more detail how one-sided violence is linked to civil war. A related explanation may be weak state structures, such as central governments that are unable to effectively control territory and mitigate violence by non-state actors. One conspicuous example is the recent atrocities by Boko Haram in Nigeria and neighboring countries.

The region with the second largest share of victims of one-sided violence is Asia, with 16 percent of all civilians killed globally. Asia is also conflict ridden, albeit without as many large-scale conflicts as are typically observed in Africa. Many of the Asian victims of one-sided violence are found in Afghanistan, India, and Myanmar. Both India and Myanmar have had a number of separate ongoing armed conflicts, with numerous active rebel groups. Most of the one-sided violence in the other regions of the world is the result of the war in Bosnia and Herzegovina (Europe), the wars in Iraq and Syria (the Middle East), and the war in Colombia (the Americas).

Africa also stands out along another dimension: the prevalence of transnational actors engaged in one-sided violence across borders. In Africa, 80 of 389 actor-years – a little over 20 percent – involve an actor that has been targeting civilians in more than one country. One notorious example is the Lord's Resistance Army (LRA), which has been active in Sudan, the DRC, the Central African Republic (CAR), and South Sudan, as well as Uganda. Another more recent example is Al Shabaab, which has been active in Kenya and Uganda, as well as Somalia. Armed actors crossing borders to engage in civilian victimization has been observed in the Middle East, too. Nine of 72 cases (12.5 percent) in this region involve actors active in more than one country. Examples include the PKK (Turkey, Iraq) and lately the Islamic State [IS] (Iraq, Syria, Jordan). In contrast, only 1 of 57 actor-years in South America involve such cross-border violence against civilians, while none of the state or non-state actors that committed one-sided violence in Europe were active in more than one country. One circumstance that contributes to the disparities in patterns across regions is that both Africa and the Middle East have experienced a number of complex internationalized civil wars (e.g., the DRC, Somalia and Sudan in Africa, and Syria and Iraq in the Middle East). Some rebel groups in these internationalized conflicts also have transnational ambitions – in particular, the IS lays claim to an Islamic Caliphate that stretches across several Middle Eastern states. In Africa, the weakness of many states and the associated porousness of borders facilitate cross-border activities by rebel groups and governments.

The Relationship between One-Sided Violence and Civil War

As we have already emphasized, the prevalence of civilian targeting is closely related to civil wars. This relationship is clearly demonstrated by the use of one-sided violence within the context of an internal armed conflict (i.e., armed contestations between a government and one of more rebel groups). Over the period from 1989–2013, 13 percent (554 of 4233) of the country-years worldwide exhibit one-sided violence, with at least one armed actor meeting the threshold of 25 civilians killed.[2] Of these instances of one-sided violence, 75 percent (418 country-years) coincide with an active armed conflict (see Table 5.1). Furthermore, 93 percent of all observations of one-sided violence occurred in countries that experienced armed conflict at some point from 1989–2013. These patterns strengthen the observation that violence against civilians and armed conflict are typically linked. Most countries around the world experience neither armed conflict nor one-sided violence, but those that do often experience both.

Figure 5.4 (see next page) shows the number of government and rebel actor-years that exhibit one-sided violence, conditional on the presence or absence of internal armed conflict. The higher prevalence of civilian targeting in civil war contexts holds both for government and rebel actors, with the difference all the more pronounced for rebels.

One point of curiosity that arises: Who are the non-state actors that commit one-sided violence during years without active internal armed conflict? Some of the perpetrators are rebel groups (or factions thereof) that engage in battles with governments at some point – just not in a given year that significant atrocities against civilians were committed. Other perpetrators are ethnic militia groups like the Mungiki in Kenya, terrorist organizations like Al-Qaida in Saudi Arabia, or criminal gangs like the Mara Salvatrucha in Honduras and the various drug cartels in Mexico. Still, the majority of one-sided violence by non-state actors is perpetrated in the context of ongoing civil wars.

Not surprisingly, one-sided violence results in more deaths in the context of civil wars. Of the total of 246,088 victims of deliberate targeting, 204,388 (83 percent) were killed in the context of a country-year with active conflict.[3] The rate of violence is also telling: across the country-years exhibiting active armed conflict, an average of 289 civilians were killed in one-sided violence, whereas the corresponding average for country-years without armed conflict is just 12 killings. A major source of the discrepancy is that the largest massacres of civilians are often perpetrated alongside – or as a direct part of – civil wars. Notable cases include the massacres by AFDL in eastern DRC in 1996–1997, the Taliban massacres

Conflict Context	Country-Years with One-Sided Violence (≥25 civilian fatalities)	Country-Years without One-Sided Violence (<25 civilian fatalities)
Civil war	418	290
No civil war	136	3,389

Table 5.1 Relationship between One-Sided Violence and Civil War, 1989–2013

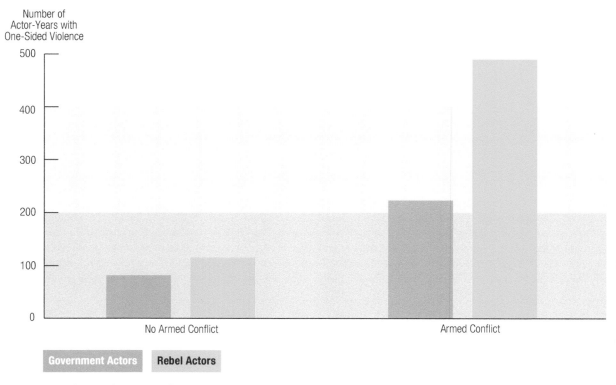

Figure 5.4 Prevalence of One-Sided Violence, by Armed Conflict Activity, 1989–2013

primarily centered around Mazar-i-Sharif in Afghanistan in 1998, and the Srebrenica massacre by Serbian forces in Bosnia and Herzegovina in 1995.

The reason for the close connection between one-sided violence and civil war is that violence against civilians often serves some strategic function in the armed conflict. Armed actors – both governments and rebel groups – often target civilians believed to support the enemy side (Fjelde and Hultman 2014; Kalyvas 2006; Valentino, Huth, and Balch-Lindsay 2004). Armed actors may direct violence at the civilian population for purposes of establishing territorial control. During the war in Bosnia, many civilians were killed during campaigns of ethnic cleansing aimed at taking control over new territories. Violence may also be used to control people through fear. Violence against civilians then serves to demonstrate to a larger audience what happens if you do not collaborate – or if you collaborate with an adversary. Violence against civilians may thus be employed to generate fear among the population. Thus, all these aspects of violence against civilians can be closely connected to civil war dynamics.

One-sided violence does not always have a strategic function. Instead, the violence may be linked to the civil war in other ways. Consider the common scenario that individual rank-and-file fighters have different motivations than elites for being involved in the civil war. Under these circumstances, lack of control over armed forces may lead to more violence, if the rank-and-file target civilians for other gains than those that may serve the goals of the group (Weinstein 2007). Use of alcohol and drugs within some fighting units may also spur such abusive behavior. In addition, civil wars can give rise to criminal activities, such as looting of natural resources or people's homes, which lead to high levels of violence against civilians (Azam 2002). Such dynamics that increase the risk for civilians are typically more prevalent in the context of a civil war, regardless of whether they are instrumental or peripheral to the conflict. Civil wars ultimately present conditions that are permissive of and conducive to all types of violence – not least, one-sided violence.

Available evidence also suggests that the prevalence of one-sided violence increases with the complexity of the conflict. In Figure 5.5 (see next page), we compare the average annual numbers of cases and fatalities from one-sided violence during armed conflicts with only one rebel actor (e.g., civil war in Mozambique involving Renamo, Maoist rebellion in Nepal) against armed conflicts with multiple rebel actors (e.g., DRC, Liberia). The results indicate that instances of one-sided violence committed by governments are more frequent during conflicts involving multiple rebel groups, but these instances do not tend to generate higher numbers of civilian victims from government violence. By contrast, cases of one-sided violence by rebels are markedly more common in conflicts with multiple rebel groups. As the number of rebel groups involved in a conflict increases, so too does the number of those groups that engage in civilian victimization and the total number of victims killed, on average.

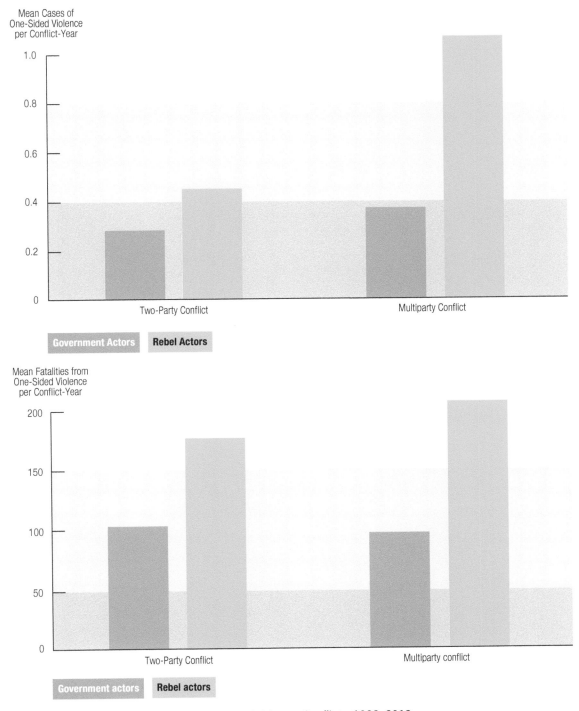

Figure 5.5 One-Sided Violence in Two-Party versus Multiparty Conflicts, 1989–2013

One potential explanation for this last result is that rebel groups may compete for support from the same civilian constituencies and in the process employ extreme tactics to appear strong, so as to change the preferences of the civilian supporters or to control resources (Boyle 2009; Wood and Kathman 2015). Yet there does not seem to be a general outbidding effect, whereby the presence of more rebel groups increases the level of civilian targeting by each group. Figure 5.6 (see next page) shows how the mean number of civilians killed by each rebel actor differs across conflicts with one, two, three, four or more rebel groups, taking into account the groups that do not kill civilians. In fact, the mean of civilian victims killed by each rebel perpetrator decreases as more actors become involved, though the total fatalities by conflict-year are still higher, since more actors engage in one-sided violence.

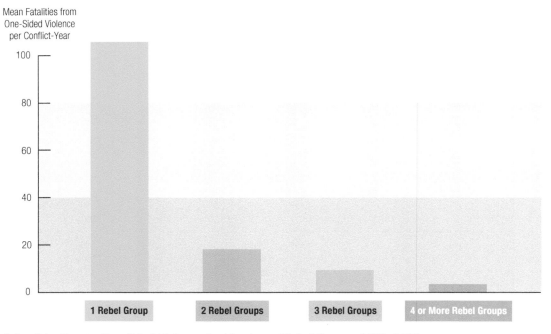

Figure 5.6 Fatalities Due to One-Sided Violence, by Number of Rebel Groups, 1989–2013

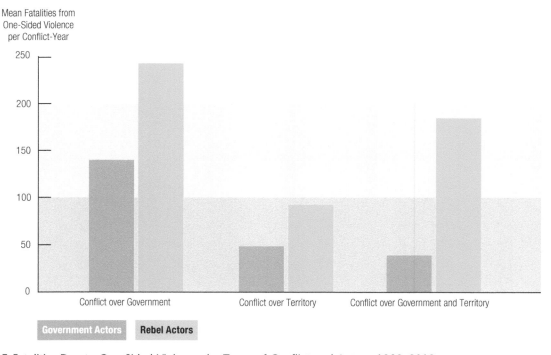

Figure 5.7 Fatalities Due to One-Sided Violence, by Types of Conflict and Actors, 1989–2013

Figure 5.7 displays the patterns of one-sided violence for different types of conflict: (1) the incompatibility concerns power over the central government of a country, (2) rebels have territorial claims on some part of a country (i.e., separatism or autonomy), or (3) both types of claims are present. The highest levels of one-sided violence are observed in civil wars where governmental power is contested. One possible reason is that the geographical scope of conflicts over political control is generally wider, involving a larger portion of the population, compared to separatist conflicts, which often have a more limited scope. As civil war violence becomes more encompassing, one-sided violence is likely to rise as well. Also, fighting in wars over government power is often more intense, killing greater numbers of people both on and off the battlefield. It may also be that territorial conflicts are likely to exhibit a more close-knit relationship between warring actors and their civilian constituencies. Where rebel groups operate in state peripheries, they might set up state-like organizations. The existence of a reciprocal relationship, based on the provision of collective goods, social services, employment, etc. in exchange for civilian support, may reduce the incentives for civilian targeting by rebel groups. Rebel groups involved in conflicts over government control may act in a more predatory manner.

Concluding Remarks

Violence against civilians is a common feature in the context of armed conflict, despite the principles of protection for non-combatants expressed in the Geneva Convention and other foundational instruments of International Humanitarian Law. The link between violence against civilians and armed conflict is rather unmistakable, whether manifesting as a strategy or a consequence of war, with the majority of deaths from one-sided violence occurring in close connection with ongoing civil wars. Current campaigns by the IS in Syria and Iraq and by Boko Haram in Nigeria and neighboring countries, in which civilians are targeted en masse and often under the guise of being infidels, illustrate the potential of instrumental and ideological rationales for such violence.

To date, the available data on one-sided violence has been focused on perpetrators. Meanwhile, comparable information on the victims is largely lacking. We know that civilian populations are often targeted on the basis of ethnic, religious, and other identities. Such targeting may be intentional and strategic in the context of a civil war where civilians are associated with – or perceived to be associated with – the other side in the conflict, or as part of broader political objectives that discriminate between identity groups. The worst-case scenario of identity-based targeting is full-blown genocide, as illustrated by the 1994 genocide in Rwanda. At present, little is known about general patterns of identity-based targeting as data on victims' identities and attributes is currently unavailable at a regional – let alone global – level.

A final point to stress is that the UCDP data about one-sided violence, on which this chapter builds, captures deliberate violent targeting of civilians. Aside from these fatalities, large numbers of civilians also die from indirect causes (e.g., starvation, disease) that may be unintentional consequences of civil wars. Indirect deaths may also be the result of deliberate policies by governments and rebel groups in various contexts. Among the well-known cases where large numbers of people died as a result of the deliberate targeting of civilian populations perceived to be associated with rebel groups are the forced resettlement of population groups in Ethiopia by the Derg regime in the 1980s, as well as the destruction of the Shia Marshlands in Iraq by the Iraqi government in the early 1990s. The current wars in Syria and Iraq serve as further examples of indirect targeting not included in the one-sided violence data, which focuses solely on death from the use of armed force. Collecting data on indirect fatalities poses serious challenges, not least in regard to establishing whether deaths were in fact deliberate. Nevertheless, a more complete picture would emerge if including all types of civilian targeting in future analyses became possible.

Notes

1 For access to the data and further information on the UCDP, see http://www.ucdp.uu.se.
2 This analysis is based on a global dataset covering all of the world's independent countries with a population of more than 250,000 over the 1989–2013 period. For the country-year comparisons, actors operating in more than one country are treated as a unique observation for each location where they are active and fatalities are divided equally by the number of countries.
3 One-sided fatalities in Namibia 1989 and South Sudan 2012 and 2013 are excluded from the analysis, since these country-years are not included in UCDP's conflict onset and incidence dataset.

References

Azam, Jean-Paul. 2002. "Looting and Conflict between Ethnoregional Groups: Lessons for State Formation in Africa." *Journal of Conflict Resolution* 46(1): 131–153.
Bellamy, Alex J. 2009. *Responsibility to Protect: The Global Effort to End Mass Atrocities*. Cambridge: Polity Press.
Boyle, Michael J. 2009. "Bargaining, Fear, and Denial: Explaining Violence against Civilians in Iraq 2004–2007." *Terrorism and Political Violence* 21(2): 261–287.
Fjelde, Hanne, and Lisa Hultman. 2014. "Weakening the Enemy: A Disaggregated Study of Violence against Civilians in Africa." *Journal of Conflict Resolution* 58(7): 1230–1257.
Kalyvas, Stathis N. 2006. *The Logic of Violence in Civil War*. Cambridge and New York: Cambridge University Press.
Pinker, Stephen, 2011. *The Better Angels of Our Nature: Why Violence Has Declined*. New York: Viking.
Valentino, Benjamin, Paul Huth, and Dylan Balch-Lindsay. 2004. "Draining the Sea: Mass Killing and Guerrilla Warfare." *International Organization* 58(2): 375–407.
Weinstein, Jeremy M. 2007. *Inside Rebellion: The Politics of Insurgent Violence*. Cambridge: Cambridge University Press.
Wills, Siobhán. 2009. *Protecting Civilians: Obligations of Peacekeepers*. Oxford: Oxford University Press.
Wood, Reed M., and Jacob D. Kathman. 2015. "Competing for the Crown: Inter-Rebel Competition and Civilian Targeting in Civil War." *Political Research Quarterly* 68(1): 167–179.

6

Non-State Actors in Civil War

David E. Cunningham, Kristian Skrede Gleditsch and Idean Salehyan

Introduction

The civil war in Syria that started in 2011 has resulted in the loss of hundreds of thousands of lives, created millions of refugees and internally displaced persons, and led to major changes in the balance of power between states and non-state groups throughout the broader region. This conflict has also prompted significant international debates about how best to respond, as well as a number of generally unsuccessful attempts to push the actors toward some compromise settlement. More generally, the Syrian civil war has attracted considerable attention around the world from scholars, policymakers, and the general public. This focus arises in part from two notable features of the conflict.

First, the war is complex, involving a very large number of actors. The "opposition" side includes a proliferation of armed non-state groups. Many of these groups operate as part of nominal alliances, such as the Syrian National Council. These alliances face difficulties, however, in coordinating the activities of the constituent organizations and often have largely opposing goals beyond their opposition to the government. Many groups, including most notably Islamic State/ Daesh (also known as the Islamic State of Iraq and Syria) and the Free Syrian Army, fight each other as well as the government and its affiliated forces. This fractionalization of armed actors is so extreme that identifying who the actors are at different points in time is challenging for observers and even direct participants in the conflict.[1]

Second, the civil war in Syria has been characterized by a large degree of transnational support and participation by actors external to Syria – both other states and non-state actors. Different opposition groups receive support from states such as Saudi Arabia and Qatar, as well as from wealthy individuals in the region and other individuals in the Arab diaspora and Muslim communities abroad. The government receives essential military support from parts of the Iranian security services, as well as the Lebanese rebel group Hezbollah. Russia has also started to provide extensive military support to the Syrian government.

The high degree of fractionalization of the Syrian opposition and the large amount of transnational involvement have important consequences for the likely course of the Syrian civil war. Empirical research has demonstrated that wars with more rebel groups are much longer, deadlier, and more resistant to international efforts at resolution (see Cunningham 2011; Pilster and Böhmelt 2014). In addition, international intervention can prolong civil wars, and rebel groups with external funding that are less dependent on local support commit greater violence toward civilians (see, e.g., Balch-Lindsay and Enterline 2000; Salehyan, Siroky and Wood 2014).

While the Syrian civil war may be extreme in terms of the degree of fractionalization and the level of external involvement, this conflict is hardly unique on those counts. In 2013, 12 out of 33 (36 percent) ongoing internal armed conflicts involved more than one rebel group.[2] These multiparty wars included conflicts in different regions of the world, including Africa, Asia and Latin America. Many prominent rebel groups that are currently active, such as Boko Haram (Nigeria), Al Qaeda in the Islamic Maghreb (Algeria), and Al Shabaab (Somalia), receive significant international backing and regularly operate across national borders.

In this chapter, we examine trends in civil conflicts, fractionalization, and transnational support to rebel groups over the post-1945 period. Our analysis, which concentrates on recent trends compared to historical averages, arrives at several main findings. While the number of civil wars has declined in recent years, the number of multiparty conflicts – those with multiple rebel actors – has actually increased, leading to a greater percentage of multiparty civil wars. The percentage of civil wars with transnational support has increased, though patterns of support to governments and rebels diverge over time. Taken together, these trends suggest that future wars are likely to be fewer in number and exhibit characteristics similar to the Syrian civil war: a proliferation of actors and a large degree of transnational involvement.

Civil Wars and Non-State Actors

Some civil wars are purely dyadic contests, fought between the government and a single rebel group. In contrast, many civil conflicts involve multiple different opposition forces challenging the state at the same time. These multiple rebel groups may cooperate with one another or the groups may fight each other and/or the government. The groups may represent similar constituencies or articulate very different demands. In Syria, for example, the conflict can be loosely characterized as involving four sides – the government, the more "moderate"/secular opposition, the strict (Sunni) Islamist opposition, and ethnic Kurdish forces. Each of the opposition sides is comprised of numerous different actors that draw on different local support bases and often receive support from different external patrons.

Figure 6.1 displays the global trends of active civil conflicts (blue line and left legend) and state–rebel group dyads (purple line and right legend) in each year since 1946. This analysis relies on data from the Uppsala Conflict Data Project (UCDP), which distinguish between conflicts over government and conflicts over territory and treat conflicts over different pieces of territory within the same state as separate "incompatibilities." This means that one country can have multiple distinct civil wars occurring simultaneously. Each of these conflicts could potentially have multiple rebel groups participating, if these groups are engaged in fighting over the same incompatibility. For example, Ethiopia had five active civil conflicts in 1980; one of the conflicts involved two rebel groups, while each of the others involved just a single rebel group. Meanwhile, Afghanistan had one civil conflict active in 1980, but this conflict involved as many as six different dyads over the years.

The downward trend in the number of conflicts since a peak in the early 1990s, clearly evident in Figure 6.1, is consistent with recent work on the decline of violence, which encompasses – but is not limited to – a decrease in the number of civil wars (see, most prominently, Pinker 2011; Goldstein 2011). In Chapter 3, Håvard Strand and Halvard Buhaug devote extensive attention to discussing the decline of war, which they likewise demonstrate was most profound from 1991–2003. Figure 6.1 also shows that the trend in the number of dyads in conflicts is similar to that of the number of conflicts. Yet the number of dyads peaked earlier, in the 1980s, which indicates that the number of actors in conflicts grew more rapidly than the number of ongoing distinct conflicts during the final stages of the Cold War.

Figures 6.2 and 6.3 (see next page) provide complementary ways of looking at these data. Figure 6.2 plots the share of conflicts in each year that involved at least two dyads. This series is somewhat jagged, with the highest shares throughout the entire period of coverage observed during the 1970s. Nonetheless, the trend is towards a greater share of conflicts involving multiple actors. The increase in the proportion of multiparty conflicts is rather dramatic – during the 1950s and early 1960s, generally between 10 and 15 percent of civil conflicts had more than one rebel group, whereas the share has typically exceeded 20 percent ever since and often been above 30 percent since the mid-1990s. Figure 6.3 plots the

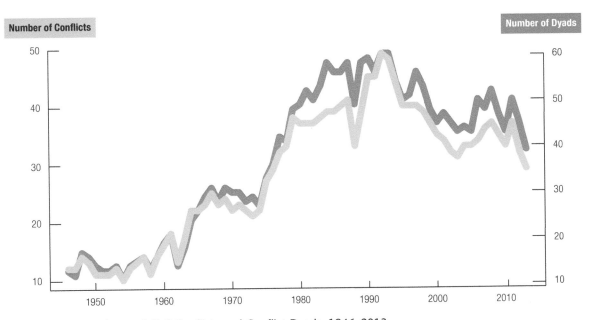

Figure 6.1 Annual Prevalence of Civil Conflicts and Conflict Dyads, 1946–2013

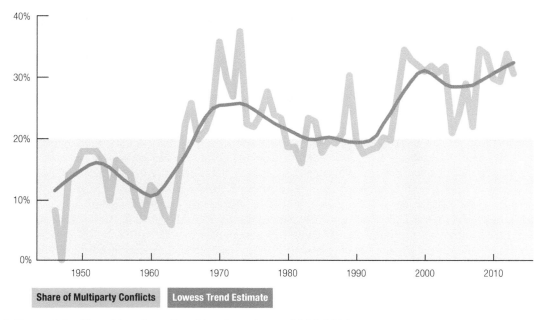

Figure 6.2 Share of Conflict with at least Two Non-State Actors, 1946–2013

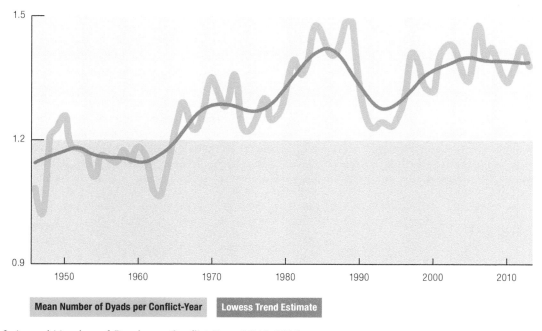

Figure 6.3 Annual Number of Dyads per Conflict-Year, 1946–2013

average number of dyads per conflict-year over time. The increasing average is again evidence of the trend towards proliferation of non-state actors in conflicts.

Taken together, the trends displayed in Figures 6.1 through 6.3 mean that current conflicts are more complex in that they are increasingly likely to involve multiple, sometimes competing, interests. Syria may be extreme in the level of opposition fractionalization. Nonetheless, the data attest to a long-term trend towards a smaller number of conflicts, but with an increasing number of rebel groups participating in them.

Transnational Dimensions

Civil wars are not purely domestic events. They also have important repercussions for the region in which they occur – and potentially for global politics in general. Refugees spill across borders, foreign actors provide funding and arms to the combatants, and rebels find sanctuary in other countries, among a range of transnational phenomena (see, e.g., Gleditsch

2007; Salehyan 2009). Some militant organizations, such as the Kachin insurgents in Myanmar, have purely local aims and do not rely on widespread support across the region. Other groups enjoy sympathy and material assistance from co-ethnics across national boundaries, such as Kurdish fighters across Iraq, Iran, Syria, and Turkey. Still other militant movements have a much broader constituency and explicitly regional and global agendas. For instance, Al-Qaeda and the Islamic State have local branches and affiliates throughout the world.

Such transnational dynamics are clearly apparent in the Syrian civil war. The government of Bashar al-Assad receives arms and support from foreign powers, including Iran and Russia. Hezbollah, the Shiite militant group from Lebanon, has also lent support to the Syrian government in its campaign to destroy the opposition. As for the opponents of the regime, the initial spark behind the movement came from the "Arab Spring" wave of protests across the region in 2011. The Free Syrian Army and other relatively moderate groups first organized in Turkey. They have since received support from foreign governments, including Saudi Arabia, Qatar, the United States, and European Union countries. Lately, the influence of the Free Syrian Army has waned as more extreme groups, linked with transnational Islamist militancy, have gained in strength. The Al-Nusra Front is affiliated with the Al-Qaeda network and attracts foreign fighters from around the world. More recently, the Islamic State – a group that split off from Al-Qaeda central – has declared the reestablishment of the Muslim Caliphate and is seeking to spread its influence to other countries.

Of course, the Syrian conflict is not unique in having an international component. The current crisis in Eastern Ukraine involves Russian irregular troops and equipment. The governments of Cameroon, Chad, and Niger are helping to fight the Nigerian Boko Haram movement. The Taliban continue to slip back and forth across the Pakistan-Afghanistan border. Moreover, the wave of Islamist militancy that has spread across Africa, the Middle East, and South and Southeast Asia is not unprecedented. During much of the twentieth century, Communist insurgencies sprang up across the world as insurgents sought to provoke a global revolution, much the same way as Jihadists pursue a global agenda.

During the Cold War, foreign support for combatants was a common phenomenon, as the United States and the Soviet Union vied for influence across the world (see, e.g., Buzan 1991). As Figure 6.4 (see next page) shows, however, markedly different trends are observed when comparing support for the rebel side and the government side during civil wars, based on the Non-State Actor data (see Cunningham, Gleditsch, and Salehyan 2013). Historically, support to rebels has been more common, with an average share well above 50 percent for most of the period, while support to the government side remained less common until the 1970s. The subsequent trends look very different: rebel support has become much less common and reached an historic low, whereas support to the government side has become steadily more common.

Foreign support for rebel organizations increased dramatically during the 1960s, then reached a plateau during the 1970s and 1980s, with approximately 70 percent of all rebel groups receiving assistance. Many such rebellions had overt geopolitical implications: for example, the United States supported anti-communist groups in Afghanistan and Nicaragua, while the Soviet Union backed leftist insurgents in Angola and Zimbabwe. Yet not all rebel groups were supported by one superpower or the other. Certain groups received support from other sources. In particular, Pakistan has backed militants in India for decades, as a way to weaken its main rival. Since the end of the Cold War, the overall level of support for the rebel side in civil wars has dropped precipitously, despite prominent cases such as Libya, Syria and Ukraine where external support is considered influential.

Contrast this with the trend toward growing foreign support of governments, which has barely abated since the collapse of the Soviet Union. Roughly 60 percent of governments received foreign support during the 1990s and 2000s, whereas only about one-third of rebel groups were receiving such support by the end of this time period. With the end of the Cold War rivalry, the international system seems to exhibit a much stronger bias toward the status quo, as reflected by diminishing support for revolution abroad and steady support for incumbents. Another prominent trend is the emergence of larger multilateral coalitions supporting the government side. This trend could be viewed as an extension beyond the core concept of international peacekeeping – helping parties settle – to more active peacemaking or counterinsurgency efforts (see, e.g., Gaibulloev, Sandler, and Shimizu 2009; Friis 2010). In Chapter 16, Deniz Cil describes these aspects in her overview of current peacekeeping operations. A contributing factor is the increase in international coalitions to offer support, often organized through regional and international intergovernmental organizations such as the UN and the African Union. Among the assortment of recent cases is the assistance from neighboring states to Nigeria in the fight against Boko Haram.

Table 6.1 (see p. 55) displays the transnational dimensions of selected conflicts that are currently active. Conflicts as diverse as the leftist insurgency in Colombia, ethnic rebellions in Central Africa and the Middle East, and Islamist violence exhibit considerable external influence. In Colombia, the FARC (Revolutionary Armed Forces of Colombia) previously enjoyed the support of Venezuela and maintained bases across the border. More recently, international support for the group has waned and the United States has been an active supporter of the government, especially as the FARC has been linked to the global drug trade. In Central Africa, the now defunct M23 rebellion was supported by Rwanda and by Tutsis across the region, while the UN Mission in the Democratic Republic of Congo (MONUSCO) worked with the government to stamp out the group. Meanwhile, the Democratic Forces for the Liberation of Rwanda (FDLR) is based in

Cunningham, Skrede Gleditsch and Salehyan

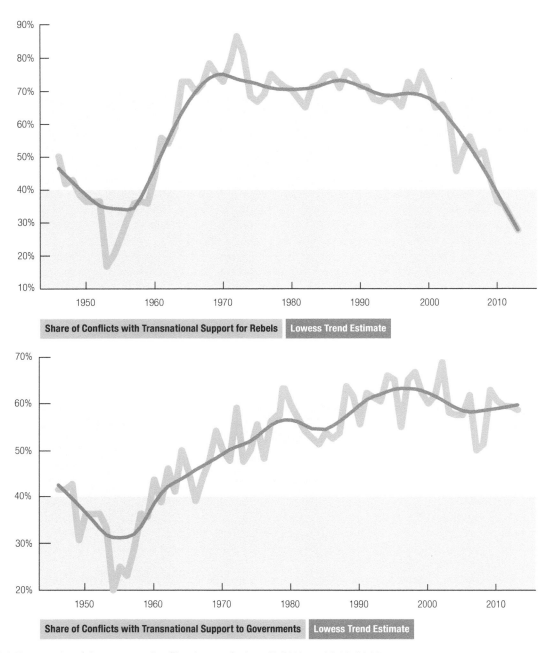

Figure 6.4 Transnational Support to Conflict Actors during Civil Wars, 1946–2013

the Democratic Republic of Congo (DRC) and largely consists of Rwandan Hutu refugees. MONUSCO also has a mandate to disarm this group, and the DRC – which has had a rocky relationship with Rwanda – sometimes cooperates in counterinsurgency efforts. As another example of transnational ethnic conflict, the Kurdish Worker's Party (PKK) has broad support among the Kurdish diaspora and maintains bases across the Middle East region as well as in Turkey. The Islamist groups share certain similarities and differences. Al-Shabaab, Boko Haram, and Al-Qaeda in the Arabian Peninsula (AQAP) all espouse a transnational Islamist ideology, but are rooted in very different circumstances. Al-Shabaab began as a domestic Somali group, but later swore allegiance to Al-Qaeda and has attracted some foreign fighters and extended activities into neighboring countries, especially Kenya. Similarly, Boko Haram was rooted in a local conflict, between southern and northern Nigeria, but has extended activities into several neighboring countries (Cameroon, Chad, Niger) – and recent reports suggest that the group is striving to establish links with foreign Islamist organizations. Unlike those two groups, AQAP saw itself as part of the global Jihadist movement from the start and has been responsible for plotting attacks well beyond its borders, including in the United States.

Location	Rebel Group	Transnational Constituency	External Participation in Conflict	External Presence of Group	External Location(s) of Group	Transnational Support for Rebel Group			Transnational Support for Government		
						Existence of Support	Type of Support	Source(s) of Support	Existence of Support	Type of Support	Source(s) of Support
Colombia	Revolutionary Armed Forces of Colombia (FARC)	None	No	No	Not applicable	None	Not applicable	Not applicable	Explicit	Military	USA
DRC	M23	Tacit	No	Some	Rwanda	Explicit	Troops	Rwanda Uganda	Explicit	Troops	MONUSCO
Nigeria	Jama'atu Ahlis Sunna Lidda' awati wal-Jihad (Boko Haram)	Explicit	Some	Some	Cameroon Chad Niger	None	Not applicable	Not applicable	Explicit	Troops	Chad Niger
Rwanda	Democratic Forces for the Liberation of Rwanda (FDLR)	Explicit	Major	Extensive	DRC	None	Not applicable	Not applicable	Explicit	Troops	DRC
Somalia	Al-Shabaab	Explicit	Minor	Some	Eritrea	Alleged	Military	Eritrea	Explicit	Military	AMISOM
Turkey	Kurdish Worker's Party (PKK)	Explicit	Major	Extensive	Iran Iraq Syria	None	Not applicable	Not applicable	Explicit	Military	USA Iraq
Yemen	Al-Qaeda in the Arabian Peninsula (AQAP)	Explicit	Major	No	Not applicable	None	Not applicable	Not applicable	Explicit	Military	USA

Table 6.1 Transnational Dimensions of Selected Conflicts

Conclusions

Over the last two decades, the world has seen a dramatic decline in the number of armed conflicts – from nearly 50 cases per year in the early 1990s to around 30 in recent years. While the overall number of wars has declined, the number of multiparty wars has not, meaning that a greater percentage of civil conflicts now involve more than one rebel group. Studies demonstrate that this feature tends to make conflicts more complex and more difficult to resolve, since multiple interests must be satisfied.

The decline in the number of wars is likely due, at least in part, to concerted international efforts at conflict management. The international community has been quite active in promoting the resolution of civil wars, with notable successes in facilitating negotiated ends to long wars in countries such as Burundi, El Salvador, Guatemala, and Mozambique, as well as between northern and southern Sudan. Deniz Cil demonstrates in Chapter 16, that the international community continues to be quite active in peacebuilding, with large multidimensional peacekeeping operations in conflict-torn countries, including the Central African Republic, Mali, Haiti, the DRC, and South Sudan.

As the proportion of multiparty wars increases, however, these successes may become less common. Civil wars with more armed actors are, on average, longer, deadlier, and more resistant to resolution than those with fewer armed actors. Consequently, multiparty wars present greater challenges to international efforts to resolve them. In the future, therefore, we may see a smaller overall number of wars, but the wars that occur, like the one ongoing in Syria, could be longer and bloodier on average, with a proliferation of actors, as a result of which international efforts to promote peaceful settlement might prove in vain.

A factor that exacerbates the challenges related to the conflict in Syria is the transnational dimensions, with a large number of foreign states, non-state actors, and wealthy individuals backing various armed actors. This high degree of external involvement has induced tensions in international bodies such as the United Nations and led to the re-shaping of regional alliances in the Middle East and beyond. A similar pattern prevails in Eastern Ukraine, with the conflict between Russian-backed separatists and a government that received at least verbal support from the United States and the European Union. Our analysis of trends in transnational support across civil wars over the last sixty years suggests, however, that Syria and Ukraine are somewhat uncommon. While support to governments has increased dramatically over the last several decades, it has declined dramatically to rebels. These trends mean that, in an increasing number of civil wars, rebels fight largely on their own against governments that receive backing from various transnational sources.

Notes

1 For example, the Uppsala Conflict Data Program states that it has "proven impossible … to distinguish between different armed groups" and thus opts for simply listing all Syrian insurgents as a single group (see http://www.ucdp.uu.se/gpdatabase/gpcountry.php?id=150#).
2 Based on the 2014 Uppsala Conflict Data Project-Peace Research Institute Oslo Armed Conflict Dataset. See Gleditsch et al. (2002); Themnér and Wallensteen (2014).

References

Balch-Lindsay, Dylan, and Andrew Enterline. 2000. "Killing Time: The World Politics of Civil War Duration." *International Studies Quarterly* 44(4): 615–642.

Buzan, Barry. 1991. *People, States, and Fear: An Agenda for International Security Studies in the Post-Cold War Era.* Boulder, CO: Lynne Rienner.

Cunningham, David E. 2011. *Barriers to Peace in Civil Wars.* Cambridge and New York: Cambridge University Press.

Cunningham, David E., Kristian Skrede Gleditsch, and Idean Salehyan. 2013. "Non-state Actors in Civil Wars: A New Dataset." *Conflict Management and Peace Science* 30(5): 516–531.

Friis, Karsten. 2010. "Peacekeeping and Counter-insurgency: Two of a Kind?" *International Peacekeeping* 17(1): 49–66.

Gaibulloev, Khusrav, Todd Sandler, and Hirofumi Shimizu. 2009. "Demands for UN and Non-UN Peacekeeping: Nonvoluntary versus Voluntary Contributions to a Public Good." *Journal of Conflict Resolution* 53(6): 827–852.

Gleditsch, Kristian Skrede. 2007. "Transnational Dimensions of Civil War." *Journal of Peace Research* 44(3): 293–309.

Gleditsch, Nils Petter, Peter Wallensteen, Mikael Eriksson, Margareta Sollenberg, and Håvard Strand. 2002. "Armed Conflict 1946–2001: A New Dataset." *Journal of Peace Research* 39(5): 615–637.

Goldstein, Joshua S. 2011. *Winning the War on War: The Decline of Armed Conflict Worldwide.* Hialeah, FL: Dutton.

Pilster, Ulrich, and Tobias Böhmelt. 2014. "Predicting the Duration of the Syrian Insurgency." *Research and Politics*, doi: 10.1177/2053168014544586.

Pinker, Steven. 2011. *The Better Angels of Our Nature: The Decline of Violence in History and Its Causes.* New York: Random House.

Salehyan, Idean. 2009. *Rebels without Borders: Transnational Insurgencies in World Politics.* Ithaca, NY: Cornell University Press.

Salehyan, Idean, David Siroky, and Reed M. Wood. 2014. "External Rebel Sponsorship and Civilian Abuse: A Principal-Agent Analysis of Wartime Atrocities." *International Organization* 68(3): 633–661.

Themnér, Lotta, and Peter Wallensteen. 2014. "Armed Conflicts, 1946–2013." *Journal of Peace Research* 51(4): 541–554.

7

Democracy, Ethnic Exclusion, and Civil Conflict

The Arab Spring Revolutions from a Global Comparative Perspective

Manuel Vogt, Nils-Christian Bormann and Lars-Erik Cederman

Introduction

The revolutions of the so-called Arab Spring constitute the most significant instances of political upheaval and regime change in the last decade. These revolutions have toppled some of the most resilient dictatorial rulers of the world. At the same time, certain popular uprisings have ushered in protracted civil conflicts, causing tremendous human suffering, as in Syria, for example. The circumstances are also significant because they raise the issue of the feasibility of achieving peaceful coexistence of different ethnic – mainly religious – groups within democratically constituted polities in a region that has been a laggard not only with regard to protecting democratic rights, but also in terms of entrenched policies and practices of ethnic exclusion and discrimination. Apart from the ethnically more homogeneous population of Tunisia, most states in the region are divided by ethnic cleavages, comprising important religious and/or linguistic minorities. In contrast to a long-lasting, worldwide trend towards ethnically inclusive governments, many regimes in the MENA region continued to rely on the dominance of specific ethnic groups, to the exclusion of others, on the eve of the Arab Spring. Thus, the introduction of democratic rule in the region may result in what one observer called a "fragmentation bomb" (Gardner 2012).

Although the events of the Arab Spring are still recent, making an evaluation of the outcomes tentative at best, political instability and violence along ethno-religious cleavages have indeed been observed with regularity throughout the MENA region. After the collapse of Muammar Gaddafi's regime in 2011 led to competitive elections in 2012, Libya has descended into civil war, with little semblance of central governance. A similar sequence transpired in Yemen: the resignation of Ali Abdullah Salei in 2012 led to a transitional government, headed by a consensus candidate for the presidential election, Abd Rabbuh Mansur Hadi, who was then ousted by a sectarian rebellion that has turned into full-scale civil war. Other cases (for example, Bahrain and Syria) only flirted with political openings, while exhibiting varying degrees of violence ranging from brutal repression of opposition mobilization to severe violent conflict – all marked by pronounced ethnic overtones.

Scholars analyzing the events of the Arab Spring have mainly focused on political institutions and the role of civil society movements (see, e.g., Lynch 2014b; for an overview, see also Lynch 2014a). Similarly, classic explanations of the link between democratic transitions and political violence have emphasized the role of institutional weakness (Huntington 1968; Mansfield and Snyder 2002). In contrast, we argue that ethnic inclusion is a key prerequisite for peaceful transitions from authoritarian to democratic regimes.

In this chapter, we examine two primary questions: How have patterns of ethnic exclusion and discrimination evolved around the world, and specifically in the Middle East and North Africa (MENA) region, before and after the Arab Spring? How do these developments relate to ethnic civil war and processes of democratization? We present some tentative answers to these questions, using the newly updated *Ethnic Power Relations* (EPR) Dataset Family (Vogt et al. forthcoming). The updates extend previous versions of the data until 2013, as well as introduce a new coding of regional autonomy regimes for ethnic groups. Our analysis reveals a clear historical association between ethnic exclusion and ethnic civil war in the MENA region. From this perspective, the violent unraveling of the popular movements of the Arab Spring cannot come as a surprise. In the light of our findings, the continuing high levels of ethnic exclusion in the MENA

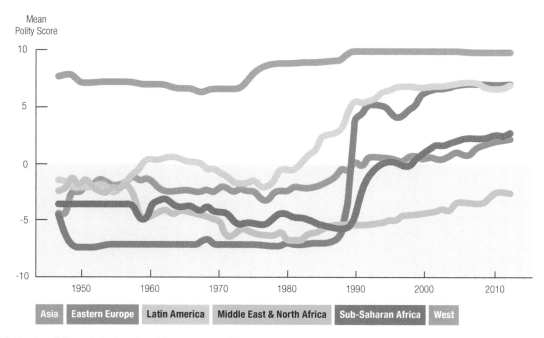

Figure 7.1 Regional Trends in Levels of Democracy, 1946–2013

Note: The figure shows the annual means of the overall Polity IV index scores (Gurr, Jaggers, and Moore 1989) for all countries in each region.

region after the Arab Spring are alarming. They suggest that the future of these states is likely to be shaped by how they will manage inter-ethnic relations in the face of potential future democratization.

Democracy and Ethnic Inclusion: The MENA Region in a Global Comparison

Before the revolutionary political changes, the MENA region was the most repressive and undemocratic in the world.[1] Other parts of the world have successively either caught up with the high level of democracy observed across the advanced industrial countries or joined in the democratic improvements experienced by many developing countries. In contrast, most states in the MENA region experienced little if any democratization. As Figure 7.1 shows, the Arab World has been – for nearly two decades – the only region where the average level of democracy falls below the midpoint of the standard Polity IV scale (Gurr, Jaggers, and Moore 1989), lagging well behind the changes in every other region. Despite a modest positive trend since 1980, more countries in the MENA region continue to lean towards strong authoritarianism than towards democracy.

The countries in the MENA region are also laggards in terms of the political inclusion of ethnic groups. Figure 7.2 (see next page) shows the annual average levels of ethnic exclusion and discrimination for the same world regions reflected in Figure 7.1, over the period from 1946–2013. This analysis is based on the updated EPR Core Dataset (Vogt et al. forthcoming). The EPR data distinguish between politically *included* and *excluded* groups based on group leaders' access to national executive power.[2] Ethnic discrimination is a particularly severe subtype of exclusion, defined as the active, intentional, and targeted discrimination of members of specific ethnic groups, with the intent of excluding them from political power based on their ethnic identity.[3] The calculations underlying Figure 7.2 rely on aggregate measures of the relative size of politically excluded or discriminated ethnic groups as a share of the overall population in each country.

In terms of the broader measure of exclusion, the regions of the world currently separate into three distinct clusters, according to the EPR dataset.

The first cluster is the West, defined here as Western Europe, plus Cyprus and the former colonies of Australia, Canada, New Zealand, and the United States. This region has been characterized by consistently low levels of ethnic exclusion since World War II.

The second cluster encompasses the regions of Latin America, Asia, Eastern Europe, and Sub-Saharan Africa, all of which are situated at the intermediate level. Of note, the abrupt initiation of democratization in Eastern Europe at the beginning of the 1990s led to a considerable increase in ethnic exclusion in that region. Sub-Saharan Africa entered the intermediate category after 1990, exhibiting the steepest decrease on the ethnic exclusion measure of any region, after experiencing decades of high levels of ethnic exclusion in the wake of transitions to independence and then during the

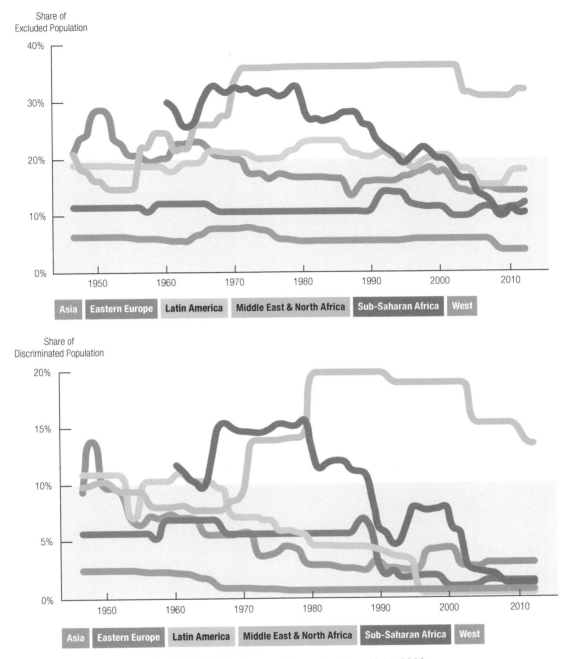

Figure 7.2 Regional Trends in Levels of Ethnic Exclusion and Discrimination, 1946–2013

Cold War era. Thus, the (favorable) impact of democratization on ethnic inclusion in Sub-Saharan Africa differed significantly from the (unfavorable) pattern observed in Eastern Europe around the same time.

The third cluster is the Arab World, which exhibits the highest values of ethnic exclusion of any region. The MENA region experienced a notable decrease in the degree of ethnic exclusion *before* the Arab Spring, as a result of power-sharing arrangements adopted in Sudan and in Iraq after the US-led invasion. Following the Arab Spring, ethnic exclusion increased slightly. Whether this constitutes the beginning of a systematic trend, similar to the developments in Eastern Europe at the beginning of the 1990s, is still too early to judge. Overall, the regimes of these countries still exclude groups that, on average, comprise over one-third of the population from access to national state power based on ethnic identity.

The picture becomes even gloomier when we examine the more narrow measure of ethnic discrimination. This practice, as defined by the EPR data, is almost completely absent in the West, while Sub-Saharan Africa again has experienced the steepest decrease in ethnic discrimination over the recent decades. The values in the MENA region have been much higher than those of all other regions since the early 1980s. In the 2000s, levels of ethnic discrimination decreased somewhat, mostly due to the end of Saddam Hussein's rule in Iraq and smaller improvements in Libya at the beginning of the Arab Spring. Nevertheless, ethnic discrimination in the MENA region is actually more prevalent today than it was 70 years ago and, on average, still affects substantial portions of these countries' populations.

Figure 7.3 maps the levels of ethnic exclusion and ethnic discrimination for each country of the MENA region in 2013.[4] Almost all countries in the region exclude at least some ethnic minorities from access to meaningful political power at the national level. Among the conspicuous examples is the highly exclusionary Assad dictatorship in Syria, which is completely based on his fellow Shia Alawites. In addition, more than half the countries in the region discriminate against ethnic segments of their populations. Certain cases are striking in this regard. In particular, two ethnic groups that experience political discrimination – Shia Arabs in Bahrain and Palestinians in Jordan – make up more than 50 percent of their respective countries' populations.

Within the MENA region, ethnic exclusion and discrimination are not uniquely Arab or Muslim phenomena. A number of the most severe instances do involve cleavages between different Arab groups or Muslim denominations – for example, Alawite Shia and other Arab groups in Syria, Jordanians and Palestinian Arabs in Jordan, and Shia and Sunni Muslims in Bahrain. Yet these phenomena are also pronounced in Israel, Turkey, and Iran, where non-Arabs exclude or discriminate against Arabs, Kurds, and other minorities. These conditions have resulted historically in a higher frequency of violent conflict across linguistic, rather than religious, divisions in the MENA region (Bormann, Cederman, and Vogt forthcoming). Moreover, as the examples of Israel and Turkey demonstrate, democratic institutions do not ensure ethnic equality in all cases. To the contrary, the dominance of the ethnic majority at the ballot box often brings about democracy's dark side (Mann 2005).

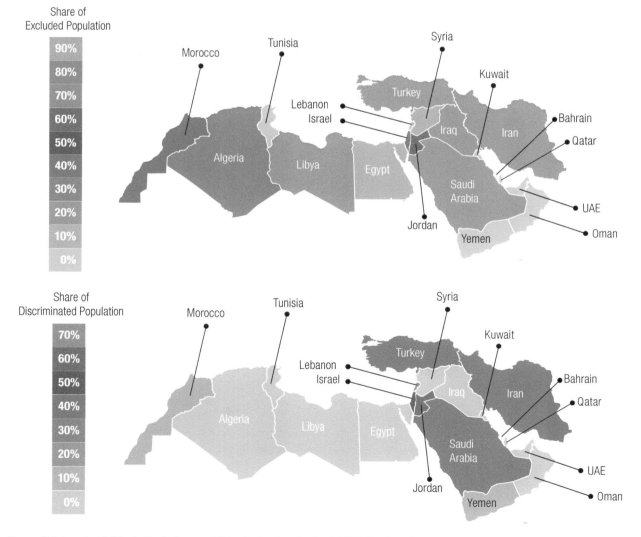

Figure 7.3 Levels of Ethnic Exclusion and Discrimination in the MENA Region, 2013

The updated EPR Core Dataset also allows us to compare regional trends in ethnic autonomy provisions. Previous versions of the dataset coded regional autonomy status as a subcategory of exclusion at the national level. To be clear, regional refers here to autonomy exercised subnationally, within a country. The 2014 version introduces a new dichotomous *regional autonomy* variable, which is coded for both excluded and power-sharing groups (Vogt et al. forthcoming).[5] A group is coded as regionally autonomous under three conditions:

1   a meaningful and active regional executive organ operates below the state level (for example, the departmental, provincial, or district level), but above the local administrative level;[6]
2   this regional entity has *de facto* (as opposed to mere *de jure*) political power; and
3   group representatives exert actual influence on the decisions of this entity, acting in line with the group's local interests.

The Kurdistan Regional Government in northern Iraq, which exercises meaningful political power at the sub-state level (Katzman 2010), is an example of a case for which a group is coded as regionally autonomous in the new EPR Core Dataset.

Figure 7.4 shows the relative size of groups with regional autonomy, as a share of the population of all groups eligible for autonomy, across the regions of the world. This analysis reveals that the MENA region also ranks last in terms of ethnic autonomy, albeit the disparity relative to other world regions is less pronounced than with the other measures discussed earlier. Autonomy provisions are even less frequent in the MENA region than in Sub-Saharan Africa, which has been identified as possessing few favorable conditions for the enactment of ethnic autonomy (Mozaffar and Scarritt 1999). This finding is noteworthy given the centrifugal forces unleashed by the current ethno-religious violence in the region, especially involving the Islamic State of Iraq and Syria (ISIS). Some have argued that in this context, ethno-federalist formulae may be a crucial institutional tool to hold together the multi-ethnic polities in the MENA region and to offer guarantees to discontented minorities in the future (Gardner 2014). At the other end of the scale, established democracies in the West provide the most autonomy to ethnically distinct groups. The other regions currently fall in the middle of the scale. Eastern Europe had been a frontrunner in terms of ethnic autonomy rights throughout much of the Cold War. Yet many autonomy regimes were abrogated amid the demise of the communist regimes and the formation of ethnically more homogenous nation-states, which are characterized by increasing levels of ethnic exclusion in the central government. The other meaningful trend over the past twenty years has been in the opposite direction: states in Latin America extended autonomy to many indigenous groups (González 2010; Van Cott 2001, 2007). Instances of such autonomy had been virtually absent in the region prior to 1990. Since then, Latin America has vaulted past both the MENA region and Sub-Saharan Africa and is now on par with Eastern Europe in terms of the extent of autonomy provided to ethnic groups.

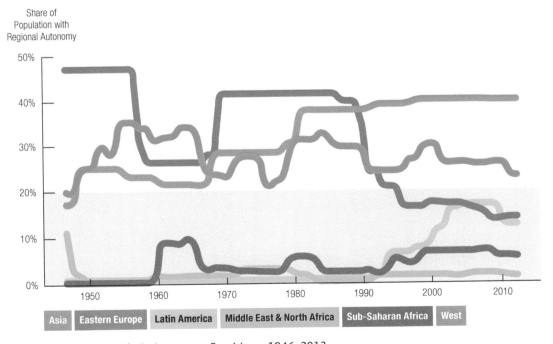

Figure 7.4 Regional Trends in Ethnic Autonomy Provisions, 1946–2013

Ethnic Exclusion and Civil Conflict

How do patterns of ethnic exclusion relate to the outbreak of civil war – arguably the most important form of political violence since World War II (Gleditsch et al. 2002)? Our analyses reaffirm existing findings that link ethnic exclusion to a higher risk of ethnic conflict both globally and for the MENA region in particular.

Specifically, we estimate the probability of civil war onset for each ethnic group-year over the period from 1946–2013. For this purpose, we rely on another component of the updated EPR Dataset Family: the ACD2EPR dataset, which identifies ethnic conflicts by linking EPR groups to rebel organizations from the 2014 version of UCDP/PRIO's Armed Conflict Database (Gleditsch et al. 2002; Themnér and Wallensteen 2014).[7] We conducted logistic regression analysis, including in our models various commonly used control variables, such as relative group size, logged measures of GDP per capita, and population figures from Hunziker and Bormann (2013), as well as cubic peace years (Carter and Signorino 2010). All ongoing conflicts are dropped from the analysis, and we only code new conflict onsets when there is at least a two-year intermission in fighting. Full results of the regression estimation are provided in Appendix 7.2.

Figure 7.5 displays the most important results from the logistic regression analysis for both the global sample of countries (purple) and a sub-sample composed of all countries in the MENA region (blue). We computed the predicted probability of ethnic civil war onset by moving the values of three key variables from "0" to "1", while holding all other variables at their respective means, medians, or modes.[8] The results make clear that the likelihood of engaging in ethnic rebellions is significantly greater among politically excluded ethnic groups, groups that experienced a recent downgrading of their power status, and groups with a history of conflict with the state. While the estimated results are less precise for the far smaller sample of ethnic groups in the MENA region,[9] they are consistent with the global pattern. Indeed, 37 of 46 (80 percent) recorded ethnic conflicts in that region were fought by excluded ethnic groups. In short, these results suggest that the violent rebellions of the past four years in Iraq, Syria, and other states of the MENA region are reflections of broader global patterns that link ethnic exclusion to ethnic conflict, as well as recurrences of historical experiences in the region.

Focusing on years of ethnic conflict incidence, Table 7.1 (see next page) shows that the group-level relationship between exclusion and the risk of ethnic conflict also holds at the country level across the MENA region. Countries that exclude larger relative shares of their population because of their ethnic identity experience more and longer spells of ethnic conflict. In this regard, Iran and Iraq lead the way, with six civil war onsets each. Countries with the highest levels of exclusion fight internal challengers during more than a third of their existence, whereas countries in the middle category spend about 20 percent of their years fighting, and states with the lowest levels of exclusion experience civil war in about 6 percent of years. These numbers even understate the true extent of conflict, since multiple challenges can occur at the same time, but are only counted once for a given country-year. Syria represents somewhat of an outlier as it only experienced three onsets of ethnic conflict during the period of observation, which is surprising given the extreme level of ethnic exclusion in the country.[10] The current civil war might unfortunately bring Syria closer to the expected count of ethnic conflict onsets.

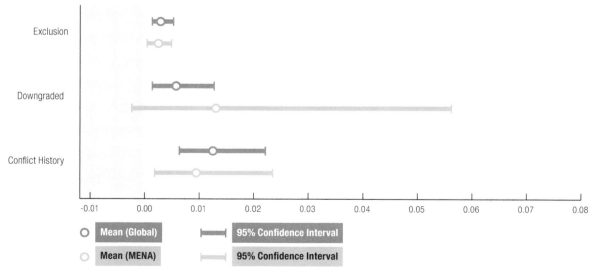

Figure 7.5 Group-Level Relationships between Ethnic Exclusion and Ethnic Conflict around the World and in the MENA Region, 1946–2013

Share of Excluded Population	Country Years without Ethnic Conflict	Country Years with Ethnic Conflict	Country Share of Years with Conflict	Conflict Onsets
High (>=40%)	223	125	35.9%	Iraq 1973, 1982, 1987, 1991, 1995 Israel 2000 Morocco 1975 Sudan 1963, 1983, 2011 Syria 1979, 2011
Medium (>=10%)	333	93	21.8%	Iran 1946, 1966, 1979, 1993, 1996, 2005 Iraq 1958, 1961, 1963 Israel 1949 Lebanon 1958, 1989 Turkey 1984
Low (<10%)	221	13	5.6%	Iraq 2004 Syria 1966 Yemen 1948, 1962, 1979, 1994
Total	**777**	**231**	**22.9%**	

Table 7.1 Country-Level Relationship between Ethnic Exclusion and Ethnic Conflict Incidence in the Middle East

Note: Fisher's exact test is significant ($p=0.000$) for the relationship between the degree of ethnic exclusion and ethnic conflict incidence.

Of the various instances of political violence following the Arab Spring, the ACD2EPR dataset only codes the Kurdish uprising in Syria as a case of ethnic civil war. This is partly a consequence of the ethnically inclusive and non-elite nature of anti-regime protests in fully or almost homogeneous states such as Tunisia, Egypt, and Libya, which did not involve claims on behalf of any distinct ethnic group. Moreover, protests in Bahrain, Morocco, and Saudi Arabia, each of which exhibit a clear ethnic dimension, either did not surpass the battle-related death criterion of UCDP or are classified as episodes of one-sided violence because only the state used violence against unarmed civilians. Finally, the ACD2EPR dataset does not code the current civil war in Iraq, which pits Sunnis against the central government, as a new conflict outbreak, but rather considers this case as part of the same conflict that has been ongoing since 2004. In the Arab monarchies and in Iraq, however, dissatisfaction among members of excluded groups is clearly on the rise (see, e.g., Wehrey 2014). Indeed, even the fundamentalist ISIS may be best understood as a reaction by the marginalized Sunni community to Shi'a dominance in Iraq (Adnan and Reese 2014). The high levels of exclusion in states such as Israel, Jordan, and Morocco, as well as the very fragile situation of the entire MENA region, make additional ethnic conflict in currently peaceful countries quite likely.

Conclusions

The states in the MENA region stand out as the most repressive regimes in the world with respect to ethnic power relations. Recent popular uprisings in the Arab region have toppled some of the most resilient dictatorial rulers of the world and are challenging the region's predominantly authoritarian political orders. Yet the decades-long exclusion of many minority and majority groups from political power has not been resolved by these democratic movements and, in fact, may block future attempts of genuine democratization. Some of the ethnically more homogeneous states embarked on major democratic reforms, including Tunisia and – for a short time – Egypt. Meanwhile, the countries marked by the highest degrees of ethnic exclusion or discrimination, including Bahrain and Syria, experienced violent uprisings that were either repressed or spiraled into protracted civil conflict.

The relationship between ethnic exclusion and conflict is not unique to the MENA region, but rather follows a global pattern. Politically excluded ethnic groups are significantly more likely to start ethnic rebellions than politically included groups. Thus, ethnic exclusion can also be expected to be a very risky political strategy on the part of rulers in this region. This suggests that ethnic inclusion and minority rights must be a central political and institutional concern if the new regimes emerging from the Arab Spring sincerely aspire to consolidate their democratization efforts. Concretely, this condition means that possibilities of political participation should be distributed equally among the population at large, independent from ethnic identity, and broad-based inter-ethnic coalitions at the elite level during this phase of political transformations will be particularly important.

Appendix 7.1: Regional Classification of Countries

Region	Countries		
Asia	Afghanistan	Kazakhstan	Republic of Vietnam
	Bangladesh	Kyrgyzstan	Singapore
	Bhutan	Laos	Sri Lanka
	Cambodia	Malaysia	Taiwan
	China	Mongolia	Tajikistan
	Fiji	Myanmar	Thailand
	India	Nepal	Turkmenistan
	Indonesia	Pakistan	Uzbekistan
	Japan	Philippines	Vietnam
Eastern Europe	Albania	Georgia	Romania
	Armenia	Hungary	Russia
	Azerbaijan	Kosovo	Serbia
	Belarus	Latvia	Serbia and Montenegro
	Bosnia and Herzegovina	Lithuania	Slovakia
	Bulgaria	Macedonia	Slovenia
	Croatia	Moldova	Ukraine
	Czechoslovakia	Montenegro	
	Estonia	Poland	
Latin America	Argentina	Ecuador	Panama
	Bolivia	El Salvador	Paraguay
	Brazil	Guatemala	Peru
	Chile	Guyana	Trinidad and Tobago
	Colombia	Honduras	Uruguay
	Costa Rica	Mexico	Venezuela
	Cuba	Nicaragua	
Middle East & North Africa	Algeria	Jordan	South Sudan
	Bahrain	Kuwait	Sudan
	Egypt	Lebanon	Syria
	Iran	Libya	Turkey
	Iraq	Morocco	Yemen
	Israel	Saudi Arabia	
Sub-Saharan Africa	Angola	Gabon	Namibia
	Benin	Gambia	Niger
	Botswana	Ghana	Nigeria
	Burundi	Guinea	Rwanda
	Cameroon	Guinea-Bissau	Senegal
	Central African Republic	Kenya	Sierra Leone
	Chad	Liberia	South Africa
	Congo-Brazzaville	Madagascar	Tanzania
	Democratic Rep. of the Congo	Malawi	Togo
	Cote d'Ivoire	Mali	Uganda
	Djibouti	Mauritania	Zambia
	Eritrea	Mauritius	Zimbabwe
	Ethiopia	Mozambique	
West	Australia	Finland	Spain
	Austria	France	Switzerland
	Belgium	Greece	United Kingdom
	Canada	Italy	United States
	Cyprus	New Zealand	

Appendix 7.2: Regression Results

Dependent Variable: Onset of Ethnic Civil War	(1) Full Sample	(2) Middle East & North Africa
INDEPENDENT VARIABLES		
Excluded Group	0.92***	0.62*
	(0.21)	(0.30)
Downgraded Group	0.78**	1.01
	(0.24)	(0.81)
Relative Group Size	1.26***	1.46***
	(0.30)	(0.37)
Ln(War History)	1.91***	1.40**
	(0.19)	(0.47)
Ln(GDP per capita)	−0.30**	−0.04
	(0.10)	(0.14)
Ln(Population)	0.07	0.47*
	(0.09)	(0.20)
Peace Years	−0.28***	−0.09
	(0.05)	(0.14)
Constant	−3.59*	−11.90***
	(1.74)	(3.49)
Cubic Splines	Yes	Yes
Observations	30876	3781
Log-Likelihood	−1129.90	−199.96
c^2	483.71	1417.73

Note: Country-clustered standard errors in parentheses. * $p < 0.05$, ** $p < 0.01$, *** $p < 0.001$

Notes

1. See Appendix 7.1 for a list of the countries considered to be part of the MENA region for purposes of this study. The table also shows the regional classification of all other countries.
2. The EPR dataset is arguably the most comprehensive data source on ethnic group inclusion. In particular, the EPR dataset covers the entire time period since World War II up to 2013, thus extending well beyond the temporal reach of other datasets on ethnic group political representation. For example, the discrimination indicators of the Minorities at Risk (MAR) dataset are available from 1980 onwards (Minorities at Risk Project 2003), while Ruedin's (2013) data on representation in legislatures only cover a single year. Although MAR offers a very detailed measurement of different types of discrimination, it is less precise on ethnic groups' political representation.
3. For a more complete and precise description of the EPR data and the power statuses of ethnic groups, see Chapter 8 in *Peace and Conflict 2014* (Cederman, Girardin, and Wucherpfennig 2014).
4. EPR treats the West Bank and the Gaza Strip as *de facto* parts of Israel and Western Sahara as part of Morocco.
5. The autonomy dimension is not coded for "monopoly" and "dominant" groups, since their political interests are assumed to be sufficiently represented at the level of the central state.
6. "Meaningful" refers to executive organs that carry out core competencies of the state, involving, for example, cultural rights (language and education) and/or significant economic autonomy (e.g., the right to levy taxes, or very substantial spending autonomy).
7. In the ACD2EPR dataset, a rebel organization is linked to an ethnic group from the EPR Core Dataset if the organization both recruited fighters from the ethnic group *and* made public claims on behalf of the group (Wucherpfennig et al. 2012).
8. The predicted probabilities and 95 percent confidence intervals were calculated with simulation methods using Clarify (King, Tomz, and Wittenberg 2000). Replication code is available on request from the authors.
9. The error term on the downgrading variable is extremely large and the effect of the variable is statistically insignificant, mainly because there were very few such instances in the MENA region during the time period that we study.
10. The first of these ethnic conflicts actually occurred during a period marked by low levels of ethnic exclusion.

References

Adnan, Sinan, and Aaron Reese. 2014. "Beyond the Islamic State: Iraq's Sunni Insurgency." *Middle East Security Report* 24, http://www.understandingwar.org/report/beyond-islamic-state-iraqs-sunni-insurgency (accessed May 7, 2015).

Bormann, Nils-Christian, Lars-Erik Cederman, and Manuel Vogt. Forthcoming. "Language, Religion, and Ethnic Civil War." *Journal of Conflict Resolution*.

Carter, David B., and Curtis S. Signorino. 2010. "Back to the Future: Modeling Time Dependence in Binary Data." *Political Analysis* 18 (3): 271–292.

Cederman, Lars-Erik, Luc Girardin, and Julian Wucherpfennig. 2014. "Exploring Inequality and Ethnic Conflict: EPR-ETH and GROWup." In David A. Backer, Jonathan Wilkenfeld, and Paul K. Huth (eds.). *Peace and Conflict 2014*. Boulder, CO: Paradigm. 74–87.

Gardner, David. 2012. "Moyen-Orient: Minorités, la bombe à fragmentation." *Jeune Afrique*, August 26–September 1, 2012: 48–51.

Gardner, David 2014. "A Federal Cure for a Shattered Middle East." *The Financial Times*, December 22.

Gleditsch, Nils Petter, Peter Wallensteen, Mikael Eriksson, Margareta Sollenberg, and Håvard Strand. 2002. "Armed Conflict 1946–2001: A New Dataset." *Journal of Peace Research* 39(5): 615–637.

González, Miguel. 2010. "Autonomías territoriales indígenas y regímenes autonómicos (desde el Estado) en América Latina." In M. González, A. Burguete Cal y Mayor, and P. Ortiz (eds). *La autonomía a debate. Autogobierno indígena y Estado plurinacional en América Latina*. Quito: FLACSO. 35–62.

Gurr, Ted Robert, Keith Jaggers, and Will H. Moore. 1989. *Polity II Codebook*. Boulder, CO: University of Colorado.

Huntington, Samuel P. 1968. *Political Order in Changing Societies*. New Haven, CT: Yale University Press.

Hunziker, Philipp, and Nils-Christian Bormann. 2013. "Size and Wealth in the International System: Population and GDP Per Capita Data for Political Science." Unpublished manuscript. ETH Zürich.

Katzman, Kenneth. 2010. "The Kurds in Post-Saddam Iraq." *CRS Report for Congress* (RS22079), http://www.fas.org/sgp/crs/mideast/RS22079.pdf (accessed June 2, 2014).

King, Gary, Michael Tomz, and Jason Wittenberg. 2000. "Making the Most of Statistical Analyses: Improving Interpretation and Presentation." *American Journal of Political Science* 44(2): 347–361.

Lynch, Marc. 2014a. "Response to Howard and Walters." *Perspectives on Politics* 12(2): 415–416.

Lynch, Marc ed. 2014b. *The Arab Uprisings Explained: New Contentious Politics in the Middle East*. New York: Columbia University Press.

Mann, Michael. 2005. *The Dark Side of Democracy: Explaining Ethnic Cleansing*. New York: Cambridge University Press.

Mansfield, Edward D., and Jack Snyder. 2002. "Democratic Transitions, Institutional Strength, and War." *International Organization* 56(2): 297–337.

Minorities at Risk Project. 2003. "Minorities at Risk (MAR) Dataset Users Manual 030703." http://www.cidcm.umd.edu/mar/margene/mar-codebook_040903.pdf (accessed July 3, 2015).

Mozaffar, Shaheen, and James R. Scarritt. 1999. "Why Territorial Autonomy Is Not a Viable Option for Managing Ethnic Conflict in African Plural Societies." *Nationalism and Ethnic Politics* 5(3–4): 230–253.

Ruedin, Didier. 2013. *Why Aren't They There? The Political Representation of Women, Ethnic Groups and Issue Positions in Legislatures*. Colchester, UK: ECPR Press.

Themnér, Lotta, and Peter Wallensteen. 2014. "Armed Conflict, 1946–2013." *Journal of Peace Research* 51(4): 541–554.

Van Cott, Donna Lee. 2001. "Explaining Ethnic Autonomy Regimes in Latin America." *Studies in Comparative International Development* 35(4): 30–58.

Van Cott, Donna Lee 2007. "Latin America's Indigenous Peoples." *Journal of Democracy* 18(4): 127–141.

Vogt, Manuel, Nils-Christian Bormann, Seraina Rüegger, Lars-Erik Cederman, Philipp Hunziker, and Luc Girardin. Forthcoming. "Integrating Data on Ethnicity, Geography, and Conflict: The Ethnic Power Relations Dataset Family." *Journal of Conflict Resolution*.

Wehrey, Frederic M. 2014. *Sectarian Politics in the Gulf: From the Iraq War to the Arab Uprisings*. New York: Columbia University Press.

Wucherpfennig, Julian, Nils Metternich, Lars-Erik Cederman, and Kristian S. Gleditsch. 2012. "Ethnicity, the State, and the Duration of Civil Wars." *World Politics* 64(1): 79–115.

8

Global Terrorism and the Deadliest Groups since 2001

Gary LaFree and Laura Dugan[1]

Introduction

This chapter reports new results from the most recent version of the Global Terrorism Database (GTD), which includes information on the characteristics of more than 125,000 terrorist attacks that occurred worldwide between 1970 and 2013 (LaFree, Dugan, and Miller 2015). We provide an update of baseline information on the distribution of terrorist attacks and fatalities around the world. In addition, we present analysis focusing on the worldwide surge in terrorist activity since the attacks of 9/11. Of the 20 deadliest terrorist groups since 2001, we classify 13 as organizations that strongly professed Islamic or Islamist motivations or goals. Our analysis highlights the extent to which these groups have come to dominate terrorism statistics in the years since the attacks of 9/11. We also review how these groups' targets, tactics, use of weapons, and regional distribution of activities compare to other extremely violent groups during the same time period.

Background on the GTD

The GTD is maintained by the National Consortium for the Study of Terrorism and Responses to Terrorism (START) at the University of Maryland. The database is currently complete through 2013,[2] with the exception of 1993 data, which were misplaced prior to the transfer of the records to START and are treated as missing when conducting the analysis in this chapter. The dataset is updated annually and made available to policymakers, analysts, scholars, and the general public through START's website (http://www.start.umd.edu/gtd). Data collection for 2014 was well underway as this chapter was being prepared. Under a contract with the US State Department, an abridged version of the GTD will support the statistical annex for the US State Department's *2014 Country Reports on Terrorism*.

For purposes of the GTD, our operational definition of terrorism is *the threatened or actual use of illegal force by non-state actors, in order to attain a political, economic, religious or social goal, through fear, coercion or intimidation*. In practice, we require that incidents be intentional, entail some level of violence or threat of violence, and be carried out by sub-national actors (for a complete description, see the GTD Codebook, available at http://www.start.umd.edu/gtd/downloads/Codebook.pdf). Thus, the GTD excludes state terrorism and genocide, topics that are important and complex enough to warrant separate attention and data collection.

To compile the GTD, including identifying and systematically recording details of terrorist attacks, START relies entirely on unclassified sources, primarily print and electronic media articles. At present, this process begins with a universe of over 1.6 million articles published daily worldwide, within which a relatively small subset of articles describe terrorist attacks. We use customized search strings to isolate an initial pool of potentially relevant articles, followed by more sophisticated machine learning techniques to further refine the search results. For this subset of articles, additional manual review is required to identify the unique events that satisfy the GTD inclusion criteria and are subsequently researched and coded according to the specifications of the GTD Codebook. For each month of data collection, about 15,000 articles are manually reviewed and about 1,500 attacks are identified and coded.[3]

Worldwide Trends in Terrorism

One of the most striking things about terrorism around the world over the past half century is how much it has changed locations. This evolution is clearly illustrated by considering total and fatal terrorist attacks worldwide since 1970. As Figure 8.1 shows, total attacks were relatively infrequent during the early 1970s, with fewer than 1,000 incidents recorded each year until 1977. We observe steady increases, however, throughout the decade; between 1970 and 1979, the number of attacks increased by more than 300 percent, from 651 to 2,661. This rise is associated especially with high levels of activity during the 1970s in Western Europe and the United States. In particular, 47 percent of all attacks during the 1970s in the GTD were located in Western Europe. Leading countries included Northern Ireland (treated here as a country, for convenience; 32 percent), Italy (22 percent), and Spain (19 percent). Meanwhile, 14 percent of all terrorist attacks recorded during the 1970s were located in the United States.

During the 1980s, the trends and locations of terrorism changed considerably. The annual frequency continued to increase throughout the 1980s up until a distinct peak in 1992 (5,078 attacks), with smaller peaks in 1984 (3,494 attacks) and 1989 (4,322 attacks). This steady rise in attacks was due in large part to a surge of attacks in Latin America. More than 55 percent of all terrorist attacks during the 1980s took place in South America (31 percent) and Central America and the Caribbean (24 percent). After 1992, the number of terrorist attacks worldwide dropped dramatically, falling to a twenty-year low in 1998. Likely the biggest reason for the drop-off was the collapse of the Soviet Union in 1991. Many of the organizations most active in committing terrorist acts in Latin America during the 1980s were left-wing groups with strong Marxist-Leninist-Maoist sympathies, including the *Sendero Luminoso* in Peru, the *Fuerzas Armadas Revolucionarias de Colombia* (FARC) in Colombia, and the *Frente Farabundo Martí para la Liberación Nacional* (FMLN) in El Salvador. Declines in attacks after 1990 were especially pronounced in El Salvador, where total attacks dropped by 82 percent from the 1980s to the 1990s, and Guatemala, where attacks dropped by 71 percent over the same period.

Figure 8.1 shows another major transition that occurred during the 2000s. Total attacks in 2000 (1,813), the year prior to the 9/11 attacks, were just a few hundred more than the corresponding figure for 1978 (1,526). Total attacks rose sharply in the aftermath of the United States and its allies invading Iraq in 2003. By 2011, total attacks (5,065) were barely less than the record level experienced in 1992. Since 2011, total attacks have shattered all previous records. In 2013, total attacks stood at 11,952, or 135 percent higher than the peak in 1992. This ebb and flow produces a pronounced U-shape pattern in total terrorist attacks from 1992–2013.

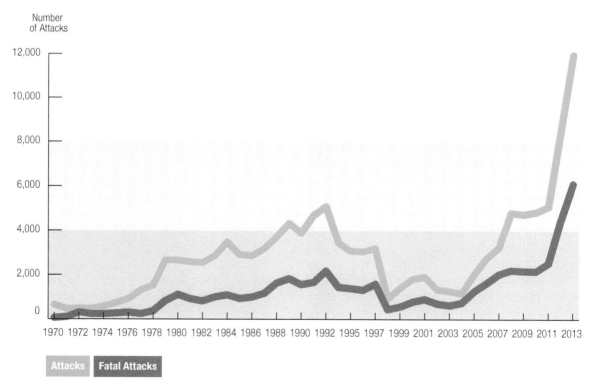

Figure 8.1 Annual Trends in Total and Fatal Terrorist Attacks, 1970–2013
Note: N (total attacks) = 125,087; N (fatal attacks) = 55,019.

On a global basis, less than half of all terrorist attacks result in fatalities: an average of 1,280 fatal attacks per year compared to 2,909 total attacks per year over the period from 1970–2013. The two time series are highly correlated (r = 0.98). Until 1979, the GTD recorded less than four hundred fatal terrorist attacks per year. Between 1978 and 1979, fatal attacks more than doubled, from 374 to 836. Throughout most of the 1980s, fatal attacks hovered close to 1,000 each year. The trend shifted again in 1988, after which fatal attacks rose to a 1992 peak of 2,173 fatal terrorist attacks. Fatal attacks then declined over time, bottoming out in 1998 with 451 fatal attacks. This drop was followed by another rise, especially after 2003, with the 1992 peak eventually surpassed for the first time in 2011, when 2,521 fatal attacks were recorded. Since 2011, fatal attacks have risen precipitously by 142 percent.

Trends in fatalities are also closely related to the regional location of terrorist attacks. This relationship is most clearly demonstrated by contrasting the 1970s and the period after 2000. As mentioned previously, around half of the terrorist attacks during the 1970s took place in Western Europe and North America. Both regions were characterized by attacks that produced relatively few fatalities. For example, attacks in Western Europe during the 1970s resulted in an average of 0.63 deaths per attack. In the 2000s, the locus of worldwide terrorist attacks shifted to the Middle East/North Africa and South Asia. These regions have been characterized by terrorist attacks that are far more lethal than those occurring in Western Europe or North America. For example, the attacks in the Middle East/North Africa since 2000 resulted in an average of 2.76 deaths – more than four times the average lethality of attacks observed in Western Europe during the 1970s.

Rank	Organization	Years Active	Fatalities		Attacks	
			Number	Average per Year	Number	Average per Year
1	Taliban	2002–2013	9,961	830	3,213	268
2	Islamic State of Iraq and the Levant (ISIL)[a]	2002–2013	8,173	681	1,199	100
3	Tehrik-i-Taliban Pakistan (TTP)	2007–2013	4,151	593	876	125
4	Boko Haram	2009–2013	3,686	737	808	162
5	Al-Shabaab	2007–2013	2,398	200	872	73
6	Maoists (India)/Communist Party of India-Maoist	2002–2013	2,320	193	1,905	159
7	Lord's Resistance Army (LRA)	2002–2011	1,988	199	171	17
8	Al-Qa'ida in the Arabian Peninsula (AQAP)	2004–2013	1,963	164	473	39
9	Liberation Tigers of Tamil Eelam (LTTE)	2002–2010	1,635	182	503	56
10	Maoists (Nepal)/Communist Party of Nepal-Maoist (CPN-M)	2002–2012	1,311	119	236	21
11	Revolutionary Armed Forces of Colombia (FARC)	2002–2013	1,277	106	877	73
12	Chechen Rebels[b]	2002–2011	1,243	124	137	14
13	Al-Qa'ida in the Lands of the Islamic Maghreb (AQIM)[c]	2002–2013	1,200	100	389	32
14	Lashkar-e-Jhangvi	2002–2013	1,015	85	82	7
15	Al-Nusrah Front[d]	2012–2013	1,010	505	67	34
16	Lashkar-e-Taiba (LeT)	2002–2013	821	68	103	9
17	New People's Army (NPA)	2002–2013	617	51	631	53
18	Al-Qa'ida	2002–2011	592	59	69	7
19	Hamas (Islamic Resistance Movement)	2002–2013	500	42	200	17
20	Haqqani Network[e]	2006–2013	490	61	66	8

Table 8.1 The Twenty Most Lethal Terrorist Organizations, 2002–2013
(Islamic terrorist groups shaded)
Note: [a] Islamic State of Iraq and the Levant includes groups that operated under different names: Tawhid and Jihad (2002–2004), Al-Qaida in Iraq (2004–2013), Islamic State of Iraq (2007–2011), and Islamic State of Iraq and the Levant (2013).
[b] Chechen rebels include Riyadus-Salikhin Reconnaissance and Sabotage Battalion of Chechen Martyrs.
[c] AQIM includes its originating organization, the Salafist Group for Preaching and Fighting (GSPC), which operated from 1999 through 2008. Also, the GTD refers to AQIM as AQLIM.
[d] The Al-Nusrah Front temporarily operated in close collaboration with the Islamic State, but on balance has maintained a separate identity and is therefore treated as a distinct organization.
[e] Although part of the Taliban family, the Haqqani Network has a distinctive organizational and operational structure and is therefore included separately.

The Most Lethal Terrorist Organizations between 2002 and 2013

To capture how the lethality of terrorism has changed since 9/11, as well as some of the consequences of this shift, Table 8.1 shows a summary of the 20 most lethal terrorist organizations in the world between 2002 and 2013. The rankings are restricted to the subset of identified attacks for which we can attribute responsibility to a specific actor.[4] The Taliban tops the rankings, followed closely by the Islamic State of Iraq and the Levant (or ISIL; we also include cases attributed to this organization's prior names, Tawhid and Jihad, al Qaida in Iraq and Islamic State of Iraq). Fifteen organizations were attributed responsibility for at least 1,000 fatalities (and 14 groups averaged at least 100 fatalities per year). Only six of these organizations operated throughout 2002–2013. Tehrik-i-Taliban Pakistan (TTP) and Boko Haram ranked as the third and fourth most deadly, despite operating for just seven and five years, respectively. In these shorter stretches, they were responsible for about half as many fatalities as the two top groups, which means that the average intensity of violence was relatively comparable. Five of the organizations on the top 20 list (LRA, LTTE, CPN-M, Chechen rebels, al Qaida) had no attributed attacks in the GTD for the last one to three years of the time series. The least deadly group on the list is the Haqqani Network, with just under 500 fatalities.

To provide further insight, we classified the 20 organizations in Table 8.1 according to whether they could be viewed as Islamic terrorist organizations. Our working definition of this term was *those organizations that committed terrorist attacks and who also strongly professed Islamic or Islamist motivations or goals*. Based on this definition, we classified 13 organizations – the Taliban, ISIL, TTP, Boko Haram, al-Shabaab, AQAP, AQIM, Lashkar-e-Jhangvi, al-Nusrah Front, Lashkar-e-Taiba, al Qaida, Hamas and the Haqqani network – as being engaged in Islamic terrorism. One set of actors that was tricky to classify is the Chechen rebels, which are composed mostly of Muslims, but their struggle has generally been presented in nationalistic, rather than religious terms. Thus, we do not classify the Chechen rebels as an Islamic terrorist group. In contrast, we classify Hamas as an Islamic terrorist group because the group frequently describes its goals and motivations in religious terms.

The results demonstrate just how consequential Islamic terrorism was to worldwide terrorism since 9/11. From 2002–2013, 13 of the 20 deadliest terrorist organizations – including five of the top six – can be classified as Islamic terrorist organizations. All of them are based in the Middle East, Africa or South Asia. Their emergence contrasts with the patterns observed in our contributions to previous editions of this book series. For example, in our chapter for *Peace and Conflict 2008*, which relied on GTD coverage from 1970–1997, we reported that 39 percent of terrorist events worldwide were linked to Latin America and 21 percent to Europe (LaFree, Dugan, and Fahey 2008: 46). During the same period, only 13 percent of attacks occurred in the Middle East/North Africa and 6 percent in Sub-Saharan Africa.

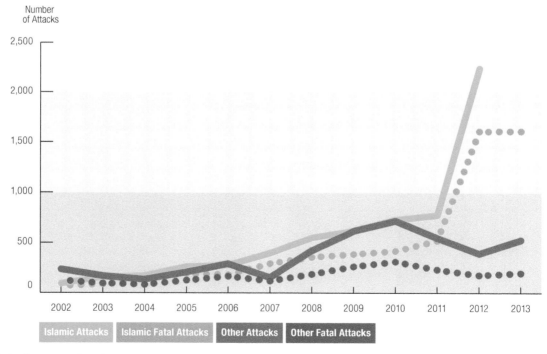

Figure 8.2 Islamic Total and Fatal Attacks Compared to Non-Islamic Total and Fatal Attacks, 2002–2013

Note: The 20 most lethal organizations committed a total of 12,831 attacks (8,417 by Islamic organizations and 4,414 by non-Islamic organizations; attacks by multiple organizations in this category are counted for both types), of which 7,930 involved fatalities (5,843 by Islamic organizations and 2,087 by other organizations).

Trends and Regional Distribution of Attacks

Next, we examine the time trends and the regional distributions of both total and fatal attacks committed by the top 20 terrorist organizations from 2002–2013. As Figure 8.2 shows, non-Islamic groups committed more attacks (235 vs. 94) and more fatal attacks (127 vs. 68) than Islamic groups in 2002. This pattern changed over the course of the 2000s, with a steady increase in total and fatal attacks by Islamic terrorist groups from 2002–2011, followed by a huge increase thereafter – of more than 2,000 percent. After 2010, the gap between Islamic and non-Islamic attacks is especially wide. In particular, attacks attributed to the deadliest Islamic groups were four times more common than attacks attributed to the deadliest non-Islamic groups in 2013, while the corresponding ratio for fatal attacks was over eight to one.

Figure 8.3 presents the share of total terrorist attacks from 2002–2013 by region (the countries and territories in each region are listed in Appendix 8.1) that were attributed to the 20 most lethal organizations, differentiating again between those that are Islamic and non-Islamic. The region with by far the highest percentage of these attacks is South Asia, comprising over half the total – more than three times as many as either the Middle East/North Africa or Sub-Saharan Africa. Of note, similar majorities of attacks by non-Islamic terrorist organizations (59 percent) and Islamic terrorist organizations (52 percent) on the top 20 list occurred in South Asia. The former is attributable especially to activity by the Liberation Tigers of Tamil Eelam (LTTE) and Maoists from both India and Nepal. Other major regions of activity for non-Islamic organizations among the top 20 are Latin America (20 percent) and Southeast Asia/Oceania (14 percent), due especially to the FARC and the New People's Army (Philippines), respectively. Nearly all of the attacks attributed to the deadliest Islamic terrorist organizations took place in just three regions: South Asia, the Middle East/North Africa and Sub-Saharan Africa. From 2002–2013, only seven attacks in other regions (two in Southeast Asia/Oceania, two in Western Europe, and three in North America) were attributed to such organizations.

Targets

Table 8.2 (see next page) presents the distribution of the targets of the 20 most lethal terrorist organizations, differentiating once more between Islamic terrorist organizations and the others, from 2002–2013. The most common targets were private citizens and property, the police, and the military, which together account for over 68 percent of the total number of attacks. In spite of our definition of terrorism emphasizing civilian targets, these results indicate that purely civilian targets – those without a more specific institutional or organizational affiliation – account for only about one-quarter of all the attacks by these especially deadly groups.

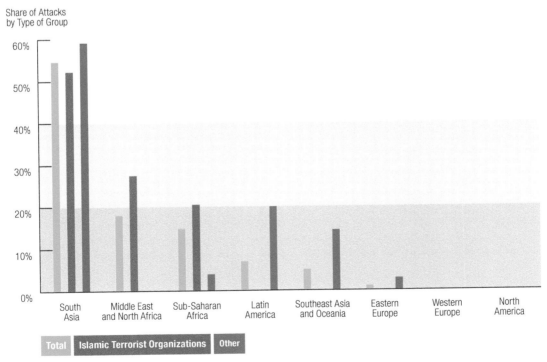

Figure 8.3 Regional Distribution of Attacks by the 20 Most Lethal Terrorist Organizations, 2002–2013

Category of Target	Share of Total Attacks (n=14,308)	Share of Attacks by Islamic Terrorist Groups (n=9,400)	Share of Attacks by Other Groups (n=4,908)
Private Citizens & Property	29.58%	29.84%	29.09%
Police	21.23%	22.26%	19.26%
Military	17.46%	20.02%	12.57%
Government (General)	14.08%	13.66%	14.88%
Business	8.00%	6.31%	11.21%
Educational Institution	3.44%	3.97%	2.45%
Religious Figures/Institutions	2.35%	3.08%	0.95%
Terrorists	1.97%	2.25%	1.45%
Government (Diplomatic)	1.28%	1.76%	0.36%
Transportation	3.50%	1.56%	7.20%
Unknown	1.28%	1.29%	1.25%
NGO	0.94%	1.19%	0.48%
Journalists & Media	0.85%	1.05%	0.48%
Utilities	1.83%	0.84%	3.72%
Telecommunication	1.56%	0.71%	3.17%
Airports & Airlines	0.50%	0.62%	0.27%
Tourists	0.28%	0.32%	0.20%
Violent Political Party	0.67%	0.31%	1.36%
Other[a]	0.28%	0.29%	0.27%
Food or Water Supply	0.26%	0.20%	0.39%
Maritime	0.16%	0.15%	0.18%

Table 8.2 Distribution of Targets of the 20 Most Lethal Terrorist Organizations, 2002–2013
Notes: According to the coding rules for the GTD, a terrorist attack can have up to three targets. All coded targets are counted in this analysis. Therefore, the columns will sum to more than 100 percent. Shaded figures indicate that the difference in shares between Islamic terrorist organizations and other organizations is statistically significant at a 0.05 level.
[a] "Other" encompasses a diverse range of targets, including refugee camps, emergency responders, and members of a wedding caravan.

In general, the targets chosen by the deadliest terrorist organizations do not differ substantially depending on whether or not they are Islamic. The top five targets are the same for both types. Our analysis does, however, identify three disparities in targeting that are statistically significant. The Islamic terrorist organizations on the list were more likely than the non-Islamic organizations to target the military, whereas the non-Islamic organizations were significantly more likely to target both businesses and transportation targets. Given that a large number of cases in the GTD since 2003 are from war-torn Iraq and Afghanistan, the importance of military targets for groups categorized as Islamic terrorists is unsurprising.

Tactics

The coding of the GTD also permits the examination of tactics used by terrorists, which are grouped into eight categories. Bombings are attacks that use explosive devices, including bombs detonated manually or by remote timer and suicide bombings. Armed assaults are in-person attacks whose primary objective is to cause physical harm or death directly on human targets, by means other than explosives. Hence, we would classify the use of an explosive or an incendiary device

Category of Tactic	Share of Total Attacks (n=13,571)	Share of Attacks by Islamic Terrorist Groups (n=8,826)	Share of Attacks by Other Groups (n=4,925)
Bombing/Explosion	48.88%	53.35%	40.37%
Armed Assault	35.79%	33.78%	39.59%
Hostage Taking (Kidnapping)	11.11%	9.38%	14.42%
Facility/Infrastructure Attack	8.45%	4.59%	15.81%
Assassination	6.41%	7.32%	4.67%
Unarmed Assault	0.46%	0.45%	0.47%
Hostage Taking (Barricade Incident)	0.37%	0.36%	0.38%
Hijacking	0.33%	0.24%	0.50%

Table 8.3 Distribution of Tactics Employed by the 20 Most Lethal Terrorist Organizations, 2002–2013

Notes: According to the coding rules for the GTD, a terrorist attack can employ up to three tactics. All coded tactics are counted in this analysis. Therefore, the columns will sum to more than 100 percent. Attacks for which no specific tactic could be determined are excluded. Shaded figures indicate that the difference in shares between Islamic extremist organizations and other organizations is statistically significant at a 0.05 level.

as a bombing, but the use of a grenade in the hands of a suicide attacker as an armed assault. Assassinations are attacks that target and kill or attempt to kill specific prominent figures. Such attacks are considered assassinations even if they are accomplished by implementing another tactic (e.g., bombing or armed assault). A recent example occurred in October 2011, when suspected members of al Qaeda in the Arabian Peninsula placed a bomb in the car of an Air Force Colonel in Yemen, killing the Colonel and two passengers. This attack was classified as an assassination, rather than a bombing, given the Colonel's prominent position. Facility or infrastructure attacks are those whose primary objective is to cause damage to non-human targets, such as buildings or monuments. Kidnappings involve hostage taking of persons or groups of persons with an intention to move and hold the hostages in a clandestine location. Barricade/hostage attacks are those whose primary objective is to obtain political or other concessions in return for the release of the hostages. Such attacks are distinguished from kidnappings because the incident is initiated and usually plays out at the target location, without holding the hostages in a separate clandestine location. Hijackings are attacks that involve the forcible takeover of vehicles, including airplanes, buses, and ships, for the purpose of obtaining some concession, such as the payment of a ransom or the release of political prisoners. Hijackings are different from barricade/hostage attacks because the target is the vehicle, regardless of whether there are people in the vehicle.

Table 8.3 shows the distribution of tactics of the 20 most lethal terrorist organizations, differentiating between Islamic terrorist organizations and other organizations, between 2002 and 2013. As we have found in previous analysis (LaFree, Dugan, and Miller 2015), bombings and armed assaults are by far the most common tactic, accounting for more than 84 percent of the total number of attacks. Hostage taking, facility attacks, and assassinations each contribute between six and eleven percent to the total. Unarmed assaults, hostage taking involving barricades, and hijacking are rare tactics, each accounting for less than one-half of one percent of the total. Islamic terrorist organizations among the top 20 rely on bombings significantly more than their non-Islamic counterparts, which instead favor armed assaults, kidnapping, and facility/infrastructure attacks more often.

Weapons

Because of high-profile terrorist incidents like those that occurred on 9/11 and more recently in London, Mumbai and Paris, as well as how terrorism is typically depicted by the media and the entertainment industry, there is an understandable tendency to think that most attacks are complex, carefully orchestrated events that rely heavily on sophisticated weaponry. In a previous contribution to *Peace and Conflict 2010*, however, we demonstrated that this image is off base. Instead, the vast majority of terrorist attacks by the deadliest groups relied on rather ordinary, accessible weapons – mostly explosives and firearms (LaFree, Dugan, and Cragin 2010).

Our conclusions also hold true for the deadliest terrorist organizations between 2002 and 2013. Table 8.4 shows the distribution of the range of weapons employed by the 20 most lethal organizations, differentiating as usual between

Category of Weapon	Share of Total Attacks (n=13,119)	Share of Attacks by Islamic Terrorist Groups (n=8,628)	Share of Attacks by Other Groups (n=4,491)
Explosives	55.76%	61.44%	44.74%
Firearms	42.58%	41.74%	44.21%
Incendiary	8.95%	5.13%	16.36%
Melee	4.35%	3.19%	6.59%
Chemical	0.26%	0.35%	0.08%
Sabotage Equipment	0.21%	0.06%	0.48%
Vehicle	0.11%	0.05%	0.23%
Fake Weapons	0.01%	0.01%	0.00%

Table 8.4 Distribution of Weapons Used in Attacks by the 20 Most Lethal Terrorist Organizations, 2002–2013

Note: According to the coding rules for the GTD, a terrorist attack can employ up to three types of weapons. All coded weapons are counted in this analysis. Therefore, the columns will sum to more than 100 percent. An "other" category is included in the analysis, but not presented. Attacks for which no weapon could be determined are excluded from the analysis. Shaded figures indicate that the difference in shares between Islamic extremist organizations and other organizations is statistically significant at a 0.05 level.

Islamic and non-Islamic. Explosives and firearms were used in more than 98 percent of all attacks where a weapon was recorded, with more attacks relying on explosives than firearms. The only other weapons that were employed in meaningful shares of attacks were incendiaries and melee attacks – where the perpetrator comes into direct contact with the target using low technology weapons such as fists or knives. Reliance on more complex weapons such as chemicals, the sabotage of equipment, and the use of vehicles and fake weapons was uncommon. Most notable, we did not identify any attacks involving the use of biological or radiological agents by the deadliest terrorist organizations during this time period.

Two statistically significant differences are observed in the use of weapons by Islamic terrorist organizations and other organizations on the list. The former rely more often on explosives, whereas the latter rely more often on incendiaries. In supplementary analysis, we also found that the use of suicide attacks was far more common among the Islamic terrorist groups (12.4 percent of attacks) than among other organizations (1.1 percent of attacks) on the list.

Conclusions

In this chapter, we examined the latest available data on terrorist activity from the GTD, with a special focus on exploring trends and patterns in recent attacks committed by the 20 deadliest terrorist organizations and evaluating differences between Islamic extremists and non-Islamic organizations. Our review indicates that both total terrorist attacks and lethal attacks increased dramatically from 1970 to the early 1990s, declined thereafter up until about 2000–2002, and then increased rapidly over the past decade. In 2013, total attacks and total fatal attacks worldwide were at their highest level since the start of the data series in 1970.

Among the most striking trends in global terrorism over the past half century is the shift away from attacks in Western Europe and North America during the 1970s, to Latin America during the 1980s, and subsequently to the concentration of attacks spanning South Asia, the Middle East/North Africa and Sub-Saharan Africa, which began to emerge during the 1990s and has intensified in recent years. These shifts in the prevalence of terrorism among various regions also had consequences for the characteristics of terrorist attacks. Most notably, terrorist attacks in Western Europe and North America during the 1970s were characterized by relatively few fatalities. By contrast, terrorist attacks concentrated in South Asia, the Middle East/North Africa and Sub-Saharan Africa during the past decade have been far deadlier.

An inescapable part of the recent history of terrorism is its connections to terrorism engaged in by groups who strongly justify their attacks through Islamic narratives. When we examine the 20 deadliest terrorist organizations in the world between 2002 and 2013, we find that 13 can be classified as organizations that strongly profess Islamic or Islamist motivations or goals. Moreover, the proportion of total and fatal attacks attributed to these deadly Islamic organizations has increased more rapidly since 2001 and especially since 2011, relative to the proportion attributed to the non-Islamic organizations on the list. Not surprisingly, the activities of these two types of organizations are associated with major differences across regions. South Asia records the highest proportion of attacks by the most lethal organizations and is the lone region of the world where both Islamist and non-Islamist organizations on the list engaged in substantial terrorist activity. By contrast, nearly all of the attributed activity in the Middle East/North Africa and Sub-Saharan Africa by the most lethal terrorist organizations has been carried out by Islamic extremist groups. Meanwhile, nearly all of the terrorist activity in Latin America, Southeast Asia/Oceania, and Eastern Europe by the most lethal terrorist organizations has been carried out by non-Islamic groups. During this period, attacks in Western Europe and North America by the most lethal terrorist organizations in the world were rare.

Limited differences in the choices of targets, tactics and weapons were observed between the Islamic and non-Islamic terrorist organizations on the list of the deadliest in the world from 2002–2013. Private citizens and property were the most common targets across the board. Likewise, bombings and armed attacks were far and away the most common tactics. Also, the five most important weapons were consistent. The Islamic organizations were significantly more likely than their non-Islamic counterparts to attack the military and less likely to attack businesses and transportation-related targets. In addition, Islamic organizations were significantly more likely to rely on bombings and suicide attacks and less likely to rely on armed assaults, kidnapping, and facility or infrastructure attacks.

Since our first contribution to the *Peace and Conflict* book series, which analyzed terrorist attacks from 1970–1997, the worldwide distribution of terrorism has changed rather dramatically. The number of attacks and the number of fatal attacks are at record levels and the locus of terrorist activity is now strongly concentrated in South Asia, the Middle East/North Africa, and Sub-Saharan Africa. Within these regions, a disproportionate number of terrorist attacks where a group can be attributed responsibility can be broadly categorized as Islamic organizations. Based on shifting trends during the past half century, however, our expectation is that the locus of terrorist attacks will not remain in South Asia and the Middle East/North Africa permanently – any more than it remained permanently in Western Europe or Latin America.

Appendix 8.1. Countries Categorized within Each Region

Region	Countries/Territories		
East and Central Asia	China	Kyrgyzstan	Taiwan
	Hong Kong	Macao	Tajikistan
	Japan	North Korea	Turkmenistan
	Kazakhstan	South Korea	Uzbekistan
Eastern Europe	Albania	Georgia	Romania
	Armenia	Hungary	Russia
	Azerbaijan	Latvia	San Marino
	Bosnia-Herzegovina	Lithuania	Serbia
	Bulgaria	Kashmir	Serbia-Montenegro
	Belarus	Kosovo	Slovak Republic
	Croatia	Macedonia	Slovenia
	Czechoslovakia	Moldova	Soviet Union
	Czech Republic	Montenegro	Ukraine
	Estonia	Poland	Yugoslavia
Latin America	Antigua and Barbuda	Dominica	Martinique
	Argentina	Dominican Republic	Nicaragua
	Bahamas	Ecuador	Panama
	Barbados	El Salvador	Paraguay
	Belize	Falkland Islands	Peru
	Bermuda	French Guiana	Puerto Rico
	Bolivia	Grenada	St. Kitts and Nevis
	Brazil	Guadeloupe	Suriname
	Cayman Islands	Guatemala	Trinidad and Tobago
	Chile	Guyana	Uruguay
	Colombia	Haiti	Venezuela
	Costa Rica	Honduras	Virgin Islands (U.S.)
	Cuba	Jamaica	
Middle East and North Africa	Algeria	Kuwait	South Yemen
	Bahrain	Lebanon	Syria
	Cyprus	Libya	Tunisia
	Egypt	Morocco	Turkey
	Iran	North Yemen	United Arab Emirates
	Iraq	Oman	West Bank and Gaza Strip
	Israel	Qatar	Western Sahara
	Jordan	Saudi Arabia	Yemen

Region	Countries/Territories		
North America	Canada	Mexico	United States
South Asia	Afghanistan	Mauritius	Sri Lanka
	Bangladesh	Nepal	Tonga
	Bhutan	New Caledonia	Vanuatu
	India	Pakistan	Wallis and Futuna
	Maldives	Seychelles	Western Samoa
Southeast Asia and Oceania	Australia	Malaysia	Solomon Islands
	Brunei	Myanmar	Singapore
	Cambodia	New Caledonia	South Vietnam
	Fiji	New Hebrides	Thailand
	French Polynesia	New Zealand	Timor-Leste
	Guam	Papua New Guinea	Vanuatu
	Indonesia	Philippines	Vietnam
	Laos	Samoa (Western Samoa)	Wallis and Futuna
Sub-Saharan Africa	Angola	Gambia	Nigeria
	Benin	Ghana	Rwanda
	Botswana	Guinea	Senegal
	Burkina Faso	Guinea-Bissau	Sierra Leone
	Burundi	Ivory Coast	Somalia
	Cameroon	Kenya	South Africa
	Central African Republic	Lesotho	Sudan
	Chad	Liberia	Swaziland
	Comoros	Madagascar	Tanzania
	Congo (Brazzaville)	Malawi	Togo
	Congo (Kinshasa)	Mali	Uganda
	Djibouti	Mauritania	Zaire
	Equatorial Guinea	Mauritius	Zambia
	Eritrea	Mozambique	Zimbabwe
	Ethiopia	Namibia	
	Gabon	Niger	
Western Europe	Andorra	Gibraltar	Netherlands
	Austria	Great Britain	Northern Ireland
	Belgium	Greece	Norway
	Corsica	Iceland	Portugal
	Denmark	Ireland	Spain
	East Germany	Italy	Sweden
	Finland	Luxembourg	Switzerland
	France	Malta	West Germany
	Germany	Isle of Man	

Notes

1 Support for this work was provided by the Department of Homeland Security (DHS) through the National Center for the Study of Terrorism and Responses to Terrorism (START), grant number N00140510629. Any opinions, findings, or recommendations in this chapter are those of the authors and do not necessarily reflect the views of DHS. We especially want to thank Erin Miller and Mike Jensen for advice on interpreting the GTD.
2 By the time we had completed the original GTD, covering 1970 to 1997, it was already 2005, meaning our data collection was eight years behind real time. As we worked to extend the data forward, we were forced to rely on older sources for the initial years beyond 1997, whereas we approached real-time data collection, using current sources, for more recent years. To the extent that newspaper and electronic media are not archived, availability of original sources may erode over time, causing underreporting or missing data. These issues are likely to be especially problematic in regards to small, regional and local newspapers. For more details, see LaFree, Dugan, and Miller (2015).
3 For a detailed discussion of the strengths and weaknesses of the GTD, see LaFree, Dugan, and Miller (2015).
4 Across the entire GTD, we are able to attribute responsibility to a specific actor in 45 percent of the identified attacks (for a complete discussion, see Chapter 5 in LaFree, Dugan, and Miller 2015).

References

LaFree, Gary, Laura Dugan, and Kim Cragin. 2010. "Trends in Terrorism, 1970–2007." In J. Joseph Hewitt, Jonathan Wilkenfeld and Ted R. Gurr (eds.). *Peace and Conflict.* Boulder, CO: Paradigm Publishers. 51–64.

LaFree, Gary, Laura Dugan, and Susan Fahey. 2008. "Global Terrorism and Failed States". In J. Joseph Hewitt, Jonathan Wilkenfeld and Ted Robert Gurr (eds.). *Peace and Conflict 2008.* Boulder, CO: Paradigm Publishers.

LaFree, Gary, Laura Dugan, and Erin Miller. 2015. *Putting Terrorism in Context: Lessons from the Global Terrorism Database.* London: Routledge.

9

Defense Spending, Arms Production and Transfers

The Political Economy of Defense in a Transitional Phase

Aude-Emmanuelle Fleurant and Yannick Quéau

Introduction

After a period of uninterrupted and significant ascent, global military expenditure has dropped by nearly two percent since 2011. This drop could suggest an easing of tensions alongside the phasing out of military intervention in Central Asia and the Middle East. Yet various factors support the hypothesis that the current down cycle is likely to be reversed in the short term.

The first and most important of these factors is the eruption of several major armed conflicts since 2011. Wars are a primary driver of defense spending. Growing demand for arms is observed in areas where insurgencies have intensified and/or there is a hardening of frictions about sovereignty over resource-rich areas. Therefore, the current security environment could signal a return to growth in military expenditures, especially for the states involved in the conflicts, neighboring countries, and major Western powers. A second factor that may reverse the current downward trend is a global expansion in demand for weapons. Arms transfers exhibit significant growth since the 2008 financial debacle.[1] Moreover, weapons imports are used to foster and accelerate the development of indigenous arms production capabilities in an increasing number of countries. The long-term sustainability of these new capabilities will likely require that these states generally maintain higher defense spending. These ambitions are also expected to motivate forays into the international arms trade, as several countries have already announced, which will contribute to greater weapons availability. Thus, available evidence tends to indicate that the main drivers of the modest decrease in military spending are not attributable to a more peaceful configuration and that the downward trend may be very short lived.

This chapter aims to clarify the current dynamics underpinning the global defense political economy and to highlight and discuss possible causes and consequences. In particular, we explore the ambiguity and conflicting nature of developments in the international defense political economy, i.e., the interaction of defense policies and postures, military spending, arms production and arms transfers, and how they relate to current dynamics of conflict and geopolitical/territorial disputes. The first section outlines major trends in defense expenditures globally and for some key regions and states. Including the latter more detailed view of the distribution of expenditures is crucial to improving understanding of recent trends and projecting future trajectories. The second section draws a portrait of the supply side and of the strategies implemented by the defense firms to face a changing geopolitical and financial environment, paying special attention to circumstances that affect arms transfers. In the concluding section, we suggest some avenues to explain and reflect on current trends.

Global Military Expenditures: Trends and Transitions

After reaching a peak at US$1.75 trillion in 2011, military expenditures worldwide have decreased at a moderate pace (see Figure 9.1 on next page). This downward trend in defense spending, on the heels of fifteen years of uninterrupted growth, hints that changes may have occurred in the global defense political economy.

Yet the small extent and recent nature of the decline – amounting to −1.9 percent between 2011 and 2014 – make it difficult to anticipate whether the trend is set to continue, or this is a temporary interruption that will be followed by a

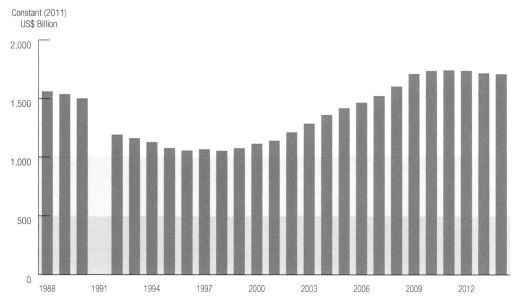

Figure 9.1 Trend in Global Military Expenditure, 1988–2014

Note: Estimating global military spending in 1991 is virtually impossible given the collapse of the Soviet Union, the second largest military spender in the world at that time.
Source: SIPRI 1988–2014 Military Expenditure Database.

new upward cycle in worldwide military spending.[2] Variations in the levels of resources allocated to defense can be interpreted as adjustments in security and defense spending priorities made by countries, as well as reflections of new national and global economic circumstances. We observe strong contradictory pressures from the strategic and economic environment that influence defense budget decisions at the national level, making forecasting longer-term trends a risky endeavor.

On the strategic side, several armed conflicts have emerged since 2012. Some of these conflicts, such as the Libyan war, insurgencies in both Mali and the Central African Republic, and the fight to counter ISIL in Iraq/Syria, have exhibited direct involvement from one or more Western powers. As major drivers of military expenditures, these conflicts put upward pressure on the budgets of all the major protagonists, both local and foreign. They may also lead neighboring countries to increase their own spending to address concerns of possible destabilization or spillover of the conflict on their territory. Indeed, the media and the academic community increasingly use the "arms races" concept to characterize regional military acquisition processes in Asia and the Middle East (Tan 2014; Beaumont 2015).

At the same time, persistent difficult economic conditions, combined with the fall in prices of commodities – especially oil – will likely curtail defense spending by certain states. This observation applies to countries in all regions of the world. It is of specific importance to Russia, the third largest military spender in the world during 2014. Russia has to deal with the potential effects of falling oil prices in combination with effects of the embargos and sanctions imposed in response to the Ukraine crisis (Perlo-Freeman et al. 2015b).

An Historical Perspective: Looking Back at the 2000s

To better understand the current situation, revisiting the dynamics prior to 2011 is useful. As Figure 9.1 illustrates, global military spending grew substantially during the period from 1999–2010. The growth was attributable mostly to two factors.

The first and most significant was major, long-term wars in Afghanistan and Iraq. Several Western countries, which are also the world's largest military spenders, participated in one or both of the conflicts. The armed forces of these countries were granted supplementary resources specifically for the war effort, contributing to increases in defense spending.[3]

A second central factor is an upsurge in funds allocated to defense in all the other regions of the world. In some cases, this growth in military expenditure supported more assertive defense policies and postures. In other cases, spending increases addressed issues of obsolescence or introduced large-scale and costly reforms such as armed forces professionalization. Most of the time, it was a combination of the two.

A further related driver of military expenditure evolution during that period was the implementation of arms modernization programs by several states in every region (*Géoéconomie* 2011). States replacing their arsenals with newer equipment face high costs associated with major weapon systems such as ships and aircraft, whether they are produced

Regional Index

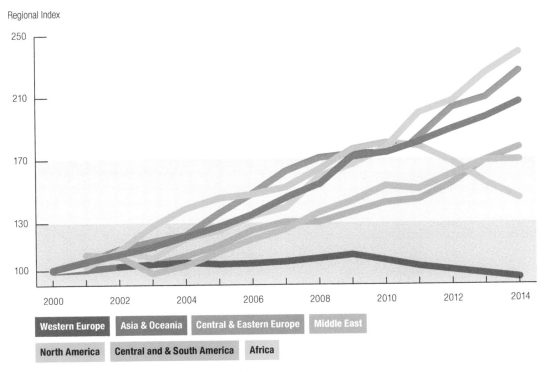

Figure 9.2 Regional Trends in Military Expenditures, 2000–2014

Notes: Expenditures are indexed by region to base 100 in 2000. All calculations are made on the basis of constant (2011) US$. Central and Eastern Europe includes Russia.
Source: SIPRI 1988–2014 Military Expenditure Database.

domestically or imported from foreign suppliers. As a result, these states have needed to dedicate significant resources to procurement accounts, the part of the defense budget dedicated to buying weapons, which in turn increased their overall defense spending. Indeed, one impetus of the upward cycle that began in 2000 was the increase in the United States military procurement budget as the Department of Defense was preparing to buy a new generation of armaments.

In addition, increases in military expenditures have been especially evident in countries with emerging economies (e.g., Brazil, Indonesia, Poland). A number of these countries have capitalized on their increasing GDPs and chosen to dedicate greater resources to defense.

Global military spending leveled off between 2010 and 2011 and then began to decline. A key precipitating event was the global economic crisis, which commenced in 2008. As Figure 9.2 shows, the decline in global military spending was almost exclusively due to reductions in the defense budgets of North American and West European countries. These cuts reflected a decrease in funding for defense organizations in the context of the implementation of austerity policies (Western Europe) and costly stimulus measures (US), as well as the gradual withdrawals of military forces from Afghanistan and Iraq. Meanwhile, military expenditures outside the Western world have continued to grow at a steady pace, except for in South America, where spending stagnated between 2013 and 2014. The offsetting trends in the Western countries and the rest of the world largely account for the modest scale of the decline in global military spending that started in 2011.

The Changing Balance among Regions

Figure 9.3 (see next page) shows that recent evolutions in military spending have eroded the indisputable enduring domination of global military spending by North America and Western Europe. The share of spending by these two regions dropped from 64 percent in 2004 to 50 percent in 2014. The regions that have expanded spending the most over the same time period – Asia, the Middle East and Africa – are currently theaters of severe tensions both between countries (territorial disputes, border skirmishes, interstate wars, foreign military interventions) and within countries (*coups d'état*, inter-group clashes, civil wars).[4]

Another important takeaway is that one or two countries stand out in most of the regions as exhibiting significant increases in military expenditure between 2000 and 2014. The leading countries include China (+416 percent) and India (+80.8 percent) in Asia, Russia (+194.4 percent) in Eastern Europe, and Brazil (+48 percent) in South America. These four countries are also known as the BRIC group of emerging economies. All four have progressively asserted themselves

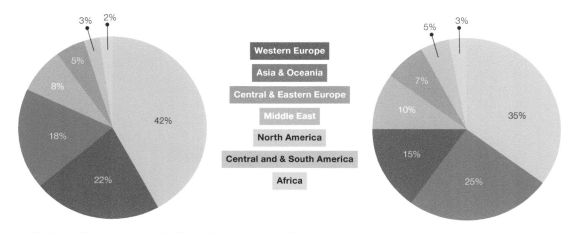

Figure 9.3 Regional Shares of Global Military Expenditures, 2004 and 2014

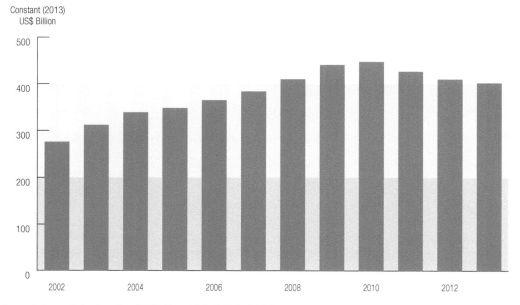

Figure 9.4 Annual Arms Sales by the SIPRI Top 100, 2002–2013

Source: SIPRI Arms Industry Database, 2014.

as regional leaders. A significant part of this quest for leadership relies on bringing their military capacities in line with their economic weight and growing influence in world affairs. Meanwhile, Africa is an exception, as drivers of growth in military spending are more numerous and dispersed.

The significant increases observed outside of the West reflect the costs of implementing policies designed to achieve selective or complete autonomy of supply in armaments, by building domestic arms production capabilities, in support of these more assertive foreign and defense policies. Their general purpose is to reduce the possibility of being cut off from access to weapons should they get into a conflict about which countries that host their major suppliers – based in Western states – disapprove. The search for capabilities also tends to indicate that military power is still very much considered by these countries as an essential instrument of foreign policy.

Trends in Arms Production and Transfers

In 2013, the combined sales of the top 100 arms companies in the world, excluding China,[5] declined by two percent in real terms, compared to 2012, to US$402 billion. As Figure 9.4 shows, this amount remains high relative to the revenues declared in 2002, but represents the fourth consecutive year of decline (Fleurant and Perlo-Freeman 2014). The 2013 decline in the total revenues of the top 100 is smaller than the one observed in 2012 (3.9 per cent).

The Traditional Dominance of Western Arms Producers

The defense industry continues to be dominated by Western producers. As Table 9.1 (see next page) shows, the top 10 ranking in terms of sales is populated entirely by US and Western European companies. These frontrunners, which capture an important share of procurement spending from their home country, make up more than half of the arms sales of the top 100. Indeed, the 68 Western companies (38 headquartered in the US, 29 in Western Europe, and one in Canada) ranked in the SIPRI top 100 are collectively responsible for close to 85 percent of the combined arms sales of the top 100 defense firms in 2013. As Figure 9.5 illustrates, the top 10 companies were major beneficiaries of large increases in procurement spending by Western countries during the 2000s, as well as an expansion of international demand during the same period.

The stability at the top of the rankings since the early 2000s confirms that Western companies still dominate the global arms production hierarchy. This enduring status is attributable to at least five primary factors.

The first is the size of the national military spending. The level of resources dedicated to weapons acquisition remains substantial – generally around 20–25 percent of total defense spending – despite difficult economic conditions that have led to decreases in total defense funding in several countries. Second, the countries where the top 10 companies are headquartered have consistently sustained significant domestic arms production capabilities since the start of the Cold War. In turn, procurement spending is funneled mostly to national producers, which are often shielded from foreign competition in order to ensure that autonomy of supply for the state is sustained. Third, because of continued high levels of military research and development investments, which started during the Cold War to build arms-production capacities, Western companies now produce the most sophisticated and technologically advanced – and therefore costly – weapons.[6] Fourth, all of the top Western companies are major exporters, which also bolsters their sales to varying degrees. Fifth, the top companies employ huge numbers of people in the manufacturing sector, relying on a highly qualified engineering and technical workforce (see Table 9.1), which are important considerations in their relationships with national governments. Defense lobbyists often leverage employment as a major argument in favor of supporting the industry as a whole. Consequently, this workforce plays a huge role in public industrial, technological and educational policies. Certain companies depend on a small number of lucrative contracts. Such companies then lobby their clients to maintain particular procurement programs on the justification of ensuring the sustainability of the jobs they provide – and the survival of the companies themselves.

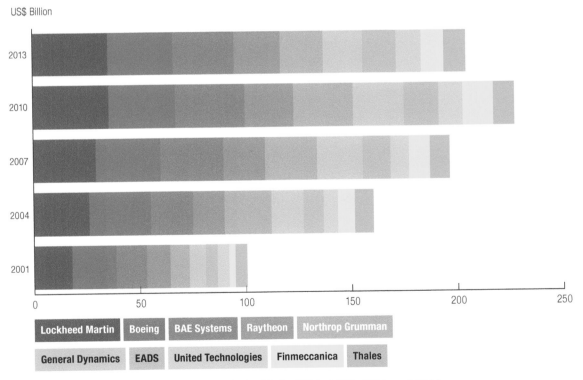

US$ Billion

Figure 9.5 Arms Sales by Major Military Companies in 2001, 2004, 2007, 2010 and 2013

Note: This list of major companies corresponds to those that made the SIPRI top 10 in 2013, as reflected in Table 9.1. EADS was renamed Airbus Group in 2014.
Source: SIPRI (2002, 2005, 2008, 2011, 2014).

2007					
Rank	Company	Country	Arms Sales (US$ millions)	Total Sales (US$ millions)	Employment
1	Boeing	USA	30,480	66,387	159,300
2	BAE Systems	UK	29,860	31,426	97,500
3	Lockheed Martin	USA	29,400	42,862	140,000
4	Northrop Grumman	USA	24,600	32,018	122,000
5	General Dynamics	USA	21,520	27,240	83,500
6	Raytheon	USA	19,540	21,301	72,100
S	BAE Systems Inc.	USA	14,910	14,908	51,300
7	EADS	Trans-Eur.	13,100	53,534	116,490
8	L-3 Communications	USA	11,240	13,961	64,600
9	Finmeccanica	Italy	9,850	18,376	60,750
10	Thales	France	9,350	16,825	61,200

2010					
Rank	Company	Country	Arms Sales (US$ millions)	Total Sales (US$ millions)	Employment
1	Lockheed Martin	USA	35,730	45,803	123,000
2	BAE Systems	UK	32,880	34,609	98,200
3	Boeing	USA	31,360	64,306	160,500
4	Northrop Grumman	USA	28,150	34,757	117,100
5	General Dynamics	USA	23,940	32,466	90,000
6	Raytheon	USA	22,980	25,113	72,400
S	BAE Systems Inc.	USA	17,900	17,903	46,900
7	EADS	Trans-Eur.	16,360	60,599	121,690
8	Finmeccanica	Italy	14,410	24,762	75,200
9	L-3 Communications	USA	13,070	15,680	63,000
10	United Technologies	USA	11,410	53,326	208,220

2013					
Rank	Company	Country	Arms Sales (US$ millions)	Total Sales (US$ millions)	Employment
1	Lockheed Martin	USA	35,490	45,500	115,000
2	Boeing	USA	30,700	86,623	168,400
3	BAE Systems	UK	26,820	28,406	84,600
4	Raytheon	USA	21,950	23,706	63,000
5	Northrop Grumman	USA	20,200	24,661	65,300
6	General Dynamics	USA	18,660	31,218	96,000
7	EADS	Trans-Eur.	15,740	78,693	144,060
8	United Technologies	USA	11,900	62,626	212,000
9	Finmeccanica	Italy	10,560	21,292	63,840
10	Thales	France	10,370	18,850	65,190

Table 9.1 The SIPRI Top 10 Arms-Producing and Military Services Companies in the World in 2007, 2010 and 2013

Adaptation by Leading Arms Producers to Changing Conditions: An Industry under Pressure

Changes in the general dynamics of military expenditure have an impact on arms producers. The impact is not necessarily straightforward. Arms producers adapt to anticipated or actual fluctuations in procurement budgets by redesigning their strategies and making specific choices on how to adapt to new economic parameters. In turn, these decisions can have significant ramifications for the evolution of the global arms market and/or national defense landscapes.

The US experience during the 1990s is a case in point. Procurement spending fell 49 percent from 1991–1997.[7] One observed response was a major wave of mergers and acquisitions, encouraged and supported financially by the federal government. The changes resulted in an unprecedented concentration of US arms producers, raising concerns about competition and the range of supply options available to the US Department of Defense (Markusen and Costigan 1999). Another consequence was a defense industry integration process in Western European countries, prompted by worries about what these new "super prime contractors" would mean for their own military industry (Adams, Cornu, and James 2001).

More recently, sales by the top 100 arms producers have decreased modestly. The dip is attributable to the circumstantial factors driving global military spending that were discussed above, namely the combined impacts of the economic crisis on procurement accounts of defense budgets and the phasing out of war-related procurement spending. These factors have primarily affected corporations based in Western countries, as can be expected considering their overwhelming domination of the top arms producers ranking.[8]

Western states have sought to manage downward pressures on defense spending, in particular by mitigating the impact of budget cuts on procurement accounts (McGerty 2015; McLeary 2015; Berteau and Ben-Ari 2012). In the US, this mitigation has been achieved partially by cancelling underperforming programs such as the Future Combat System (FCS), which was deemed less in line with the administration's new priorities,[9] in order to secure other projects such as the F-35 combat aircraft (Chandrasekaran 2013). In some Western European countries, where procurement funding is already considered too low to fully support the defense industrial base, military procurement and investment funds were shielded from large reductions to an extent, with cuts focused instead on reducing military and civil personnel spending (Fleurant 2012). These policy decisions can have direct benefits to arms producers. For example, France's shipbuilder DCNS benefited from a strong commitment by the French government to maintain procurement spending (République française 2013).

More generally, many of the top arms producers based in the major military industrial powers have fared well despite a stringent fiscal environment. A key to ongoing success has been the implementation of adaptation strategies, which has helped producers stay near the top of the rankings by ensuring new and/or growing streams of revenue.

First, a majority of the major Western producers have diversified by targeting the penetration of so-called "adjacent markets," i.e., markets that display similar features and norms to those of the defense market (Lemer and Thomas 2011). The process is mainly presented as a way to maintain revenues – and returns to shareholders – without straying too far from core military business. In markets where defense and non-defense production actually intersect, such as cybersecurity, diversification is presented as a way to sustain defense capabilities. More generally, diversification also reflects changing demand worldwide, linked to new threat assessments made by defense and security agencies, where activities such as cybersecurity, mass surveillance, and border monitoring and control have become priorities.[10]

Second, major Western arms producers have devoted increased effort to export markets. The search for new markets is hardly novel. European companies have faced narrower domestic markets for longer than their US counterparts and thus turned earlier to exports to augment sales.[11] For example, French shipbuilder DCNS – mentioned earlier – has benefited heavily from export sales (République française 2013). Meanwhile, US companies have moved more slowly to accord greater priority to export sales. These companies continue to be the largest arms exporters in the world since the collapse of the Soviet Union. Yet international sales still constitute a modest share of sales by US companies, which remain highly dependent on demand from the US Department of Defense. Domestic military spending during the 2000s was sufficiently robust to support sales at high levels. A new phenomenon is the recent, rapid growth in military expenditures and demand for weapons in several parts of the world, which has invigorated the interest of the major arms companies in international sales. They take note of large, expanding markets in countries such as Brazil, India, and Saudi Arabia, making them priorities for export sales.

The attention to export markets has important implications. A number of arms companies have established a long-term presence in buying countries (Dehoff, Dowdy and O Sung Kwon 2014). In addition, growth in exports increases the influence of international customers in the sales of arms producers and may weaken their links to domestic markets (Bitzinger 1999). The interest in exports has also altered the balance of power in ways that are largely favorable to clients in the global arms market. This shift has registered with importing countries, which can take advantage of fierce competition between suppliers by requesting lower prices or more advantages, in the form of offsets (see below), from bidders.[12]

The "Rest": Leveraging a Favorable Balance of Power in the Global Arms Market

The focus on Western companies brushes over the fact that companies based elsewhere have substantially increased their sales over the past 10 years. A chief reason is that several countries are openly pursuing strategies to become bigger actors in the international defense trade. These countries span all regions of the world. The countries are active as both suppliers and clients. An emphasis of their strategies is to improve domestic arms production.

In particular, Russia – the second largest arms exporter (Wezeman and Wezeman 2015) – renewed its military industrial ambitions in the late 2000s. The shift followed a decade during which its arms production capabilities were significantly diminished. Taking advantage of strong economic growth and infusions of funds from high oil prices, the Putin government adopted a comprehensive and costly modernization program, looking to upgrade simultaneously the quality of Russia's weapons and of its arms industry. Russian companies have benefited greatly from the country's major defense modernization projects. Ten Russian firms appeared in the SIPRI top 100 for 2013, together accounting for US$31 billion in sales – an increase of 20 percent compared to 2012.[13] Of note, Almaz-Antey, a producer of air defense missiles systems, is now ranked 12th, with US$8 billion of arms sales in 2013.[14] To reach these goals, Russia has selectively turned to Western suppliers to fulfill some technological gaps, especially in information technology and more advanced electronic systems.[15]

Meanwhile, companies from Singapore, South Korea and Turkey have recently entered the list of top 100 arms producers. They climbed up the rankings in part due to strong domestic orders, but also because of some successes with exports. In addition, evidence indicates that sales by Chinese arms-producing companies have increased significantly over the past 10 years. For now, however, a lack of reliable data about arms sales by major Chinese conglomerates makes accurate assessment and comparison to the rest of the world impossible.

The Influence of Offsets

A key part of the broader strategy often adopted by emergent countries in the international arms industry is offset policies (Anderson 2009). Generally speaking, offsets are a contractual mechanism by which a foreign supplier winning a major contract for a public market is required to reinvest a certain percentage of the value of that contract in the client country's economy and industry.[16] In practice, offsets are considerable in scale, with the potential to accumulate to billions of dollars over a decade, as shown in Figure 9.6.[17]

When offsets are directly linked to the activities of a contract, such as by requiring that parts for a weapon system be produced and/or assembled in the purchasing country, they can become a useful lever to expedite development of domestic arms production capacities. Given the offset proposal is often a decisive criterion in a winning bid, Western

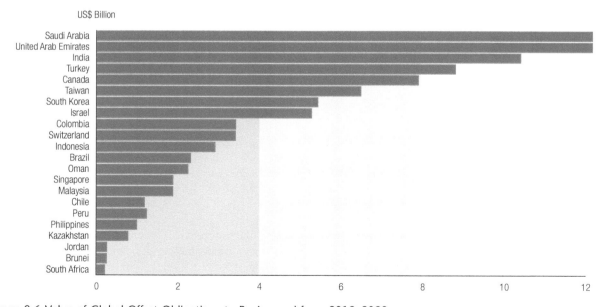

Figure 9.6 Value of Global Offset Obligations to Be Accrued from 2012–2022

Notes: These results are a conservative assessment based on existing proprietary datasets covering the procurement programs of 23 defense markets: Argentina, Brazil, Brunei, Canada, Chile, Colombia, India, Indonesia, Israel, Jordan, Kazakhstan, Malaysia, Oman, Peru, Philippines, Saudi Arabia, Singapore, South Africa, South Korea, Switzerland, Taiwan, Turkey, and the UAE.
Source: Jane's 2013.

exporters have little choice other than to satisfy demands, which often involve local production, transfers of technology and know-how, partnerships with local companies and/or their integration in the foreign company's supply chains, in order to win procurement competitions. A good example is the Prosub program in Brazil. One part of the submarine is built in France, the other part in Brazil, where the final assembly takes place. The contract also envisions transfers of technologies, training, and engineering guidance, with the purpose of enabling Brazil to acquire the necessary know-how to design its next generation of submarines by itself. In connection with the requirements of offsets, Western producers have been induced to establish a long-term presence in various client countries. Another by-product is that when offsets are designed to support greater national defense production capabilities, they raise the level of militarization of the manufacturing base in client countries.

Consequences of Supply-Side Adjustments

The strategies implemented to address the changing market conditions of the 2000s have important repercussions for the supply side of arms production. A key factor in this regard is the global arms trade, which has grown over the past decade (see Figure 9.7).

The push towards export sales is supporting a process of internationalization of the arms industry. As mentioned above, the combination of military spending patterns and the multiplication of offset requirements has led arms producers to strengthen their footprint in client countries by opening factories and training centers, partnering with local companies, and integrating them into supply chains (Ungaro 2013). These developments apply mostly to Western arms companies. At the same time, some emerging producers are approaching export markets with offers of local production. For example, Brazil has targeted the African market and met with some success (Pelzer 2014).

This evolution makes monitoring activities of the arms industry increasingly difficult, for multiple reasons. Production and assembly of weapons systems is becoming more dispersed, lessening visibility. Also, the content of offset agreements is not made public, as they are considered proprietary information by the supplying companies. Therefore, what benefits are agreed upon and what is being transferred can be hard to establish. Partly because of this lack of transparency, offsets are widely considered a major conduit of corruption.

Another consequence of the role of exports and offsets is growing concern among traditional Western defense industrial powers about the sustainability of their military technological advantage. Offsets, in particular, can erode this advantage and create competitors in the longer term, given the transfer of production, technologies, skills, and know-how to client countries. Two widely cited illustrations are South Korea, which is actively involved in the international market to sell its training aircraft following 30 years of developing its aerospace industry with the support of US companies, and Turkey, which is becoming an increasingly important actor in the armored vehicles market (Hogg and Sezer 2015).

Figure 9.7 Trend in International Exports of Major Weapons, 2000–2014
Source: SIPRI Arms Transfers Database.

The intensification of competition and the possibility of losing the so-called "military edge" have prompted pressing requests by industry and lawmakers in military industrial powers to increase funding for military research and development (R&D). Investments in R&D support development of new generations of armaments, which typically feed into new procurement cycles (Fleurant 2008), creating conditions for higher military spending in the future in categories where the vast majority of the funds is funneled to the industry.

In the US, defense officials share the misgivings about a possible shrinking of the country's military technical supremacy (Hagel 2014). In early 2015, US Secretary of Defense Ashton Carter announced a new strategy to address this issue, especially in light of indications of China's improvement in military equipment, as well as generally greater availability of and access to weapons and weapons components, which are now supplied by civil companies or by ministries of defense through international sales (Carter 2015). Similarly, European military industrial powers are engaged in ongoing discussions about states raising their military R&D budgets, which have been deemed largely insufficient for several years. Major European producers are also considering increasing their in-house R&D, even as they actively lobby both the states where they have facilities and some European agencies to dedicate funds to support military R&D performed in companies.

Thus, the desire to secure and enhance arms production capabilities dominates supply-side dynamics in both the West and the Rest. Offsets are creating conditions of greater dispersion of arms production capabilities, as well as establishing potential new sources of supply in the international market. All emerging suppliers have stated goals of exporting production when their industries are sufficiently mature.[18]

Current available data suggest that this point has not yet been reached. Imports have actually intensified in regions that have simultaneously experienced high GDP growth and increases in conflicts and disputes – most notably, Asia and the Middle East. As a result, these regions have become the largest recipients of arms transfers by a significant margin (see Figure 9.8). The statistics underscore that national production capabilities in these regions remain limited and turning to foreign suppliers remains essential. Acquiring national production capabilities is an expensive proposition, especially for ambitious weapons programs, and a challenge to pursue and accomplish amid the tense geopolitical environment.

Meanwhile, the major arms producers are far from passive actors. They have vested interests in maintaining a high level of spending for defense procurement and R&D. These motives lead companies to promote to their clients – states – ideas for new, more advanced military equipment to wage future wars, including weapons that are often tailored to address scenarios emerging from pessimistic assessments of the security environment.[19] Companies on both sides of the North Atlantic also consistently lobby governments – with some success – to streamline administrative burdens related to obtaining authorization for weapons exports, in order to ease and expedite transfers. Another argument in favor of cutting red tape to reduce delays in obtaining export licenses, the intensification of competition in the international market, has led several countries to establish defense export promotion agencies to support their own companies in key markets (Béraud-Sudreau et al. 2015). In addition, as was discussed above, the arms industry continues to leverage its status as a major employer. This consideration, however, can occasionally run up against competing national security interests. A good illustration is the recent discussion surrounding France's transfer of a Mistral class amphibious assault ship to Russia in the context of the Ukraine crisis. Both the authorities of the shipyards and the unions involved in production of the ship

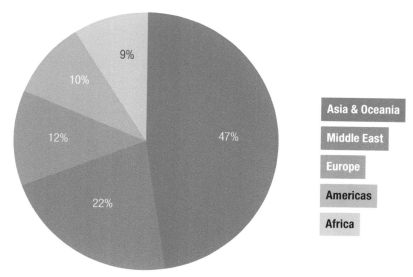

Figure 9.8 Regional Distribution of Arms Imports, 2010–2014
Source: SIPRI Arms Transfers Database.

advocated strongly in favor of carrying out the transaction, arguing that the necessity of maintaining jobs, skills, and know-how justified the sale, which was ultimately exempted from the embargo (Isbister and Quéau 2014).

Conclusion: A Pessimistic View of the Future

The global defense market appears to have entered a new – and possibly transitional – phase. The indications that the current downturn may be short lived come from all dimensions of the global defense political economy, i.e., trends in military expenditure, the behavior of the arms industry, and transformations of the international market.

The modest decline of world military spending since 2011 is the result of conflicting trends at the global level. Large Western military spenders – especially the US – have reduced their defense budgets, while the rest of the world has grown, leading to an erosion of the Western share of total military expenditures. Western companies' domination of the arms production hierarchy endures, but some emerging actors are, for now, successfully penetrating the global arms market. These observations reflect trends in both spending, including ambitious arms acquisition programs developed by several countries outside the West, and arms transfers, which show significant increases globally and regionally. Countries in Asia, the Middle East, and South America have become very attractive clients for arms producers faced with shrinking domestic markets, shifting the balance of power in the arms market to buyers.

This shift has provided importers with the leverage to demand greater benefits, including offsets, from their defense suppliers. In several cases, these benefits pursue the specific goal of building national arms-producing capabilities to achieve some level of autonomy of supply and to support more assertive foreign and defense policies. Both traditional leaders of the defense markets and emerging producers have stated goals of exports. As a result, the current dynamic has created greater dispersion of arms production capabilities and weapons availability in the international market.

The relationship between arms production capabilities and the likelihood of violent conflict is far from straightforward. That said, greater dissemination of weapons and the acquisition of better performing and lethal arsenals could significantly exacerbate existing tensions in regions already under considerable pressures from unresolved disputes or insurgencies. Availability of numerous and modern armaments within a country is not necessarily a cause of conflict. Yet it sends a message of possible hardening of conflict – a signal sometimes strengthened by apparent arms races – and widens the scope of options available to decision makers for any dispute settlement. Perceived advantages of these weapons may also be a critical element in decisions to use force.

A central policy instrument to prevent or manage conflict escalation remains better monitoring of arms transfers and production capabilities. Such measures have demonstrated that they create necessary conditions to open and maintain dialogues between stakeholders, by promoting transparency that can mitigate perceptions of military threats. Monitoring also supports alternatives to arms races, to address thorny defense issues, and more generally promotes an agenda of restraint in transfers based on a variety of factors such as respecting human rights or prohibiting sales of weapons to countries at war.

A complication, however, is that monitoring and reporting of defense spending, arms transfers, and arms production have met with growing challenges in recent years. Indeed, transparency in the global defense political economy has suffered. The number of countries reporting their military expenditure to the UN register has steadily declined. Some post-Cold War conventional arms control treaties have been denounced or are disregarded, which also leads to the loss of their monitoring/reporting mechanisms. Reporting of arms sales – both domestic and international – by producers and by states is increasingly fuzzy. Instead, they now tend to agglomerate "defense and security" sales in a bigger ensemble. Even more worrisome, high-profile arms sales in early 2015 to governments with very questionable human rights records raise questions about the willingness to push for alternatives to supplying arms to address conflict. They also call into question agreed-upon fundamental principles of conventional arms trade controls.[20] The Arms Trade Treaty is a positive exception to this trend. Given this treaty recently entered into force, its impact cannot yet be evaluated.

Legitimizing Military Spending, Arms Production and Arms Transfers

Tensions, disputes, and violent conflicts are primary drivers of arms transfers and support the search for autonomy of supply, but they only partially explain the current changes in the global defense political economy. Indeed, most of South America has been experiencing a stable and peaceful environment for some time. Nevertheless, Brazil, Chile, and Venezuela have all increased their defense spending, and are pursuing goals of military industrialization. Growth of GDP, by itself, cannot explain the decision to dedicate resources to defense, indicating that other factors may be at play. One of these factors is the resort to military instruments to address a wider range of security issues, which has led to a growing militarism, i.e., "the idea that national security and military security are one and the same" (Jackson 2012).

Part of this evolution can be traced back to post-Cold War choices in adjusting to a radically changed geopolitical environment. In the early 1990s, the concept of *uncertainty* was widely used in defense and security policies of major military industrial powers to characterize an international environment where the major threat – a large-scale confrontation between two major nuclear and conventional powers – disappeared in a very short time frame, but numerous destabilizing trends justified a certain level of military preparedness. Today, this concept has become a justification for states to prepare for all possible risks to national security – the "unknown unknowns" memorably referenced by former US Secretary of Defense Donald Rumsfeld in a February 2002 news briefing. This widening of threat assessments supports advocates of high military and national security spending. In other words, if during the 1990s, *uncertainty* was used to protect the military budgets from even more severe cuts, it progressively became a tool justifying the allocation of more resources to a broader and more militarized security agenda (Stohl 2012).

In the Western world, the media and significant segments of the academic and think-tank communities tend to support this pessimistic, all-hazards approach. Current trends in the global defense political economy are mostly interpreted as Western countries – especially European states in the NATO context – devoting insufficient resources to military spending, which are regularly characterized as being "too low." In contrast, high levels of resources allocated to defense in several countries are rarely presented as being "too high." Indeed, an all-hazards approach has no clear limits, by definition, exactly like its costs.

Notes

1 According to SIPRI data, the volume of arms transfers for the 2010–2014 period is 16 percent higher than for 2009–2013 and 45 percent higher than the volume of transfers during the 2000–2004 period. See Wezeman et al. 2015.
2 For a thorough review of current dynamics of global military expenditure, see Perlo-Freeman et al. 2015a.
3 See US Department of Defense budgets from 2003 to 2014, available online at http://comptroller.defense.gov/budgetmaterials.aspx.
4 Here, one could cite many examples: skirmishes at the border between India and Pakistan, sovereignty disputes in the South China Sea, operations to counter Boko Haram in Nigeria and ISIL in Syria, Iraq and Northern Africa, wars in Yemen and Ukraine, etc.
5 The data excludes China due to the lack of reliable sources on the country and its major defense companies.
6 Russia is the only non-Western arms-producing country that could be included in this group, but only for a few select systems such as combat aircraft.
7 Taking figures based on US constant FY2016 dollars from the peak of procurement spending in 1987 through 1997, the decrease was 67 percent (US Department of Defense 2015: 160).
8 The top 10 companies' share of the total arms sales in the top 100 is just over 50 percent (US$206 billion). Huge differences exist between the firms on the list: in 2013, arms sales by world leader Lockheed Martin were more than 3.5 times those of 10th ranked Thales. See Table 9.1 and Figure 9.5.
9 Among the reasons Secretary Gates canceled the land system program were cost overruns and delays, severe technical issues spanning a few wars, and the "rebalance" to Asia (essentially a maritime theater). Several items of equipment designed under the FCS have survived the program's cancellation, sustained under new names.
10 See, for instance, the border monitoring and control programs in both Brazil and Saudi Arabia (Wasserbly 2014; Binnie 2014).
11 Some of the European forays into foreign markets specifically targeted the growing US market of the 2000s. The US military market is not easy to penetrate for foreign producers, but remains very attractive considering the sheer size and the technological audacity of some projects. During the 2000s, the companies that established a strong foothold in the US were primarily from the UK and Italy.
12 An example is the Indian multirole combat aircraft, one of the largest programs (US$20 billion) ever launched for international competition. The stakes for combat aircraft producers were very high and competition pitted every combat aircraft producer against one another. The winning company – French Dassault – was selected partly due to its offset proposal, which included some production and assembly in India as well as technology transfers. As is often the case for India, however, the program has been cancelled.
13 Any impact due to the conflict in Ukraine is very limited – and may never materialize. We will have to wait for the data collected on 2014 to evaluate whether this crisis has a tangible effect on Russian arms sales.
14 Almaz-Antey increased sales revenue by 34 percent in 2013. Others notable performances among Russian companies include Tactical Missiles Corporation (+118 percent) and United Aircraft Corporation (+20 percent).
15 One of the lessons learned from the Russo-Georgian conflict in 2008 was that the Russian forces lacked modern command-and-control systems to coordinate their actions.
16 For a general overview of the different forms offsets can take, as well as a presentation of current offset obligations of US arms companies, see US Department of Commerce 2015.
17 Offsets have attracted a lot of attention in the past few years, but they are far from a novelty in the defense market. In the post-World War II period, the US used offsets, through NATO, to facilitate and expedite the rearmament of Western Europe. Rebuilding parts of the European arms industry was also an important means by which to address a perceived rising military threat from the Soviet Union. See US Congress 1990.
18 An example is the Brazilian company Embraer, with its KC-390 medium-size military transport aircraft.
19 Annual reports from major arms-producing companies are instructive in that regard. See also the Foreword of the Chairman of the Joint Chiefs of Staff to the United States National Military Strategy, published in June 2015 (Joint Chiefs of Staff 2015).
20 An example of the complexities that can arise is sales by France of military patrol ships, frigates, and combat aircraft to the government of Abdel Fattah el-Sisi, who became Egypt's president following a coup d'état in 2013. The government has conducted mass execution of political opponents, mostly from the Islamist movement, based on the justification of Egypt's need to fight against ISIL (Julien 2015).

References

Adams, Gordon, Christopher Cornu, and Andrew James. 2001. "Between Cooperation and Competition: The Transatlantic Defense Market." Chaillot Paper no. 44, April 2001. Paris: Western European Union Institute for Security Studies.

Anderson, Guy (ed.). 2009. "Quid Pro Quo: The Changing Role of Offset in the Global Defence Market." *Jane's Industry Quarterly*, October.

Beaumont, Peter. 2015. "The $18bn Arms Race in Helping to Fuel Middle East Conflict." *The Guardian*, April 23. http://www.theguardian.com/world/2015/apr/23/the-18bn-arms-race-middle-east-russia-iran-iraq-un.

Béraud-Sudreau, Lucie, et al. 2015. *The Extra-EU Defence Exports' Effects on European Armaments Cooperation*. Study. Directorate-General for External Policies, European Parliament. June.

Berteau, David J., and Guy Ben-Ari (eds). 2012. *European Defense Trends 2012: Budgets, Regulatory Frameworks, and the Industrial Base*. Washington, DC: Center for Strategic and International Studies. http://csis.org/files/publication/121212_Berteau_Euro DefenseTrends2012_Web.pdf.

Binnie, Jeremy. 2014. "Saudi Arabia Inaugurates Northern Border Security Project." *IHS Jane's Defence Weekly*, September 11.

Bitzinger, Richard. 1999. "Globalization in the Defense Industry: Challenges and Opportunities." In Ann R. Markusen and Sean S. Costigan (eds), *Arming the Future: A Defense Industry for the 21st Century*. New York: Council on Foreign Relations Press. 305–333.

Carter, Ashton B. 2015. "Secretary of Defense Message: Message from Secretary Ashton Carter to all Department of Defense Personnel." US Department of Defense. February 17.

Chandrasekaran, Rajiv. 2013. "F-35's Ability to Evade Budget Cuts Illustrates Challenge of Paring Defense Spending." *Washingtonpost.com*, March 9. http://www.washingtonpost.com/world/national-security/f-35s-ability-to-evade-budget-cuts-illustrates-challenge-of-paring-defense-spending/2013/03/09/42a6085a-8776-11e2-98a3-b3db6b9ac586_story.html.

Dehoff, Kevin, John Dowdy, and O Sung Kwon. 2014. "Defense Offsets: From 'Contractual Burden' to Competitive Weapon." McKinsey Insights and Publications, June 2014.

Fleurant, Aude-Emmanuelle. 2008. "Convergences et divergences des stratégies de quatre Etats: la dynamique post-Guerre froide." Dissertation presented to the Political Science Department, University of Quebec in Montreal.

Fleurant, Aude-Emmanuelle. 2012. "Moteurs et conséquences des mutations de l'industrie de défense américaine." In Yves Bélanger et al., *Les mutations de l'industrie de défense: regards croisés sur trois continents – Amérique du Nord – Europe – Amérique du Sud*. Cahier de l'IRSEM no. 10. Paris: Institut de recherche stratégique de l'Ecole militaire. 24–80.

Fleurant, Aude-Emmanuelle and Sam Perlo-Freeman. 2014. "The SIPRI Top 100 Arms-Producing and Military Services Companies, 2013." *SIPRI Fact Sheet*, December 2014. http://www.sipri.org/research/armaments/production/recent-trends-in-arms-industry/Fact%20Sheet%20Top100%202013.pdf.

Géoéconomie. 2011. "La révolution des industries de défense." *Géoéconomie*, 57 (Spring).

Hagel, Chuck. 2014. "Secretary of Defense Speech: Reagan National Defense Forum Keynote." US Department of Defense. November 15.

Hogg, Jonny, and Can Sezer. 2015. "Erdogan Aims to Turn Turkey into a Major Defense Industry Power." *Reuters*, May 27. http://www.reuters.com/article/2015/05/27/us-turkey-election-defence-idUSKBN0OC0FT20150527.

Isbister, Roy, and Yannick Quéau. 2014. *An Ill Wind? How the Sale of Mistral Warships to Russia Is Undermining EU Arms Transfer Controls*. Briefing. London: Saferworld; Bruxelles: Groupe de recherche et d'information sur la paix et la sécurité (GRIP). November. http://www.saferworld.org.uk/resources/view-resource/865-an-ill-wind-how-the-sale-of-mistral-warships-to-russia-is-undermining-eu-arms-transfer-controls.

Jackson, Susan T. 2012. "The National Security Exception, the Global Political Economy and Militarization." In Kostas Gouliamos and Christos Kassimeris (eds.), *The Marketing of War in the Age of Neo-militarism*. New York: Routledge. 214–235.

Joint Chiefs of Staff, US Department of Defense. 2015. "The National Military Strategy of the United States of America 2015." June. http://www.jcs.mil/Portals/36/Documents/Publications/National_Military_Strategy_2015.pdf.

Julien, Gérard. 2015. "Vente des Rafale à l'Egypte: un contrat qui fait grincer des dents." *France 24*, February 14. http://www.france24.com/fr/20150214-video-rafale-vente-dassault-france-egypte-ong-amnesty-international-droit-homme-al-sissi.

Lemer, Jeremy, and Helen Thomas. 2011. "Defense Groups Diversify amid Budget Cuts." *Financial Times*, September 20. http://www.ft.com/intl/cms/s/0/5afbfd70-d240-11e0-9137-00144feab49a.html#axzz3flY7rCWt.

Markusen, Ann R., and Sean S. Costigan (eds.). 1999. *Arming the Future: A Defense Industry for the 21st Century*. New York: Council on Foreign Relations Press.

McGerty, Fenella. 2015. "French Defence Budget Boost Swaps a 7% Cut for a 4% Jump." *IHS Jane's 360*, April 29. http://www.janes.com/article/51079/french-defence-budget-boost-swaps-a-7-cut-for-a-4-jump.

McLeary, Paul. 2015. "US Budget Request Will Change Drastically, Experts Say." *Defensenews.com*, February 2. http://www.defensenews.com/story/defense/policy-budget/budget/2015/02/01/fiscal-2016-defense-department-budget-request-will-change/22599163/.

Pelzer, Michael. 2014. "Bullets from Brazil: Growing Military Industrialism in Latin America." Washington Office on Latin America (WOLA), March 21. http://www.wola.org/commentary/bullets_from_brazil_0.

Perlo-Freeman, Sam, et al. 2015a. "Military Expenditure." In *SIPRI Yearbook 2015*. Oxford: Oxford University Press.

Perlo-Freeman, Sam, et al. 2015b. "Trends in World Military Expenditure, 2014." *SIPRI Fact Sheet*, April 2015. http://books.sipri.org/product_info?c_product_id=496.

République française. 2013. "Loi no 2013–1168 du 18 décembre 2013 relative à la programmation militaire pour les années 2014 à 2019 et portant diverses disposition concernant la défense et la sécurité nationale." *JORF* no. 0294, 19 décembre 2013, page 20570, texte 1. http://legifrance.gouv.fr/affichTexte.do?cidTexte=JORFTEXT000028338825&dateTexte=&categorieLien=id.

Stohl, Michael. 2012. "US Homeland Security, the Global War on Terror and Militarism." In Kostas Gouliamos and Christos Kassimeris (eds), *The Marketing of War in the Age of Neo-militarism*. New York: Routledge. 124–144.

Tan, Andrew. 2014. *The Arms Race in Asia: Trends, Causes and Implications*. London: Routledge.

Ungaro, Alessandro R. 2013. "Trends in the Defence Offsets Market." Paper presented at the 17th Annual International Conference on Economics and Security, Stockholm, June. http://www.sipri.org/research/armaments/milex/ICES2013/papers/archive/ungaro-trends-in-the-defence-offsets-market.

US Congress, Office of Technology Assessment. 1990. *Arming our Allies: Cooperation and Competition in Defense Technology OTA-ISC-449*. Washington, DC: US Government Printing Office. https://www.princeton.edu/~ota/disk2/1990/9005/900501.PDF.

US Department of Commerce, Bureau of Industry and Security. 2015. *Offsets in Defense Trade: Nineteenth Study*. March.

US Department of Defense, Office of the Undersecretary of Defense – Comptroller. 2015. *National Defense Budget Estimates for FY 2016*. March.

Wasserbly, Daniel. 2014. "Brazilian Army Launches Border Monitoring System." *IHS Jane's Defence Weekly*, November 13.

Wezeman, Pieter D., and Siemon T. Wezeman. 2015. "Trends in International Arms Transfers, 2014." *SIPRI Fact Sheet*, March 2015. http://books.sipri.org/files/FS/SIPRIFS1503.pdf.

Wezeman, Siemon T., Sam Perlo-Freeman and Pieter D. Wezeman. 2015. "Developments in Arms Transfers, 2014." In *SIPRI Yearbook 2015*. Oxford: Oxford University Press.

10

Global Trends in the Implementation of Intrastate Peace Agreements

Jason Michael Quinn and Madhav Joshi

Introduction

Peace agreements to end civil wars, which were once infrequent, have become far more common over the recent decades. At the same time, peace agreements have become more substantive in terms of prescriptions for institutional and policy reforms and interventions into political practice. Peace agreements vary considerably in terms of the numbers and types of provisions they contain. Likewise, differences are observed in the extent to which provisions are actually implemented in practice. Both dimensions of variation are vital to scrutinize because of the potential implications for the durability of peace and other conditions during the post-conflict period.

In this chapter, we examine the content and implementation of peace agreements intended to resolve civil wars around the world. The analysis is based on the Peace Accords Matrix (PAM) database and dataset. These online public information resources (http://www.peaceaccords.nd.edu) emerge from the PAM project, the mission of which is to support practitioners, policy-makers, and researchers in the study of peace agreements and peace processes by providing comparative data on the content and implementation outcomes of accords in both qualitative (preferred by practitioners) and quantitative (preferred by social scientists) forms. The project, based at the Kroc Institute for International Peace Studies at the University of Notre Dame, is organized with a practice component (with two active conflict mediators) and a research component (with two principal investigators [authors]).[1] In the following sections, we discuss the background to the project, describe the PAM database and dataset in greater detail, provide an overview of patterns and trends of implementation of peace agreements since 1989, and reflect on future areas of research.

Prior Research on Accord Implementation and Data Limitations

Walter's (1997: 335) influential article on the barriers to civil war settlements argued that settlements were rare "because credible guarantees on the terms of the settlement are almost impossible to arrange by the combatants themselves." Her analysis was predicated on the relative paucity of negotiated bargains to end civil wars, compared to interstate wars. This juxtaposition of outcomes no longer holds true. Figure 10.1 (see next page) displays the numbers of civil conflicts and of peace accords negotiated in such conflicts, based on data compiled by the Uppsala Conflict Data Program and UN Peacemaker, respectively. As is evident, civil war peace agreements have lately become much more common than in previous decades. Their prevalence began to tick upward in the mid-1980s, then accelerated with a dramatic surge in agreements accompanying the end of the Cold War that accompanied an unprecedented number of ongoing negotiations. The number of agreements per year peaked in 1994, when negotiations in Bosnia and Herzegovina, Georgia, Guatemala, and Papua New Guinea alone resulted in a total of 19 accords. The number of accords then declined significantly until 2000. A parallel decline can be seen in the number of active civil conflicts from 52 in 1992 to 28 in 2003. After 2003, the number of accords rose slightly and has remained fairly steady (with the exception of 2008, which saw the negotiation of 17 partial agreements on separate issues in Kenya and Uganda).

Bell (2006: 373) catalogues the explosion of civil war peace agreements after 1989, attributing the trend to a growing global awareness of the problem of civil war, as well as an increasingly accepted view among domestic and international actors of "the peace agreement as a binding document." Meanwhile, Fazal (2013: 699) charts the decline of peace agreements in interstate wars, arguing that nation-states are reluctant to sign peace treaties in wars with other nation-states

Number of Cases

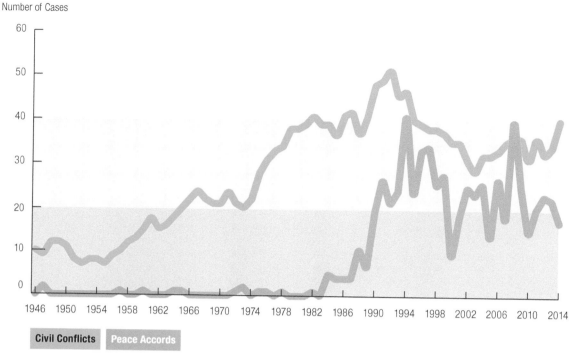

Figure 10.1 Trends in Civil Conflicts and Peace Agreements, 1946–2014

because they expect to be "unequivocally obliged to pay the costs of compliance and to bear the consequences of non-compliance." Together, these analyses suggest that the absence of credible guarantees to secure the terms of intrastate agreements is not the problem it used to be. In our view, the increase in frequency of intrastate agreements is ultimately due to the increased expectation that the negotiated provisions will be implemented.

The content of peace agreements to end civil wars has become more substantive over time, as the purpose of agreements has evolved, within lengthier negotiation processes. Civil war settlements negotiated during the Cold War contained few reforms that would require much of an implementation process. Virtually none of the accords negotiated during the 1940s and 1950s contained what could be considered political reforms. During the 1970s and 1980s, the shares of agreements with any such reform provisions rose to 25 percent and then 33 percent, respectively. During the 1990s and 2000s, the shares of reform-minded agreements jumped further to 56 percent and 61 percent.[2] Currently, the signing of a final agreement in civil war negotiations is often held up as a culminating historic moment in a peace process and the implementation of the agreement takes a highly legitimized array of social and political reforms and puts them at the center of national politics.

Thus, the practice around reaching settlements to civil wars has shifted in meaningful ways, toward the regularity of agreements that embed tangible ambitions of change. All of these circumstances heighten the value of taking stock of the provisions of agreements, evaluating the extent to which they are implemented, and assessing the resulting consequences.

Over the last 15 years, many empirical studies have addressed variation in the types of provisions found in peace agreements and considered the post-agreement effects on levels of violence. We know of only three studies, however, where the authors collected and analyzed comparative data concerning the implementation of the provisions central to the theory at hand. Hoddie and Hartzell (2003) examined 16 peace agreements between 1980 and 1996 that called for the integration of rebel combatants into the national military. They found that renewed civil war was avoided in seven of the eight cases where military integration was fully implemented. Jarstad and Nilsson (2008) show that implementation of power-sharing provisions in peace agreements produced strong significant effects on future conflict behavior, unlike the mere presence of such provisions. Despite these promising findings, only one subsequent study has generated any new data on the implementation of peace agreements. These data likewise concern powersharing arrangements (Ottmann and Vüllers 2014). Meanwhile, little attention has been paid to gathering systematic data on implementation of other provisions of peace agreements. The lack of such data represents a clear, conspicuous gap in research, especially when viewed against the backdrop of recent global trends in the prevalence and diverse purposes of peace agreements to end civil wars.

The Peace Accords Matrix Implementation Database and Dataset

The PAM project is home to the largest existing collection of data on the implementation of intrastate peace agreements. Coverage extends to comprehensive peace agreements (CPAs) signed since 1989. The data collection centers around a typology of different types of provisions appearing in these agreements. For each agreement, information about the existence of provisions and the extent of their implementation in practice is compiled and coded. The resulting database and dataset are then resources for empirical research.

Case Selection

Naturally, most inquiries about peace agreements, whether undertaken by scholars, policy-makers or practitioners, are motivated by a desire to better understand their post-accord effects. When conducting any comparative analysis of this sort, sampling parameters and case selection are critically important. Accords have different purposes and the extent and specific content of agreements, as well as stakeholder expectations about when, where and how that content will be implemented, are tied to those purposes. Comparing agreements that are very different in context and purpose would not necessarily be appropriate. Instead, a more logical comparison to make is among agreements with similar contexts and purposes.

For purposes of the PAM project, we identified a sample of peace agreements that qualify as comprehensive in nature. This identification is based on characteristics of the negotiation process that produced the agreement. To be considered comprehensive, the written agreement had to be produced through negotiations that included the government and the main rebel group(s). This criterion excludes agreements between the government and tertiary factions of the opposition. For example, we do not include the 1999 Kosovo accord or any of the accords concerning the Nicaraguan civil war from 1989 and 1990, because they were not produced from negotiations that included both conflict actors. In addition, the negotiations that produced the accord must have addressed the major issues underlying the dispute and done so in a manner that is reflected in explicit provisions in the agreement. This criterion distinguishes comprehensive agreements from ceasefire agreements, framework agreements, process agreements, and partial agreements. In those instances where negotiating actors released separate agreements on various conflict issues as they were negotiated, which were later reaffirmed in a final agreement, we consider this last agreement to be a comprehensive case. As it happens, CPAs frequently subsume an assortment of previous non-comprehensive agreements. In Guatemala, for example, negotiations between the warring parties produced 16 accords over seven years. We consider the last agreement, the Accord for a Firm and Lasting Peace, which subsumes the prior agreements, to be comprehensive. In Liberia, negotiations produced 11 accords that in the end became the Accra Agreement, which we consider to be a comprehensive agreement.

To avoid selecting on dependent variables of interest, our sampling approach does not consider post-accord outcomes, such as ongoing violence and the extent of implementation, as criteria. Each CPA that is included in the PAM dataset can be followed by violence or a lack of violence, as well as by a successful implementation process, a partial implementation process, or a failing implementation process – gauged down to the level of individual types of provisions. All of our CPA cases were negotiated in an effort to end an armed conflict resulting in at least 25 battle-related deaths in one calendar year, therefore meeting UCDP's criteria of an intrastate armed conflict (Pettersson and Wallensteen 2015). Based on these selection criteria, the dataset tracks the implementation of 34 CPAs from 1989 through 2015; the last CPA case was actually negotiated in March 2007. Table 10.1 (see next page) lists these 34 agreements and the date of their signing.

Typology of Provisions

Within the content of agreements, we isolated 51 types of provisions, each defined in terms of a goal-oriented reform falling within a relatively discrete policy domain. To organize the provisions constructively and facilitate comparison, we group them into several categories. Under the *Security* category are eight types of provisions that range from military and police reform to the handling of paramilitary groups. The *Institutions* category encompasses a wide spectrum of reforms about the executive branch, the judiciary, and civil administration, as well as constitutions, transitional power-sharing arrangements, and dispute resolution mechanisms. The *Rights* category includes provisions about self-determination, citizenship, education, minority rights, and women's rights. The remaining two categories, *External Actors* and *Other Arrangements*, cover 15 different types of provisions, including UN Transitional Authority, UN Peacekeeping, verification, referendums, ratification mechanisms, and arms embargoes. The typology of provisions was the result of an inductive process aimed at capturing all of the main aspects observed across contemporary comprehensive peace agreements. Table 10.2 (see p. 94) outlines the full set of provisions that are coded, organized by category.

Country	Name of Accord	Date of Accord
Angola	Lusaka Protocol	November 15, 1994
Angola	Luena Memorandum of Understanding	April 4, 2002
Bangladesh	Chittagong Hill Tracts Peace Accord (CHT)	December 2, 1997
Bosnia and Herzegovina	General Framework Agreement for Bosnia and Herzegovina	November 21, 1995
Burundi	Arusha Peace and Reconciliation Agreement for Burundi	August 28, 2000
Cambodia	Framework for a Comprehensive Settlement of the Conflict	October 23, 1991
Congo	Agreement on Ending Hostilities in the Republic of Congo	December 29, 1999
Côte d'Ivoire	Ouagadougou Political Agreement (OPA)	March 4, 2007
Croatia	Erdut Agreement	November 12, 1995
Djibouti	Accord de paix et de la reconciliation nationale	December 26, 1994
Djibouti	Agreement for the Reform and Civil Concord	May 12, 2001
El Salvador	Chapultepec Peace Agreement	January 16, 1992
Guatemala	Accord for a Firm and Lasting Peace	December 29, 1996
Guinea-Bissau	Abuja Peace Agreement	November 1, 1998
India	Memorandum of Settlement (Bodo Accord)	February 20, 1993
Indonesia	MoU between Republic of Indonesia and the Free Aceh Movement	August 15, 2005
Lebanon	Taif Accord	October 22, 1989
Liberia	Accra Peace Agreement	August 18, 2003
Macedonia	Ohrid Agreement	August 13, 2001
Mali	National Pact	January 6, 1991
Mozambique	General Peace Agreement for Mozambique	October 4, 1992
Nepal	Comprehensive Peace Agreement	November 21, 2006
Niger	Agreement Between the Republic Niger Government and the ORA	April 15, 1995
Papua New Guinea	Bougainville Peace Agreement	August 30, 2001
Philippines	Mindanao Final Agreement	September 2, 1996
Rwanda	Arusha Accord	August 4, 1993
Senegal	General Peace Agreement between Republic of Senegal and MFDC	December 30, 2004
Sierra Leone	Abidjan Peace Agreement	November 30, 1996
Sierra Leone	Lomé Peace Agreement	July 7, 1999
South Africa	Interim Constitution	November 17, 1993
Sudan	Sudan Comprehensive Peace Agreement	January 9, 2005
Tajikistan	General Agreement on Peace and National Accord in Tajikistan	June 27, 1997
Timor-Leste (East Timor)	Agreement on the question of East Timor	May 5, 1999
United Kingdom	Northern Ireland Good Friday Agreement	April 10, 1998

Table 10.1 Comprehensive Peace Agreements, 1989–2015

Institutions [13 provisions]

Boundary Demarcation

Civilian Administration Reform

Constitutional Changes

Decentralization Federalism

Dispute Resolution Committee

Electoral or Political Reform

Executive Branch Reform

Inter-Ethnic State Relations

Judiciary Reform

Legislative Branch Reform

Powersharing – Transitional Govt.

Territorial Powersharing

Truth or Reconciliation Mechanism

Security [8 Provisions]

Ceasefire

Demobilization

Disarmament

Military Reform

Paramilitary Groups

Police Reform

Prisoner Release

Reintegration

External Arrangements [7 Provisions]

Commission to Address Damages/Loss

Intl. Arbitration Commission on Land

Regional Peacekeeping Force

UN Peacekeeping Force

UN Transitional Authority

UN, Intl., or Internal Verification

Withdrawal of Troops

Rights [15 Provisions]

Amnesty

Children's Rights

Citizenship

Cultural Protections

Education Reform

Human Rights

Indigenous Minority Rights

Internally Displaced Persons

Media

Minority Rights

Official Language and Symbol

Refugees

Reparations

Right of Self-Determination

Women's Rights

Other Arrangements [8 Provisions]

Provision for Review of Agreement

Ratification Mechanism

Arms Embargo

Detailed Implementation Timeline

Donor Support

Economic and Social Development

Independence Referendum

Natural Resource Usage

Table 10.2 Classification Scheme of Provisions in Comprehensive Peace Agreements

Coding Process

Extensive information on the characteristics of these agreements was compiled through a three-stage coding process. The first stage involved performing content analysis on the 34 CPAs. Each accord was carefully read and coded according to the typology of provisions described above. The effort was not aimed at classifying all of the text within the accords. Rather, the text that is most pertinent to each category, if any, was identified. A provision may be coded only once per accord, no matter the number of stipulations within the provision. Certain accords contain multiple provisions for a given type. Only one provision of a particular type is coded for a given accord. For example, provisions about executive branch reform and judicial reform – both of which fall into the Institutions category – can be coded separately, but only one provision about executive branch reform would be coded. If an accord calls for multiple changes to be made to the executive branch, these would appear as stipulations under one provision. In total, 724 provisions were identified across the sample of 34 accords, which works out to an average of 23 provisions per accord.

The second stage involved researching the history of the implementation process for every identified provision in each agreement and writing annual chronological narratives covering the major events in each peace process. We track implementation for ten years, since implementation processes routinely run past the five-year mark, but seldom last longer than a decade.[3] The most common sources of information were Lexis-Nexis Academic, the UN Secretary-General's Reports to the Security Council, Refworld documents, and journal articles and books on specific conflicts and accords. Covering the major implementation events occurring each year for ten years for 724 provisions would yield a maximum of 7,240 qualitative narratives. At present, the total number is slightly less than 7,240, for multiple reasons. Although agreements are followed for a period of up to ten years, this point had yet to be reached for a couple of cases. In addition, full implementation of many of the 724 provisions was accomplished before the 10-year mark was reached. Once full implementation is reached, the annual coding reflects only the presence or absence of a reversal of what has already been implemented.

The third stage involved research assistants turning the collection of annual narratives into a dataset amenable for statistical analysis. For each identified provision, trained coders read the associated narratives, starting with the first year in the sequence, and coded, year by year, the level of implementation on a four-point scale: [0] not initiated, [1] minimal implementation, [2] intermediate implementation, and [3] full implementation.[4]

The method of determining the degree of implementation each year centers on the concept of a viable implementation rate. *Initiation* represents some observable start in the process of implementation. A viable implementation rate is one that, if continued at the current rate for the remainder of the current year, could reasonably produce full implementation by the end of the following year. We chose this approach because it best approximates contemporaneous observation of the process by stakeholders to the accord. Stakeholders value full implementation and do not necessarily have the luxury of retrospective analysis when evaluating implementation progress. Therefore, we directed our coders to assume the position of a stakeholder observing events taking place and to ask whether a reasonable person could argue, based on what has transpired to a given point in time, that the stipulations called for under this provision will likely reach full implementation in the future. The *minimal implementation* code is meant to capture non-viable processes – that is, implementation was initiated, but is not on track for a timely completion. *Intermediate implementation* implies that the process is likely to be completed by the end of the following year, if continued at the same pace. *Full implementation* means that the process was complete or almost complete as of a given year.

We also code reversals in progress toward implementation of an accord. Reversals capture a deliberate dismantling by the government or the rebels of what was previously implemented. Two degrees of reversals are coded. A minor reversal constitutes a change within an implementation category. An example is the early suspension of the demobilization process in Cambodia in 1992, which resulted in the release of the troops who had entered the camps up to that point.[5] A major reversal constitutes a change in implementation level, going down the scale in an unfavorable sense, from one year to the next. An example is the suspension of the power-sharing arrangement in Northern Ireland from 2002–2007 due to perceived IRA non-compliance with the accord.[6] As a result of this circumstance, the coding of power-sharing was downgraded from full to minimum implementation.

Data Utilization

The structure of the PAM data allows researchers to study the implementation of peace agreements at several different levels of analysis. Researchers can focus on a particular peace agreement and all of the provisions contained in that agreement, or study one type of provision across agreements. Alternatively, researchers can study groups of related provisions and their joint implementation. Each of these different ways of aggregating and disaggregating the data can also be studied longitudinally, as the dataset is organized as a time series.

The online database is designed to facilitate comparative analyses of cases, by enabling users to identify a given type of provision and quickly examine every CPA adopted from 1989–2012 that contains this type of provision. After selecting a provision, the relevant original text from the accord is displayed, followed by the annual narratives outlining the chronology of implementation events. In short, users can see at a glance what the CPAs included in the database stipulate about any of the covered categories of provisions and what was done to put those stipulations into practice.

In the research context, many features of the database and dataset are novel, including the diversity of provisions that are followed, the longitudinal nature of the data, and how long the implementation process is tracked (10 years). As a consequence, users are able to examine the implementation of CPAs related to civil wars in ways that were previously infeasible.

Patterns of Implementation

In this section, we provide a cross-sectional view of the 724 provisions negotiated in the 34 CPAs. This analysis reflects the highest level of implementation of each provision either after 10 years or as of the last year of observation. In this context, the PAM data can provide insights into the types of reforms that face greater and lesser forms of resistance in societies emerging from civil war.

We favor approaching problems of CPA implementation using a principal-agent framework, given that CPAs are designed to change the policy status quo and are negotiated and subsequently implemented by different sets of actors. Principal-agent theory is frequently employed in a context of domestic power struggles over the future policy status quo (Miller 2005; Pinto and Oliveira 2008). For example, Persson, Rothstein, and Teorell (2013) use principal-agent theory to explain the failures of anti-corruption reform efforts in developing nations. In such a framework, three sets of actors are most relevant: (1) the principals, or those actors mandated to seek implementation; (2) the agents tasked with carrying out implementation; and (3) actors within the government agencies and bureaucracies that are likely to be adversely impacted by implementation. In this framework, high implementation outcomes are generally expected in processes characterized by high membership overlap between groups 1 and 2. Low implementation outcomes are expected in processes characterized by high membership overlap between groups 2 and 3, based on the logic that the implementing agents themselves will be negatively impacted by the reforms.

Figure 10.2 displays the extent of implementation of the 724 individual provisions, by category. The highest share of full implementation is observed for provisions under an external actor or third-party mandate. Of the 64 provisions in this category, 81 percent were fully implemented, whereas only 4 percent were not initiated. A different pattern is observed for rights-related provisions: of the 176 cases in this category, 39 percent were fully implemented and 32 percent were not initiated or minimally implemented. For each of the remaining categories (Institutions, Security, Other), the outcomes are bifurcated, with roughly half of the provisions not achieving full implementation.

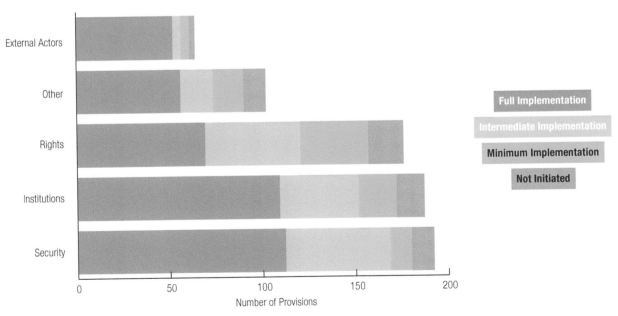

Figure 10.2 Frequency and Extent of Implementation of Provisions in Comprehensive Peace Agreements, by General Category

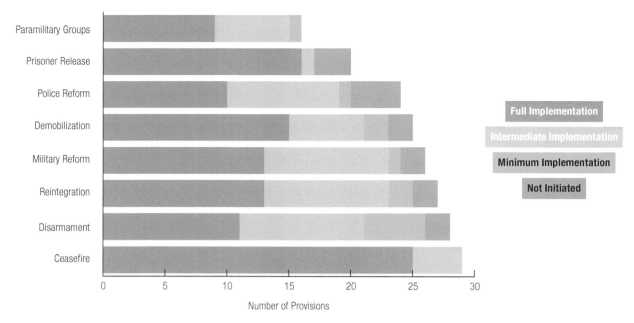

Figure 10.3 Frequency and Extent of Implementation of Security Sector Provisions in Comprehensive Peace Agreements

Figure 10.3 shows the frequency and implementation of Security Sector provisions across the 34 CPAs. Several broad patterns are evident. At one end of the spectrum, when a CPA contains a ceasefire provision, the warring parties comply with its stipulations in a large majority of cases. Although accords containing only a ceasefire are frequently unstable, this is not the case when the ceasefire is bundled with other provisions within CPAs. At the other end of the spectrum, the implementation of police reform appears to be the most difficult to achieve. The narratives associated with these cases of non-initiation suggest a high degree of overlap between the implementing agents and those likely to be negatively impacted by the reforms. For example, the 1997 General Agreement in Tajikistan called for members of the United Tajik Opposition to be incorporated into law-enforcement agencies on the basis of a 30 percent quota; however, neither the judicial system nor the police were ultimately integrated. In the Philippines, the forces of the Philippine National Police (PNP) stationed in the Autonomous Region of Muslim Mindanao were due to be placed under the control of the ARMM Regional Government under the provisions of the 1996 Mindanao Final Agreement; after a decade, however, this stipulation had yet to be implemented.[7] Similarly, a key priority in the 1997 CHT Accord in Bangladesh was to establish a local CHT district police force that better reflected the ethnic composition of the CHT and its indigenous communities; as of 2007, however, nothing had been implemented in this regard (Chowdhury 2002; PCJSS 2013).

Figure 10.4 (see next page) displays results for the 13 types of provisions calling for institutional reform. One interpretation of the results is that certain types of institutional reforms, such as changing the constitution or changing a boundary, only make it out of negotiations and into the resulting agreement when enough support for them exists to ensure high rates of future implementation. Consistent with this argument, the actors whose support would be needed for implementation of particular institutional reforms to occur may tend to have disproportionate influence on the negotiations. The evidence on this count is stronger with regard to the executive and legislative branches, but less so with the judiciary (and related truth and reconciliation mechanisms). Perhaps the same is not true of other types of provisions that negotiating parties are prepared to include in the agreement, but their future implementation is uncertain. For example, a mixed record of implementation can be seen for provisions whose implementation requires the actions of a larger number of spatially dispersed agents (decentralization/federalism, civilian administration reform).

Figure 10.5 (see next page) displays the frequencies of the 15 types of rights-related provisions and their highest recorded level of implementation across the 34 CPAs. Both the lowest and highest levels of implementation observed thus far are found within this category. Provisions for media reform and education reform are relatively common, but rarely implemented in full; they also have the highest instances of non-initiation of any provisions. Conversely, the results suggest that amnesty provisions typically make it into a CPA only when they have enough support to ensure full implementation.

This last finding leads to a practical question: what are the implications of low or delayed implementation if amnesty is usually negotiated with the expectation that it will be implemented? Here again, we can investigate the consequences of implementation dynamics for peace processes by exploring patterns in the quantitative data in conjunction with the associated qualitative narratives. Clear case evidence exists that problems over implementing amnesties created a serious

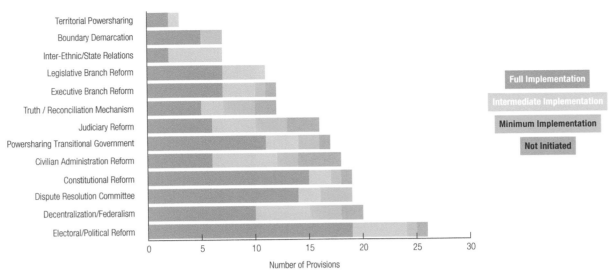

Figure 10.4 Frequency and Extent of Implementation of Institutional Reform Provisions in Comprehensive Peace Agreements

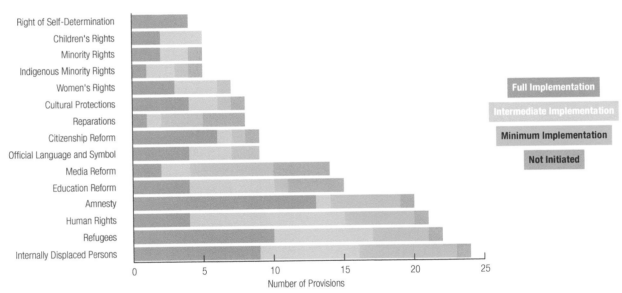

Figure 10.5 Frequency and Extent of Implementation of Rights-Related Provisions in Comprehensive Peace Agreements

strain in several cases and contributed to renewed civil war in at least two cases. In Tajikistan, the 1997 agreement stipulated that "The President and the Commission on National Reconciliation shall adopt the reciprocal-pardon act as the first political decision to be taken during the initial days of the Commission's work." One month later, President Rakhmonov and United Tajik Opposition (UTO) leader S. A. Nuru reaffirmed the high priority of the General Amnesty Act in a Protocol of Mutual Understanding. Yet those within the government and judicial system who were tasked with implementing the amnesty provision later insisted on reviewing UTO soldiers and detainees on a case-by-case basis. By the end of the next year (1998), only 399 individuals had been granted amnesty. According to Grant Smith (1999: 245), the US Ambassador to Tajikistan at the time and a negotiator in the Inter-Tajik Talks, the peace process was greatly jeopardized in 1998:

> The UTO asserted that its forces could not give up their weapons and demobilize before the opposition received the 30 per cent of governmental positions due to it ... The UTO also argued that the amnesty process should be completed prior to demobilization and disarmament, so that UTO fighters would know where they stood with the law before surrendering their weapons. The government, for its part, maintained that because the UTO had failed to live up to obligations in the ceasefire agreements ... UTO members could not be trusted with ministerial positions until after implementation of the entire military protocol.

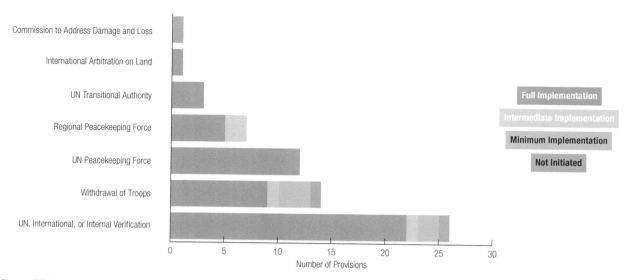

Figure 10.6 Frequency and Extent of Implementation of External Actor Provisions in Comprehensive Peace Agreements

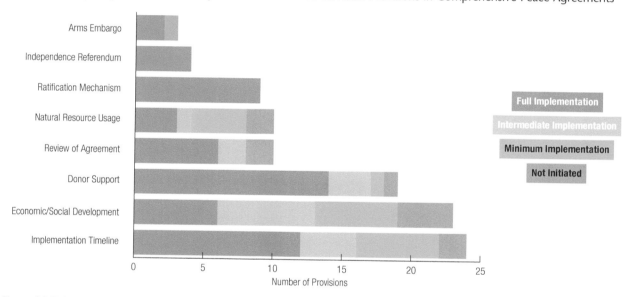

Figure 10.7 Frequency and Extent of Implementation of Other Provisions in Comprehensive Peace Agreements

Ambassador Smith further noted that UTO fighters were leaving the demobilization camps and violence was escalating as a direct consequence of delayed implementation of the amnesty and power-sharing provisions of the accord. In March and April 1998, several dozen people were killed in clashes between bands of UTO troops and army units near Romit and Dushanbe, which qualifies as a case of renewed armed conflict based on UCDP's 25 battle-related death threshold.

Figure 10.6 displays the results for seven types of provisions related to external actors. As previously highlighted, this group of provisions exhibits the highest levels of implementation. There are only two instances of non-initiation in this category, and five cases where implementation was coded as minimal. Both cases of non-initiation followed Sierra Leone's 1996 Abidjan Accord. A natural conclusion is that a third-party actor is unlikely to agree to undertake measures such as establishing an arbitration commission, verification mission, or peacekeeping mission, and then fail to implement that pledge. Another aspect of the dynamics is that external actors tend to occupy a position of greater independence, vis-à-vis the conflict and the actors involved. As a result, external actors are not relying on other actors with whom they have been at odds to reach an agreement and to facilitate implementation. Instead, external actors can do more to self-implement these provisions, generally requiring at most certain accommodations and forms of coordination from the conflict actors.

That said, implementation of third-party mandates is not straightforward in all cases. One conspicuous instance of non-implementation occurred in Sierra Leone, where a neutral international monitoring group was not established because Sierra Leone People's Party and Kamajor troops (pro-government) engaged in military offensives against Revolutionary

United Front (RUF) (rebel) positions immediately after the November 1996 peace accord. As a result, foreign troops supporting the government against the RUF were not immediately withdrawn as stipulated by the accord. After the government fell in May 1997, troops from Ghana, Guinea, Ivory Coast, and Nigeria fought to restore ousted President Kabbah to power. In 1998, the former government ousted the RUF/Armed Forces Revolutionary Council government and full-scale civil war renewed. Thus, non-implementation of the provision for the withdrawal of foreign troops ended up having a critical impact on the ultimate outcome in this case.

Finally, Figure 10.7 (see previous page) shows the implementation levels for eight types of provisions that call for a variety of other actions. Ratification mechanisms and independence referendums are process-oriented (vs. outcome-oriented) provisions, and in all cases the planned process was carried out. Another noteworthy finding is the under-utilization of review of agreement provisions. This result is surprising in as much as conflict actors often spend years in negotiations trying to reach acceptable terms, yet most agreements do not contain robust support structures to facilitate their implementation. Where such structures have been included, most envisioned retrospective evaluation of progress, without permitting intervention let alone correction in the event of non-implementation.

Conclusion and Future Research

For countries caught in a trap of conflict and associated underdevelopment, achieving better governance through the implementation of consensus-based reforms is likely a prerequisite to break the cycle and advance in more favorable directions. Yet civil war settings are often worst-case scenarios for achieving implementation of policy reforms. Identifying instances where implementation has been accomplished and understanding better why this result was possible, as well as assessing the implications, would go a long way towards promoting more effective outcomes in the aftermath of conflict.

In this chapter, we examined patterns, trajectories and trends in the implementation of CPAs following civil wars, using novel PAM data resources, which are designed expressly for these purposes. The findings present interesting questions for future study concerning the negotiation and implementation of peace accords, particularly in the area of selection effects. Many provisions are presumably included in agreements with the expectation that they will be implemented, because the actors who hold the power to further or frustrate such outcomes have expressed sufficient support. Yet the data show that implementation is hardly a foregone conclusion: consider that progress on provisions is ultimately left incomplete in substantial numbers of cases, as well as that a failure to initiate the process is observed in plenty of other cases. Are these cases where optimistic expectations of implementation were later foiled by spoilers? Or are some provisions included with very little expectation of implementation – or even with an advance expectation that implementation will fail? What about the provisions absent from agreements: are some measures not included in accords due to pessimism about their future prospects for implementation?

These questions point to multi-stage causal processes in which provisions are not randomly assigned to peace agreements, but rather the provisions are determined in ways that are endogenous to the complex dynamics of both conflict and negotiations, which can also influence post-accord implementation. This raises interesting possibilities whereby negotiators anticipate principal-agent problems associated with the implementation of certain measures, which could affect their negotiating strategies. Similarly, rebel negotiators may try to anticipate those areas where fierce resistance to implementation is likely, so as to maximize the chances of implementation for those concessions they are able to secure. These orientations can produce the paradoxical expectation that reforms in peace agreements may be directed at policy jurisdictions where they are either most likely or least likely to be implemented.

Notes

1 The two practitioners are John Paul Lederach, who has several decades of mediation experience working in civil conflicts in Latin America, Africa, and Asia, and Francisco Diez, who is a professional mediator working in Latin America and is the author of *International Mediation in Venezuela.*

2 These figures are estimates derived from UN Peacemaker for accords signed before 1975 and from Högbladh (2012) for accords signed after 1975 (based on the variable *Political Provisions* being coded 1).

3 Adopting the 10-year time period for evaluating the implementation of peace agreements also mirrors practice of key actors in this space. For instance, USAID's Office of Conflict Management and Mitigation considers countries to be "conflict-affected" for a period of ten years following the end of active armed conflict.

4 During the training period, we had at least three cases coded by two different coders and achieved inter-coder reliability in excess of 90 percent.

5 "Second Phase of Ceasefire, May–November 1992," United Nations, Cambodia – UNTAC Background, accessed July 22, 2015, http://www.un.org/en/peacekeeping/missions/past/untacbackgr2.html#two.

6 "Timeline: Northern Ireland Assembly," BBC News, January 21, 2013, http://news.bbc.co.uk/2/hi/uk_news/northern_ireland/7932068.stm.

7 As of 2008, the processes remained ongoing. See "Title V: Public Order and Security, Chapter 1: Philippine National Police Regional Command for the ARMM," accessed August 24, 2012, http://armm.gov.ph/armm-content/uploads/2013/03/MMA% 20Act%20No.%20287.pdf, p. 19.

References

Bell, Christine. 2006. "Peace Agreements: Their Nature and Legal Status." *American Journal of International Law* 100(2): 373–412.

Chowdhury, Bushra Hasina. 2002. "Building Lasting Peace: Issues of the Implementation of the Chittagong Hill Tracts Accord." *Unpublished manuscript for the Program in Arms Control, Disarmament, and International Security*, University of Illinois at Urbana-Champaign.

Fazal, Tanisha M. 2013. "The Demise of Peace Treaties in Interstate War." *International Organization* 67(4): 695–724.

Hoddie, Matthew, and Caroline Hartzell. 2003. "Civil War Settlements and the Implementation of Military Power-Sharing Arrangements." *Journal of Peace Research* 40(3): 303–320.

Högbladh, Stina. 2011. "Peace Agreements 1975–2011: Updating the UCDP Peace Agreement Dataset", in Thérése Pettersson and Lotta Themnér (eds.), 2012, *States in Armed Conflict 2011*. Department of Peace and Conflict Research Report no. 99. Uppsala: Uppsala University. 39–56.

Jarstad, Anna K., and Desiree Nilsson. 2008. "From Words to Deeds: The Implementation of Power-Sharing Pacts in Peace Accords." *Conflict Management and Peace Science* 25(3): 206–223.

Miller, Gary J. 2005. "The Political Evolution of Principal-Agent Models." *Annual Review of Political Science* 8: 203–225.

Ottmann, Martin, and Johannes Vüllers. 2015. "The Power-Sharing Event Dataset (PSED): A New Dataset on the Promises and Practices of Power-Sharing in Post-conflict Countries." *Conflict Management and Peace Science* 32(3): 327–350.

Parbatya Chattagram Jana Samhati Samiti (PCJSS). 2013. "Report on the Implementation of the CHT Accord". Kalyanpur: Parbatya Chattagram Jana Samhati Samiti.

Persson, Anna, Bo Rothstein, and Jan Teorell. 2013. "Why Anticorruption Reforms Fail: Systemic Corruption as a Collective Action Problem." *Governance* 26(3): 449–471.

Pettersson, Thérése, and Peter Wallensteen. 2015. "Armed Conflicts, 1946–2014." *Journal of Peace Research* 52(4): 536–550.

Pinto, Rogerio F., and Jose Antonio Puppim De Oliveira. 2008. "Implementation Challenges in Protecting the Global Environmental Commons: The Case of Climate Change Policies in Brazil." *Public Administration and Development* 28(5): 340–350.

Pressman, Jeffrey Leonard, and Aaron Bernard Wildavsky. 1984. *Implementation*. Berkeley, CA: University of California Press.

Smith, Grant R. 1999. "Tajikistan: The Rocky Road to Peace." *Central Asian Survey* 18(2): 243–251.

United Nations Peacemaker. http://peacemaker.un.org/.

Walter, Barbara. 1997. "The Critical Barrier to Civil War Settlement." *International Organization* 51(3): 335–364.

11

Why States Repress

Evaluating Global Patterns of Abuse with the Political Terror Scale

Reed M. Wood, Mark Gibney and Peter Haschke

Introduction

The Political Terror Scale (PTS) is one of the earliest and most commonly used cross-national quantitative indicators of state-sponsored repression.[1] More specifically, this index provides a standards-based measure of abuses of physical integrity. The PTS was created in the early 1980s and has been updated annually ever since. The latest version of the dataset covers 192 countries and territories for the years 1976–2014.[2] PTS datasets are posted online (www.politicalterrorscale.org) for open public access.

Academics and practitioners rely on the PTS data to gauge the extent of state repression and to track patterns and trends around the world. In particular, the dataset has been widely employed in quantitative analyses that seek to uncover the causes and implications of state-sponsored abuse. Figure 11.1 shows the number of known citations of the PTS in items published each year between 1997 and 2015.[3] This inventory does not represent a complete list of all studies referencing

Number of Citations

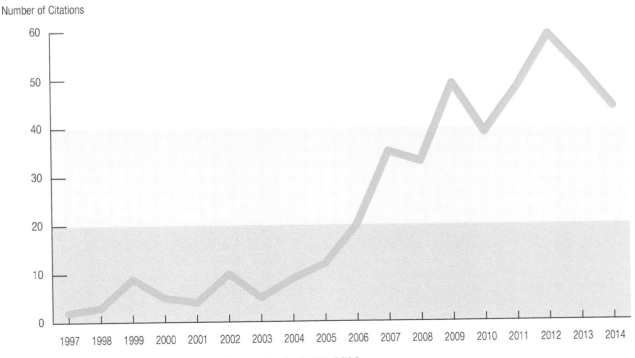

Figure 11.1 Annual Citations of the Political Terror Scale, 1997–2015

the PTS; the actual number is expected to be higher, due to circumstances where the data are used, but not explicitly cited. These results highlight the frequency with which the PTS is used, which has increased over time, especially since 2003.

This chapter begins by describing in detail the conceptualization of repression and the coding scheme used for purposes of the PTS. We then review core findings of analysis of the PTS data, in relation to contexts of civil conflict, differences in regime types, and differences in levels of development. In addition, we discuss spatial patterns and trends over time.

Conceptualizing and Measuring "Repression"

The concept and coding scheme for the PTS were initially adapted from a "political terror" scale published in the 1980 edition of the Freedom House Yearbook (Gastil 1980). At the outset, an important point to emphasize is that the PTS measures repression only with reference to violence, in the form of actual violations of physical integrity, such as torture, political imprisonment, summary executions, and disappearances. Thus, the PTS is not intended to capture the full range of political repression, including those other aspects that may not necessarily involve violence, such as restrictions on individuals and groups, threats of coercion, and suppression of dissent. In addition, the PTS aims to capture only violations committed by official agents of the state or by actors under the control of agents of the state. This criterion excludes violations carried out by private actors who are not under such direct influence of the state (e.g., domestic abuse, mob violence, terrorist attacks). Admittedly, the distinction between state and non-state actors is often blurry in practice. That said, the coding of cases is highly attentive to the nature of any relationship that can be established between actors committing violations and the state.

The Freedom House scale that serves as the basis for the PTS roughly accounted for the level of abuse committed by state in terms of five distinct categories:

Level 1: Countries … under a secure rule of law, people are not imprisoned for their views, and torture is rare or exceptional … Political murders are extremely rare …

Level 2: There is a limited amount of imprisonment for nonviolent political activity. However, a few persons are affected; torture and beating are exceptional. … Political murder is rare …

Level 3: There is extensive political imprisonment … Execution or other political murders and brutality may be common. Unlimited detention, with or without trial, for political views is accepted …

Level 4: The practices of Level 3 are expanded to larger numbers. Murders, disappearances, and torture are part of life … In spite of its generality, on this level terror affects primarily those who interest themselves in politics or ideas.

Level 5: The terrors of Level 4 have been extended to the whole population … The leaders of these societies place no limits on the means or thoroughness with which they pursue personal or ideological goals.

These category descriptions served as the basis for the original coding of the PTS (see Gastil 1980; also Stohl, Carleton, and Johnson 1984). The coding procedures were formally developed, refined, and standardized by the researchers who subsequently developed and maintained the dataset (see Stohl, Carleton, and Johnson 1984; Gibney and Dalton 1996; Wood and Gibney 2010).

Thus, the PTS gauges the overall extent and severity of state-sponsored physical integrity abuses in each country in each year using a five-category index. On this scale, countries scoring a "1" witnessed very few violations during the year: examples are Norway or Canada in most years. This score does not mean the absence of abuses – even the best-performing states occasionally commit abuses. By contrast, a score of "5" indicates gross and systematic human rights violations: examples of this category are Rwanda in 1994 or the Sudan throughout much of the 2000s. Countries receiving this score do not exhibit identical patterns of abuses; they merely qualify as having evidence of the most serious abuses.

The country-year scores are assigned based on three dimensions of state-sponsored abuses: *scope, intensity*, and *range*. In the process, the methodology ultimately collapses a concept that is inherently multidimensional into a one-dimensional measure. The limitations of this approach are quite obvious and have been discussed elsewhere (e.g., McCormick and Mitchell 1997). Regardless, readers should know that coders do attempt to account for these multiple dimensions in the coding process. The multidimensionality of both the underlying concept and the scoring process means that there are multiple "paths" to the same score. Two states may receive the same score, reflecting key similarities in the level of abuses that they exhibit, even though the actual patterns of abuse within the country might be quite different. Consider, for example, one hypothetical state that engages in systematic torture of detainees and another hypothetical state that repeatedly fires on protesters throughout the year, but only occasionally engages in torture in custody. Both states might receive the same score (probably a "4"), but for different reasons.

Scope refers to the type of violence being carried out by the state. The main types of violence tracked in the coding have traditionally been torture, summary executions, disappearances, and political imprisonment. Yet the PTS also considers other violent measures, such as forced evictions. The death penalty and prison conditions warrant special mention. In terms of the former, the PTS is confined to state-sponsored killings that take place outside normal judicial proceedings. These "extrajudicial" killings include killings of political enemies by death squads, the unlawful use of lethal force by the police, the intentional killing of civilians during combat operations, and other arbitrary deprivations of life by state actors. The PTS does not consider state-sanctioned executions that occur after trials conforming to international standards. What distinguishes a "legal" execution from an "extrajudicial" one is not always easy to determine, but a sincere effort to do so is made as part of the construction of the PTS. In terms of prison conditions, the PTS will measure unlawful acts carried out while in detention, torture being the most common, but it does not consider whether a country's prisons are considered to be "harsh" or "life threatening" as a general matter, which is an all-too-common occurrence in so many countries.

Intensity refers to the frequency of abuse – essentially how widespread are the incidents of torture; how many summary executions and disappearances; how many political prisoners; and approximately how many individuals were forcibly evicted from their homes? The sources of information on which the coding relies (see below) seldom provide exact numbers. Dependable figures are realistically impossible to obtain on a consistent basis. Rather, the coders must make educated guesses, using conventions, based on the language presented in the sources. Another consideration is that the PTS makes a concerted effort to factor in the size of a country. In that way, a thousand political prisoners in a populous country such as China says something much different about abuses of physical integrity than this same number of cases in a much smaller country.

Range refers to the proportion of the population that is targeted for abuse. This dimension serves as one of the distinguishing features between Levels 4 and 5. The former score is generally applicable to countries where violence is directed against those who participate in the political life of the country, whereas the latter score is reserved for pervasive, society-wide violence. In practice, the two scores often capture the distinction between selective violence and more indiscriminate forms of violence. For example, a state that routinely detains and tortures members of the political opposition or fires upon student protesters might receive a score of "4", provided this was the extent of violence during the year and apolitical, "average" citizens were generally not at risk of abuse. A country where physical abuses are routinely perpetrated against citizens not involved in politics, including bystanders, may instead receive a score of "5". Often, these scores are assigned when there is evidence of "scorched earth" counterinsurgency policies or summary executions of persons based on class or ethnic affiliation (as opposed to merely political involvement).

The PTS scores are coded based on material obtained from two independent sources: the U.S. State Department *Country Reports on Human Rights Practices* (SD) and the Amnesty International *Annual Report* (AI). Each of these sources is released on an annual basis. Both sources supply information about the human rights conditions in countries around the world during the previous year. For the most part, the information is highly similar across these two reports, as well as consistent in treatment across countries and over time. Yet some important disparities are observed. Most notably, information was less detailed and some bias was evident in the reports during the Cold War, resulting in the SD reports being generally more critical of socialist states and less critical of US allies, compared to the AI reports (Poe, Carey, and Vazquez 2001). Figure 11.2 (see next page), which shows the smoothed average annual scores based on the SD and AI reports, reveals a significant disparity for the 1970s and 1980s.[4] After 1990, the average scores based on the two reports tended to converge over time, continuing a long-term trend evident since 1975, suggesting that the Cold War biases have diminished. A potential worry is that new biases might emerge in connection with the global War on Terror, which might show up with SD reports being generally more critical of Arab and Muslim states and generally less critical of Western countries and US allies, compared to the AI reports. This concern does not appear to have been realized in practice: the disparity in average annual scores has remained small and actually narrowed since 2001.

Nonetheless, each country is assigned two separate scores each year, one based on the SD Report and the other based on the AI Report, to take account of any differences in how countries are viewed by the two sources, including specific differences about individual countries and systematic differences about sets of countries. In the construction of an index for each year for each report, countries are evaluated as if the sources are accurate and complete. Thus, any biases exhibited in the annual reports of the two organizations should be evident in the indices. The advantage of summarizing the reports through a coding scheme is that information about human rights practices can then be compared and used to test various hypotheses with statistical techniques in both cross-national and longitudinal contexts.

The long-standing reliance on the SD and AI reports is at least partly pragmatic. When the PTS was developed, these two reports were the only annual sources characterizing human rights practices with coverage of large numbers of countries. Since 1989, Human Rights Watch (HRW) has also published an annual report on human rights practices in individual countries. The HRW report, however, does not cover nearly the number of states as either the SD or AI sources. In the absence of an AI Report published in 2014, the PTS will be providing HRW scores for calendar year 2013.

Average Annual Score

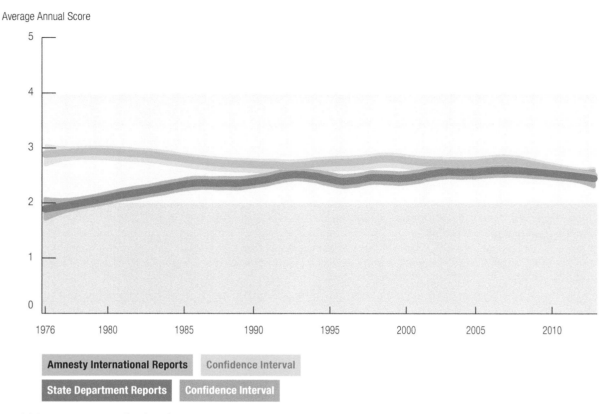

Figure 11.2 Average Annual Political Terror Scale Scores, 1976–2014

Review of Core Findings

To highlight the utility of the index, we reflect on a few of the most consistent findings from the vast body of research on state repression of physical integrity rights. Our overview focuses predominantly on the influence of political and social conflict, state political institutions, and economic development on cross-national variations in state repression. While not all of the studies discussed below relied on the PTS as their measure of abuse,[5] many (if not most) have. More important, this overview highlights the types of theoretical and empirical questions that the PTS and similar measures can help to address.

State Repression in the Context of Political and Social Conflict

Perhaps the most consistent finding in the literature on state repression is that political and social conflicts contribute to an increase in state abuses.[6] Existing studies almost invariably find that protests, riots, terrorism, and other challenges to state authority result in an increase in state repression (e.g., Davenport 1995; Gartner and Regan 1996; Piazza and Walsh 2009; Poe and Tate 1994). The theoretical justification for this result is that incumbent leaders will be inclined to respond to challengers' threats by increasing repression, in the expectation that the strategy will help them secure or recover their authority (e.g., De Nardo 1985). Gurr (1986) has gone further and argued that the existence of groups perceived as threats to the leaders' authority is a necessary condition for repression, not just a sufficient condition or a frequent correlate. Moreover, threat perception and repression are closely linked, and regime repression tends to increase as the magnitude of the challenge and its perceived likelihood of ousting the incumbent increases (e.g., Poe 2004; see also Ritter 2014). Christian Davenport (2007) has termed this relationship "the law of coercive responsiveness," highlighting the tit-for-tat nature of regime responses to domestic challengers.

Even in the presence of threats, state repression varies in response to the tactics adopted by challengers. In particular, states may meet nonviolent dissent with coercion (e.g., curfews and arrests), but repression escalates most dramatically where dissidents rely on violent tactics (Carey 2010; Moore 2000). State repression becomes most severe and widespread when states experience protracted insurgencies or plunge into full-scale civil war (e.g., Poe and Tate 1994). Indeed, with few exceptions, the states that receive the worst PTS scores (5) are those involved in these types of active domestic armed conflicts. Figure 11.3 compares the mean PTS scores for states involved in internal armed conflicts and those at peace, using the civil war data from the Correlates of War (COW) project (Sarkees and Wayman 2010). As the figure

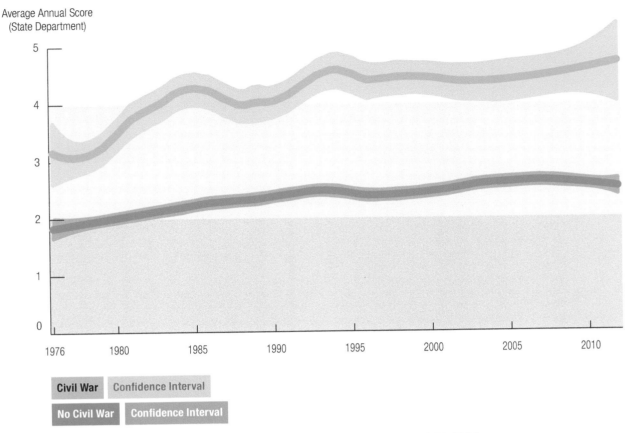

Average Annual Score
(State Department)

Civil War   Confidence Interval

No Civil War   Confidence Interval

Figure 11.3 Average Annual Political Terror Scale Scores, by Civil Conflict Status, 1976–2014

demonstrates, states involved in civil conflicts are significantly more abusive. The fact that the highest levels of state repression, on average, are observed within states facing serious domestic threats, such as insurgencies and civil wars, is unsurprising. The result emphasizes the strategic context as motivation for repression.

A second common finding is the link between illiberal political institutions and state repression. By contrast, liberal democratic regimes, which are premised on human dignity and respect for individual rights and freedoms, typically display the lowest levels of physical violations (e.g., Howard and Donnelly 1986). Past empirical analyses have demonstrated that more democratic states are less abusive than their more autocratic counterparts (Henderson 1991; Poe and Tate 1994). Figure 11.4 (see next page) evaluates this relationship, using the Polity IV dataset (Marshall, Jaggers, and Gurr 2011), distinguishing countries as democracies if they received a score of "7" or higher on the Polity2 indicator. The results clearly illustrate the link between regime type and state repression, with autocracies, on average, receiving a PTS score that is nearly one category worse than their democratic counterparts.

While the presence of robust democratic institutions has a clear constraining effect on state repression, the relationship between democracy and repression is not necessarily linear. A "murder in the middle" hypothesis suggests that so-called "anocracies" – states that are neither fully institutionally democratic nor fully autocratic – are actually the most abusive of all (e.g., Fein 1995; Regan and Henderson 2002). The primary logic is the differences in opportunities for dissent, as well as general fragility of such institutionally inconsistent regimes. Because of the absence of political competition and strong constraints on civil liberties in full autocracies, citizens generally have few opportunities to challenge the incumbent regime. By contrast, mixed regimes often allow some level of political competition, including regular multiparty elections, and even tolerate some forms of political mobilization and organization, as well as public dissent. When dissent exceeds expectations and threatens the social order or when opposition challenges draw broad support, the incumbent regime often turns to violence as a means to reassert control. For example, state repression spikes during election years in non-democratic states, whereas elections have little impact on repression in full democracies (Davenport 1997). While the available evidence indicates that anocracies may be the most repressive regimes, full democracies are consistently the least repressive regimes. Indeed, Davenport and Armstrong (2004) find a clear threshold effect for democracy, below which institutional measures of democracy have no impact on repression, but above which there is a clear suppressive effect.

Average Annual Score
(State Department)

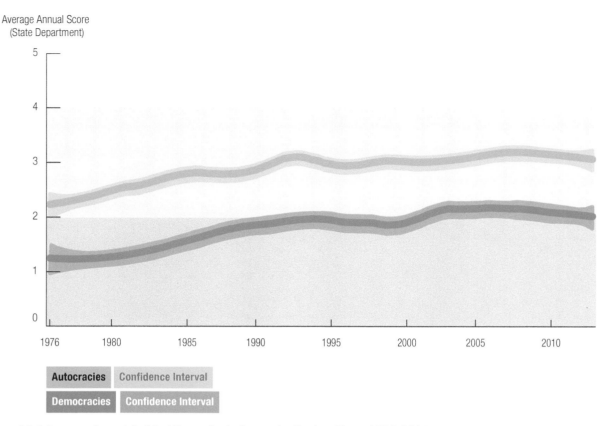

Figure 11.4 Average Annual Political Terror Scale Scores, by Regime Type, 1976–2014

The conclusion that democracies engage in the lowest levels of repression represents another in a long line of normative justifications for the diffusion of democracy throughout the international system. The basic logic is that spreading democracy improves respect for human rights around the world. Yet, the process of democratization is rarely linear and can be quite uncertain, particularly when democracy is strongly pushed or imposed by external actors. For this reason, studies have also considered how processes of regime change and other political transitions influence patterns of abuse. On the one hand, moves to democracy may dampen repression, in so far as new or evolving institutions place increasing constraints on executive actors and citizens exercise power to remove unpopular and abusive leaders through elections. On the other hand, the transition from rigid autocracies to more liberal forms of government creates new opportunities for political challenges and dissent. Where these challenges outpace the leadership's willingness to make concessions, incumbents may resort to repression in order to maintain their authority. Previous studies also highlight how the process of transition often leads to increased internal competition and conflict, especially when previous excluded political groups – particularly ethno-nationalist groups – attempt to secure a position in the emerging political order (e.g., Snyder 2000). Where such conflicts arise, repression is more likely to follow, because groups that have traditionally been in power seek to maintain this status and the authority and benefits it confers. The empirical evidence about the impact of transition processes is mixed. Some studies find that the process of democratic transition reduces repression (Zanger 2000), whereas others do not detect a general relationship (Davenport 2004).

Many previous studies also highlight the important roles that economic development plays in influencing the extent to which incumbent regimes and their security forces rely on physical repression to maintain control and suppress dissent (Poe and Tate 1994). As Figure 11.5 (see next page) highlights, wealthier states are far less likely than poorer states, all else being equal, to engage in harsh physical repression. The results show that states with an estimated GDP per capita above the global mean typically score one category better on the PTS than do their relatively poorer counterparts. From a theoretical perspective, this robust result reflects two mechanisms.

The first mechanism derives from the traditional view that poverty is as a prime source of popular grievances. The logic is that poverty leads to the dissatisfaction with the state, increasing the odds of challenges to the status quo, including violent challenges such as terrorism and civil conflict. As discussed above, such challenges typically provoke a coercive response from incumbent regimes. While most states will increase repression in response to challenges, the extent of the increase is likely conditioned by the bargaining power of domestic opponents, the willingness and ability of the state to

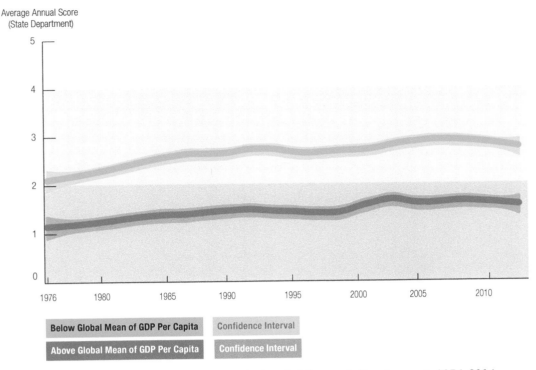

Average Annual Score
(State Department)

Below Global Mean of GDP Per Capita   Confidence Interval

Above Global Mean of GDP Per Capita   Confidence Interval

Figure 11.5 Average Annual Political Terror Scale Scores, by Level of Economic Development, 1976–2014

make concessions, and the expected cost/benefit calculus of using repression as an alternative. Leaders of wealthier states who can successfully bargain with domestic constituents, as well as fear electoral repercussions from the use of violence against the population, are therefore less likely to engage in significant repression against their citizens (Young 2009).

The second mechanism relates to state coercive capacity. Economic development often correlates with high levels of bureaucratic and institutional capacity. Wealthy states also tend to possess superior coercive capacity compared to their less developed counterparts. Coercive capacity is often viewed in terms of the state using physical violence to repress citizens. Yet states with the most robust coercive capacity should be able to suppress both violent threats and non-violent opposition with the least amount of violence. Such states can effectively gather intelligence on threats, target dissident leaders directly, and preempt popular protests before they create instability. Higher levels of state capacity have been found empirically to dampen state abuses of physical integrity violations (Englehart 2009). The Soviet Union and its client states are good examples of this phenomenon. Widespread dissatisfaction with the leadership was observed in those countries during the 1980s, but the states were able to successfully deter popular mobilization and violent challenges through superior intelligence gathering and the existence of large, well-trained, well-equipped professional security, intelligence and police forces.[7] More recently, the United States and European countries have not dramatically escalated repression in the wake of transnational and domestic terror attacks, largely because they have the capabilities and resources to effectively pursue threats with greater precision.[8] Another plausible mechanism is that economic development reduces physical integrity rights violations by increasing the state's ability to check agents in its employ, through monitoring and accountability, and reducing the incentives of agents to abuse coercive power (Englehart 2009; Haschke 2014).

Spatial and Temporal Patterns

State-sponsored repression is not a constant. As can be expected, therefore PTS scores vary around the world, by country and region. At the same time, the trends have not followed the same trajectories, in some cases getting better, but in other cases worsening. To illustrate both the spatial and temporal patterns of abuse captured in the PTS, Figure 11.6 (see pp. 112-113) shows the PTS scores for each state in the international system at various time points. The four maps comprising this figure present the PTS scores for the years 1981, 1991, 2001 and 2011, coded from the SD reports for each state included in the dataset.[9] These maps help to demonstrate some of the patterns that underlie the core findings discussed in previous sections.

As Figure 11.6 demonstrates, significant cross-regional variation in state conduct is present. Throughout the three decades illustrated, countries in North America and Europe, the more economically developed states of Northeast Asia, and Australia and New Zealand consistently receive the best scores (reflecting the lowest levels of abuse). Meanwhile,

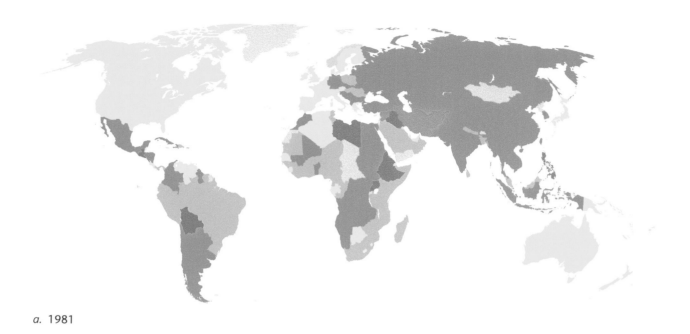

a. 1981

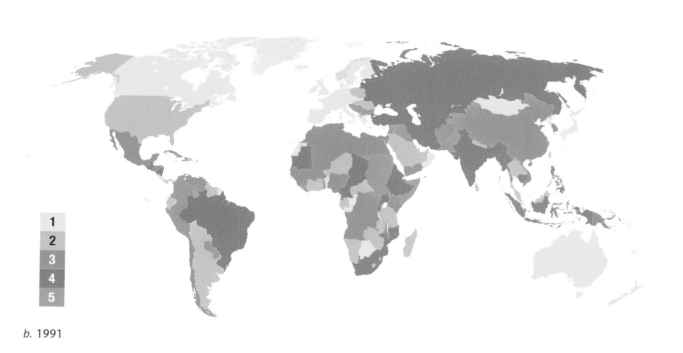

b. 1991

Figure 11.6 Political Terror Scores, by Country, in 1981, 1991, 2001, and 2011

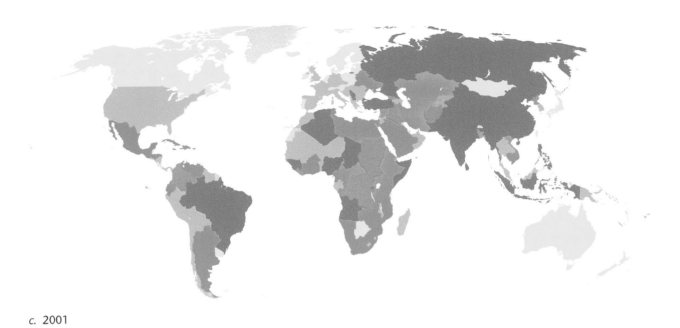

c. 2001

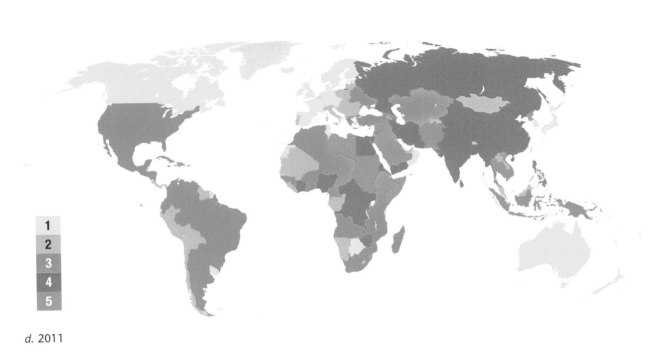

d. 2011

Figure 11.6 Political Terror Scores, by Country, in 1981, 1991, 2001, and 2011

states in South Asia and the Middle East, as well as some states in Sub-Saharan Africa, consistently receive the worst scores. This consistent regional clustering of patterns of state repression may be attributable to several explanations, encompassing a number of considerations that we addressed in the analysis presented earlier.

First, civil wars and other forms of internal unrest are rare in the regions of the world where physical violations by states are also uncommon. Thus, the map also helps to highlight the close relationship between the absence of internal conflict and a lack of state repression. Second, the regions with the least physical violations by the state are not only the most stable, they are the most democratic. This pattern emphasizes the importance of political, social, and cultural norms about violence and respect for human rights. Indeed, some scholars have found that such factors can influence state actions. At least one study found, however, that Muslim-dominated countries typically experience lower levels of state repression compared to the rest of the world, after controlling for other factors (De Soysa and Nordås 2007). A third factor is state capacity. The maps demonstrate fairly convincingly that the wealthiest regions in the international system are consistently the least repressive. This factor may help to account for the counter-intuitive findings about Muslim-dominated countries: many of them are conflict prone and/or undemocratic, but also wealthy because of natural resource endowments.

The maps further illustrate that levels of abuse are not constant across regions or over time. Some regions that were initially quite repressive have improved significantly, while other regions that were comparatively calm have seen state brutality rise considerably in a relatively short time. Variations in domestic conflict and political institutions, both of which cluster regionally, contribute to these inter-regional disparities in trends of state repression. As we previously discussed, transitions to democracy can influence reductions in state repression, particularly in countries where democratic institutions become well established.

Consider, for example, the countries in Central and Eastern Europe, which became increasingly democratic following the collapse of the Soviet Union and the end of the Cold War. As Figure 11.6 illustrates, state repression generally declined in most of these states between 1981 and 1991. Such achievements, however, are hardly permanent. In short order, Belarus and Ukraine resumed their former levels of repression, due in part to the failure of strong democratic institutions to take hold. By contrast, democratic institutions became increasingly institutionalized in states such as Bulgaria, the Czech Republic, and Poland, leading to the maintenance of low levels of repression.

To more clearly illustrate the role that democratization can play in shaping trends in repression, Figure 11.7 (see next page) compares the PTS scores of the Czech Republic and Belarus from 1978–2013. In the graphs, yellow dots represent the scores for years in which either country was considered an autocracy, while red dots represent the scores for years in which the state was considered democratic. The purple lines represent the trend in scores over time.[10] Both countries began the period as part of larger multinational, Socialist states that were members of the Eastern Bloc. At the time, their respective PTS scores were roughly comparable; conditions were actually somewhat worse in the Czech Republic than in Belarus. The scores initially followed a downward trend – far steeper in the Czech Republic than in Belarus – toward less physical repression. After the collapse of the Soviet Union, the Czech Republic immediately democratized, and repression continued to drop, quickly reaching levels comparable to those observed across Western Europe. The experience in Belarus was completely different. A modest favorable trend was observed during the 1980s. Immediately following the dissolution of the Soviet Union, Belarus enjoyed a few years of democratic governance that coincided with relatively limited repression, but lacking any further improvement in conditions. Thereafter, the country was unable to sustain democracy and within 15 years repression had returned to the levels previously observed in the late-1970s.

Thus, democratization and transitions in the broader political context are not guarantees of change, even in similarly situated countries. Instead, individual countries' experiences can vary considerably depending on how events unfold and the extent to which changes in political institutions are durable and accompanied by a more wholesale transformation of the relationship between state and society.

A trend similar to that of the Czech Republic was observed in the Southern Cone of South America. During the late-1970s and early 1980s, Argentina, Chile, and Uruguay were ruled by repressive military regimes, which frequently engaged in abuses such as the torture and disappearance of dissidents. By the late-1980s, each country had democratized, and to a large extent this transformation of political life has taken hold across much of the region, as evidenced by the low PTS scores, indicative of scant state repression.

As we discussed repeatedly above, internal political and social conflict is often a primary driver of state repression. The combination of non-democratic political institutions and low state capacity increases the likelihood that domestic dissent prompts disproportionate coercion from the state, which can quickly escalate into violent internal conflict such as terrorism, insurgency, or civil war. With few exceptions, the states that receive the worst PTS scores in any year are those involved in ongoing violent internal conflicts, which is consistent with the argument that threats to incumbent authority motivate state violence. Plenty of examples are available to demonstrate how the outbreak of internal violence can lead to increases in repression, whereas the resolution of conflicts typically helps to reduce repression.

Figure 11.8 (see p. 116) illustrates these patterns using the cases of Liberia and Sierra Leone. In the early 1980s, both countries exhibited relatively low levels of state-sponsored repression of physical integrity rights. By the early 1990s,

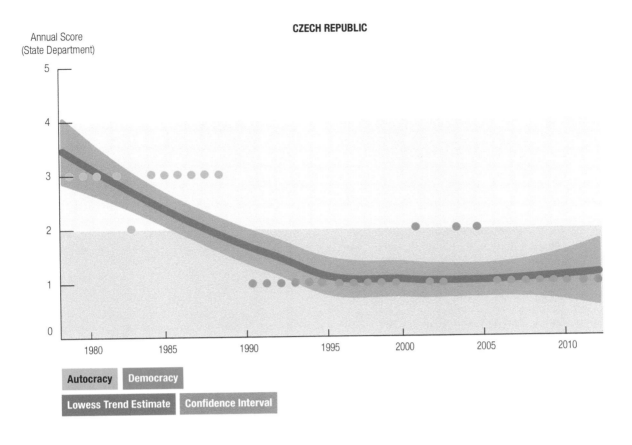

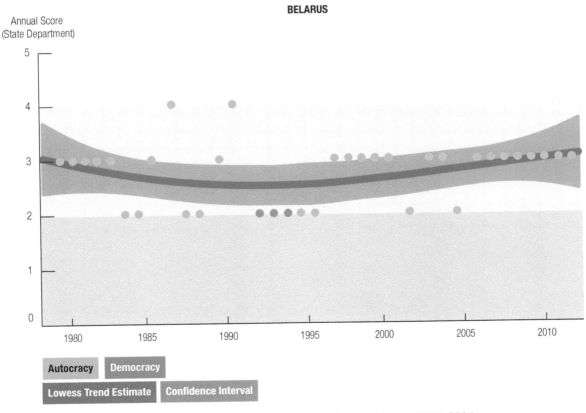

Figure 11.7 Annual Political Terror Scale Scores for the Czech Republic and Belarus, 1976–2014

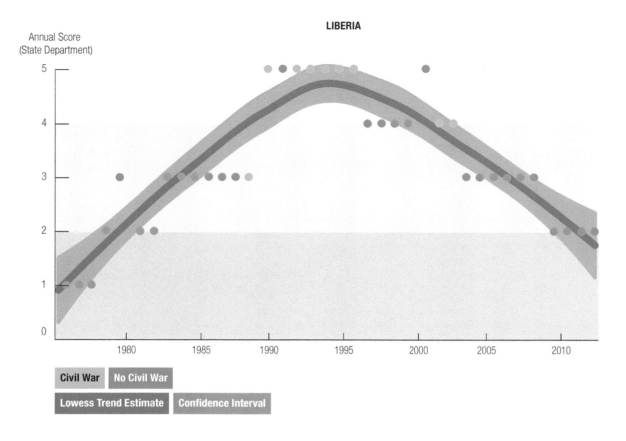

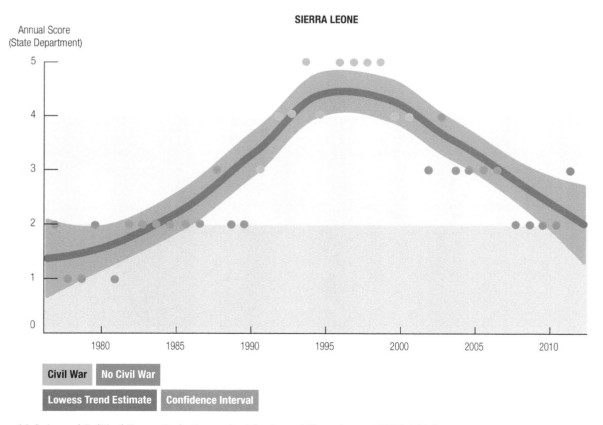

Figure 11.8 Annual Political Terror Scale Scores for Liberia and Sierra Leone, 1976–2014

however, a series of interconnected civil conflicts plagued the region. For more than a decade, the governments of Liberia and Sierra Leone used their security forces and state-allied militias to carry out widespread, systematic abuses of citizens' physical integrity rights. Fortunately, repression abated following the terminations of these countries' respective civil wars, partly as the result of assistance from international peacekeeping missions. Of note, the trendlines presented in Figure 11.8 show that the decline in state repression actually began before the civil wars terminated in Liberia (1997, though with a recurrence in 2003) and Sierra Leone (2002).

These examples also demonstrate that civil war and state repression are not synonymous. Instead, state repression can fluctuate during civil conflicts and may spike at points when the state feels especially threatened. Such repression in response to conditions can occur early on in a conflict (as an effort to squelch the threat), emerge progressively over time (in so far as the threat gets worse), or materialize at the late stages (of conflict as an endgame maneuver to shut down a threat once and for all, as a last-gasp measure, or for fear of what will ensue during the post-conflict transition).

While the resolution of conflict should lead to a rapid reduction in repression, the effect appears most robust when the international community has assisted in the peace process, including via post-conflict peacekeeping and peacebuilding operations. This impact is evident when comparing cases in which the international community played a key role in the cessation of the conflict through a negotiated settlement and the maintenance of post-conflict peace to cases where wars terminated through the defeat of one side and without international assistance. Both of the cases highlighted in Figure 11.8 eventually terminated through negotiated settlements and with the assistance of the international community. By contrast, Sri Lanka's recent civil war ended through the defeat of the domestic challengers (the LTTE) and without substantial international intervention or assistance. As Figure 11.9 illustrates, repression has remained quite high despite the end of the conflict in late-2009. Peacekeeping and other forms of international assistance and involvement do not necessarily lead to immediate dramatic reductions in repression. Yet the available evidence suggests they can help reduce state violence and promote post-conflict stability, which should help to reduce state repression during the years immediately following conflict (e.g., Kathman and Wood 2014; Murdie and Davis 2010).

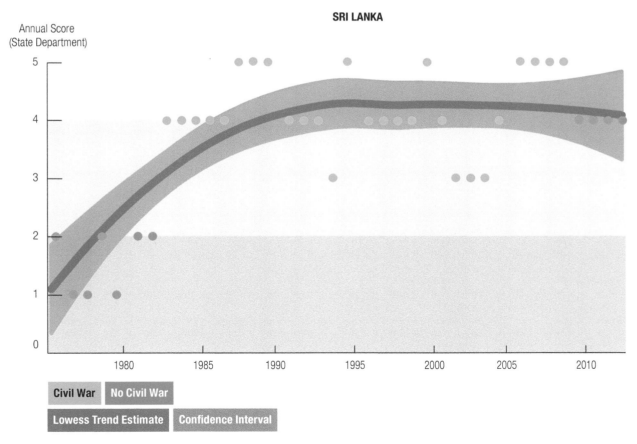

Figure 11.9 Annual Political Terror Scale Scores for Sri Lanka, 1976–2014

Conclusion

The Political Terror Scale remains an essential resource for both scholars and advocates in the field of human rights, improving understanding of why physical integrity rights remain under assault. As measured by this index, global levels of abuses of physical integrity rights remained relatively stable from 1976–2014. During this period, the average country around the world experienced extensive political imprisonment or a recent history of such imprisonment. In addition, extra-judicial executions or other political murders and brutality are often common and unlimited detention – with or without a trial – for political views is accepted in the average country. Several major factors contribute to variation across countries and regions and over time in violations of physical integrity rights. These violations are substantially more common and severe during periods of civil conflict. Democracies are generally more committed to and better at protecting physical integrity rights than their autocratic counterparts. Finally, the degree to which physical integrity rights are respected is highly conditional on levels of economic development.

Notes

1 The use of the word "terror" might cause some confusion because of the association that term now has with international terrorism, particularly since September 11, 2001. The "political terror" measured by the PTS is the violence carried out by a state against its own citizens.
2 The latest release of the PTS covers 184 countries in 2014. The number of countries for which scores are generated varies for previous years based on the availability of the source documents required to perform the coding.
3 The data were taken from Google Scholar's citation database.
4 The lines shown represent fitted values from a local polynomial regression (Loess) smoother with a low span parameter. Values approximate annual means. Shaded areas represent the confidence interval around the smoothed lines.
5 All figures in this section rely on PTS scores, based on coding of SD reports.
6 The reverse may also be true. Repression can lead to an increase in dissent and protest behavior (see Lichbach 1987; Davenport 2007a).
7 The Soviet Union certainly engaged in physical repression, including torture and arbitrary imprisonment during this time. Moreover, it had engaged in widespread and systematic abuses during earlier decades. By the 1970s and 1980s, however, repression was relatively mild, especially considering the depth of popular discontent with the state.
8 State repression did increase following the 9/11 attacks. The increase was relatively restrained, however, compared to escalations in repression observed in other states following terrorist attacks (or armed violence). In this case, the restraint is a product of both state capacity and the presence of robust democratic institutions.
9 Where the SD scores are missing, we substituted the AI scores.
10 Here again, the lines represent fitted values from a local regression (Loess) smoother. Shaded areas represent the confidence interval around the smoothed line.

References

Carey, Sabine C. 2010. "The Use of Repression as a Response to Domestic Dissent." *Political Studies* 58(1): 167–186.
Davenport, Christian. 1995. "Multidimensional Threat Perception and State Repression: An Inquiry into Why States Apply Negative Sanctions." *American Journal of Political Science* 39(3): 683–713.
Davenport, Christian. 2007. *State Repression and the Democratic Peace*, Cambridge: Cambridge University Press.
Davenport, Christian 2007a. "State Repression and Political Order." *Annual Review of Political Science* 10: 1–23.
Davenport, Christian, and David Armstrong. 2004. "Democracy and the Violation of Human Rights: A Statistical Analysis from 1976 to 1996." *American Journal of Political Science* 48(3): 538–554.
De Nardo, James. 1985. *Power in Numbers: The Political Strategy of Protest and Rebellion*. Princeton, NJ: Princeton University Press.
De Soysa, Indra, and Ragnild Nordås. 2007. "Islam's Bloody Innards? Religion and Political Terror, 1980–2000." *International Studies Quarterly* 51: 927–943.
Englehart, Neil A. 2009. "State Capacity, State Failure, and Human Rights." *Journal of Peace Research* 46(2): 163–180.
Fein, Helen. 1995. "More Murder in the Middle: Life-Integrity Violations and Democracy in the World." *Human Rights Quarterly* 17(1): 170–191.
Gartner, Scott, and Patrick Regan. 1996. "Threat and Repression: The Non-linear Relationship between Government and Opposition Violence." *Journal of Peace Research* 33(3): 273–287.
Gastil, Raymond D. 1980. *Freedom in the World: Political Rights and Civil Liberties*. Piscataway, NJ: Transaction Publishers.
Gibney, Mark, and Matthew Dalton. 1996. "The Political Terror Scale." *Policy Studies and Developing Nations* 4(1): 73–84.
Gurr, Ted Robert. 1986. "The Political Origins of State Violence and Terror: A Theoretical Analysis." In Michael Stohl and George Lopez (eds). *Government Violence and Repression: An Agenda for Research*. Westport, CT: Greenwood Press.
Haschke, Peter. 2014. "Democracy and the Human Right to the Physical Integrity of the Person." Unpublished PhD dissertation. University of Rochester.
Henderson, Conway W. 1991. "Conditions Affecting the Use of Political Repression." *Journal of Conflict Resolution* 35(1): 120–142.
Howard, Rhoda E., and Jack Donnelly. 1986. "Human Dignity, Human Rights and Political Regimes." *American Political Science Review* 80(3): 801–817.
Kathman, Jacob D., and Reed M. Wood. 2014. "Stopping the Killing during the 'Peace': Peacekeeping and the Severity of Postconflict Civilian Victimization." *Foreign Policy Analysis*, April. doi: 10.1111/fpa.12041.

Lichbach, Mark Irving. 1987. "Deterrence or Escalation? The Puzzle of Aggregate Studies of Repression and Dissent." *Journal of Conflict Resolution* 31(2): 266–297.

Marshall, Monty G., Keith Jaggers, and Ted Robert Gurr. 2011. *Polity IV Project: Political Regime Characteristics and Transitions, 1800–2010, Dataset Users' Manual*. Center for Systemic Peace.

McCormick, James M., and Neil J. Mitchell. 1997. "Human Rights Violations, Umbrella Concepts, and Empirical Analysis." *World Politics* 49(4): 510–525.

Moore, Will H. 2000. "The Repression of Dissent: A Substitution Model of Government Coercion". *Journal of Conflict Resolution* 44(107): 107–127.

Murdie, Amanda, and David R. Davis. 2010. "Problematic Potential: The Human Rights Consequences of Peacekeeping Interventions in Civil Wars." *Human Rights Quarterly* 32(1): 50–73.

Piazza, James A., and James Igoe Walsh. 2009. "Transnational Terror and Human Rights." *International Studies Quarterly* 53(1): 124–148.

Poe, Steven. 2004. "The Decision to Repress: An Integrative Theoretical Approach to the Research on Human Rights and Repression." In Steven Poe and Sabine C. Carey (eds). *Understanding Human Rights Violations: New Systematic Studies*. Burlington, VT: Ashgate Press.

Poe, Steven, and Neal Tate. 1994. "Repression of the Human Right to Personal Integrity in the 1980s: A Global Analysis." *American Political Science Review* 88(4): 853–872.

Poe, Steven C., Sabine C. Carey, and Tanya C. Vazquez. 2001. "How Are These Pictures Different? A Quantitative Comparison of the US State Department and Amnesty International Human Rights Reports 1976–1995." *Human Rights Quarterly* 23(3): 650–677.

Regan, Patrick M., and Errol A. Henderson. 2002. "Democracy, Threats and Political Repression in Developing Countries: Are Democracies Internally Less Violent?" *Third World Quarterly* 23(1): 119–136.

Ritter, Emily Hencken. 2014. "Policy Disputes, Political Survival, and the Onset and Severity of State Repression." *Journal of Conflict Resolution* 58(1): 143–168.

Sarkees, Meredith Reid, and Frank Wayman. 2010. *Resort to War: 1816–2007*. Thousand Oaks, CA: CQ Press.

Snyder, Jack L. 2000. *From Voting to Violence: Democratization and Nationalist Conflict*. New York: Norton & Company.

Stohl, Michael, David Carleton, and Stephen Johnson. 1984. "Human rights and US Foreign Assistance from Nixon to Carter." *Journal of Peace Research* 21(3): 215–226

Wood, Reed M., and Mark Gibney. 2010. "The Political Terror Scale (PTS): A Re-Introduction and a Comparison to CIRI." *Human Rights Quarterly* 32(2): 367–400.

Young, Joseph K. 2009. "State Capacity, Democracy, and the Violation of Personal Integrity Rights." *Journal of Human Rights* 8(4): 283–300.

Zanger, Sabine C. 2000. "A Global Analysis of the Effects of Political Regime Changes on Life Integrity Violations, 1977–1993." *Journal of Peace Research* 37(2): 213–233.

12

Foreign Aid and Conflict

What We Know and Need to Know

Bradley Parks, Caroline Bergeron and Michael J. Tierney

Introduction

The *World Development Report 2011* calls attention to the fact that "one-and-a-half billion people live in areas affected by fragility, conflict, or large-scale, organized criminal violence, and no low-income fragile or conflict-affected country has yet to achieve a single United Nations Millennium Development Goal" (World Bank, 2011). In order to confront this long-standing challenge, donors of foreign aid have invested billions of dollars in fragile and conflict-affected (F/CA) countries over the recent decades. Between 2003 and 2007, the US government invested approximately $32 billion in reconstruction funds in Iraq alone (Berman, et al., 2011).

Donors provide money to F/CA countries to build or bolster states that govern effectively; maintain peace, security, and the rule of law; create employment opportunities; and provide critically important public services (e.g., education, health, etc.), as well as to address humanitarian crises. In principle, therefore, such aid should help to mitigate the potential for conflict, limit the scope, severity and duration of conflict when it does transpire, and facilitate the implementation and sustainability of transitions from conflict to peace. Yet there is growing concern that foreign aid can also have a number of negative, unintended effects in F/CA countries, potentially provoking, prolonging, or intensifying conflict. Aid secured by a government might ease its budget constraint and thereby increase military spending, which might make the government more willing to employ military force against political opponents. Aid appropriated by rebel groups might be used to fuel an insurgency or win the allegiances of the local population. Finally, aid may be lost due to corruption or wasted due to ineffective programming.

The complex nature of these multi-directional relationships between aid, conflict, and development poses a significant challenge to researchers and practitioners alike. We not only need to better understand when aid to F/CA countries is most likely to achieve its intended purposes, but also how international development and humanitarian agencies can avoid inadvertently doing harm in these settings.

Over the last decade, a growing number of studies have highlighted the differential effects of aid in F/CA countries that result from variation in the sources, types, implementers, and locations of aid. This chapter seeks to describe the current state of the literature. We start by discussing existing cross-national research that treats countries as the relevant units of analysis. We then turn our attention to a more recent line of empirical inquiry that investigates the topic from a subnational perspective. Finally, we conclude by identifying key gaps in the existing state of knowledge and potentially fruitful avenues for future research.

Cross-National Research on Aid's Impact in Conflict and Post-Conflict Settings

Whether the provision of external assistance diminishes or promotes conflict is not obvious. Theoretical arguments and empirical evidence exist on both sides of this debate. The lack of consensus in the literature likely follows from the fact that there is little agreement on the most appropriate data or models for testing hypotheses, but also that this is a very complex set of issues and the relationships are likely contingent and endogenous. Therefore, the next generation of scholarship on this topic will need to clearly identify the conditions under which aid ameliorates or exacerbates conflict – or has no discernible impact.

There are several reasons aid might decrease the incidence of conflict. Collier and Hoeffler (2002) provide evidence that aid does not directly impact intrastate conflict, but can reduce the probability of civil war in so far as aid affects economic growth and primary commodity export dependence. Likewise, other studies have found that aid, to the extent that it increases economic growth and state capacity (and state legitimacy), could reduce the probability of conflict (Fearon 2004; Miguel et al. 2004; de Ree and Nillesen 2009; Nielsen et al. 2011; Savun and Tirone 2012). Aid could plausibly reduce the reliance of the state on natural resource revenues, thereby cutting off a potential source of funding for insurgent groups and other armed factions (Collier and Hoeffler 2004). In addition, aid might reduce conflict by giving the government a softer budget constraint, thus allowing the government to more effectively deter insurgent groups through increased military spending (Collier and Hoeffler 2002; Collier and Hoeffler 2007). A softer budget constraint could also make it easier for the government to buy off rebels (Azam and Mesnard 2003; Azam 2006; Nielsen et al. 2011). Savun and Tirone (2012) provide complementary evidence; they find that, in the face of an exogenous economic shock, the provision of aid can have a conflict-suppressing effect.[1] De Ree and Nillesen (2009) find no relationship between aid flows and the *onset* of civil conflict; however, they do find that increased aid reduces the duration of civil conflict.

At the same time, there are reasons to think aid might increase the probability of conflict. Aid could strengthen the incentive for rebels and would-be rebels to engage in conflict, in order to capture the spoils of military victory (Grossman 1992; Azam 1995). Nielsen et al. (2011) present evidence that rapid withdrawals of foreign aid can increase the likelihood of civil war. Yet Strange et al. (2015) show that rapid reductions in Western aid are only likely to induce conflict in the absence of sufficient alternative funding from China. Similarly, Gutting and Steinwand (2015) find that negative aid shocks are less likely to result in violent political conflict in a country characterized by high levels of donor fragmentation.

Most existing studies treat aid as an undifferentiated resource transfer. A separate line of research adopts the premise that aid designed for different purposes can be expected to have different effects – and therefore the use of granular, disaggregated data is appropriate and will yield new insights. Indeed, when scholars divide aid by sector, their analyses yield more nuanced empirical results. Research in this vein has produced evidence that particular types of aid can dampen conflict and violence. For example, Savun and Tirone (2011) find that civil conflict is less likely when democratizing states receive high levels of democracy assistance. Young and Findley (2011) find that aid directed to education, health, civil society, and conflict prevention can be an effective means of fighting terrorism. A number of studies offer contrasting results. Military aid, which frees up domestic resources for security purposes and increases the coercive capabilities of the state (Collier and Hoeffler 2002; Collier and Hoeffler 2007), is associated with a higher likelihood of intrastate conflict (Sollenberg 2012). Similarly, a large body of qualitative research suggests that humanitarian aid can inadvertently promote conflict by providing armed groups with access to lootable or otherwise appropriable resources (De Waal 1994; Omaar and De Waal 1994; Pendergast 1996; de Waal 1997; Jok 1999; Anderson 1999, 2000; Terry 2002; Kenyon Lischer 2005; Metelits 2010; Polman and Waters 2010; Mampilly 2011; Kevlihan 2013). Several quantitative studies provide corroborating evidence that humanitarian aid can indeed prolong conflict (Narang 2014, 2015; Nunn and Qian 2014).

Scholars have not only focused attention on the impact of aid before and during periods of conflict. The question of whether post-conflict aid reduces the likelihood of future conflict is also important, since over half of all countries that exhibit conflict at any given time have also experienced conflict in the previous 10 years (Collier and Hoeffler 2002). Collier et al. (2008) find that the risk of relapse declines substantially when a post-conflict country experiences economic recovery and receives UN peacebuilding funds. By contrast, Walter (2010) does not find that aid reduces the probability of a post-conflict country relapsing into conflict. She speculates that these null findings may be the result of endogeneity, whereby the most conflict-prone countries also receive the most aid.

A substantial related literature examines the effectiveness of aid in achieving development goals in post-conflict settings. Elbadawi et al. (2008) find that aid-induced appreciations of the real exchange rate are less severe in post-conflict settings, thereby rendering aid more effective. Adam, et al. (2008) suggest that aid to post-conflict countries might be relatively more effective because it is often used to curb inflation, by reining in fiscal deficits accumulated during the conflict. Duponchel (2008) estimates that the optimal aid-to-GDP ratio (in terms of economic growth) for a post-conflict country is 4.8 percent, but finds that most post-conflict countries have substantially lower aid-to-GDP ratios. Thus, the problem may not be that aid is ineffective, but that a critical mass of aid is often not allocated. This conclusion contrasts with the findings of Collier and Hoeffler (2004). They provide evidence that the capacity of countries to productively absorb foreign aid during the first three years following the end of a conflict is no different than in other countries that are not conflict affected. They also show, however, that absorptive capacity is roughly twice as high in post-conflict countries over the seven years following the initial three-year period, which highlights the importance of timing. They also suggest that too much aid too soon after conflict will lead to substantial waste, unless strong policies and institutions are established. An obvious implication is that aid is better suited to facilitate long-term rebuilding than immediate recovery in the aftermath of conflict. Girod (2012) suggests another conditional finding: aid is most effective in post-conflict countries lacking geostrategic significance and access to natural resource rents. She explains that governments confronting these conditions are more desperate for income and thus have stronger incentives to meet donors' development goals, whereas governments with significant access to unearned income – in the form of natural resource rents and powerful, geostrategic patrons – have fewer incentives to put foreign aid to effective use.

Despite a recent increase in the number of cross-country empirical studies that seek to unpack the complex causal relationships between aid and conflict, this literature raises as many questions as it answers. In particular, the research does not yet establish definitively which specific types of development interventions work to limit the potential of violence in pre-conflict, active conflict, and post-conflict settings. Nor does the literature shed much light on causal mechanisms. Another critical knowledge gap is how different types of development assistance affect the incentives and behaviors of different actors *within* a country.

The Subnational Distribution and Impact of Aid in Conflict and Post-Conflict Settings

In response to these limitations of the cross-country empirical literature, a new generation of research has emerged to explore the aid-conflict nexus through *subnational* analysis. While some of these studies are observational and others are experimental, they are consistent with the advice for those studying political violence that "the most promising avenue for new empirical research is on the subnational scale, analyzing conflict causes, conduct, and consequences at the level of armed groups, communities, and individuals" (Blattman and Miguel 2010). The logic applied here is that relationships between aid and conflict can and ought to be observed at lower levels of aggregation, especially to identify important sources of variation within countries.

To start, an important consideration is that donors' choices about where to locate aid can be a function of conflict conditions in different places at different times. These decisions are complex. On one hand, aid may be more likely to flow to areas of ongoing or recent conflict, which can create many different types of needs for assistance: among other things, violence destroys infrastructure, reduces investment in productive enterprises, depresses economic growth, and erodes social trust and cohesion (Cerra and Saxena 2008; Lis 2014; Findley 2011). Fragile areas that have a high probability of relapsing into conflict may create the "pull" conditions that draw in assistance. On the other hand, aid may be more likely to flow to stable, peaceful areas, since operating in conflict zones is more dangerous and difficult for aid agencies and their staff (Lis 2014; Fast 2014). Thus, aid could be disproportionately sited either in conflict zones or in peaceful areas, depending on the factors that influence the decision-making processes of individual donors working in specific countries and contexts.

In order to rigorously evaluate the nature and direction of these and other potential causal relationships, spatially disaggregated and time-varying information on aid and conflict is required. Until relatively recently, such data were not available. Over the last five years, however, subnational data collection initiatives have rapidly expanded in number, scope, and accessibility. In particular, AidData (www.aiddata.org) is a major source of subnationally geocoded data on aid projects around the world. Sources of subnationally geocoded conflict data include the Armed Conflict Location and Event Data (ACLED) Project, the Uppsala Conflict Data Program's Georeferenced Events Dataset (UCDP GED), the Social Conflict Analysis Database (SCAD), and the Integrated Crisis Early Warning System (ICEWS) Project. These subnationally georeferenced data are increasingly being leveraged to unpack the relationships between aid and conflict.[2]

Among the instances was Findley et al. (2011), which used subnationally georeferenced data on aid projects in Sub-Saharan Africa during conflict-affected years from 1989–2008. They find that aid fungibility has a differential impact on violence, conditional on subnational location: aid to state capitals and nearby areas (where incumbent regimes enjoy substantial relative power advantages) will increase state capacity and deter conflict, whereas aid directed to areas further away from the main locus of state power will promote competitive rent-seeking and local violence. Along similar lines, Weezel (2015) uses geocoded data from AidData and UCDP GED and a first-difference identification strategy to estimate aid's impact on conflict. He finds that the overall relationship between aid and conflict intensity is weak at the district and provincial levels. When aid is decomposed, however, statistically significant relationships cutting in opposite directions are observed. More fungible sources of aid (e.g., budget support) correlate with increased conflict, whereas less fungible sources of aid (e.g., road and technical assistance projects) are associated with reduced conflict. These results are consistent with the idea that fungible aid provides greater opportunities for rent-seeking and theft, while less fungible sources of aid increase the opportunity costs of rebellion.

Strandow et al. (2014) rely on the same data, but employ a different method of causal inference (propensity score matching) to estimate aid's impact on conflict. They find that areas receiving high levels of aid experience more military fatalities than areas receiving low levels of aid (or no aid). This result suggests that the prospect of gaining access to aid may motivate combat between warring factions. Wood and Sullivan (2015) employ a similar matching method to analyze subnationally geocoded aid and conflict data. They find that (humanitarian) aid induces rebel violence, but not state violence.[3] Crost et al. (2014) provide corroborating evidence from the Philippines, using a regression discontinuity design:

the possibility of a given village receiving World Bank project funding increased the likelihood of insurgent violence. They argue that this evidence supports the hypothesis that "insurgents try to sabotage [aid] program[s] because [the program's] success would weaken their support in the population." Beath et al. (2013) make a similar argument based on analysis of data from a randomized evaluation of a community-driven development program in Afghanistan. In contrast, Felter et al. (2013) find that a conditional cash transfer program diminished the influence of insurgents and reduced violence in Philippine villages. Their results suggest that foreign aid *projects* may be more conflict-prone and vulnerable to predation by rebels, whereas direct cash transfer programs may provide fewer rent-seeking opportunities and thus not encourage violence. Of course, cash is more fungible than any other type of aid, but if cash is transferred directly to poor and vulnerable households in a targeted and discreet manner, it can apparently lower the likelihood of conflict.

Findley et al. (2011) also suggest that the likelihood of conflict might plausibly be reduced by certain types of aid interventions, including labor-intensive development programs (e.g., public works) that increase the opportunity costs of engaging in violent activity, as well as programs that are explicitly geared towards promoting social cohesion and dispute resolution. The support for these arguments is mixed. Iyengar et al. (2011) find that labor-intensive development spending reduced insurgent violence in Iraq. Berman et al. (2011) generate what could be a contradictory result: when unemployment is high, insurgent attacks against the military go down. Of course, a low level of unemployment is not the same thing as the presence of labor-intensive development programming. Therefore, future research will be needed to sort out these findings that do not fit together comfortably.

Other subnational studies have sought to identify the impact of aid programs specifically intended to reduce existing conflict. Drawing upon a novel source of subnational data on the Commanders Emergency Response Program (CERP) in Iraq, Berman et al. (2011) find that US assistance targeted to areas with high levels of expected violence was effective in reducing conflict. Adams (2014) produces similar estimates of the CERP's effectiveness in Afghanistan. Such assistance proved particularly effective when supplied in modest amounts (less than $50,000) and accompanied by the provision of technical expertise (Berman et al. 2011; Berman et al. 2013). In addition, evidence exists that the violence-reducing effect of CERP was amplified in communities benefiting from a stronger military presence, which suggests that more secure development projects are generally more successful development projects (Berman et al. 2013). Meanwhile, van der Windt and Humphreys (2014) find that development projects in the Democratic Republic of Congo that sought to adhere to the "do no harm" principle actually helped to curb violence.

Finally, a number of subnational studies have been conducted on the effectiveness of post-conflict aid programs that are explicitly designed to reduce the likelihood of relapse into conflict. Many of the results are encouraging. Campbell et al. (2014) designed an impact evaluation of UN Peacebuilding Fund (PBF) activities in Burundi from 2007–2013 by creating matched sets of rural settlements that are similar in many respects, but for the presence or absence of PBF activity. According to their analysis, PBFs substantially improved inter-group social cohesion among returning ex-combatants, IDPs, and their host communities. Likewise, Fearon et al. (2009) provide evidence from a randomized evaluation in Liberia that community-driven development projects can improve social cohesion. An important caveat is that these two studies do not assess the relationship of aid to conflict outcomes. Instead, the dependent variables in the analyses are intermediate factors that are believed to favorably influence conflict potential and dynamics. One study that explores conflict outcomes more directly is Blair et al. (2014). They demonstrate that mass education campaigns promoting the use of alternative dispute resolution institutions can reduce land disputes and violence, while at the same time inadvertently increasing non-violent interpersonal conflict.

Research Frontiers

The growing body of work described in this chapter has made significant progress in evaluating and demonstrating the conditional effects of various factors that shape the relationship between aid and conflict. Of particular note, recent, dramatic improvements in the availability of more complete, accurate, and granular data are being leveraged to provide fresh insights about the complex causal relationships between aid and conflict. Yet plenty of "low-hanging fruit" still remains and demands immediate attention.

First, researchers have begun to discover that detecting whether, when, and how different types of aid have differential impacts on various conflict outcomes is significantly easier when appropriate data are collected, categorized and analyzed. This effort is progressing, but remains seriously underdeveloped. The new empirical insights reviewed in this chapter are based on limited disaggregation of aid into very broad sectors. Expecting all of a given type of aid to have similar effects makes little theoretical sense. Meanwhile, the available data does not foreclose differentiation. Rather, studying sub-types of aid is feasible. For example, AidData's purpose and activity coding scheme permits disaggregation of the data well beyond the major types of aid (Tierney, et al. 2011). To date, however, few scholars have sought to use more highly disaggregated data in analysis of relationships between aid and conflict.[4] Further disaggregation of aid (and conflict) will potentially yield greater knowledge about conditional effects.

Second, a growing literature demonstrates that the channels through which aid is delivered (e.g., IGO, NGO, private firm, recipient government) can have an impact on the nature of both aid allocation and development outcomes (Dietrich 2013; Atkinson 2014; Reinhardt 2015), but only a small qualitative literature explores the impact of the delivery channel on conflict outcomes. For example, Tzifakis and Huliaras (2015) argue that outsourcing post-conflict aid projects to INGOs and private security companies leads to increased conflict compared to similar situations where the donor government implements the project. These findings rest primarily on case study analysis of the US and UK policies in the post-9/11 era. Systematic, large-N empirical research should be undertaken, capitalizing on new data, to establish the generality of such claims, which should help to explain how the channel of delivery or the implementing agent of an aid-funded development activity might shape conflict dynamics at the national or sub-national level (Dietrich 2013). This research is crucial because many of the hypotheses reviewed in this chapter rely upon assumptions about the ease with which aid can be used to increase support for the government, redirected for purposes not intended by the donor, or looted by rebel groups. The type of agent selected to administer an aid project can plausibly have a substantial effect on whether aid is effective, re-purposed, or misappropriated. Explorations of the links between these and other effects related to aid delivery and conflict behavior are only in the preliminary stages.

Third, in spite of dramatic improvements in the quantity, quality and scale of spatially disaggregated data on both aid and conflict events, few studies have attempted to capture spatial diffusion or contagion effects (Lyall, et al. 2013). Progress on this front has been slowed by the limited attention given to spatial-temporal causal inference models (Warren 2015). As data become available with more geographic density and at higher degrees of spatial precision (e.g., shifting from countries to latitude and longitude coordinates), the challenges become evident. In particular, assumptions of observational independence are rarely appropriate when analyzing spatial data, especially on neighboring localities. The workhorse tools of causal inference (e.g., difference-in-differences, propensity score matching, regression discontinuity) do well when there are no (or few) spatial contagion effects. At present, however, these tools are less well suited when spatial patterns must either be controlled for or modeled directly. Models that suitably account for spatial contagion represent an important methodological frontier for those who study the complex relationships between aid and conflict.

Fourth, the emergence of non-traditional aid donors has arguably re-shaped the global development regime and the geopolitical landscape in aid-receiving countries (Mawdsley et al. 2014), but these circumstances are not reflected in most existing research. Much of what we think we know about aid and conflict is derived from inferences about aid from OECD donors, because we have data on aid from OECD donors. Aid from non-Western donors has traditionally been overlooked in analyses. Concerns about such an omitted variable are mitigated to the extent that aid from non-Western donors is small. If, instead, aid from non-Western donors is increasing more rapidly than any other source on the planet, as recent evidence indicates, then empirical studies need to accommodate this fact. The consequences of doing so can be significant. As we discussed earlier, a key result of Findley et al. (2011), that sudden withdrawals of Western aid dramatically increase the probability of civil war in recipient countries, disappears for those countries receiving high levels of Chinese foreign aid (Strange et al. 2015). With aid from China and other non-traditional donors on the rise, collecting and analyzing data comparable to that for OECD donors (cross-national, time-series, disaggregated by sector, subnationally georeferenced) will be increasingly important. Consequently, the next generation of research on the relationship between aid and conflict will hinge on recent efforts to compile granular data on the location of non-traditional aid projects (Dreher et al. 2015).

The map in Figure 12.1 (see next page) illustrates the potential for subnational analyses that could compare the distribution of traditional Western aid to Chinese aid in the Democratic Republic of the Congo. A quick visual examination identifies differences. Western projects are frequently located in conflict zones, whereas Chinese projects are not. In addition, Western projects are numerous and small, while Chinese aid projects are fewer in number, but significantly larger. This particular map does not represent the sectoral distribution of aid. The associated data show, however, that Western aid funded humanitarian relief, health clinics, peace-building, refugee resettlement, and technical assistance, in contrast to the Chinese government funding infrastructure, transportation, and mineral extraction projects. Any inferences about "aid in general" drawn from either of these two samples alone would misrepresent the reality on the ground. If anyone still needs justification to improve the quality of data on non-traditional donors, compelling reasons are clearly revealed on this map.

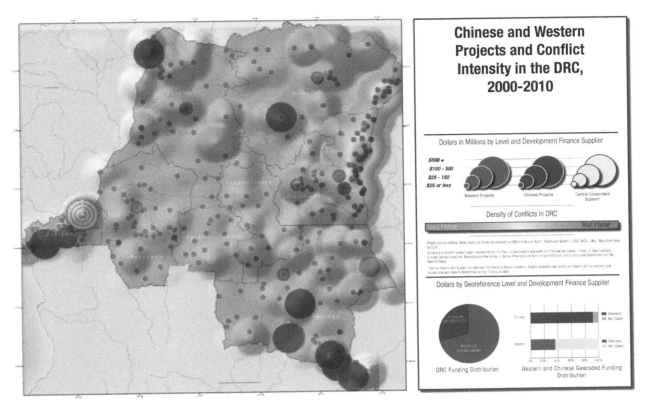

Figure 12.1 Chinese and Western Aid Projects and Conflict Intensity in the Democratic Republic of the Congo, 2000–2010
Source: AidData.

Notes

1 Dal Bó and Dal Bó (2011) find that the impact of an exogenous shock on conflict is mediated by whether the shock occurs in a capital-intensive or labor-intensive sector.
2 The authors are involved in a collaboration, based at the University of Maryland and funded by the Minerva Initiative of the US Department of Defense, to study the relationship between development aid and resilience to intrastate armed conflict.
3 Dube and Naidu (2014) find that military assistance increases political violence by paramilitary groups in Colombia.
4 For exceptions, see Young and Findley (2011) and Ziaja (2013).

References

Adam, Christopher, Paul Collier, and Victor A.B. Davies. 2008. "Postconflict Monetary Reconstruction." *World Bank Economic Review* (22)1: 87–112.
Adams, Greg. 2014. "Conflict of Interest: Military-Led Development Insights from Afghanistan for Warfighters, Development Practitioners, and Policy Makers." MPA Thesis. Cambridge, MA: Harvard University.
Anderson, Mary B. 1999. *Do No Harm: How Aid can Support Peace – or War*. Boulder, CO: Lynne Rienner Publishers.
Anderson, Mary B. 2000. "Aid: A Mixed blessing." *Development in Practice* 10(3–4).
Atkinson, James E. 2014. "Signals, Channels, and Political Connections in Government Disaster Response." PhD Dissertation. University of Michigan.
Azam, Jean-Paul. 1995. "How to Pay for Peace? A Theoretical Framework with References to African Countries." *Public Choice* 83 (1–2): 173–184.
Azam, Jean-Paul, and Alexandra Delacroix. 2006. "Aid and the Delegated Fight against Terrorism." *Review of Development Economics* 10(2): 330–344.
Azam, Jean-Paul, and Alice Mesnard. 2003. "Civil War and the Social Contract." *Public Choice* 115(3–4): 455–475.
Beath, Andrew, Fotini Christia, and Ruben Erikolopov. 2013. "Randomized Impact Evaluation of Afghanistan's National Solidarity Programme." World Bank Other Operational Studies no. 16637. The World Bank.
Berman, Eli, Jacob N. Shapiro, and Joseph Felter. 2011. "Can Hearts and Minds Be Bought? The Economics of Counterinsurgency in Iraq." *Journal of Political Economy* 119: 766–819.
Berman, Eli, Michael Callen, Joseph H. Felter, and Jacob N. Shapiro. 2011. "Do Working Men Rebel? Insurgency and Unemployment in Afghanistan, Iraq, and the Philippines." *Journal of Conflict Resolution* 55(4): 496–528.
Berman, Eli, Joseph H. Felter, Jacob N. Shapiro, and Erin Troland. 2013. "Modest, Secure, and Informed: Successful Development in Conflict Zones." *American Economic Review* 103(3): 512–517.

Blair, Rob, Christopher Blattman, and Alexandra Hartman. 2014. "How to Promote Order and Property Rights under Weak Rule of Law? An Experiment in Changing Dispute Resolution Behavior through Community Education." *American Political Science Review* 108(1): 100–120.

Blattman, Christopher, and Edward Miguel. 2010. "Civil War." *Journal of Economic Literature* 48(1): 3–57.

Campbell, Susanna, Tracy Dexter, Michael Findley, Stephanie Hofmann, Josiah Marineau, and Daniel Walker. 2014. "Independent External Evaluation: UN Peacebuilding Fund: Project Portfolio in Burundi." United Nations Peace Building Fund.

Cerra, Valerie, and Sweta Chaman Saxena. 2008. "Growth Dynamics: The Myth of Economic Recovery." *American Economic Review* 98(1): 439–457.

Collier, Paul. 2009. "Post-Conflict Recovery: How Should Strategies Be Distinctive?" *Journal of African Economies* 18(1): i99–i131.

Collier, Paul, and Anke Hoeffler. 2002. "AID, Policy and Peace: Reducing the Risks of Civil Conflict." *Defence and Peace Economics* 13(6): 435–450.

Collier, Paul, and Anke Hoeffler. 2004. "Aid, Policy and Growth in Post-Conflict Societies." *European Economic Review* 48(5): 1125–1145.

Collier, Paul, and Anke Hoeffler. 2007. "Unintended Consequences: Does Aid Promote Arms Races?" *Oxford Bulletin of Economics and Statistics* 69: 1–28.

Collier, Paul, Anke Hoeffler, and Måns Söderbom. 2008. "Post-Conflict Risks." *Journal of Peace Research* 45(4): 461–478.

Crost, Benjamin, Joseph Felter, and Patrick Johnston. 2014. "Aid under Fire: Development Projects and Civil Conflict." *American Economic Review* 104(6): 1833–1856.

Dal Bó, E., and P. Dal Bó. 2011. "Workers, Warriors, and Criminals: Social Conflict in General Equilibrium." *Journal of the European Economic Association* 9(4): 646–677.

de Ree, Joppe, and Eleonora Nillesen. 2009. "Aiding Violence or Peace? The Impact of Foreign Aid on the Risk of Civil Conflict in Sub-Saharan Africa." *Journal of Development Economics* 88: 301–313.

De Waal, Alex. 1994. "Dangerous Precedents? Famine Relief in Somalia, 1991–1993." In J. Macrae and A. Zwi (eds). *War and Hunger: Rethinking International Responses to Complex Emergencies*. London: Save the Children and Zed Books.

De Waal, Alex. 1997. *Famine Crimes: Politics and the Disaster Relief Industry in Africa*. London: African Rights & the International African Institute in association with Oxford: James Currey, and Bloomington: Indiana University Press.

Dietrich, Simone. 2013. "Bypass or Engage? Explaining Donor Delivery Tactics in Foreign Aid Allocation." *International Studies Quarterly* 57(4): 698–712.

Dreher, Axel, Andreas Fuchs, Roland Hodler, Bradley Parks, Paul Raschky, and Michael J. Tierney. 2015. "Aid on Demand: African Leaders and the Geography of China's Foreign Assistance." CESifo Working Paper no. 5439, July 2015.

Dube, Oeindrila, and Suresh Naidu. 2014. "Bases, Bullets and Ballots: The Effect of US Military Aid on Political Conflict in Colombia." National Bureau of Economic Research, Working Paper no. 20213.

Duponchel, M. 2008. "Can Aid Break the Conflict Trap?" Mimeo.

Elbadawi, Ibrahim A., Linda Kaltani, and Klaus Schmidt-Hebbel. 2008. "Foreign Aid, the Real Exchange Rate, and Economic Growth in the Aftermath of Civil Wars." *The World Bank Economic Review* 22(1): 113–140.

Fast, Larissa. 2014. *Aid in Danger: The Perils and Promise of Humanitarianism*. Philadelphia: University of Pennsylvania Press.

Fearon, James D. 2004. "Why Do Some Civil Wars Last So Much Longer Than Others?" *Journal of Peace Research* 41(3): 275–303.

Fearon, James D., Macartan Humphreys, and Jeremy M. Weinstein. 2009. "Can Development Aid Contribute to Social Cohesion after Civil War? Evidence from a Field Experiment in Post-Conflict Liberia." *American Economic Review* 99(2): 287–291.

Felter, Joseph H., Benjamin Crost, and Patrick Johnston. 2013. "Conditional Cash Transfers, Civil Conflict and Insurgent Influence: Experimental Evidence from the Philippines." Unpublished paper.

Findley, Michael G., Josh Powell, Daniel Strandow, and Jeff Tanner. 2011. "The Localized Geography of Foreign Aid: A New Dataset and Application to Violent Armed Conflict." *World Development* 39(11): 1995–2009.

Girod, Desha M. 2012. "Effective Foreign Aid Following Civil War: The Nonstrategic-Desperation Hypothesis." *American Journal of Political Science* 56(1): 188–201.

Grossman, Hershel. 1992. "Foreign Aid and Insurrection". *Defence Economics* 3: 275–288.

Gutting, Raynee S., and Martin C. Steinwand. 2015. "Donor Fragmentation, Aid Shocks and Violent Political Conflict." *Journal of Conflict Resolution*, August 10. doi: 10.1177/0022002715595701.

Iyengar, Radha, Jonathan Monten, and Matthew Hanson. 2011. "Building Peace: The Impact of Aid on the Labor Market for Insurgents." National Bureau of Economic Research, Working Paper no. 17297.

Jok, Jok Madut. 1999. "Militarization and Gender Violence in Southern Sudan." *Journal of Asian and African Studies* 34: 427–442.

Kenyon Lischer, Sarah. 2005. *Dangerous Sanctuaries, Refugee Camps, Civil War, and the Dilemmas of Humanitarian Aid*. Ithaca, NY: Cornell University Press.

Kevlihan, Rob. 2013. *Aid, Insurgencies and Conflict Transformation: When Greed is Good*. London: Routledge.

Lis, Piotr. 2014. "Terrorism, Armed Conflict and Foreign Aid." *Peace Economics, Peace Science and Public Policy* 20(4): 655–667.

Lyall, Jason, Graeme Blair, and Kosuke Imai. 2013. "Explaining Support for Combatants during Wartime: A Survey Experiment in Afghanistan." *American Political Science Review* 107(4): 679–705.

Mawdsley, Emma, Laura Savage, and Sung-Mi Kim. 2014. "A 'Post-Aid World'? Paradigm Shift in Foreign Aid and Development Cooperation at the 2011 Busan High Level Forum." *Geographical Journal* 180: 27–38.

Miguel, Edward, Shanker Satyanath, and Ernest Sergenti. 2004. "Economic Shocks and Civil Conflict: An Instrumental Variables Approach." *Journal of Political Economy* 112(4): 725–753.

Narang, Neil. 2014. "Humanitarian Assistance and the Duration of Peace after Civil War." *Journal of Politics* 76(2): 446–460.

Narang, Neil. 2015. "Assisting Uncertainty: How Humanitarian Aid Can Inadvertently Prolong Civil War." *International Studies Quarterly* 59(1): 184–195.

Nielsen, Richard A., Michael G. Findley, Zachary S. Davis, Tara Candland, and Daniel L. Nielson. 2011. "Foreign Aid Shocks as a Cause of Violent Armed Conflict." *American Journal of Political Science* 55: 219–232.

Nunn, Nathan, and Nancy Qian. 2014. "US Food Aid and Civil Conflict." *American Economic Review* 104(6): 1630–1666.

Omaar, Rakiya, and Alexander de Waal. 1994. *Rwanda: Death, Despair, Defiance*. African Rights.

Reinhardt, Gina. 2015. *Brands and Bypass: Getting Aid Donors What They Want*. College Station: Texas A&M University.

Savun, Burcu, and Daniel C. Tirone. 2011. "Foreign Aid, Democratization, and Civil Conflict: How Does Democracy Aid Affect Civil Conflict?" *American Journal of Political Science* 55(2): 233–246.

Savun, Burcu, and Daniel C. Tirone. 2012. "Exogenous Shocks, Foreign Aid, and Civil War." *International Organization* 66: 363–393.

Sollenberg, Margareta. 2012. "A Scramble for Rents: Foreign Aid and Armed Conflict." Dissertation. Uppsala University. Retrieved from http://uu.diva-portal.org/smash/record.jsf?searchId=1&pid=diva2:512.

Strandow, Daniel, Michael G. Findley, and Joseph K. Young. 2014. "Foreign Aid and the Intensity of Violent Armed Conflict." Unpublished working paper.

Strange, Austin, Axel Dreher, Andreas Fuchs, Bradley Parks and Michael J. Tierney. 2015. "Tracking Under-Reported Financial Flows: China's Development Finance and the Aid-Conflict Nexus Revisited." *Journal of Conflict Resolution*, September 20. doi: 10.1177/0022002715604363.

Tzifakis, Nikolaos, and Asteris Huliaras. 2015. "The Perils of Outsourcing Post-Conflict Reconstruction: Donor Countries, International NGOs and Private Military and Security Companies." *Conflict, Security and Development* 15(1): 51–73.

Van der Windt, Peter, and Macartan Humphreys. 2014. "Crowdseeding in Eastern Congo: Using Cell Phones to Collect Conflict Events Data in Real Time." *Journal of Conflict Resolution*, November 4. doi:10.1177/0022002714553104.

Walter, B. 2010. "Conflict Relapse and the Sustainability of Post-Conflict Peace." Background Paper for the World Development Report 2011.

Warren, T. Camber. 2015. "Explosive Connections? Mass Media, Social Media, and the Geography of Collective Violence in African States." *Journal of Peace Research* 52(3): 297–311.

Weezel, Stijn Van. 2015. "A Spatial Analysis of the Effect of Foreign Aid in Conflict Areas." AidData Working Paper no. 8. Williamsburg, VA: AidData.

Wood, Reed, and Christopher Sullivan. 2015. "Doing Harm by Doing Good? The Negative Externalities of Humanitarian Aid Provision during Civil Conflict." *Journal of Politics* 77(3): 736–748.

World Bank. 2011. *World Development Report 2011: Conflict, Security, and Development*. Washington, DC: The World Bank.

Young, Joseph K., and Michael G. Findley. 2011. "Can Peace Be Purchased? A Sectoral-Level Analysis of Aid's Influence on Transnational Terrorism." *Public Choice* 149: 365–381.

Ziaja, S. 2013. "Fuel or Water to the Fire? Democracy Aid and Political Instability." Paper prepared for the CRS/ENCoRe conference.

13

The Peace and Conflict Instability Ledger

Ranking States on Future Risks

David A. Backer and Paul K. Huth

Introduction

This chapter presents the latest results of the Peace and Conflict Instability Ledger. The focus of the analysis is the ranking of countries around the world according to their estimated risk of experiencing significant bouts of political instability during the three-year period of 2014–2016. Those risk estimates are obtained using a statistical forecasting model, developed based on historical data. The statistical model confirms strong correlations between the onset of instability and several factors. The most current data available for these factors, from the individual countries, are plugged into the forecasting model, yielding projections of the risk that they face in the future. Once again, the findings illuminate a concentration of serious vulnerabilities in Sub-Saharan Africa and South Asia. Awareness of these risks, as well as where they worsened and improved, is an important resource in conflict preparedness and management.

Methodology

The Ledger represents a synthesis of leading research on conceptualizing, explaining, and forecasting political instability. The definition of instability established by the Political Instability Task Force (PITF) is employed.[1] This definition guided the PITF's compilation of state failure events during 1955–2006, which encompass a wide variety of types, including adverse regime changes, revolutionary wars, ethnic wars, genocides and politicides. While the set of events is heterogeneous, they share a fundamental similarity: their onset signals the arrival of a period in which government's capacity to deliver core services and to exercise meaningful authority has been disrupted, threatening its overall stability.

The specification of the Ledger's forecasting model involved identifying risk factors for instability on which agreement about their relative importance was consistent among researchers. Empirical studies demonstrate historical associations between instability and five risk factors in four domains of government and society that comprise the forecasting model.[2] Table 13.1 (see next page) provides a brief overview of the theoretical relationship between each of these factors and the risk of instability. A fuller discussion is given in an earlier edition of *Peace and Conflict* (Hewitt 2008).

Leveraging these relationships, the Ledger uses results from a statistical model to obtain risk scores for all 165 countries with a population of at least 500,000 in 2013. This analysis employs annual observations for each country for every year that data exist for all five risk factors. Each observation records whether a given country experienced an onset of instability in any of the subsequent three years. The data can thereby be analyzed to assess the empirical relationship between the five factors and the risk of future instability. To maintain comparability with the results presented in past editions of *Peace and Conflict*, we continue to estimate the model using "training data" from 1950–2003. The logistic regression procedure produces weights for the five factors that reflect the relative influence each has on explaining future instability. For the updated Ledger, we then apply the weights to 2013 data – the last year for which complete data are available for all five factors – to produce a forecast indicating the risk of instability at any time during the period 2014–2016. In the absence of significant change to any of the five factors, risks change only gradually from year to year. Therefore, a high-risk country that experiences no major structural or institutional changes to its regime, socioeconomic status, or security situation in the period 2014–2016 will likely remain at high risk during and beyond this forecast period.

The full listing of results for all 165 countries is presented in the appendix at the end of the chapter (see Table 13.5). The tabulation includes an indication of the performance of each country on each of the risk factors, which enables a

Factor	Domain	Description
Institutional Consistency	Political	Institutional consistency refers to the extent to which the institutions comprising a country's political system are uniformly and consistently autocratic or democratic. Political institutions with a mix of democratic and autocratic features are inconsistent, a common attribute of polities in the midst of a democratic transition. Based on a series of findings reported in the academic literature, we expect regimes with inconsistent institutes to be more likely to experience political instability (Gurr 1974; Gates, et al. 2006; Hegre, et al. 2001)
Economic Openness	Economic	Economic openness is a gauge of the extent to which a country's economy is integrated with the global economy. Countries that are more tightly connected to global markets have been found to experience less instability (Hegre, et al. 2003; Goldstone, et al. 2000).
Infant Mortality Rates	Economic and Social	The infant mortality rates serve as a proxy for a country's overall economic development, its level of advancement in social welfare policy, and its capacity to deliver core services to the population. In this respect, this indicator taps into both the economic and social domains of a country. Research findings reported by the PITF have been especially notable for the strong relationship found between high infant mortality rates and the likelihood of future instability (Esty, et al. 1999; Goldstone et al. 2005).
Militarization	Security	Instability is most likely in countries where the opportunities for armed conflict are greatest. When the infrastructure and capital for organized armed conflict are more plentiful and accessible, the likelihood for civil conflict increases (Collier and Hoeffler 2004). Extensive militarization in a country typically implies that a large portion of the society's population has military skill and training, weapons stocks are more wisely available, and other pieces of military equipment are more diffused throughout the country. the likelihood of instability is greater in this setting because increased access to and availability of these resources multiplies the opportunities for organizing and mobilizing.
Neighborhood Security	Security	The likelihood of political instability in a state increases substantially when a neighboring state is currently experiencing armed conflict. This risk is especially acute when ethnic or other communal groups span across borders. A number of studies have shown that neighborhood conflict is a significant predictor of political instability (Sambanis 2001; Hegre and Sambanis 2006; Goldstone, et al. 2005).

Table 13.1 Factors in Model of the Risk of Large-Scale Instability Events

quick assessment of how these indicators relate to the ultimate risk estimates. In this fashion, the full Ledger table also serves as a diagnostic tool, offering information about all countries so that comparisons can be drawn about how the levels of each factor influence risk.

To ease interpretation of the results, the Ledger presents each country's likelihood of future instability as a risk ratio. The risk ratio gives the relative risk of instability in a country compared to the average estimated likelihood of instability for the members of the Organization for Economic Cooperation and Development (OECD). The OECD supplies a worthwhile baseline because its membership is widely viewed to contain the most stable countries in the world. To illustrate, Bangladesh's estimated probability of experiencing instability in the next three years is 0.090, which yields a relative risk ratio of 12.0 given that the average estimated probability of OECD countries experiencing an instability event during the 2014–2016 period is 0.0075. The analysis indicates that Bangladesh's risk of instability is about 12 times that of the OECD.

The risk ratios are estimated with varying levels of confidence, depending on the particular attributes of a given country. This is a standard, but underappreciated, aspect of statistical inferences. For example, in the historical analysis underlying the Ledger, infant mortality rates were found to be positively related to the onset of instability. The level of uncertainty for that estimate was sufficiently small to rule out the possibility that the model was pointing erroneously to a positive relationship when the "true" relationship was actually negative (or nonexistent). Yet uncertainty around the estimate remains. The uncertainty exists because certain countries with high infant mortality rates have not experienced instability (e.g., Malawi, Saudi Arabia, or Bolivia), while certain countries with a low rate of infant mortality have experienced instability (e.g., Israel). These cases that deviate from the normal pattern introduce "noise" in the estimated relationship between instability and infant mortality rates. This kind of uncertainty accompanies each of the estimates for the variables in the model. Based on the results of the analysis, the amount of uncertainty surrounding the estimate of instability risk for an individual country can be computed. The Ledger reports a single best estimate of the overall risk of instability for each country. In addition, the Ledger reports the level of uncertainty, in terms of a confidence range of values within which the best estimate lies. Statistically speaking, the "true" risk of instability lies within this range with a 95 percent probability.

Countries are assigned to different risk categories, according to the procedure described in Box 13.1. This procedure establishes meaningful risk categories. Within a given category, a solid empirical basis exists to indicate that the identified states are comparable in terms of risk. Meanwhile, states assigned to different categories are expected to face distinct levels of risk. In particular, states in lower-risk categories are unlikely to have a true risk in excess of that of countries assigned to higher-risk categories. The graphical display of the confidence range shows how it extends across risk categories. For some countries, the range is confined largely or entirely within one category. For other countries, large segments of the range extend across multiple categories, which suggests that assessments of these countries' risk of instability should be more cautious.

Box 13.1 Classification of Countries into Risk Categories

Information about the risk scores and the confidence ranges are the basis of the classification of countries into separate risk categories, using the following approach:

- The list of 165 countries is sorted from highest to lowest risk scores.

- The country with the highest risk score (Somalia) anchors the first group of countries.

- Moving down the list, any country for which the upper bound on its confidence range is higher than Somalia's risk score of 28.6 is assigned to the same group as Somalia. Such an overlap indicates that there is little difference in these countries' respective risk scores

- The initial country on the list with an upper bound on its confidence range that is less than Somalia's score begins a new group. In this instance of the Ledger, the country is Pakistan.

- Moving further down the list, any country with an upper bound greater than Pakistan's risk score of 19.3 would be grouped with Pakistan.

- The first two groups are combined to form the "highest risk" category.

- Moving down the list in a similar manner, the third group of states (beginning with Guinea-Bissau) will be assigned to the "high risk" category, the fourth group (beginning with Namibia) makes up the "moderate risk" category, the fifth group (beginning with Guatemala) makes up the "some risk" category, and all remaining countries are assigned to the "low risk" category.

- The risk score for the last country in a category serves as a threshold for characterizing the portion of a confidence range that falls into that category. For example, the last country in the highest risk category, Chad, has a risk score of 12.9. Therefore, a confidence range that spans 12.9 falls into multiple categories.

This approach allows for clearer delineation of categories, relying on the statistical estimates.

Like any statistical model, the Ledger is not a perfect prediction tool. Yet empirical evidence demonstrates that it is relatively reliable: for every several cases the analysis forecasts correctly, one is forecast incorrectly. Only a share of these incorrect forecasts will be false negatives: instances of instability in places not anticipated by applying the results of the model. Events that are unusual – unprecedented, some might argue – will be among these anomalies.

For instance, *Peace and Conflict 2014* discussed the events that came to be known as the Arab Spring – a wave of mass protests, beginning in early 2011, that affected multiple countries in both North Africa (Egypt, Libya, Tunisia) and the Middle East (Bahrain, Jordan, Syria, Yemen). The fact that these events occurred at all, especially on such a scale within and across countries, and advanced as far as they did, even resulting in political transitions in several cases, came as a surprise to many, not least those used to long-standing, entrenched autocratic regimes across the region. In other words, the countries were not generally forecast to be places of significant upheaval, including by the Peace and Conflict Instability Ledger (Hewitt 2012). Part of the explanation is that this analysis of risk focuses on the prospects of instability at a level beyond what has been observed in most of the aforementioned countries. The projections of the Ledger were admittedly inaccurate in the cases of Libya and Syria, both of which descended into full-scale civil war. Neither of these countries conformed to the historic tendencies exhibited by most consolidated autocracies, where such devastating conflict is actually outside the norm. Elsewhere in the region, circumstances have been consistent with expectations. There has been serious turmoil, without bringing about the wholesale collapse of governments and the complete disruption of the provision of basic services, the risk of which is what the Ledger was specifically designed to gauge.

Thus, we continue to maintain confidence in the Ledger. At the same time, we acknowledge the need for and continue to explore ways of improving the reliability of forecasting instability.

Results

Figure 13.1 shows how the countries in the analysis were classified according to their estimated risk scores, corresponding to the full results presented in the appendix. A quick glance at the map offers an overview of the geographic landscape of the risk of instability. Africa remains the most serious concern. Of the 46 African countries covered in the Ledger, 29 (63 percent) qualify for either the high or highest risk category. Of the countries worldwide in those categories, African countries comprise 76 percent (29 of 38). A similar concentration of states qualifying at high or highest risk exists in South Asia, a grouping that contains Afghanistan and Pakistan, which are pivotal because their situations can have direct repercussions for global trends in terrorism.

Table 13.2 (see next page) lists the countries with the top 25 risk scores. Since the publication of *Peace and Conflict 2014*, this group has undergone some changes. Five countries (Bhutan, Gabon, Nepal, South Sudan, Timor-Leste) have dropped out of the top 25. Other countries have taken their place (Angola, Papua New Guinea, Sudan, Zambia, Zimbabwe). Both sets of countries were split between Africa and Asia. The net effect leaves 19 African countries in the top 25 listing, an increase from the 17 reported in *Peace and Conflict 2014*, but the same as reported in *Peace and Conflict 2012*. As recently as 2010, however, 22 African countries were in the top 25. Thus, the uptick is notable, but not necessarily cause for alarm, especially given the values for underlying risk factors are subject to fluctuation from year to year.

The risk scores among countries that were previously in the highest or high risk categories generally declined, though the difference is modest. According to *Peace and Conflict 2014*, 46 countries were classified in those two categories, and these countries had an average risk score of 13.0. In the latest estimates, the average for the same set of countries is 12.7.

Equally important, this result does not mean that all the underlying factors improved in all the countries. Instead, there is fluctuation in both unfavorable and favorable directions over time. Some countries experienced shifting political situations that greatly amplified the risk of instability. For example, nine countries faced neighborhood conflicts that were not present just two years prior. Also, Somalia gained partial democratic status to accompany irregular institutions. Elsewhere, evolving circumstances substantially lowered the risk of instability. In particular, the neighborhood conflict that confronted Guinea-Bissau dropped below the threshold level in 2013. As a broader backdrop, improving conditions were prevalent and often coincided among the set of at-risk countries. In 45 of the 46 countries, infant mortality rates dropped, demonstrating developmental progress. Also, 42 of the countries reduced their levels of militarization and 16 countries exhibited increased economic openness.

Figure 13.1 Risk of Large-Scale Instability Events in 2014–2016, by Country

Rank	Country	Risk Score
1	Somalia	28.6
2	Afghanistan	27.1
3	Djibouti	21.6
4	Congo, Dem. Rep.	21.4
5	Mali	19.8
6	Pakistan	19.3
7	Nigeria	18.8
8	Côte d'Ivoire	18.6
9	Guinea	17.7
10	Burundi	16.9
11	Zimbabwe*	16.4
12	Sierra Leone	15.7
13	Niger	15.2
14	Central African Republic	14.9
15	Angola*	14.0
16	Benin	13.8
17	Haiti	13.6
18	Mozambique	13.3
19	Chad	12.9
20	Guinea-Bissau	12.5
21	Zambia*	12.3
22	Bangladesh	12.0
23	Papua New Guinea*	11.8
24	Sudan*	11.1
25	Iraq	11.0

Table 13.2 Top 25 Countries in Estimated Risk of Instability, 2014–2016
Note: * New to the top 25 in the most recent rankings.

In sum, looking back at the set of countries that qualified in either of the top two risk categories from *Peace and Conflict 2014*, the picture is mixed, yet has cause for optimism. Despite the worsening of the security environment in a significant number of cases, there was a general trend toward less militarization within risk-prone countries. Regression toward more autocratic practices was rare. Pervasive gains in the social and economic domains present another positive sign.

To appreciate how changing circumstances can influence risk estimates, consider the countries that experienced significant change over the last five years. Table 13.3 (see next page) lists the 10 countries with the largest increases in risk scores over the past five years. The first row for each country presents the estimated risk score for the forecast period of 2009–2011, generated based on 2008 data. The second row for each country presents the latest risk score for the 2014–2016 forecast period.

In many of the cases, the increase in risk can be traced to a single factor: a transition to more democratic governance that led to classification as a partial democracy. Among the 10 countries that experienced the greatest increase in risk over the past five years, nine were classified as partial democracies according to 2013 data, including six that were not in this

Forecast Period	Country	Risk Ratio	Net Change	Regime Consistency	Partial Democracy	Infant Mortality	Economic Openness	Militarization	Neighborhood War
2009–11	Zimbabwe	5.7		16	✗	58	110%	399	✗
2014–16		16.4	10.6	16	✓	55	86%	359	✓
2009–11	Côte d'Ivoire	8.5		0	✗	81	87%	104	✗
2014–16		18.6	10.1	16	✓	71	91%	82	✓
2009–11	Somalia	18.6		0	✗	102	19%	80	✓
2014–16		28.6	10.1	25	✓	90	19%	105	✓
2009–11	Bangladesh	2.7		36	✗	43	43%	149	✓
2014–16		12.0	9.3	16	✓	33	46%	141	✓
2009–11	Guinea	8.5		1	✗	77	75%	184	✗
2014–16		17.7	9.2	16	✓	65	83%	105	✓
2009–11	Gabon	2.2		16	✗	46	91%	472	✗
2014–16		9.9	7.7	9	✓	39	94%	401	✗
2009–11	Sudan	4.1		16	✗	58	44%	373	✓
2014–16		11.1	7.0	4	✗	51	26%	696	✓
2009–11	Afghanistan	24.7		0	✗	79	73%	348	✓
2014–16		27.1	2.4	0	✓	70	55%	1082	✓
2009–11	Senegal	9.0		49	✗	50	79%	155	✗
2014–16		10.5	1.5	49	✓	44	74%	132	✓
2009–11	Benin	12.4		49	✗	66	47%	89	✗
2014–16		13.8	1.4	49	✓	56	52%	92	✓

Table 13.3 Largest Five-Year Increases in the Risk of Instability Events

Notes: Infant mortality represents deaths per 1,000 live births. Economic openness column refers to the percentage of a country's GDP accounted for by the value of its imports plus exports. Militarization refers to the number of active military personnel per 100,000 people. The symbol ✓ means "yes" and the symbol X means "no."

position five years prior. The degree of democratization is a welcome development because it brings more desirable qualities to governance (e.g., greater citizen participation, broader competition for leadership positions, and more expansive civil liberties). For many observers, though, the heightened dangers of instability during this period are often underappreciated. Partial democracies are at greater risk for instability than autocracies or full democracies. Repressive tactics adopted by autocratic governments often smother the potential for significant political instability. Coherent and mature democracies possess the capacity to address group grievances and manage the competition between groups that vie for political power and other resources, thereby reducing the risks of instability. Partial democracies typically possess neither the qualities of full autocracies nor those of democracies, leaving them more vulnerable to the drivers of instability (Gates et al. 2000; Hegre et al. 2001; Fearon and Laitin 2003; Pate 2008). Indeed, the historical data over the past half-century show a strong empirical relationship between partial democracy and the future onset of instability.

Another major factor for these countries with the greatest increases in instability risk was the external security environment. According to the 2013 data, nine of the ten countries were exposed to war in a neighboring country, whereas just four were in this position as of 2008. Every instance where the external security environment worsened compounded the effects of political changes observed domestically that were unfavourable in terms of instability risk.

Table 13.4 presents a list of five countries that showed the largest improvement in relative risk scores, based on a comparison of forecasts for 2014–2016 to those for 2009–2011. Most of these countries were partial democracies before. Only Guinea-Bissau experienced a shift away from this status, which had the effect of reducing the risk of instability relative to before. All made advances in social development and reductions in militarization. The extent of economic openness actually decreased in most of these countries, which is unfavorable in terms of risk. Changes in the external security environment only made a difference to risk estimates in the case of Nigeria.

Conclusion

The latest risk estimates from the Peace and Conflict Instability Ledger offer some positive news for the set of countries most vulnerable to conflict or instability. Average levels of risk have declined across the set of countries qualifying as highest or high risk. Certain of the factors that heighten risks – such as, partial democratic transitions and significant worsening of socioeconomic conditions – were largely absent in the world's most vulnerable states. In fact, improvements

Forecast Period	Country	Risk Ratio	Net Change	Regime Consistency	Partial Democracy	Infant Mortality	Economic Openness	Militarization	Neighborhood War
2009–11	Guinea-Bissau	22.3		36	✓	89	19%	396	✗
2014–16		12.5	−9.8	1	✗	78	17%	378	✗
2009–11	Iraq	16.8		0	✓	31	81%	1961	✓
2014–16		11.0	−5.7	9	✓	28	67%	531	✓
2009–11	Pakistan	24.5		25	✓	76	36%	551	✓
2014–16		19.3	−5.2	49	✓	69	33%	520	✓
2009–11	Sierra Leone	20.8		49	✓	120	39%	199	✗
2014–16		15.7	−5.2	49	✓	107	108%	172	✗
2009–11	Nigeria	23.5		16	✓	88	65%	107	✓
2014–16		18.8	−4.7	16	✓	74	31%	93	✗

Table 13.4 Largest Five-Year Decreases in the Risk of Instability Events
Notes: Infant mortality represents deaths per 1,000 live births. Economic openness column refers to the percentage of a country's GDP accounted for by the value of its imports plus exports. Militarization refers to the number of active military personnel per 100,000 people. The symbol ✓ means "yes" and the symbol X means "no."

in socioeconomic conditions and reductions in the extent of militarization were commonplace, in some cases helping to offset increased vulnerabilities in other areas, such as the emergence of neighborhood conflict.

These findings have important implications for the notable hotspots of instability around the world, including the countries experiencing turmoil, violence, and in certain instances political change as a result of the Arab Spring, as well as many others in Africa and South Asia. In these settings, the hope that accompanies the removal of long-standing autocratic regimes should be tempered by a recognition of the challenges ahead. The early stages of any democratic reforms should be monitored closely because the dangers for observing significant instability events will be especially high – Egypt is a clear example. The historical evidence indicates that two types of political change can lower this risk. One is a return to strong autocratic rule. The ability to maintain stability is often advanced as a justification for intrusions on democracy, as with the Egyptian military deposing President Morsi. Of course, this change has been accompanied by considerable violence, which might only die down as the result of the military tightening its grip. Additional examples from the Middle East and North Africa (e.g., Syria) demonstrate that even strong autocratic regimes do not always inoculate countries against major instability such as civil war. Instead, the other political change that tends to reduce the risk of instability in a more robust and sustainable manner is continuing a trajectory towards full-fledged democracy. Reaching that point is hard, however, if key actors prove unwilling to countenance electoral competition with the legitimate prospect for alternation of power, as well as protections of rights, tolerance, inclusiveness, participation, accountability, and the other hallmarks of democracy. Libya presents a conspicuous example of these challenges. The analysis also emphasizes that other ways exist of mitigating the risks of instability, which may help to offset negative circumstances or sluggish performance on the political front. In particular, it is vital to enhance the delivery of core social services (health, education, etc.), economic benefits (jobs, trade, infrastructure development, etc.), and security (demilitarization, reduction in crime). Doing so will enhance the likelihood that a government is viewed as legitimate, reducing the chances of popular upheaval, intergroup antagonism, and armed rebellion.

Ultimately, the key to effective policy responses to heightened risks of instability depends heavily on an ability to trace back from the estimate to the particular factors that exert the most influence on it. The Peace and Conflict Instability Ledger places an emphasis on making information about the risk estimates as accessible and interpretable as possible, so that diagnosing the foundations of these risks can be more effective. Moreover, by explicitly reporting confidence ranges associated with each country estimate, the Ledger offers policymakers enhanced leverage for making more confident assertions about the substantive importance of any year-to-year change observed in a particular country, which is crucial for making precise assessments about progress in at-risk countries. This chapter suggests how information from the Ledger can be used to help clarify risk trends in a particular country. Employed alongside the detailed information available to country experts, the Ledger can be a powerful tool in any policy maker's toolkit for assessing risk levels across countries.

Appendix

Table 13.5 presents the detailed results of the Peace and Conflict Instability Ledger. The notes provide a description of the information in the table, including the color codes.

Regional Rank 2016	Regional Rank 2014	Country	Regime Consistency	Partial Democracy	Infant Mortality	Economic Openness	Militarization	Neighborhood War	Risk Category	Risk Score	Confidence Range		Active Armed Conflict in 2014
Sub-Saharan Africa												
1	6	Somalia								28.6	21.2 - 36.7		✓
2	2	Djibouti								21.6	12.9 - 33.2		
3	5	Congo, Dem. Rep.								21.4	13.4 - 31.8		✓
4	8	Mali								19.8	12.8 - 29.0		✓
5	13	Nigeria								18.8	13.3 - 26.0		✓
6	10	Cote d'Ivoire								18.6	11.3 - 28.3		
7	3	Guinea								17.7	10.9 - 26.5		
8	4	Burundi								16.9	11.7 - 23.1		
9	22	Zimbabwe								16.4	10.2 - 24.8		
10	9	Sierra Leone								15.7	8.4 - 26.2		
11	7	Niger								15.2	9.5 - 22.0		
12	11	Central African Rep.								14.9	8.8 - 23.5		
13	32	Angola								14.0	7.5 - 22.9		
14	16	Benin								13.8	9.0 - 20.0		
15	14	Mozambique								13.3	8.4 - 19.7		
16	15	Chad								12.9	7.1 - 20.8		
17	1	Guinea-Bissau								12.5	8.3 - 18.0		
18	27	Zambia								12.3	7.5 - 18.4		✓
19	18	Sudan								11.1	7.0 - 16.3		
20	23	Malawi								10.5	6.1 - 17.0		
21	26	Senegal								10.5	6.4 - 15.7		
22	24	Burkina Faso								10.1	5.8 - 16.3		
23	17	Gabon								9.9	5.7 - 15.7		
24	20	Kenya								9.6	5.7 - 15.0		
25	28	Lesotho								9.5	4.8 - 16.4		
26	19	Liberia								9.5	5.5 - 14.9		
27	29	Cameroon								8.8	5.2 - 13.6		
28	34	Ghana								7.9	4.5 - 12.9		
29	30	Comoros								7.8	4.3 - 12.7		
30	35	Namibia								7.7	4.5 - 12.3		✓
31	25	Ethiopia								7.7	4.6 - 12.1		
32	21	Uganda								7.5	4.3 - 12.0		✓
33	37	South Africa								6.7	3.9 - 10.4		

Regional Rank 2016	Regional Rank 2014	Country	Regime Consistency	Partial Democracy	Infant Mortality	Economic Openness	Militarization	Neighborhood War	Risk Category	Risk Score	Confidence Range		Active Armed Conflict in 2014
Sub-Saharan Africa (continued)												
34	31	Tanzania								6.4	3.5 - 10.8		
35	33	Togo								6.1	3.7 - 9.9		
36	40	Botswana								6.0	3.6 - 9.8		
37	12	South Sudan								5.6	3.1 - 9.0		✓
38	36	Eritrea								4.5	2.3 - 7.6		
39	38	Madagascar								4.4	2.6 - 7.1		
40	39	Mauritania								4.2	2.0 - 7.6		
41	42	Rwanda								3.0	1.4 - 5.8		
42	43	Equatorial Guinea								2.4	1.3 - 4.1		
43	44	Congo, Rep.								2.0	0.9 - 3.9		
44	41	Gambia, The								1.9	1.0 - 3.3		
45	45	Swaziland								1.8	1.0 - 3.2		
46	47	Mauritius								0.7	0.3 - 1.3		
Asia, Australia & the Pacific												
1	1	Afghanistan								27.1	17.2 - 40.1		✓
2	2	Pakistan								19.3	13.5 - 26.2		✓
3	4	Bangladesh								12.0	7.3 - 18.1		
4	8	Papua New Guinea								11.8	7.8 - 16.9		
5	5	Nepal								10.9	7.0 - 15.6		
6	3	Bhutan								9.6	5.8 - 14.8		
7	7	India								8.8	5.1 - 13.4		✓
8	6	Timor-Leste								7.2	4.2 - 11.7		
9	10	Tajikistan								6.0	3.4 - 9.6		
10	9	Cambodia								5.8	3.1 - 10		
11	14	Indonesia								4.9	3.0 - 7.4		
12	13	Sri Lanka								4.8	2.0 - 9.9		
13	11	Myanmar								4.5	2.2 - 8.1		✓
14	16	Philippines								4.5	2.6 - 7.3		✓
15	12	Korea, Dem. Rep.								4.4	1.6 - 9.6		
16	15	Kyrgyz Republic								3.9	2.1 - 6.6		
17	17	Solomon Islands								3.9	2.2 - 6.6		
18	19	Laos								3.6	2.1 - 5.7		
19	18	Thailand								3.2	1.7 - 5.8		✓

Regional Rank 2016	Regional Rank 2014	Country	Regime Consistency	Partial Democracy	Infant Mortality	Economic Openness	Militarization	Neighborhood War	Risk Category	Risk Score	Confidence Range		Active Armed Conflict in 2014
Asia, Australia & the Pacific (continued)
20	20	Malaysia	●	●	●	●	●	●	●	2.3	1.0 - 4.8	▮▭	
21	22	Mongolia	●		●	●	●	●	●	2.1	1.0 - 3.8	▮▭	
22	23	Turkmenistan	●		●	●	●	●	●	1.9	1.1 - 3.2	▮▮	
23	21	Uzbekistan	●		●	●	●	●	●	1.5	0.8 - 2.7	▮▮	
24	25	Kazakhstan	●		●	●	●	●	●	1.0	0.4 - 2.1	▮▮	
25	27	Fiji	●		●	●	●	●	●	1.0	0.4 - 2.0	▮▮	
26	24	Korea, Rep.	●	●	●	●	●	●	●	1.0	0.3 - 2.2	▮▮	
27	26	China	●		●	●	●	●	●	0.7	0.3 - 1.7	▮▮	
28	28	Vietnam	●		●	●	●	●	●	0.7	0.3 - 1.4	▮	
29	29	Singapore	●		●	●	●	●	●	0.6	0.1 - 1.5	▮▮	
30	31	New Zealand	●		●	●	●	●	●	0.4	0.2 - 0.8	▮	
31	32	Australia	●		●	●	●	●	●	0.3	0.1 - 0.7	▮	
32	30	Japan	●		●	●	●	●	●	0.3	0.1 - 0.8	▮	
Eastern Europe
1	1	Armenia	●	●	●	●	●	●	●	6.9	3.7 - 11.8	▭ ▮▭	
2	2	Kosovo	●	●	●	●	●	●	●	6.4	3.0 - 12.2	▭ ▮▭	
3	4	Russian Federation	●	●	●		●	●	●	4.6	1.9 - 9.2	▮▭ ▮ ▮	✓
4	3	Georgia	●	●	●	●	●	●	●	3.6	1.8 - 6.4	▮▮▭	
5	5	Ukraine	●	●	●	●	●	●	●	2.9	1.3 - 5.7	▮▮▭	✓
6	7	Bulgaria	●	●	●	●	●	●	●	2.3	1.1 - 4.1	▮▮▭	
7	6	Albania	●	●	●	●	●	●	●	2.3	1.2 - 4.0	▮▮▭	
8	10	Romania	●	●	●	●	●	●	●	2.1	1.0 - 3.7	▮▮▭	
9	8	Moldova	●	●	●	●	●	●	●	2.1	1.0 - 3.8	▮▮▭	
10	11	Latvia	●	●	●	●	●	●	●	2.0	0.9 - 4.1	▮▮▭	
11	9	Azerbaijan	●		●	●	●	●	●	1.8	0.9 - 3.1	▮▮	✓
12	12	Montenegro	●	●	●	●	●	●	●	1.4	0.6 - 2.8	▮▮▭	
13	14	Serbia	●	●	●	●	●	●	●	1.3	0.5 - 2.7	▮▮	
14	13	Macedonia, FYR	●	●	●	●	●	●	●	1.0	0.4 - 2.3	▮▮	
15	15	Bosnia&Herzegovina	●		●	●	●	●	●	0.9	0.3 - 2.2	▮▮	
16	16	Croatia	●	●	●	●	●	●	●	0.8	0.3 - 1.9	▮▮	
17	17	Estonia	●	●	●	●	●	●	●	0.7	0.2 - 1.7	▮▮	
18	18	Czech Republic	●	●	●	●	●	●	●	0.5	0.2 - 1.3	▮	
19	19	Poland	●		●	●	●	●	●	0.5	0.2 - 1.0	▮	

Regional Rank 2016	Regional Rank 2014	Country	Risk Score	Confidence Range	Active Armed Conflict in 2014
Eastern Europe (continued)					

Regional Rank 2016	Regional Rank 2014	Country	Risk Score	Confidence Range	Active Armed Conflict in 2014
		Eastern Europe (continued)			
20	20	Lithuania	0.4	0.1 - 0.9	
21	21	Slovak Republic	0.4	0.1 - 0.7	
22	22	Belarus	0.3	0.1 - 0.9	
23	23	Hungary	0.3	0.1 - 0.7	
24	24	Slovenia	0.2	0.1 - 0.5	
		Latin America & the Caribbean			
1	1	Haiti	13.6	8.2 - 21.5	
2	4	Ecuador	7.0	3.9 - 12.0	
3	5	Guyana	7.0	4.2 - 10.5	
4	3	Suriname	6.9	3.7 - 11.8	
5	2	Bolivia	6.8	4.1 - 10.4	
6	17	Venezuela, RB	6.0	2.8 - 11.5	
7	7	Dominican Republic	5.0	3.0 - 8.0	
8	6	Guatemala	5.0	3.0 - 7.6	
9	9	Colombia	4.6	2.4 - 7.7	✓
10	8	Brazil	4.4	2.3 - 7.4	
11	10	Peru	3.7	2.0 - 6.1	
12	12	Honduras	3.7	2.0 - 6.2	
13	11	Mexico	3.5	1.8 - 5.9	
14	13	Nicaragua	3.1	1.7 - 5.1	
15	15	Argentina	3.1	1.5 - 5.5	
16	14	Paraguay	3.0	1.6 - 4.8	
17	16	El Salvador	2.8	1.5 - 4.9	
18	18	Jamaica	2.3	1.2 - 4.1	
19	19	Panama	1.3	0.6 - 2.4	
20	20	Trinidad and Tobago	1.1	0.6 - 2.0	
21	21	Uruguay	0.8	0.4 - 1.4	
22	22	Costa Rica	0.6	0.3 - 1.1	
23	23	Chile	0.6	0.2 - 1.1	
24	24	Cuba	0.3	0.1 - 1.0	
		Middle East & North Africa			
1	1	Iraq	11.0	6.6 - 17.7	✓
2	2	Yemen, Rep.	5.6	3.5 - 8.5	✓

Regional Rank 2016	Regional Rank 2014	Country	Regime Consistency	Partial Democracy	Infant Mortality	Economic Openness	Militarization	Neighborhood War	Risk Category	Risk Score	Confidence Range		Active Armed Conflict in 2014
		Middle East & North Africa (continued)											
3	3	Algeria					●	●		4.5	2.2 - 7.8		✓
4	6	Turkey		●				●	●	4.5	2.6 - 7.1		
5	5	Jordan				●		●		3.6	1.8 - 6.7		
6	4	Lebanon		●			●	●	●	3.5	1.6 - 6.7		✓
7	8	Morocco					●	●		2.0	0.8 - 3.9		
8	9	Egypt, Arab Rep.					●			1.9	0.7 - 4.2		
9	7	Tunisia						●		1.8	0.9 - 3.2		
10	10	Iran, Islamic Rep.				●	●	●		1.1	0.4 - 2.2		
11	11	Libya				●		●		1.0	0.3 - 2.5		✓
12	13	Oman					●			0.6	0.2 - 1.4		
13	12	Syrian Arab Republic								0.6	0.2 - 1.3		✓
14	14	Israel					●			0.6	0.2 - 1.2		
15	17	Saudi Arabia					●			0.6	0.3 - 1.1		
16	16	Kuwait					●			0.5	0.2 - 1.2		
17	19	United Arab Emirates			●	●				0.3	0.1 - 0.6		
18	18	Qatar								0.2	0.1 - 0.6		
19	15	Bahrain				●	●			0.2	0.1 - 0.5		
		North Atlantic											
1	1	United States					●			0.8	0.3 - 1.6		
2	2	Belgium		●		●				0.7	0.2 - 1.6		
3	3	Greece					●	●		0.5	0.2 - 1.1		
4	4	Canada						●		0.5	0.2 - 1.1		
5	5	France								0.4	0.1 - 0.9		
6	7	Cyprus					●			0.4	0.1 - 0.8		
7	6	United Kingdom								0.3	0.1 - 0.7		
8	8	Spain								0.3	0.1 - 0.7		
9	11	Norway					●			0.3	0.1 - 0.7		
10	14	Portugal				●				0.3	0.1 - 0.7		
11	10	Italy								0.3	0.1 - 0.7		
12	12	Finland					●			0.3	0.1 - 0.7		
13	9	Switzerland			●					0.2	0.1 - 0.6		
14	15	Germany								0.2	0.1 - 0.6		
15	13	Austria								0.2	0.1 - 0.5		

Regional Rank 2016	Regional Rank 2014	Country	Regime Consistency	Partial Democracy	Infant Mortality	Economic Openness	Militarization	Neighborhood War	Risk Category	Risk Score	Confidence Range	Active Armed Conflict in 2014
						North Atlantic (continued)						
17	16	Netherlands								0.2	0.1 - 0.5	
16	17	Denmark								0.2	0.1 - 0.5	
18	18	Ireland								0.2	0.1 - 0.5	
19	19	Sweden								0.2	0.1 - 0.5	
20	20	Luxembourg								0.1	0.0 - 0.3	

Table 13.5 The Peace and Conflict Instability Ledger

Notes and Explanations for the Peace and Conflict Instability Ledger

The Ledger reflects a theoretical model that relates the future likelihood of instability events in a given country to five risk factors. A statistical analysis, using "training data" for more than 160 countries during the period of 1950–2003, found that all of these factors are strongly associated with the future risk of instability. Based on the estimates from the model for the causal weight assigned to each factor, data from 2013 – the last year for which complete data are available for all of the factors – are used to produce a forecast indicating the risk of instability in the period 2014–2016. The notes below describe the information presented in the table, including the factors and the color codings they are assigned, which reflect a country's standing based on 2013 values.

(1) **Regional Rank (2016):** Rank of the country's risk score within the region, according to the analysis reported here in *Peace and Conflict 2016*.

(2) **Regional Rank (2014):** Rank of the country's risk score within the region, according to the analysis reported in *Peace and Conflict 2014*.

(3) **Country:** The Ledger examines only those countries with populations greater than 500,000 in 2013.

(4–5) **Regime Consistency and Partial Democracy:** The risk of future instability is related to the extent to which the institutions comprising a country's political system are consistently autocratic or democratic. Political institutions with a mix of democratic and autocratic features are deemed inconsistent, a common attribute of polities in the midst of a democratic transition (or a reversal from democratic rule to more autocratic governance). Regimes with inconsistent institutions are expected to be more likely to experience political instability. In the Ledger, highly consistent democracies (Polity score greater than or equal to 6) and autocracies (Polity score less than or equal to − 6) receive a green marker. A red marker is assigned to regimes with inconsistent characteristics that also qualify as partial democracies according to PITF. Regimes with these characteristics have been found to have the highest risk for instability. A yellow marker is assigned to partial autocracies because the propensity for instability in these regimes is somewhat less than in partial democracies.

(6) **Infant Mortality:** This indicator serves as a proxy for overall governmental effectiveness in executing policies and delivering services that improve social welfare in a country. High rates are associated with an increased likelihood of future instability. Countries with the best records (scoring in the bottom quartile of infant mortality rates) are indicated with a green marker. Countries with the worst records (scoring in the highest quartile) are indicated with a red marker. Countries falling in between these two groups are indicated with a yellow marker.

(7) **Economic Openness:** Integration with global markets reduces the likelihood of political instability and armed conflict. Policies that integrate global and domestic markets can produce higher growth rates and sometimes reduce inequality, thereby lessening common drivers for civil unrest related to economic grievances. The measure for economic openness employed here is the proportion of a country's GDP accounted for by the value of all trade (exports plus imports). Countries with economic openness in the lowest quartile are considered to be at the highest risk and designated with a red marker. The highest quartile of countries is at low risk and assigned a green marker. Countries whose economic openness falls in between these two groups are assigned a yellow marker.

(8) **Militarization:** Instability is most likely in countries where the opportunities and means for conflict are greatest. In societies where the infrastructure and capital for organized armed action are more plentiful and accessible, the likelihood of civil conflict is higher. The Ledger measures militarization as the number of individuals in a country's active armed forces as a percentage of the country's total population. Countries with militarization scores in the bottom quartile are

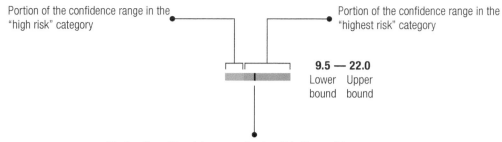

Portion of the confidence range in the "high risk" category

Portion of the confidence range in the "highest risk" category

9.5 — 22.0
Lower   Upper
bound   bound

The location of the risk score estimate within the confidence range is depicted with a vertical black line. In this example, the estimate is **15.2**. The location of the risk score estimate does not necessarily fall at the midpoint of the confidence range.

Figure 13.2 Understanding the Instability Risk Confidence Ranges

indicated with a green marker. Countries in the top quartile are indicated with a red marker. Countries with levels of militarization that fall in between those two groups are indicated with a yellow marker.

(9) Neighborhood War: Countries with neighbors that are engaged in armed conflict (internal or interstate) face a higher risk of instability. Regional armed conflict can have spillover and contagion effects, especially when ethnic or other communal groups span across borders. The most recent data released from the Uppsala Conflict Data Program is used to determine the conflict status of states in 2013. For a neighbor to be considered involved in armed conflict, the conflict must produce 25 or more battle-related fatalities per year. Neighbors are defined on the basis of shared borders. A red marker indicates when at least one neighboring country is involved in armed conflict. A green marker indicates the absence of armed conflict in all neighboring countries.

(10) Risk Category: Based on their risk score (see Box 13.1), countries are placed in one of five categories: highest risk (red), high risk (orange), moderate risk (yellow), some risk category (green), or low risk (blue).

(11) Risk Score: The results from estimating a statistical model using global data from the period 1950–2003 are applied to data from 2013 to obtain a three-year forecast for each country of the relative risk (compared to an average member of the OECD) of experiencing instability during for the period 2014–2016.

(12) Confidence Range: The confidence range provides information about the degree of uncertainty corresponding to a country's estimated risk score. Statistically speaking, the "true" risk of instability is expected to fall within this range with a 95 percent probability. In the bars presenting the confidence ranges, the widths of each bar and any constituent segments are drawn to scale. When the bar is one color, the confidence range is confined to a single risk category. In cases where the confidence range spans multiple risk categories, the different colors of the segments of the bar reflect the extent of the overlap with those categories. The color blue indicates the low risk range, green the some risk range, yellow the moderate risk range, orange the high risk range, and red the highest risk range. Figure 13.2 illustrates how to read the information contained in the graphic for each country's confidence range, using a sample country (Niger).

(13) Active Armed Conflict in 2014: A red check mark indicates that a country was involved in an armed conflict as of December 31, 2014, according to information compiled by the Uppsala Conflict Data Program. This designation means that there was a contested incompatibility between the government and at least one other armed group, resulting in at least 25 battle-related deaths in 2014 and a cumulative total of at least 1,000 battle-related deaths since the start of the conflict.

Notes

1 The initial compilation of state failure events was done in 1994–1995 at the University of Maryland's Center for International Development and Conflict Management, under the direction of Ted Robert Gurr. The roster of genocides and politicides was provided by Barbara Harff. The PITF presents full definitions for adverse regime change, revolutionary war, ethnic war, genocide, and politicide in Esty et al. (1999).
2 Significant contributions to this literature include Collier et al. (2003); Collier and Hoeffler (2004); Esty et al. (1999); Fearon and Laitin (2003); Goldstone et al. (2005); Hegre and Sambanis (2006); Hegre et al. (2001); King and Zeng (2001); Sambanis (2002, 2004); and the United States Agency for International Development (2005).

References

Collier, Paul, V. L. Elliot, Håvard Hegre, Anke Hoeffler, Marta Reynal-Querol, and Nicholas Sambanis. 2003. "Breaking the Conflict Trap: Civil War and Development Policy." World Bank Policy Research Report. Oxford: Oxford University Press.

Collier, Paul, and Anke Hoeffler. 2004. "Greed and Grievance in Civil War." *Oxford Economic Papers* 56(4): 563–595.

Esty, Daniel C., Jack Goldstone, Ted R. Gurr, Barbara Harff, Marc Levy, Geoffrey D. Dabelko, Pamela T. Surko, and Alan N. Unger. 1999. *The State Failure Task Force Report: Phase II Findings*. McLean, VA: Science Applications International Corporation (SAIC).

Fearon, James D., and David Laitin. 2003. "Ethnicity, Insurgency, and Civil War." *American Political Science Review* 97(1): 75–90.

Gates, Scott, Håvard Hegre, Mark P. Jones, and Håvard Strand. 2006. "Institutional Inconsistency and Political Instability: Polity Duration, 1800–2000." *American Journal of Political Science* 50: 893–908.

Goldstone, Jack A., Ted R. Gurr, Barbara Harff, Marc A. Levy, Monty G. Marshall, Robert H. Bates, David L. Epstein, Colin H. Kahl, Pamela T. Surko, John Ulfelder, and Alan N. Unger. 2000. *The State Failure Task Force Report: Phase III Findings*. McLean, VA: Science Applications International Corporation.

Goldstone, Jack A., Robert H. Bates, Ted R. Gurr, Michael Lustik, Monty G. Marshall, Jay Ulfelder, and Mark Woodward. 2005. "A Global Forecasting Model of Political Instability." Paper presented at the Annual Meeting of the American Political Science Association, Washington, DC, September 1–4.

Gurr, Ted R. 1974. "Persistence and Change in Political Systems, 1800–1971." *American Political Science Review* 68(4): 1482–1504.

Hegre, Håvard, and Nicholas Sambanis. 2006. "Sensitivity Analysis of Empirical Results on Civil War Onset." *Journal of Conflict Resolution* 50(4): 508–535.

Hegre, Håvard, Tanja Ellingsen, Scott Gates, and Nils Petter Gleditsch. 2001. "Toward a Democratic Civil Peace? Democracy, Political Change, and Civil War, 1816–1992." *American Political Science Review* 95(1): 33–48.

Hegre, Håvard, Ranveig Gissinger, and Nils Petter Gleditsch. 2003. "Globalization and Internal Conflict." In Gerald Schneider, Katherine Barbieri, and Nils Petter Gleditsch (eds). *Globalization and Armed Conflict*. Lanham, MD: Rowman and Littlefield Publishers.

Hewitt, J. Joseph. 2008. "The Peace and Conflict Instability Ledger: Ranking States on Future Risk." In J. Joseph Hewitt, Jonathan Wilkenfeld, and Ted R. Gurr (eds.). *Peace and Conflict 2008*. Boulder, CO: Paradigm Publishers.

Hewitt, J. Joseph. 2012. "The Peace and Conflict Instability Ledger: Ranking States on Future Risk." In J. Joseph Hewitt, Jonathan Wilkenfeld, and Ted R. Gurr (eds.). *Peace and Conflict 2012*. Boulder, CO: Paradigm Publishers.

King, Gary, and Langche Zeng. 2001. "Improving Forecasts of State Failure." *World Politics* 53(4): 623–658.

Pate, Amy. 2008. "Trends in Democratization: A Focus on Instability in Anocracies." In J. Joseph Hewitt, Jonathan Wilkenfeld, and Ted R. Gurr (eds.). *Peace and Conflict 2008*. Boulder, CO: Paradigm Publishers.

Sambanis, Nicholas. 2001. "Do Ethnic and Non-Ethnic Civil Wars Have the Same Causes? A Theoretical and Empirical Inquiry (Part 1)." *Journal of Conflict Resolution* 45(3): 259–282.

Sambanis, Nicholas 2002. "A Review of Recent Advances and Future Directions in the Quantitative Literature on Civil Wars." *Defense and Peace Economics* 13(3): 215–243.

Sambanis, Nicholas 2004. "What Is a Civil War? Conceptual and Empirical Complexities of an Operational Definition." *Journal of Conflict Resolution* 48(6): 814–858.

United States Agency for International Development. 2005. *Measuring Fragility: Indicators and Methods for Rating State Performance*. Washington, DC: United States Agency for International Development.

14

New Developments in Measuring the Welfare Effects of Conflict Exposure at the Micro Level

Tilman Brück, Patricia Justino and Philip Verwimp

Introduction

The effects of violent conflict may register at the individual and household levels through a variety of direct and indirect channels (Justino 2009). Diverse modalities of violence and varied timings of exposure to violence affect how different individuals and households experience conflicts. Yet these complex relationships are rarely studied in detail due to a shortcoming of existing socio-economic surveys: a lack of comprehensive micro-level information on conflict processes. This gap forces researchers to rely on less than optimal measures of violent conflict when assessing the welfare effects of conflict. In particular, some of the commonly used measures, such as the number of battle-related deaths per country per year, are often narrowly measured at high levels of aggregation, which means they are clearly inadequate substitutes for rich micro-level data.

Seeking to improve the quality of research and resulting insights, the Households in Conflict Network has recently developed the "Conflict Exposure Module" (CEM). The main purpose of the CEM is to propose ways of collecting systematic and comprehensive information on conflict processes within socio-economic surveys conducted in conflict-affected countries.[1] We seek to accomplish that aim by capturing the ways in which people experience the many dimensions of violent conflict. This chapter provides an introductory overview of the CEM. We begin by discussing the principles that guided the development. Next, we review the segments of the CEM. Finally, we conclude with thoughts about future utilization.

Guiding Principles

The CEM has been designed to take advantage of the two main approaches to linking conflict processes to socio-economic outcomes at the micro level. The first approach is to rely on high-quality data from individuals, which requires large-scale surveys to collect detailed and nuanced answers from respondents about the circumstances under which they were exposed to violence, the severity of the exposures, and associated effects. The second approach is to link conflict-related information in socio-economic surveys to separate conflict event databases. This requires the collection of time- and location-specific information about when and where events occur, as part of surveys, so the responses can be matched to corresponding information in the event databases.

In developing the CEM, we owe much to the recent emergence of literature on the micro-level impact of conflict, especially studies based on surveys purposely designed for the study of conflict (e.g., Blattman and Miguel 2010; Justino, Brück, and Verwimp 2013; Justino 2012). We have advocated that the design of socio-economic surveys in conflict-affected contexts be guided by four principles, which are discussed in turn below.[2]

Breadth and depth of answers. Asking respondents to report on how different aspects of conflict have affected them at different times is an important first step to achieving better comprehension of conflict dynamics at the micro level. Too few socio-economic surveys conducted in conflict-affected countries extend the range of answer choices and provide the scope for sufficient detail, to afford respondents opportunities to explain more precisely how conflict has actually affected them. This shortcoming is important because it limits the ability to appreciate specific mechanisms whereby violent conflict may affect micro-level outcomes, rather than just simply establishing a correlation between the two.

Sensitivity to the timing of events. Carefully recording information on when and where events occurred allows researchers to attribute socio-economic outcomes to particular conflict dynamics, as well as to grasp how conflict evolves over time and space. Matching survey data to independent data on conflict events is an important way of assessing the existence, nature and magnitude of potential reporting biases. Yet obtaining such independent data at adequately disaggregated levels of analysis is often infeasible, if not impossible. Also, these other sources of data are hardly immune to biases related to how the data is collected and reported. An intent of the CEM is to collect time-specific information across all main sections of a survey questionnaire, in order to better align answers to major changes in the dynamics of a given conflict process and to other events and circumstances.

Sensitivity to the type and intensity of violence. Surveys in conflict-affected areas should be attuned to characteristics of violence (Kalyvas 2006). Each conflict creates a heterogeneous landscape of experiences and hardships, which vary according to individual circumstances and the strategies employed by different armed actors and their factions and units. Sensitivity to this variation requires multiple questions that ask about different types of violence and answer categories that go beyond simple binaries by including a range that encompasses levels of intensity of the violence. This approach also allows researchers to evaluate the effects of the nature and degrees of conflict on behavior and welfare – in contrast to earlier identification strategies relying merely on certain aspects of the conflict having been present or not (typically deaths in the household, displacement, or destruction of major assets).

Comprehensiveness. Surveys often focus too narrowly on selected categories of violence and fail to account for the multi-dimensional nature and impact of violent conflict. Instead, surveys should cover a wide range of channels through which violent conflict may influence a number of outcomes at the micro level. One simple way is to include questions on conflict across the various sections of these surveys, rather than limiting the angle of inquiry to a small number of restricted questions (for instance, on the destruction of dwellings or deaths in the household), as currently is the norm. The CEM demonstrates how to adopt such empirical strategy. Surveys should also be comprehensive *within* answer categories, by considering a broader range of answer choices when feasible, to allow for disaggregation.

The Conflict Exposure Module

To reiterate, the main objective of the CEM is to allow researchers to identify the main direct and indirect channels whereby conflict may affect individual and household welfare and behavior outcomes. These channels – based on the theoretical framework proposed in Justino (2009) – include household composition, economic welfare, household activities (including coping strategies), displacement, health and nutrition outcomes, education outcomes and decisions, perceptions of security, life satisfaction, and future expectations. We discuss these channels below. For reasons of space, we illustrate some (but not all) of the channels with extracts from the CEM. In this regard, priority is given to the channels that are not as well developed in existing household surveys. The full CEM, including a complete list of sections and proposed answer categories, is available in Brück, et al. (2013).

Changes in demographic characteristics. Under normal conditions, changes in the composition of households typically take place through a limited number of modes, including birth, death, marriage, and migration. Violent conflicts add other modes and variants to the list. Conflicts are regularly accompanied by circumstances that have a bearing on who is in the household, such as imprisonment, abductions, (forced) disappearances, hostage-taking, forced or voluntary internal displacement, (forced) recruitment, and forced marriage and sexual relationships. Household composition may also be influenced by the physical destruction of property, threats, and a general environment of insecurity, which can cause members of the household to flee or eliminate the household altogether at a given location. Another way of capturing conflict-related changes in household demographic characteristics is to probe in depth the causes of death in the household, as well as the reasons for additions in household members. The links of changes to conflict are not necessarily obvious on the surface. Instead, establishing these links may require connecting the dots or making reasonable inferences under the context (e.g., relatives or friends join a household from other areas that are/were heavily affected by the conflict). Timing is also a crucial factor in identifying how changes in household composition may be linked with conflict processes.

Table 14.1 (see next page) offers an illustrative example of how conflict-related questions could be made more explicit in a standard socio-economic module about changes in household composition. This example shows how answer options that capture important population movements due to violence and other aspects of conflict exposure **could** potentially be added to more standard survey questions.

Economic welfare. Important measures of household economic welfare include income status, food consumption, and asset endowments. Conflict and violence can directly and indirectly affect the ability of households to generate income or assets or access basic needs (Bozzoli and Brück 2009; Ibáñez and Moya 2009; Justino 2009). This may occur through a wide assortment of means, including the lack of employment opportunities, the destruction of infrastructure, restricted

A1	A2	A3.1
In case [NAME] joined, what was the cause of joining?	**In case [NAME] died, what was the cause of death?**	**In case [NAME] has left, what was the reason for leaving?**
1. Married into household 2. Divorce, separation or widowed 3. Cannot live in house 4. Education **5. Security or threats** 6. More work opportunities 7. Discrimination **8. Experienced violence** 9. Other	1. Malaria 2. HIV/AIDS 3. Other disease 4. Malnutrition 5. Accident **6. Death in combat violence** **7. Death in non-combat violence** 8. Natural death 9. Suicide 10. Other	1. Divorce, separation or widowed 2. Left to get married **3. Left because of the conflict or threat of violence** **4. Was taken (abducted, kidnapped) by armed movement** **5. Joined armed movement voluntarily** 6. Left for work **7. Imprisoned** 8. Left for education **9. Other suspected violent way of going missing** **10. Left for political reasons/protest** 11. Other peaceful move 12. Other

Table 14.1 Changes in Household Demographic Characteristics

Source: Extract from Conflict Exposure Module (Brück, Verwimp and Tedesco 2013).

markets and physical and labor resources, curtailed investment capital, payment of protection and other forms of revenue-extraction imposed by different armed factions, military service, social restrictions, health effects, uncertainty, and insecurity. Measuring declines in food consumption among conflict-affected households is particularly important in order to capture instances of extreme shocks to welfare and to reveal which households are most vulnerable. Assets may also be mechanisms of self-insurance in risky environments, but even where available any assets are often at risk of being destroyed or looted during violent conflict (Bundervoet, Verwimp, and Akresh 2009; Justino 2009). Existing surveys tend to focus on large-scale asset losses, such as the destruction of household dwellings. Other assets (e.g., livestock, agricultural tools, seeds, etc.) may be of considerable importance for understanding the economic security of households living in areas of conflict and violence, how they may adapt to conflict, and what losses are driven by conflict exposure. Capturing these considerations requires adding questions about assets that are theoretically relevant in conflict settings, as well as meaningful for each local context being studied.

Activities during conflict. Households may employ *ex-ante* coping strategies, anticipating changes in circumstances by adjusting their behavior before the conflict takes place (e.g., exchanging livestock for more fungible assets). Households may also employ *ex-post* strategies in response to insecurity and violence. These strategies may include broad changes in consumption and investment, as well as changes in more specific items such as crops and livestock. Strategies can also involve reliance on social networks and external assistance. Interactions between household members and combatants may also serve to protect households physically and economically during conflict. Some household members opt to join the police, the military, or rebel groups (Annan and Blattman 2009; Humphreys and Weinstein 2008; Justino 2009). In addition, households may try to engage in local self-protection. Inclusion of questions on changing roles and affiliations in socio-economic surveys conducted in conflict-affected countries can supply important indicators of local political transformation processes, which are underexplored in the literature (Justino 2009). Table 14.2 (see next page) illustrates questions that may capture some of these important dynamics of changing household activities.

Displacement. Population displacement, including refugee flows, is among the most visible impacts of modern conflicts. An important dimension of displacement warranting attention, which research typically overlooks, is that only certain people move, while others – sometimes the majority – choose to remain in place despite the outbreak of the conflict (Justino 2009; Kalyvas and Kocher 2009). Meanwhile, not enough is known about the challenges displaced people face (Ibáñez and Moya 2009). More systematic understanding of displacement experiences will require in-depth knowledge about the reasons why individuals leave their homes in conflict-affected contexts, where people move, what happens to them in the process, how many times they have been displaced, whether displaced people intend to return to their homes, what happens when they do, and how they respond to situations faced upon return. When tracking displacement experiences, sensitivity to timing is particularly important. Table 14.3 (see next page) provides some suggestions on how household surveys could include a number of questions aimed at capturing experiences of different types of population movements associated with conflict.

C1.1	C1.2	C2.1
Have you or your household members changed your activities as a result of violence?	**Compared to before the conflict [SPECIFY PERIOD OF TIME IN CONTEXT] does your household [INSERT ACTIVITY HERE] more, less or about the same?**	**Did any members of your household take any of the following steps in/during [SPECIFY PERIOD OF TIME]?**
1. Yes 2. No	1. Engage in social networks (groups, community) 2. Save money 3. Engage in investment 4. Borrow money or ask for loan 5. Depend on transfers and assistance from government, NGOs or church 6. Grow cash crops 7. Raise livestock 8. Send children to work 9. Migrate for salary 10. Eat daily meals 11. Eat quality meals 12. Share food 13. Consume reserved seeds 14. Sell livestock or other goods 15. Share tenancy 16. Work (part-time versus full-time) 17. Engage in education	**1. Joined the official police** **2. Joined a rebel group** **3. Joined the military** **4. Paid contribution to rebel groups** **5. Tried to bribe governmental officials or rebels** **6. Joined or established community policing/neighborhood watch** **7. Got a weapon** 8. Reduced visits to market **9. Got guard dog or employed watchmen** **10. Improved house security** 11. Sold furniture/assets or livestock 12. Had children migrate out of the community 13. Became more active member of the community 14. Became less active member of the community 15. Used connections with influential people 16. Used traditional remedies 17. Others, please specify

Table 14.2 Household Activities during Conflict
Source: Extract from Conflict Exposure Module (Brück, Verwimp, and Tedesco 2013).

D4	D8	D9
What was the main reason for you to move to the new place or current location?	**If you were forced to leave, who forced you to leave your original place of residence?**	**Why did you stay in the place you lived despite the outbreak of conflict?**
1. To look for work 2. Marriage/family reasons **3. Threat of violence or physically forced to leave** **4. Political reasons** 5. Famine 6. Disease **7. Property destroyed** **8. Property occupied** 9. Community disputes: land 10. Community disputes: water 11. Community disputes: ethnic 12. Community disputes: other 13. Lack of land 14. Other reason	**1. Government army soldiers** **2. Rebel group** **3. Militia members** **4. Bandits** 5. Neighbors 6. Household member(s) 7. Others	1. Had to take care of the family 2. Had to take care of work, production or agriculture 3. Was ill 4. Had no money 5. Waited for other family members to join 6. Thought it would be over soon 7. No transport available 8. Infrastructure destroyed (e.g. roads) 9. Was forced to stay by others 10. Was involved in fights/violence 11. Other

Table 14.3 Displacement
Source: Extract from Conflict Exposure Module (Brück, Justino, Verwimp, and Tedesco 2013).

Health and education. Gauging the physical impact of violent conflicts is a very delicate task. Before attempting to identify physical harms inflicted by violence, an in-depth understanding of the types of violence employed in different conflicts is an essential prerequisite. The types may include any combination of physical, verbal, psychological and/or sexual violence. Some types may be common across conflicts, while others may be context specific. Another challenge is that perspectives about what constitutes violence and understandings of what qualifies under each of the types differ across cultures and contexts. Even small differences in the meaning might impede comparisons across settings. To address the challenges, survey enumerators must be trained to be sensitive to variations in meaning, while working within the framework of specific answer codes. Many existing household surveys conducted in conflict-affected countries contain a number of variables that capture physical harms caused by violence (see survey in Brück et al. 2013). Surveys could often be improved by making answer categories more comprehensive and sensitive to conflict intensity, attempting to identify whether those experiencing harm are combatants or civilians, and establishing as best as possible the timing and locations of incidents of violence. At the same time, these questions may lead to the identification of perpetrators of violence and must be asked with care.

Conflict also affects dimensions of human capital such as education. Following Blattman and Miguel (2010: 42), vital information to collect includes whether conflict affects household accumulation of human capital, as well as "in what ways, how much, for whom, and how persistently." Most existing surveys tend to include questions about school disruption due to conflict; this is one of the most developed areas of research on the consequences of conflict. Other questions could be included in surveys to probe related aspects such as how persistently education has been interrupted and the specific reasons for school absences (e.g., fear, insecurity, economic needs of the household), which may help to document the nature of exposures to conflict and the associated effects. Such questions would advance understanding considerably because they identify both the direct effects of conflict on education and the channels shaping those effects – the latter is often missing in existing studies.

Perceptions of security, life satisfaction and expectations. Even long after the official end of war, people may still be – or feel – under threat. Perceptions of safety that reflect current conditions, as well as being linked to past violence, may affect individual and household behavior. Capturing these perceptions is important to examining why individuals and households employ certain types of coping strategies over others during and after a conflict. Therefore, surveys in conflict-affected countries should address how individuals and households perceive their own security, regardless of whether the conflict is ongoing or has ended. Exposure to conflict may also have a significant impact on life satisfaction and expectations about the future (Bozzoli, Brück, and Muhumuza 2012). These sentiments, in turn, may affect how people recover from exposures to violence. Here, a multidisciplinary perspective is particularly useful, combining questions around emotions, as well as more attitudinal and behavioral dimensions such as expectations and time discount rates. We believe that this area of research will exhibit major advances over the next few years, with diverse teams coming together to investigate various dimensions of recovery from conflict.

Conclusions

The CEM is a comprehensive tool to measure how individuals and households experience past or recent violent conflict. This tool can act as a template for adapting and expanding existing socio-economic surveys to be more conflict sensitive. Many socio-economic surveys in conflict-affected areas are too selective in their attention, missing important features in the process. Instead, surveys should aim for a comprehensive treatment of the multi-faceted ways in which violent conflict may affect different individuals and households. The CEM, appropriately adapted to local conditions, can serve as a general model for investigating the impact of violent conflict, comparatively across countries, on a number of attributes and outcomes at the micro level, including household demographics, economic welfare, coping strategies, physical harm, displacement, education, perceptions, attitudes, and expectations. We expect this module – if successfully adopted across multiple surveys – to significantly contribute to understanding of conflict dynamics at the micro level as well as patterns of socio-economic development in conflict-affected areas.

Notes

1 Two examples are the Living Standards Monitoring Surveys, collected by the World Bank, and the Demographic and Health Surveys.
2 For more detailed discussion of these principles, see Brück, Justino, Verwimp, and Tedesco (2013), and Brück, et al. (2013).

References

Annan, Jeannie, Christopher Blattman, and Roger Horton. 2006. "The State of Youth and Youth Protection in Northern Uganda: Findings from the Survey for War Affected Youth." A report for UNICEF Uganda. September 2006.

Blattman, Christopher, and Jeannie Annan. 2009. "The Consequences of Child Soldiering." *Review of Economics and Statistics* 92(4): 882–898.

Blattman, Christopher, and Edward Miguel. 2010. "Civil War." *Journal of Economic Literature* 48(1): 3–57.

Bozzoli, Carlos, and Tilman Brück. 2009. "Agriculture, Poverty and Post-War Reconstruction: Micro-Level Evidence from Northern Mozambique." *Journal of Peace Research* 46(3): 377–397.

Bozzoli, Carlos, Tilman Brück, and Tong Muhumuza. 2012. "Movers or Stayers? Understanding the Drivers of IDP Camp Decongestion During Post-Conflict Recovery in Uganda." DIW Discussion Papers no. 1197.

Brück, Tilman, Patricia Justino, Philip Verwimp, and Andrew Tedesco. 2013. *The Conflict Survey Sourcebook*. Washington, DC: The World Bank.

Brück, Tilman, Patricia Justino, Philip Verwimp, Alexandra Avdeenko, and Andrew Tedesco. 2013. "Measuring Conflict Exposure in Micro-Level Surveys." HiCN Working paper no. 153. The Households in Conflict Network.

Bundervoet, Tom, Philip Verwimp, and Richard Akresh. 2009. "Health and Civil War in Rural Burundi." *Journal of Human Resources* 44(2): 536–563.

Humphreys, Macartan, and Jeremy M. Weinstein. 2008. "Who Fights? The Determinants of Participation in Civil War." *American Journal of Political Science* 52(2): 436–455.

Ibáñez, Ana Maria, and Andrés Moya. 2010. "Vulnerability of Victims of Civil Conflicts: Empirical Evidence for the Displaced Population in Colombia." *World Development* 38(4): 647–663.

Justino, Patricia. 2009. "Poverty and Violent Conflict: A Micro-Level Perspective on the Causes and Duration of Warfare." *Journal of Peace Research* 46(3): 315–333.

Justino, Patricia. 2012. "War and Poverty." In Michelle Garfinkel and Stergios Skaperdas (eds). *Handbook of the Economics of Peace and Conflict*. Oxford: Oxford University Press. Chapter 27.

Justino, Patricia, Tilman Brück, and Philip Verwimp (eds). 2013. *A Micro-Level Perspective on the Dynamics of Conflict, Violence and Development*. Oxford: Oxford University Press.

Kalyvas, Stathis N. 2006. *The Logic of Violence in Civil War*. Cambridge: Cambridge University Press.

Kalyvas, Stathis N., and Matthew Adam Kocher. 2007. "How Free Is 'Free-Riding' in Civil Wars? Violence, Insurgency, and the Collective Action Problem." *World Politics* 59(2): 177–216.

Active Armed Conflicts in 2014

Margareta Sollenberg

Introduction

This chapter summarizes the origins and evolution of armed conflicts that were active in 2014, as recorded by the Uppsala Conflict Data Program (UCDP). Descriptive profiles are provided of active armed conflicts that reached the level of war either in 2014 or in one or more previous years.[1] War is defined as those armed conflicts that have resulted in at least 1,000 battle-related deaths in a calendar year. This chapter is compiled based on information included in the UCDP Conflict Encyclopedia, as well as various UCDP datasets (www.ucdp.uu.se). The details about armed conflict activity in 2014 also draw on the most recent publications about the UCDP data (Pettersson and Wallensteen 2015; Melander 2015).

UCDP Definitions and Data

The UCDP defines armed conflict as a contested incompatibility that concerns government or territory, or both, where the use of armed force between two parties results in at least 25 battle-related deaths in a calendar year. Of these two parties, at least one has to be the government of a state.[2] Conflicts are differentiated by type:

- *Interstate armed conflict:* conflict between two or more states.
- *Internationalized intrastate armed conflict:* conflict between the government of a state and internal opposition groups, with intervention from other states in the form of troops.
- *Intrastate armed conflict:* conflict between the government of a state and internal opposition groups.

Conflicts are also divided into two categories according to their intensity:

- *War:* at least 1,000 battle-related deaths recorded in a calendar year.
- *Minor armed conflict:* at least 25 battle-related deaths but fewer than 1,000 deaths, recorded in a calendar year.

Countries may experience more than one active conflict in the same year, fought over different incompatibilities. Therefore, the number of active conflicts may exceed the number of countries that are locations of active conflicts.

UCDP data are compiled mainly using secondary written sources, including news reports as well as human rights reports. The fatality estimates reported in the data are conservative best estimates. This characterization means the data are not likely to be exhaustive depictions of all violence that may have occurred in a conflict. Some violence goes unreported, or the perpetrators remain unknown. The figures for battle-related deaths discussed here do not include deaths in non-state conflict (i.e., fighting between non-state actors where no government is involved) or from one-sided violence (i.e., international targeting of unarmed civilians by state or non-state actors).[3] UCDP compiles separate data on those types of violence.

Summary

In 2014, 40 armed conflicts were active. Of these conflicts, 17 have never been recorded as wars involving the current combatant parties. This chapter covers the remaining 23 conflicts, which were active in 21 locations across the world in 2014. Here is an overview of some pertinent details about these conflicts:

- Two of the conflicts erupted in 2014, both in Ukraine;
- Three of the conflicts restarted in 2014 after having been inactive in 2013: Azerbaijan vs. Nagorno-Karabakh & Armenia; India vs. Pakistan; and Israel vs. Hamas & PIS;
- 11 of the conflicts were wars – causing more than 1,000 deaths – in 2014 itself, which is almost double the number of wars in 2013 (6);
- 15 of the conflicts were over control of government, compared to eight over territory;
- Only one conflict was an interstate conflict (India vs. Pakistan), whereas all of the others were intrastate conflicts;
- Exactly half of the intrastate conflicts were internationalized, with one or both warring sides receiving troop support from other states;
- Overall, the conflicts resulted in 99,027 battle-related deaths, ranging from a low of 37 (India vs. Pakistan) to a high of 53,948 (Syria vs. Syrian Insurgents); and
- Of the 21 conflicts with a history of being active prior to 2014 (i.e., excluding the two conflict onsets in Ukraine), 14 of the conflicts escalated in terms of a recorded change in the severity of the violence (i.e., battle-related deaths) between 2013 and 2014, just four deescalated, and the other three conflicts remained relatively stable.

Meanwhile, five armed conflicts that had been active in 2013, and which at some point had been recorded as wars, terminated by 2014: Ethiopia (Oromiya), Myanmar (Karen), Myanmar (Shan), Mozambique, and Turkey (Kurdistan).

Profiles of Active Armed Conflicts

Box 15.1 Afghanistan & ISAF vs. Taliban	
Side A	Government of Afghanistan, International Security Assistance Force (ISAF)
Side B	Taliban
Incompatibility	Government
Type of Conflict	Internationalized intrastate
First Year of Conflict	1978
Status in 2014	Ongoing
Intensity in 2014	War
Battle-Related Deaths in 2014	12,311
Trajectory of Conflict in 2014	Escalating

Afghanistan has been embroiled in continuous civil war since 1978. The civil war has involved a number of different warring parties and changing alliances after the Soviet invasion of 1979 and even more so after the Soviets withdrew in 1989. The Mujahideen, which had constituted the opposition against the Soviet forces, ultimately took power in 1992 after the collapse of the communist Najibullah government. Civil war continued, however, pitting new constellations of Mujahideen forces against each other.

The current civil war involves the Taliban, which first surfaced in 1994 and later took power in September 1996, proclaiming the Islamic Emirate of Afghanistan. Groups that had been part of or at least loyal to the overthrown government united against the Taliban, under the banner of the Northern Alliance. Following the September 11, 2001 terrorist attacks, the US-led multinational coalition invaded Afghanistan in October 2001, after which the Northern Alliance – heavily backed by its international allies – rapidly overthrew the Taliban government. Since late-2001, the Taliban have been battling the government of Afghanistan as well as the US-led multinational coalition.

The conflict against the Taliban escalated in 2013 and continued to escalate in 2014, when over 12,000 battle-related deaths were recorded – the highest number on record during the post-1989 period. The Afghan security forces suffered an increasing burden of fatalities, as they assumed the full responsibility for security in Afghanistan. International forces continued their planned withdrawal and the International Security Assistance Force (ISAF) mission was officially terminated in December 2014. As part of the new mission "Operation Resolute Support," however, security agreements with the US and NATO allowed for 12,000 soldiers to remain in the country in 2015.

Box 15.2 Algeria vs. AQIM	
Side A	Government of Algeria
Side B	AQIM (al-Qaida Organization in the Islamic Maghreb)
Incompatibility	Government
Type of Conflict	Intrastate
First Year of Conflict	1991
Status in 2014	Ongoing
Intensity in 2014	Minor
Battle-Related Deaths in 2014	107
Trajectory of Conflict in 2014	Deescalating

Algeria gained independence from France in 1962, after a bloody war of independence. Following 27 years of socialist one-party rule, Algeria held its first multiparty local elections in 1990, in response to growing public unrest. By then, an Islamist political party, the Islamic Salvation Front (FIS), had surfaced as the main opposition force in the country. FIS won the first round of parliamentary elections in 1991, in response to which the army canceled the second round of the elections. Amid increasing political violence, FIS was outlawed in March 1992. These events marked the beginning of the plunge into a civil war that remains ongoing, as well as a period characterized by military rule and a series of successive army-backed regimes. The conflict in Algeria has involved a number of different armed Islamist groups, each with their own strategies and religious beliefs, but all sharing the goal of establishing an Islamic state.

One of the first Islamist groups to take up arms was the Armed Islamic Movement (MIA), via its Islamic Salvation Army (AIS) wing, which emerged in 1992. FIS realized that it had lost the initiative in favor of groups choosing to engage in armed struggle and opted to endorse MIA in 1993. The Armed Islamic Group (GIA), which was later the major insurgent force in the civil war, also formed in 1992. GIA's radical political agenda – rejecting democracy and pluralism and viewing jihad as an end in itself – contrasted sharply with that of FIS. GIA subsequently splintered into even more extremist factions, most notably the Salafist Group for Preaching and Combat (GSPC), which appeared in 1998. In January 2007, the group changed its name to AQIM (al-Qaida Organization in the Islamic Maghreb), in the process confirming its allegiance to al-Qaida.

The Algerian conflict escalated to civil war in 1993, exhibiting increasing brutality over time. The army's countermeasures became more and more ruthless, resulting in gross human rights abuses. In the latter half of the 1990s, GIA engaged in extensive targeting of civilians, which came to be a dominant feature of the armed struggle. The AIS declared a unilateral ceasefire in 1997 and later disbanded. The intensity of the violence decreased in 2002. By 2004, the main armed group fighting against the Algerian government was the GSPC.

Conflict activity involving the GSPC has been fairly consistent over the years. The largest numbers of deaths were observed in 2000 and 2003, after which fatalities decreased. This trend reversed in 2007, as a result of an increase in attacks by what had become AQIM. This group also changed tactics to favor high-impact attacks, notably suicide bombings. In 2008, the conflict continued along the same lines, but by 2009 suicide attacks diminished, presumably due to their costs in terms of popular support. Battle-related fatalities still rose in 2009, almost reaching the level recorded in 2003. Since then, fatalities from the violence have consistently declined.

The conflict in Algeria remained active during 2014, though with the lowest number of battle-related fatalities since the early 1990s. The majority of the violence took place in the mountainous Kabylie region. Violence was also observed on the Tunisian border, as well as in the Saharan desert. The tactics of AQIM remained the same as previous years, with small-scale attacks on security forces and widespread use of IEDs.

Box 15.3 Azerbaijan vs. Nagorno-Karabakh & Armenia	
Side A	Government of Azerbaijan
Side B	Republic of Nagorno-Karabakh, Armenia
Incompatibility	Territory (Nagorno-Karabakh)
Type of Conflict	Internationalized intrastate
First Year of Conflict	1991
Status in 2014	Recurring
Intensity in 2014	Minor
Battle-Related Deaths in 2014	46
Trajectory of Conflict in 2014	Escalating

The region of Nagorno-Karabakh in Azerbaijan is mainly populated by Armenians and its territorial status has long been disputed. Nagorno-Karabakh was part of Armenia at the beginning of the 20th century, but the area was transferred to Azerbaijan in the 1920s. During the Soviet era, the underlying conflict in the area was suppressed. With new Soviet policies in the late-1980s, the conflict re-emerged. In 1988, the regional council in Nagorno-Karabakh voted for the integration of the region into Armenia. In late-1989, Armenia declared the enclave to be part of a unified Armenian republic, which neither the Soviet central government nor the Azerbaijani Republic accepted as legal. These moves were followed by a two-year war between Armenia and the Soviet Union over Nagorno-Karabakh.

After the dissolution of the Soviet Union and Azeri independence in 1991, the conflict continued and intensified, with fighting between the Armenia-supported Republic of Nagorno-Karabakh and the government of Azerbaijan. The fighting had resulted in several thousand deaths by the time a ceasefire agreement was finally concluded in 1994. At the time of the agreement, the Nagorno-Karabakh authorities had *de facto* control over the Nagorno-Karabakh region, as well as substantial Azeri territories, including most of the strategic heights around Nagorno-Karabakh. Despite the truce, which had effectively ended large-scale fighting, sporadic clashes continued along the border.

The first peace talks were initiated in 1992. Subsequently, numerous rounds of talks between the two parties have taken place. Since 2004, talks have been organized under a framework known as the "Prague Process," with meetings between the Armenian and Azerbaijani presidents and the Minsk Group of the Organization for Security and Cooperation in Europe (OSCE). Yet no formal negotiations on the core conflict issues have been initiated. Thus, the process has left unresolved several key questions, including the return of refugees, Nagorno-Karabakh's interim status, and the process for determining the final status of the region.

In 2014, tensions between Azerbaijan and Nagorno-Karabakh increased significantly. Skirmishes escalated on the ceasefire line, the so-called Line of Contact, particularly during the summer of 2014. The fighting was far from the level of intensity observed in the early 1990s, but still produced more fatalities than in any year since the 1994 ceasefire. Russian-led talks between the Presidents of Armenia and Azerbaijan were held in September, followed by OSCE-sponsored talks in October. Neither of these interactions managed to relieve tensions.

Box 15.4 Colombia vs. FARC	
Side A	Government of Colombia
Side B	FARC (Fuerzas Armadas Revolucionarias de Colombia: Revolutionary Armed Forces of Colombia)
Incompatibility	Government
Type of Conflict	Intrastate
First Year of Conflict	1964
Status in 2014	Ongoing
Intensity in 2014	Minor
Battle-Related Deaths in 2014	113
Trajectory of Conflict in 2014	Deescalating

Colombia has been plagued by large-scale political violence along the left-right spectrum since the initiation of *la Violencia* in 1948, which turned into a decade of widespread violence pitting numerous non-state armed groups against each other. Most of the violence took place in rural areas, involving landowners and peasants.

In the mid-1960s, left-wing guerilla groups began forming; some were based on rural self-defense groups formed during *la Violencia*. The most important of these groups was the Revolutionary Armed Forces of Colombia (FARC), which has remained the largest insurgent organization up until today. Other groups followed suit, notably the National Liberation Army (ELN), which unlike FARC had more of an urban-based profile. In the late-1970s, guerillas had begun financing their armed struggle with income from coca cultivation and violence also spread to urban areas. By the 1980s, the government of Colombia was fighting several left-wing groups and violence intensified. Some smaller rebel groups subsequently signed agreements with the government, leaving FARC and ELN as the main parties at war with the government from the 1990s onwards.

The conflict became more complex with the involvement of a number of right-wing paramilitary groups targeting left-wing guerillas, as well as civilians allegedly sympathizing with the guerillas. The United Self-Defense Forces of Colombia (AUC) was formed in 1997 as an umbrella organization for local paramilitary groups and was later revealed to have links with government officials. All parties involved in the war in Colombia have extensively targeted civilians, whom they claim support the other side.

Attempts at solving the conflict and ending the violence have failed to yield a comprehensive peace accord thus far. Some agreements were signed with both FARC and ELN in the late-1990s. Yet none of these agreements was associated with an observable decline in violence. Instead, conflict further intensified up until the mid-2000s. Negotiations initiated in 2005 began to have an effect on the intensity of the conflict. Although the talks were interrupted intermittently by outbursts of violence, the trend of decreasing violence has been consistent since 2006. The demobilization of the AUC, which was completed by 2006, also played a role in reducing tensions. Peace talks with FARC, with the express aim to deal with additional political issues such as land reform, began in Oslo in 2012 and were ongoing as of the end of 2014. Violence still continued in 2013–14, but at a significantly lower level than in previous decades.

Box 15.5 Democratic Republic of the Congo vs. APCLS & PARC-FAAL

Side A	Government of the DRC
Side B	APCLS (*Alliance des patriotes pour un Congo libre et souverain*: Alliance of Patriots for a Free and Sovereign Congo), PARC-FAAL (*Parti pour l'action et la reconstruction du Congo–Forces armées alléluia*: Party for Action and the Reconstruction of the Congo-Allelujah Armed Forces)
Incompatibility	Government
Type of Conflict	Intrastate
First Year of Conflict	2012
Status in 2014	Ongoing
Intensity in 2014	Minor
Battle-Related Deaths in 2014	56
Trajectory of Conflict in 2014	Deescalating

The Democratic Republic of the Congo (DRC), formerly Zaire, has been torn by intertwined and complex conflicts on regional, national, and local levels. Various rebel factions have been fighting the government, fighting each other, attacking civilians and engaging in infighting. These different types of violence have resulted in huge numbers of fatalities, not the least from violence between non-state armed groups and from civilian targeting.

The first phase of civil war began as an armed rebellion in 1996–1997, led by the Alliance of Democratic Forces for the Liberation of Congo (AFDL) and supported by the governments of Rwanda and Uganda. The mobilization of AFDL had been triggered by the genocide in Rwanda in 1994 and its consequences for neighboring provinces in Zaire. President Mobutu, who had ruled Zaire since 1965, was eventually toppled by AFDL in May 1997. The new regime, however, was soon at war again, this time with the Congolese Rally for Democracy (RCD) and the Congolese Liberation Movement (MLC). The war ultimately involved at least seven African countries and as a result became known as Africa's first World War. After years of negotiations, the parties concluded a final peace agreement in 2003. In 2006, DRC's first democratic elections were held.

The next phase of war in the DRC broke out after the 2006 elections. This phase pitted the National Congress for the Defence of the People (CNDP), allegedly supported by the government of Rwanda, against the DRC government. The conflict ended in an agreement on March 23, 2009, but was restarted in 2012 by the M23 movement, which was dissatisfied with implementation of the peace agreement. M23 was defeated in November 2013 by the DRC government with heavy backing from the UN Force Intervention Brigade (see also under "Uganda").

In 2014, only two armed groups were active and fighting was very limited compared to previous years. In 2013, the Alliance of Patriots for a Free and Sovereign Congo (APCLS), a small group that had earlier fought in support of the government, changed sides and joined the fight against it. APCLS remained active in 2014. The other group active in 2014 was the Party for Action and the Reconstruction of the Congo-Allelujah Armed Forces (PARC-FAAL), often referred to as Mai Mai Yakutumba, a Mai Mai militia based in South Kivu. Occasional clashes between this group and the DRC armed forces had occurred since 2009, but this violence only escalated to the level of producing more than 25 deaths in one year during 2014.

Box 15.6 India vs. Kashmir Insurgents

Side A	Government of India
Side B	Kashmir insurgents
Incompatibility	Territory (Kashmir)
Type of Conflict	Intrastate
First Year of Conflict	1990
Status in 2014	Ongoing
Intensity in 2014	Minor
Battle-Related Deaths in 2014	177
Trajectory of Conflict in 2014	Stable

The insurgency in Kashmir (the Indian part of Kashmir, formally known as Jammu and Kashmir) originates in the state's disputed accession to India following partition in 1947. The so-called Line of Control (LoC), the ceasefire line agreed upon through UN mediation in 1949 after the first war over Kashmir, has effectively defined the *de facto* borders of Kashmir, dividing it between Indian- and Pakistani-controlled sections.

In the 1970s, a militant opposition movement emerged with secessionist demands for Indian Kashmir. Dissent was temporarily mitigated by democratic policies implemented in the early 1980s. By 1988, however, progress was reversed and non-violent channels for expressing discontent became more limited. Support for militant outfits advocating violent secession from India increased dramatically. A series of anti-government demonstrations and strikes, as well as violent attacks on government targets, launched in July 1988, marked the onset of the Kashmir insurgency, which escalated into war in 1990. Since then, the insurgency in Kashmir has been the most important internal security issue in India. The conflict has involved a range of groups and factions, collectively referred to as "Kashmir insurgents," fighting against the Indian government. Although the insurgents originally included movements advocating Kashmiri independence from both India and Pakistan, groups favoring union with Pakistan have subsequently been dominant. India has repeatedly accused Pakistan of fueling the insurgency. More broadly, the matter of Kashmir has been continuously closely intertwined with the interstate conflict between India and Pakistan.

The conflict over Kashmir has deescalated significantly since 2005. Nevertheless, active violence was observed in 2014, affecting a large number of districts in the state. Fighting occurred along the LoC, as well as in other areas.

Box 15.7 India vs. Pakistan	
Side A	Government of India
Side B	Government of Pakistan
Incompatibility	Territory (Kashmir)
Type of Conflict	Interstate
First Year of Conflict	1948
Status in 2014	Recurring
Intensity in 2014	Minor
Battle-Related Deaths in 2014	37
Trajectory of Conflict in 2014	Escalating

India and Pakistan have fought a series of wars since independence from Britain and partition in 1947. Large-scale wars were fought immediately after independence in 1947–1948 and again in 1965, 1971, and 1999.

The unsettled territorial status of the strategically and symbolically important state of Kashmir has remained at the core of the incompatibility between India and Pakistan up until today (see further under the profile of "India"). The interstate conflict between India and Pakistan has become increasingly intertwined with the Kashmir insurgency, which first reached 25 deaths in a year in 1989. A number of Kashmiri rebel groups have allegedly been supported by Pakistan. Increased tension in the interstate conflict has often tended to spill over into increased tension in the intrastate conflict, and vice versa. A clear illustration of this dynamic is the Kargil war of 1999, which was triggered by large-scale movement of Kashmiri militants into Kashmir, allegedly under the auspices of Pakistan. Tensions were reduced in 2003, when a formal truce between the two parties came into place and dialogue was initiated. The continuing dialogue has resulted in little substantive change, but both parties have continually reaffirmed their commitment to dialogue and peaceful relations. Despite this, sporadic fighting between the respective armed forces, the Indian Border Security Force and the Pakistan Army, has continued across the disputed LoC.

Fighting in 2014 surpassed the 25 battle-related deaths threshold for the first year since 2003. Skirmishes on the LoC escalated in the summer of 2014 and continued into 2015, accompanied by increasingly hostile political rhetoric between the newly elected Indian Prime Minister Modi and the Pakistani government. As in previous years, each side blamed the other for having initiated the skirmishes.

Box 15.8 Iraq, et al. vs. IS	
Side A	Government of Iraq, Australia, Bahrain, Belgium, Canada, Denmark, France, Jordan, the Netherlands, Saudi Arabia, United Arab Emirates, United Kingdom, United States of America
Side B	IS (Islamic State)
Incompatibility	Government
Type of Conflict	Internationalized intrastate
First Year of Conflict	2004
Status in 2014	Ongoing
Intensity in 2014	War
Battle-Related Deaths in 2014	12,598
Trajectory of Conflict in 2014	Escalating

Iraq has been involved in a number of different wars in the past decades. The latest is a civil war that has engulfed most of the country since 2003.

Following the victory by USA, UK and Australia against Iraq in the 2003 military intervention, Saddam Hussein's regime was replaced by a new Iraqi government. Forces from a coalition of countries remained in Iraq to support the new government. Violence soon commenced and would involve a number of different groups in the coming years, most of which had religious agendas. Fighting in Iraq has been fierce since 2004, which was a particularly bloody year in the conflict, but violence declined after 2006. A new phase of escalation began in 2013, which culminated in unprecedented levels of violence in 2014. In addition to the war with the government, various conflicts between armed groups have occurred throughout the war, accompanied by extensive killings of civilians.

During the first years of the conflict, the main opposition armed forces were the Sunni group Ansar al-Islam, the Shi'ite group Al-Mahdi Army, and an al-Qaida-affiliated organization that later became known as the Islamic State of Iraq (ISI) and is known today as the Islamic State (IS). The government of Iraq has engaged in heavy fighting with several armed groups, particularly the Al-Mahdi Army in southern Iraq during 2004. Since the onset of the war, however, the bulk of the violence has involved the ISI.

ISI was formed as the Jama'at al-Tawhid wa'al-Jihad, led by Abu Mus'ab al-Zarqawi. The group changed its name to Tanzim Qa'idat al-Jihad fi Bilad al-Rafidayn (TQJBR) in the fall of 2004, when it also pledged allegiance to al-Qaida (see further under the profile of "United States of America"). On October 15, 2006, the official formation of ISI was declared. Al-Zarqawi was killed in June 2006. Thereafter, the leadership of ISI was formed by representatives from several different factions.

From 2004–2009, the Iraqi government was supported by troops from a US-led multinational coalition. During these years, the foreign troops provided the majority of the armed forces on the government side. On June 30, 2009, responsibility for security in Iraq was handed over to the Iraqi government and by the end of July, only US forces remained. With the official termination of "Operation Iraqi Freedom" on August 31, 2010, the US combat mission in Iraq ended. The last US troops were withdrawn from Iraq in December 2011.

In April 2013, ISI changed its name to the Islamic State in Iraq and al-Sham (ISIS), signaling the group's widened territorial claims, which also included Syria (see further under the profile of "Syria"). The violence between the Iraqi government and ISIS escalated in 2013, with ISIS increasing attacks on both military and civilian targets, especially during the second half of the year.

Fighting escalated dramatically in 2014, making the Iraqi war the second most intense conflict in 2014 after the war in Syria. At least 12,000 people were killed. ISIS carried out large-scale attacks and seized vast areas, including Mosul, Iraq's second largest city. A dispute with al-Qaida caused the expulsion of ISIS from the larger al-Qaida network in 2014. The group also changed its name to IS (Islamic State) and announced that it had established a caliphate in parts of Iraq and Syria. In response to IS advances and in face of mounting reports of various types of atrocities, the US and a number of other countries commenced air strikes against the group.

Box 15.9 Israel vs. Hamas & PIJ	
Side A	Government of Israel
Side B	Hamas, PIJ (Palestinian Islamic Jihad)
Incompatibility	Territory (Palestine)
Type of Conflict	Intrastate
First Year of Conflict	1949
Status in 2014	Recurring
Intensity in 2014	War
Battle-Related Deaths in 2014	1,665
Trajectory of Conflict in 2014	Escalating

Competing claims on the territory of Palestine have been made since ancient times. The state of Israel was created in this territory in 1948, following a UN decision to divide the existing British mandate into Palestinian and Israeli entities. Neighboring Arab countries opposed the creation of Israel and war ensued. Further interstate conflicts occurred in the decades that followed, notably in 1967 and 1973, when Israel occupied or annexed the territories of the Gaza Strip and the West Bank.

ı resistance to Israeli rule existed from the creation of the state of Israel. The first large Palestinian armed
ɡanization, Fatah, was formed in 1959. Additional organizations followed suit. An umbrella organization, the
.iberation Organization (PLO), was formed in 1964. Other organizations subsequently formed, including
lamic Jihad (PIJ) and Hamas in the 1980s. Both of these organizations have opposed the PLO and its main
member-based organization Fatah as leaders of the Palestinian struggle.

Violent demonstrations against Israeli occupation, the Intifada, were initiated in 1987. This uprising, in turn, was followed by the start of peace negotiations between the Israeli government and the PLO, leading to the Oslo Accord of
1993, which created the Palestinian Interim Self-Government Authority. Peace nevertheless remained distant. With the
Second Intifada, which began in 2000, progress in the peace process stalled.

In 2006, Hamas won the Palestinian elections, which resulted in increasing tensions with Fatah. As a consequence, the
Gaza Strip became controlled by Hamas and the West Bank by Fatah. Hamas rule in the Gaza Strip also led to an escalation of the conflict with Israel. "Operation Cast Lead," launched by Israel on the Gaza Strip from December 2008 to
January 2009, generated the highest numbers of fatalities in this conflict since 1982. A ceasefire was put in place in January
2009, after which fighting dropped significantly.

Fighting escalated dramatically again in 2014, to even higher levels of intensity, as a result of "Operation Protective
Edge," which was launched in July 2014. Peace negotiations had broken down in April. After the kidnapping and murder
of three Israeli youths in June, which was blamed on Hamas, violence escalated to levels not seen for decades. Israel
launched aerial bombings, as well as a ground incursion. Hamas engaged in frequent rocket attacks against Israel. Due to
these actions, over 1,600 people were killed. The distribution of the deaths was highly uneven: about 1,600 deaths – a
large majority being of civilians – were recorded on the Palestinian side, compared to 68 deaths on the Israeli side. After
two months of almost daily attacks, a ceasefire was agreed upon in late-August 2014, brokered through Egyptian efforts.

Box 15.10 Myanmar vs. KIO

Side A	Government of Myanmar
Side B	KIO (Kachin Independence Organization)
Incompatibility	Territory (Kachin)
Type of Conflict	Intrastate
First Year of Conflict	1961
Status in 2014	Ongoing
Intensity in 2014	Minor
Battle-Related Deaths in 2014	83
Trajectory of Conflict in 2014	Deescalating

A number of ethnic groups have been in conflict with the government of Myanmar (previously Burma) since independence in 1948. The Kachin ethnic group, based in the far north and straddling the border with China and India, had
already been involved in discussions about autonomy for Kachin areas prior to independence. Autonomy did not materialize once the country gained independence and discontent grew among the Kachin population, which saw few
resources being allocated to the development of Kachin-dominated areas.

Mobilization for armed struggle among the mainly Christian Kachin population was finally triggered by new government policies in 1960, which included a campaign for "Burmanisation" and an explicit goal of making Buddhism the state
religion. In 1961, the Kachin Independence Organization (KIO) was formed and commenced its armed campaign for
independence. In 1989, the aging leadership of KIO decided to change their goal from independence to greater autonomy within Myanmar. After several failed attempts at ceasefires and negotiations, a permanent ceasefire between the
government and KIO was announced in October 1993. KIO was given formal authority over the territory it controlled,
with the right to create a local civil administration. While the ceasefire held for almost two decades, little integration
occurred between the KIO-controlled areas and the rest of Myanmar. The Kachin Independence Army (KIA), the armed
wing of KIO, remained in place. Meanwhile, the government and local police forces rejected any attempts at political
settlement. After the new constitution came into force in 2007, several ethnic representatives that had participated in the
drafting process, including KIO, declared their disappointment with the contents. KIO was meant to reform its armed
force into an army-controlled Border Guard Force, but refused and tensions between the two sides increased.

The government eventually sent forces into the area in 2011, which led to the breakdown of the 1993 ceasefire agreement and a renewal of fighting. Several rounds of Chinese-sponsored talks were held during 2011 and 2012, but these failed to produce a new ceasefire agreement. In 2012, the fighting between the government and KIA escalated across both Kachin and Shan states. Government forces used heavy weapons and occasionally airstrikes against the rebels. The fighting resulted in the deaths of hundreds of government soldiers and rebels, as well as the displacement of tens of thousands of civilians. Several rebel organizations representing other ethnic groups joined in the fighting on the KIO side. Fighting continued in 2013 and 2014, though at a lower level of intensity than in both 2011 and 2012. Talks also took place in 2013 and 2014, but failed to produce an end to the fighting.

Box 15.11 Nigeria, et al. vs. Boko Haram	
Side A	Government of Nigeria, Cameroon, Chad, Niger
Side B	Jama'atu Ahlis Sunna Lidda'awati wal-Jihad (or Boko Haram)
Incompatibility	Government
Type of Conflict	Internationalized intrastate
First Year of Conflict	2009
Status in 2014	Ongoing
Intensity in 2014	War
Battle-Related Deaths in 2014	4,621
Trajectory of Conflict in 2014	Escalating

Since independence, Nigeria has experienced different forms of conflict related to divisions between Muslims and Christians. The Muslim population is mainly concentrated in the north, and a number of northern states have adopted Sharia law since 1999.

Jama'atu Ahlis Sunna Lidda'awati wal-Jihad, commonly known as Boko Haram, was formed in 2002 in Maiduguri of Borno state in northern Nigeria. The founders of the group were reportedly inspired by the Taliban of Afghanistan. Boko Haram seeks to topple the Nigerian government and set up strict Islamic rule. Until 2009, Boko Haram was relatively unknown. In late-July of that year, the group launched an attack on a police station, marking the beginning of armed conflict with the government. The violence culminated as the security forces lay siege to the Boko Haram's base in Maiduguri, in the course of which the rebel leader Mohammed Yussuf was captured and killed. The government reported that most of the group's members had been killed or captured. Yet some managed to escape and later made threats of renewed violence. After the death of Yussuf, the leadership and cohesion of the group became unclear, with indications that the group had split into different factions. Many believe the main faction of the group since Yussuf's death has been led by Abubakar Shekau, who was Yussuf's deputy leader.

Boko Haram resurfaced in late-2010 and intensified its attacks on state targets in 2011. The geographical scope of attacks soon widened beyond Maiduguri and the group's tactics became increasingly deadly. The government responded by strengthening its security force presence in Maiduguri and surrounding areas and declaring a state of emergency for parts of northern Nigeria bordering Cameroon, Chad, and Niger. The conflict escalated throughout 2012, in terms of both geographical scope and the number of people killed. In particular, Boko Haram stepped up its attacks on civilians. The group's operations expanded to cover all of northern Nigeria. Security forces carried out a number of offensives and were able to inflict serious losses on Boko Haram. Nevertheless, the group was able to establish control over some areas of Borno state by early 2013, in connection with which violence continued to escalate. In May 2013, the government declared a state of emergency for the three northeastern states of Nigeria and launched a large-scale military offensive, involving ground troops as well as fighter jets. The army forced the rebels to retreat to the border areas with Cameroon and Niger, in the immediate aftermath of which violence declined. Boko Haram soon managed to stage new attacks and killings intensified again.

Fighting further escalated in 2014, with the security situation in the northern part of the country deteriorating. Boko Haram made rapid territorial gains in August and September, then announced the establishment of an Islamic caliphate in areas under its control in November. The group persisted in its fight against the Nigerian military and large-scale attacks against civilians. In October, the government announced that a ceasefire deal had been signed, which was denied by Boko Haram leader Abubakar Shekau, and attacks continued thereafter.

Box 15.12 Pakistan vs. TTP, et al.	
Side A	Government of Pakistan
Side B	TTP (Tehrik-i-Taliban Pakistan: Taliban Movement of Pakistan), Lashkar-e-Islam (Army of Islam), IMU (Islamic Movement of Uzbekistan), Jamaat-ul-Ahrar (The Freedom Fighters Group)
Incompatibility	Government
Type of Conflict	Intrastate
First Year of Conflict	2007
Status in 2014	Ongoing
Intensity in 2014	War
Battle-Related Deaths in 2014	2,951
Trajectory of Conflict in 2014	Escalating

Pakistan has experienced years of political instability and several shifts between military dictatorship and democracy since independence in 1947. After an insurgency involving the Mohajirs – Urdu-speaking settlers who left India after partition – in the 1990s, Pakistan has been involved in conflict with Islamist groups since 2007. The role of religion in Pakistan had been a contested issue since independence, with segments of society favoring a more Islamist-oriented system of governance. By the time conflict erupted in 2007, groups pressing for such reforms had become increasingly prominent, as well as militant. This tendency was particularly evident in the areas along the Afghan border: the Khyber Pakhtunkhwa (KP) province, previously known as the North-West Frontier Province, and the Federally Administered Tribal Areas (FATA).

The main Islamist organization, the Taliban Movement of Pakistan (TTP), was established on December 14, 2007. The goals of the TTP were to enforce Sharia law, unite against NATO forces in Afghanistan, and perform defensive jihad against the Pakistani army. Since then, TTP has engaged the Pakistani military in battles primarily in northwestern Pakistan. Areas under TTP control have long been a sanctuary for al-Qaida, the Afghan Taliban, and a number of other Islamist groups from across Asia. TTP militants have also been involved in operations in Afghanistan and maintain close ties with the Afghan Taliban. Heavy fighting between the government and the TTP took place throughout 2008, followed by further escalation in 2009. The Pakistani government launched several offensives across the KP province and FATA, which dislodged TTP from controlling territory in most regions. TTP responded by committing bomb attacks in population centers in the south of the country. Throughout 2009, US mounted air attacks on al-Qaida (see further in the profile of "United States of America"). As al-Qaida hideouts often coincided with TTP camps, these attacks also struck hard on TTP. Meanwhile, another Islamist group became active in 2009: the Lashkar-e-Islam (Army of Islam). Although this group remained active in the following years, the vast majority of fatalities in the conflict resulted from fighting involving the TTP.

High-intensity conflict continued throughout 2010 and fighting was particularly heavy along the Afghan border. Despite a relative decline in fatalities compared to 2009, terrorist attacks spread beyond FATA and KP and were increasingly carried out in major cities and in the Punjab province of Pakistan. The TTP also claimed responsibility for a number of attacks against NATO supply convoys. Conflict continued in the same areas during 2011 and 2012, but the level of intensity declined slightly. By 2012, the TTP had split and the TTP-Tariq Afridi faction joined the conflict as a separate organization. The conflict further deescalated in 2013, when TTP seemed to have been weakened by US drone attacks.

In 2014, violence increased again. During the first half of the year, peace talks were held with the TTP, which led to a reduction in hostilities. These talks created rifts in the organization, however, leading to the emergence of a TTP splinter group, the Jamaat-ul-Ahrar. Peace talks collapsed in June when the TTP and the Islamic Movement of Uzbekistan (IMU), a group that has challenged the governments in both Uzbekistan and Tajikistan and is fighting alongside the Taliban in Afghanistan, carried out an attack against Karachi International Airport. Despite serious infighting and a massive government offensive, the TTP carried out a terrorist attack against a school in Peshawar in December 2014, severely damaging the prospects for future negotiations.

Box 15.13 The Philippines vs. ASG & BIFM	
Side A	Government of the Philippines
Side B	ASG (Abu Sayyaf Group), BIFM (Bangsamoro Islamic Freedom Movement)
Incompatibility	Territory (Mindanao)
Type of Conflict	Intrastate
First Year of Conflict	1972
Status in 2014	Ongoing
Intensity in 2014	Minor
Battle-Related Deaths in 2014	280
Trajectory of Conflict in 2014	Stable

The conflict in Mindanao dates back to colonial times and the formation of the Moro identity and the idea of an independent Moro homeland in Southern Philippines. It was not until the late-1960s, however, that Moro nationalists began organizing an Islamist-oriented independence struggle.

In May 1968, the Mindanao Independence Movement (MIM) was formed in the province of Maguindanao. Its aim was the creation of an independent state in Mindanao. Parts of the youth section of MIM later formed the Moro National Liberation Front (MNLF), under the leadership of Nur Misuari. The first MNLF offensive was staged in 1972. MNLF was the main rebel group fighting the government in Mindanao throughout the 1970s and 1980s. In some years, fighting was intense. By 1976, the MNLF had dropped its demands for independence in favor of seeking autonomy. This shift led to splits within the organization and the birth of the more radical Islamist Moro Islamic Liberation Front (MILF), which took up arms in 1986, developed into the main Moro rebel group, and still remains active. Other groups also formed, including the Abu Sayyaf Group (ASG) based on the islands of Basilan and Jolo. ASG has been fighting the government since 1993 and has become infamous for targeting civilians, including internationals.

Negotiations between the government and MNLF commenced in the 1970s. A four-year round of talks, initiated in 1992, ultimately resulted in the Final Peace Agreement signed by the government and MNLF on September 2, 1996. MILF did not participate in the 1996 agreement, but had committed not to obstruct peace.

Fighting decreased in subsequent years, as low-level talks between MILF and the government were held. Despite the start of formal negotiations in 1999, the government declared all-out war against the Moro groups in 2000. Government offensives during the first half of the year resulted in MILF leaving the negotiations in June 2000. Fighting spiraled in 2000, resulting in heavy death tolls. The remainder of the 2000s then oscillated between periods of negotiations, de-escalation, and ceasefires, and periods of escalation. Particularly intense conflict activity was recorded in 2003.

After MILF proclaimed a unilateral ceasefire in 2009, which coincided with ongoing negotiations, fighting between MILF and the government dropped off markedly. ASG remained active and a splinter from MILF, the Bangsamoro Islamic Freedom Movement (BIFM), took up arms in August 2012. The BIFM had been formed in response to MILF dropping the demand for full independence; BIFM vowed to continue the fight for a separate Moro homeland. The government and MILF finally signed the Comprehensive Agreement on the Bangsamoro (CAB) in March 2014, ending their conflict. Meanwhile, both ASG and BIFM remained active in 2014.

Box 15.14 The Philippines vs. CPP	
Side A	Government of the Philippines
Side B	CPP (Communist Party of the Philippines)
Incompatibility	Government
Type of Conflict	Intrastate
First Year of Conflict	1969
Status in 2014	Ongoing
Intensity in 2014	Minor
Battle-Related Deaths in 2014	190
Trajectory of Conflict in 2014	Stable

The origins of the conflict with the Communist Party of the Philippines (CPP) can be traced to the Huk Rebellion of 1946–1954, which was led by activists from the Filipino Communist Party (PKP). Inspired by the successful revolutions in China and Cuba and fueled by reactions to increasing US involvement in the Philippines, PKP members led by Jose Maria Sison set out to revive armed struggle in the 1960s. Consequently, the Maoist Communist Party of the Philippines (CPP) was established in 1968 and its military wing, New People's Army (NPA), has engaged in armed rebellion since 1969.

Over the following years, NPA kept expanding. In 1972, President Ferdinand Marcos declared countrywide martial law to suppress the "state of rebellion." By the mid-1980s, CPP mustered more than 25,000 fighters, who were active in 80 percent of the country's 73 provinces.

In the early 1990s, fighting decreased. The military was preoccupied with internal struggles and several peace initiatives were launched. The CPP was also weakened by internal divisions and diminishing international support. Conflict activity kept decreasing as formal peace negotiations were held in the mid-1990s and general amnesties led to a decline in CPP military strength.

After Joseph Estrada became President in 1998 and the economic crisis of 1998–1999, criticism of the government increased and the different factions of CPP united. These circumstances led to another escalation of the conflict in the early 2000s. After several rounds of failed negotiations in 2004, President Gloria Arroyo ordered an all-out war against CPP in 2006, with the stated aim of wiping it out by 2010. The rebels responded with an intensification of the struggle. Despite a decrease in rebel troop size, due to battle casualties and surrenders, NPA continued to inflict losses on the Philippine Armed Forces, as well as on civilians. By the end of the 2000s, however, NPA had been severely weakened and its troop size was at the lowest level since the mid-1990s.

Formal talks were resumed in 2011 for the first time since 2004. Talks broke down in early 2013, over the release of detained CPP members, and have not been resumed since. During the second half of 2014, however, back-channel engagement to prepare for future peace talks was conducted in the Netherlands. A traditional Christmas ceasefire was announced in December 2014, yet fighting continued unabated throughout the rest of the year.

Box 15.15 Somalia, et al. vs. Al-Shabaab	
Side A	Government of Somalia, Burundi, Djibouti, Ethiopia, Ghana, Kenya, Nigeria, Sierra Leone and Uganda
Side B	Al-Shabaab (The Youth)
Incompatibility	Government
Type of Conflict	Internationalized intrastate
First Year of Conflict	2006
Status in 2014	Ongoing
Intensity in 2014	War
Battle-Related Deaths in 2014	1,140
Trajectory of Conflict in 2014	Escalating

The armed conflict in Somalia dates back to the beginning of the 1980s, when armed clan-based opposition groups were formed to overthrow the increasingly repressive regime of President Siad Barre. In January 1991, President Barre was ousted from power. In the power vacuum after Barre's fall, various clan-based militias began to compete violently for control of the government. This conflict pushed Somalia towards state collapse. Fighting has raged almost non-stop since 1991, with numerous armed groups involved. UN and US troops were deployed in Somalia from 1992–1995, but failed to stem the violence. During several periods, Somalia has lacked a functioning government, particularly during the second half of the 1990s.

Several attempts at forging a central administration have been made, such as the 2000 Transitional National Government (TNG). In response to the establishment of the TNG, several opposition factions united in the Somali Reconciliation and Restoration Council (SRRC) in 2001. Another attempt at a central administration came in the form of the 2004 Transitional Federal Government (TFG), which resulted from negotiations led by the Intergovernmental Authority on Development (IGAD).

The Mogadishu-based part of the TFG was soon pushed out of the city by an expanding network of local Islamic courts, which evolved into the Supreme Islamic Council of Somalia (SICS). Subsequently SICS declared its opposition to the government as well as to its ally, Ethiopia. Most of the territory of southern Somalia soon became controlled by SICS. Worried by developments, the government of Ethiopia sent troops in 2006 to aid the Somali government, and together they pushed SICS back towards Mogadishu. SICS later retreated further to the south, where fighting continued. By January 2007, there were reports of al-Qaida operatives fighting alongside SICS, which prompted US air strikes. During the spring of 2007, attacks on government targets and Ethiopian troops in Mogadishu occured on almost a daily basis. Later in 2007, SICS was absorbed into the Alliance for the Re-Liberation of Somalia (ARS), a new anti-Ethiopian and anti-TFG umbrella group launched in Eritrea.

The security situation in Somalia deteriorated further in 2008, when the insurgency grew in scope, intensity, and complexity. UN-hosted talks in mid-2008 brought promise, but eventually proved fruitless. The presence of Ethiopian troops in Somalia remained the most divisive issue, eventually prompting a split in the ARS. The worsening security situation, political infighting in the TFG, and the announced intention of Ethiopia to withdraw its troops left the TFG significantly weakened.

By 2008, Al-Shabaab had become the main insurgent actor fighting government troops and their Ethiopian ally. Al-Shabaab emerged from the Islamist camp as an independent organization in 2007. Since then, much of the territory in southern and central Somalia has fallen under the control of Al-Shabaab, which has imposed strict Sharia law. This organization has the most far-reaching aims of any of the Islamist opposition organizations in Somalia, seeking to establish a global Islamic caliphate. Al-Shabaab initially enjoyed popularity for reestablishing order after years of chaos. The organization's harsh policies, however, prompted a drop in public support. During 2012–2013, Al-Shabaab's power declined, partly because of increased pressure from the African Union Mission in Somalia (AMISOM), but also due to internal struggles. Military pressure forced Al-Shabaab to change tactics from holding territory to guerilla warfare. This shift has also led to an increase in attacks on civilians. In 2013, the Somali National Army was able to push Al-Shabaab from many of its previous strongholds.

In 2014, a similar pattern of conflict continued, though with slightly higher fatalities. The Somali army, together with AMISOM troops, continued efforts to drive out Al-Shabaab from several strongholds, forcing the organization to relocate further south.

Box 15.16 South Sudan & Uganda vs. SPLM/A-In Opposition	
Side A	Government of South Sudan and Uganda
Side B	SPLM/A-In Opposition (Sudan People's Liberation Movement/Armyi-In Opposition)
Incompatibility	Government
Type of Conflict	Internationalized intrastate
First Year of Conflict	2011
Status in 2014	Ongoing
Intensity in 2014	War
Battle-Related Deaths in 2014	1,667
Trajectory of Conflict in 2014	Escalating

South Sudan became an independent state on July 9, 2011, after a referendum on the status of the territory was held in January 2011. The referendum was stipulated in the Comprehensive Peace Agreement of 2005, which ended the conflict between the government of Sudan and the Sudan People's Liberation Movement (SPLM) (see further in the profile of "Sudan").

From the outset, the new government of South Sudan was challenged by two rebel groups: the South Sudan Democratic Movement/Army (SSDM/A) and the South Sudan Liberation Movement/Army (SSLM/A), both of which were supported by the government of Sudan. Civil war has been ongoing in South Sudan ever since. The country has also experienced an interstate conflict (below the level of war) with Sudan over its common border, as well as various conflicts between non-state actors.

The fighting with SSDM/A mainly took place in Jonglei state, accompanied by some clashes in the neighboring Upper Nile state. Negotiations held with the SSDM/A resulted in a peace agreement in February 2012, which ended the fighting with this group. The SSLM/A continued to fight until 2013. In late-April 2013, a presidential pardon to all rebels active in South Sudan was announced, an offer which the SSLM/A accepted.

Although the fighting between the government and SSDM/A and SSLM/A terminated, violence did not end. Instead, two new groups entered the conflict: the SSDM/A-Cobra faction and the Sudan People's Liberation Movement/Army-In Opposition (SPLM/A-In Opposition). The SSDM/A-Cobra faction was involved in fighting in Jonglei state in 2013, after which clashes subsided. A far higher intensity of violence was recorded in fighting involving the SPLM/A-In Opposition. This conflict started in mid-December 2013, with a battle between different factions of the presidential guard. One of the factions was loyal to the sitting president, Salva Kiir, while the other faction was loyal to the former vice-president Riek Machar, who had been ousted from the government in July 2013. The fighting started in the capital city of Juba, but quickly spread to other areas of South Sudan. Battles were particularly fierce in the strategically important states of Bor, Malakal, and Unity. The fighting started only in mid-December, but over 1,100 people were recorded as being killed by the end of the year. The actual number of people killed may have been even higher, given the situation was chaotic, with several different types of violence observed simultaneously.

The conflict continued in 2014, when fighting between the government and SPLM/A-In Opposition reached the level of war. Much of the fighting was concentrated to three key cities with oil resources: Bor, Malakal and Bentiu, which changed hands multiple times during the year. Both sides retaliated by targeting civilians, often along ethnic lines. Attempts at IGAD-led negotiations took place in Addis Ababa throughout the year. Several ceasefires were declared, only to be breached by the conflict parties.

Box 15.17 Sudan vs. SARC, et al.

Side A	Government of Sudan
Side B	SARC (Sudanese Awakening Revolutionary Council), SRF (Sudan Revolutionary Front), Darfur Joint Resistance Forces
Incompatibility	Government
Type of Conflict	Intrastate
First Year of Conflict	1983
Status in 2014	Ongoing
Intensity in 2014	Minor
Battle-Related Deaths in 2014	856
Trajectory of Conflict in 2014	Escalating

Sudan has suffered from civil war, involving a variety of rebel groups, for over 30 years. The conflict is primarily rooted in the centralization of economic and political power in the capital, Khartoum, and the marginalization of peripheral areas. Religious and cultural divisions, as well as access to natural resources, have also played important roles in fueling the conflict.

The violence began in the south, where the main rebel organization was the SPLM. This phase was ended with a peace agreement in 2005 and subsequent independence for South Sudan in 2011. Since 2003, the civil war has mainly centered on Darfur in the western part of the country.

In Darfur, the government initially faced challenges from two rebel groups: the Sudan Liberation Movement/Army (SLM/A) and the Justice and Equality Movement (JEM). Both of these groups were striving to change the political system in the direction of democracy, equality, and decentralization. Aside from the fighting between the rebel groups and the army, a government-aligned Arab militia known as the Janjaweed has been wreaking havoc, killing large numbers of civilians and precipitating a massive refugee crisis in the Sudan-Chad border area.

Both SLM/A and JEM negotiated with the government from 2003–2005. These negotiations resulted in the establishment of an African Union (AU) peacekeeping force, although efforts to conclude power-sharing and security arrangements stalled. Fighting deescalated significantly in 2005. Violence increased again in 2006, amid a deteriorating humanitarian situation, intra-rebel fighting, and rebel group fragmentation. The most important contributing factor was discontent with the Darfur Peace Agreement (DPA), signed by the Government of Sudan and a faction of SLM/A in May 2006. Fragmentation – particularly of the SLM/A, but also of JEM – continued in 2007. Despite the numerous splits, the different groups often cooperated militarily against government troops. An umbrella movement called the United Resistance Front (URF) was later formed, which unified some of the SLM/A factions. The deteriorating situation led to an international response in 2007. Joint UN/AU meditation had little success during the year, but a hybrid UN/AU peacekeeping force began to deploy in Darfur.

The impending referendum about independence for southern Sudan meant a risk of war between the north and the south. Given the ongoing conflict in Darfur, the government of Sudan wanted to avoid a two-front war. Consequently, the government set out to crush the Darfurian rebel resistance in 2010, which resulted in the highest levels of violence since 2006.

In late-2011, the Sudan Revolutionary Front (SRF) was formed as an alliance between JEM, SLM/A, and other groups based in South Kordofan and Blue Nile states, which border with South Sudan. SRF has since fought in Darfur in the west, as well as in the southern states.

The SRF coalition continued to fight the government in 2014. A new alliance of rebel groups, the Darfur Joint Resistance Forces, also emerged. In addition, a former Janjaweed leader established a new political movement called Sudanese Awakening Revolutionary Council (SARC), which fought the government in 2014. Negotiations took place between the government and SRF, producing a framework agreement for future dialogue.

Box 15.18 Syria vs. Syrian Insurgents	
Side A	Government of Syria
Side B	Syrian insurgents
Incompatibility	Government
Type of Conflict	Intrastate
First Year of Conflict	2011
Status in 2014	Ongoing
Intensity in 2014	War
Battle-Related Deaths in 2014	53,948
Trajectory of Conflict in 2014	Escalating

The conflict in Syria began after a popular uprising in March 2011 as part of the Arab Spring. The Syrian government, led by President Bashar al-Assad, struck out against the largely peaceful protests with gunfire, mass arrests, and torture. As brutality increased, so did the number of defectors from the army. These army defectors formed the basis for the creation of the Free Syrian Army (FSA), a loosely organized umbrella organization composed of various recently formed militia groups, in July 2011. FSA began engaging in battles in September 2011 and was already posing a considerable challenge to the government in the fall of 2011. Fragmentation of the opposition was soon evident, however, and new groups continuously formed. In 2012, radical Sunni Islamist groups such as Jabhat al-Nusra li al-Sham and Ahrar al-Sham emerged. These groups grew in strength, and reports surfaced about foreign fighters joining, notably from the war in Iraq. By this time, the Syrian regime was fighting several rebel groups ranging from separatist Kurdish groups to jihadist groups fighting to establish an Islamic caliphate. The proliferation of armed groups has since continued, with an unknown number of armed actors present on the battlefield. Groups vary greatly in size and ideology, and their relationships to one another are frequently fluid.

Much of the fighting in the conflict has been confined to urban areas, towns, and villages across Syria. Government forces have indiscriminately shelled populated areas associated with different rebel groups, causing large numbers of deaths. Violence continued on a massive scale throughout 2013 and affected most areas of the country. The regime lost its first provincial capital, al-Raqqa, to the rebels in early March 2013. Aided by Lebanese-based Hezbollah, government forces later took the strategically located town of al-Qusayr. The military has relied heavily on aerial bombardment, as seen in the massive assault of Aleppo in late-2013.

Another important development during 2013 was the advance of the Islamic State in Iraq and al-Sham (ISIS), originally an Iraqi organization, into Syria (see above in the profile of "Iraq"). ISIS took control of large swaths of territory, mainly in the north, and eventually clashed with other rebel groups. These clashes added to the number of conflicts among non-state armed groups that were active in Syria, occurring parallel to the main conflict between these groups and the government.

Also in 2013, the Sunni-Shia sectarian divide became increasingly significant of the conflict, with the mainly Sunni rebels pitted against the Shia-supported government. Furthermore, the regional dimension of the war became more pronounced, with several neighboring countries providing support to one or the other of the warring sides.

The conflict in Syria continued at an exceptionally high level of intensity throughout 2014. Aerial bombardments continued. Reports of chemical warfare in the northern part of the country also surfaced. Severe inter-rebel fighting took place between the Islamic State (IS, previously known as ISIS) and other rebel groups. The IS also fought the regime and made large territorial advances, including taking control of regime bases in the Aleppo, Raqqah, and al-Hasakah provinces.

The complexity of the Syrian war, with a multitude of warring parties engaged in conflict with the government as well as with each other, and the relative lack of independent reporting make it difficult to estimate reliable death tolls from the war. The number reported by UCDP – 53,948 – is a conservative estimate arrived at by triangulating various summary figures and subtracting deaths known to have occurred in non-state conflict, as well as all civilian deaths. Many civilians are likely to have been killed in fighting between the government and rebels, which means that this number is likely to be an underestimation. In fact, it was clear by the end of 2014 that fatalities in the Syrian war were the highest of any civil war since the end of the Cold War. In addition, estimates indicate that almost half of Syria's population was displaced, either internally or across the Syrian border, primarily into Jordan, Lebanon, and Turkey. Entering into 2015 all attempts at finding a political solution had failed.

Box 15.19 Uganda, et al. vs. ADF & LRA	
Side A	Government of Uganda, Democratic Republic of the Congo, and South Sudan
Side B	ADF (Alliance of Democratic Forces), LRA (Lord's Resistance Army)
Incompatibility	Government
Type of Conflict	Internationalized intrastate
First Year of Conflict	1980
Status in 2014	Ongoing
Intensity in 2014	Minor
Battle-Related Deaths in 2014	864
Trajectory of Conflict in 2014	Escalating

A large portion of Uganda's post-independence history has been characterized by violence. Rebel groups have been involved in continuous warfare against successive regimes since 1978. The 1970s and 1980s witnessed a number of violent regime changes, with Milton Obote (president from 1966–1971 and 1980–1985) and Idi Amin (president from 1971–1979) among the main principals. This period ended when the National Resistance Movement (NRM) took power in 1986, after a five-year guerilla war. Since then, NRM leader Yoweri Museveni has been the president of Uganda.

The Museveni regime was soon challenged by remnants of the former Obote regime. In addition, a new rebellion erupted in 1986, with the emergence of the Holy Spirit Movement (HSM), a group driven by its own version of Christian ideology, in northern Uganda. HSM's lack of success on the battlefield led to the formation of a related but competing group led by Joseph Kony in 1987. This group eventually became the Lord's Resistance Army (LRA). After initial military setbacks, the LRA was able to take its armed struggle to a new level in the 1990s with the support of the government of Sudan, which led to a regionalization of the conflict. Boosted with resources provided by Sudan, but short on manpower, LRA resorted to a tactic that has made the group infamous: forced recruitment of children. Relations between Uganda and Sudan improved from 2000 onwards, effectively ending Sudanese support for LRA. Subsequently, the LRA returned to northern Uganda, where violence surged in 2002.

Meanwhile, the Alliance of Democratic Forces (ADF) emerged in western Uganda in late 1996, vowing to fight against the government. Like the LRA, the ADF attacked indiscriminately, killing and abducting large numbers of civilians. The ADF has had access to rear bases in the DRC throughout its armed struggle. In 1998, Uganda intervened in the conflict in the DRC in pursuit of the ADF. The main outcome was the dispersion of ADF forces and a geographical spread of the conflict. Beginning in 2000, the government destroyed several ADF bases in eastern DRC and the activity of the group subsequently diminished.

Negotiations with the LRA were initiated in 2006, but the peace process was ultimately a failure. The LRA launched new attacks toward the end of 2008. The government, supported by forces from the DRC and southern Sudan, responded by launching "Operation Lightning Thunder" into the DRC. After the offensive, LRA forces scattered across the CAR, the DRC and southern Sudan and fighting decreased. The LRA still remained a regional threat. In 2013, troops operating under AU command carried out a number of operations against LRA targets, but these efforts were hampered by the chaos engulfing the CAR and South Sudan. Nevertheless, the LRA seems to have been weakened and few battles involving its forces were reported in 2014.

By contrast, violence involving the ADF surged in 2014. The ADF had stepped up its attacks in North Kivu in 2013. DRC armed forces responded by launching an offensive against ADF in December 2013. With the aid of the UN Force Intervention Brigade, a multinational force set up in 2013 to fight the various rebel groups active in the DRC, several hundred ADF troops were killed and a number of the group's bases were destroyed.

Box 15.20 Ukraine vs. Donetsk People's Republic and Russia	
Side A	Government of Ukraine
Side B	Donetsk People's Republic, Russia
Incompatibility	Territory (Donetsk)
Type of Conflict	Internationalized intrastate
First Year of Conflict	2014
Status in 2014	New
Intensity in 2014	War
Battle-Related Deaths in 2014	1,996
Trajectory of Conflict in 2014	Not applicable

In November 2013, Ukraine was set to sign an association agreement with the EU. President Viktor Yanukovych decided to abandon this process only a few days before the agreement was to be signed. Instead, he chose to deepen ties with Russia. In response, mass protests unfolded in Kiev. The protests started as an unorganized demonstration, but the opposition – named Maidan after the Independence Square in Kiev – soon became more coherent. Maidan created a military force and called for the resignation of the government. By the end of January 2014, Maidan had occupied a large number of administrative buildings. Although the government resigned on January 28, the opposition continued to call for the president to step down. In late-February 2014, Yanukovych fled to Russia after having been dismissed by the Parliament.

The pro-Western change in government, combined with Russia's annexation of Crimea in March 2014, triggered the mobilization of a pro-Russian movement in the eastern parts of Ukraine. This process escalated into a series of territorial conflicts. One of the organizations formed by pro-Russian elements was the Donetsk People's Republic (DPR), which demanded sovereignty over Donetsk Oblast in April 2014. This assertion led to a military confrontation with Ukrainian armed forces, which resulted in large numbers of deaths. Both sides undertook extensive military operations, including tank offensives, and engaged in heavy shelling.

In the first weeks of the conflict, many major towns in the area fell under the control of the rebels. Military and police bases were overrun, with rebels obtaining access to weaponry and equipment. The army – disorganized and with low morale – put up little resistance. By early May 2014, the DPR had secured sufficient territory to be able to run a referendum for independence of the region. The DPR formally declared independence from Ukraine on May 12. The Ukrainian army regrouped and reorganized and by mid-May 2014, was back on the offensive. In early July 2014, about half of the territory that the DPR had controlled was back under control of the Ukraine government. Escalating warfare led to events such as the downing of the civilian airliner MH17 on July 17, 2014. The Ukrainian side, as well as the US and EU, consistently accused Russia of providing extensive military arms and direct troop support to the separatists.

Sollenberg

An OSCE-negotiated ceasefire between Ukraine and the DPR was reached on September 5, 2014. The agreement also included another separatist group, the Lugansk People's Republic (LPR), which was cooperating with the DPR. The agreement soon fell apart. Subsequently, the two separatist groups, which had previously fought for Donetsk and Lugansk separately, merged and effectively ceased to exist in their previous form (see further below in the profile of "Ukraine vs. United Armed Forces of Novorossiya").

Box 15.21 Ukraine vs. United Armed Forces of Novorossiya & Russia

Side A	Government of Ukraine
Side B	United Armed Forces of Novorossiya, Russia
Incompatibility	Territory (Novorossiya)
Type of Conflict	Internationalized intrastate
First Year of Conflict	2014
Status in 2014	New
Intensity in 2014	War
Battle-Related Deaths in 2014	1,558
Trajectory of Conflict in 2014	Not applicable

On September 16, 2014, a union between the DPR and the armed forces of the LPR was announced. The new group, the United Armed Forces of Novorossiya, claimed a territory larger than Donetsk and Lugansk Oblast combined: Novorossiya. Since the territorial claims differ from those of the DPR and the LPR, this conflict is considered new, rather than a continuation of the previous conflicts (see above in the profile of "Ukraine vs. Donetsk People's Republic").

A ceasefire signed with the Ukrainian government on September 19, 2014 did not prevent fighting from continuing at high intensity. Warfare included heavy shelling of Donetsk and Lugansk towns by both sides, resulting in daily casualties among both fighting forces and civilians. Bloody clashes also occurred near government-held areas, such as Donetsk Airport, and in the important communications node of Debaltseve. By December 2014, the ceasefire had completely collapsed. At the end of the year, even more intense fighting had begun over the airport and in Debaltseve, and shelling had intensified.

The conflicts in Ukraine have pitted the US and EU against Russia, creating a deadlock in diplomatic relations. After the annexation of Crimea, sanctions were imposed on Russian individuals and organizations, and further measures were applied throughout the year. Russia has bolstered its military presence along the border with Ukraine and – notwithstanding denials by the Russian government – provided arms and troop support to pro-Russian rebels. In December 2014, Ukraine decided to drop its non-aligned status and announced the intent to apply for NATO membership.

Box 15.22 United States of America, et al. vs. Al-Qaida

Side A	Government of the USA, Afghanistan and Pakistan
Side B	al-Qaida (The Base)
Incompatibility	Government
Type of Conflict	Internationalized intrastate
First Year of Conflict	2001
Status in 2014	Ongoing
Intensity in 2014	Minor
Battle-Related Deaths in 2014	103
Trajectory of Conflict in 2014	Escalating

Starting in 2001, the United States has engaged the al-Qaida network in an intrastate conflict with foreign involvement. This conflict constitutes an untraditional case of internal armed conflict, where most of the violent activity has taken place outside of the US. Troops from over 20 different countries have been involved.

The intrastate conflict between the government of the US and al-Qaida began on September 11, 2001, when al-Qaida operatives attacked US civilian and military targets in New York City and Washington DC. Except for the 9/11 attacks, no violence has taken place on US soil. Instead, fighting has mainly been located in Afghanistan and Pakistan, but also Saudi Arabia, Somalia, Yemen and most recently Syria. In some of these locations, the bulk of fighting has been carried out by US allies, rather than by US forces. The conflict reached the level of war in 2001, as a result of the attacks in the US and subsequent operations against al-Qaida in Afghanistan.

Al-Qaida was formed in 1988 by volunteer forces fighting alongside the rebels in Afghanistan. After the withdrawal of Soviet troops in 1989, al-Qaida declared continued *jihad* in defense of Islamic movements. Al-Qaida founder, Usama bin Laden, became increasingly critical of the US, focusing particularly on its military presence in the Islamic world. A stated goal in connection with the 9/11 attacks was to force the US to abandon its overseas involvement, specifically in the Middle East.

US President George W. Bush responded to the 9/11 attacks by declaring the "War on Terror" and specifically a war on al-Qaida. Several other countries soon joined the US government in its fight against terrorism. On October 7, 2001, the US launched "Operation Enduring Freedom," targeting suspected al-Qaida bases in Afghanistan, after the Taliban government had rejected the request of extradition of al-Qaida leaders based in Afghanistan. The operation also included troops from Australia, Canada, France, Germany, Italy, Poland, Turkey, and the United Kingdom, while other countries offered additional support.

After the Taliban government of Afghanistan was defeated in November 2001, US attacks on al-Qaida intensified. Most surviving al-Qaida operatives fled across the Pakistani border in 2002–2003, while others regrouped in Saudi Arabia. The dispersion of the al-Qaida network resulted in a temporary lull in conflict activity in 2003. When the conflict resumed in 2004, almost all the activity took place in the Pakistani tribal areas and Saudi Arabia. In particular, the border region between Afghanistan and Pakistan was the scene of most of the activity from 2005–2008. Also a limited number of missile strikes were launched in Somalia. In September 2008, a new front was opened as al-Qaida operatives launched attacks on the US embassy in Yemen. These attacks later evolved into a battle between al-Qaida in the Arabian Peninsula (AQAP) and the government of Yemen (see further under the profile of "Yemen").

Fatalities rose in 2009 due to an increasing use of US drone attacks targeting al-Qaida operatives in the tribal areas of Pakistan. In May 2011, Usama bin Laden was killed by US special forces in his hideout in Pakistan. In 2013, conflict activity – the majority of which was US drone attacks – remained clustered in Afghanistan, Pakistan, and Somalia. In 2014, however, most activity took place in Syria, with only a lesser share in Afghanistan and Pakistan. By 2014, core al-Qaida operatives had established a presence in Syria and US military forces conducted a number of air strikes in September and November on al-Qaida's Khorasan group, which is closely cooperating with Jabhat al-Nusra li al-Sham, active in the Syrian civil war (see further under the profile of "Syria").

Box 15.23 Yemen & United States of America vs. AQAP & Ansaruallah	
Side A	Governments of Yemen and the USA
Side B	al-Qaida in the Arabian Peninsula (AQAP), Ansaruallah
Incompatibility	Government
Type of Conflict	Internationalized intrastate
First Year of Conflict	2009
Status in 2014	Ongoing
Intensity in 2014	War
Battle-Related Deaths in 2014	1,660
Trajectory of Conflict in 2014	Escalating

Throughout the 1990s and the beginning of the 2000s, al-Qaida (see the profile of "United States of America") had been active on a low level in both Saudi Arabia and Yemen. Al-Qaida in Yemen was considerably strengthened in February 2006, when key al-Qaida members escaped from Sana'a prison. The group recruited new members and set up new bases in Yemen.

In January 2009, local al-Qaida branches in Saudi Arabia and Yemen merged and formed al-Qaida in the Arabian Peninsula (AQAP), with the aim of establishing an Islamic State in the Arabian Peninsula. After the creation of AQAP, the Yemeni government came under increased pressure from neighboring countries, as well as the US, to prevent AQAP from gaining further ground. The first battles between the Yemeni government and AQAP took place in 2009. The US launched its first missile strikes on AQAP strongholds in Yemen toward the end of that year.

In 2010, battles between government forces and AQAP became more frequent. The group also conducted several attacks on foreign targets. Fears that AQAP would pose a threat also outside Yemen led to an increased international focus. Pledges were made by a number of countries, including those of the G8, to support the government of Yemen's efforts to fight AQAP.

In 2011, the armed conflict escalated dramatically, with battles in urban areas displacing tens of thousands of people. Demonstrations in Sana'a during the Arab Spring had weakened the government of Yemen and kept it preoccupied with repressing public unrest. AQAP launched a large-scale offensive in March 2011, resulting in the capture of vast territory in Abyan governorate in southern Yemen. AQAP encountered resistance, however, from the Yemeni military in the Abyan capital of Zinjibar, where fighting raged for the remainder of 2011. In the meantime, calls for the resignation of President Saleh, which were reinforced by US pressure, finally induced him to step down in November 2012. An interim president, Mansour al-Hadi, took over early in 2012.

The conflict escalated even further in 2012. The government intensified its efforts to retake territory in the south. AQAP responded by large-scale bombings, striking even in the capital of Sana'a. As a result of AQAP advances in Abyan, many local tribes had joined the weakened and deeply divided Yemeni army, which proved decisive for eventually pushing back the militants. By the end of the summer, AQAP had lost most of its strongholds. Following these setbacks, AQAP shifted tactics to high-profile assassinations and suicide attacks. Violence escalated again in 2014, but the conflict was not as intense as in 2012, despite a number of deadly attacks. As in previous years, the US continued to carry out drone strikes against AQAP.

The Yemeni government was also challenged by a new actor in 2014. In March, the group Ansaruallah (commonly referred to as The Huthis) called for the government's resignation. Ansaruallah, which had been formed in the mid-1990s by the northern Huthi tribe, initially strived for socioeconomic justice and an end to Huthi discrimination. The group had been involved in intermittent clashes in northwestern Yemen since 2004. During the early spring of 2014, Ansaruallah advanced south towards the capital Sana'a, where it arranged demonstrations in mid-August. The peaceful protests transformed into armed clashes on September 18. Three days later, Ansaruallah took control of most of the capital. A peace agreement, which included provisions for the formation of a new government and a ceasefire, was later concluded. In November 2014, the new government was sworn in. Despite the fact that Ansaruallah's demands had been met, its troops remained in the capital by the end of the year.

Notes

1 This criterion for case selection differs from the one used in the corresponding chapters of previous editions of *Peace and Conflict*. In those chapters, the profiles covered all conflicts that had accumulated a total of at least 1,000 battle-related deaths, whether in a single calendar year (war) or over time (intermediate armed conflict).
2 For in-depth definitions of key concepts, see www.pcr.uu.se/research/ucdp/definitions/.
3 Analysis of patterns and trends in one-sided violence is presented in Chapter 5.

Reference

Melander, Erik. 2015. Organized Violence in the World 2015. *Uppsala, Sweden: Department of Peace and Conflict Research*, Uppsala University. www.pcr.uu.se/digitalassets/61/61335_ucdp-paper-9.pdf.
Pettersson, Thérèse, and Peter Wallensteen. 2015. "Armed Conflicts, 1946–2014." *Journal of Peace Research* 52(4): 536–550.

16

United Nations Peacekeeping Missions Active in 2014

Deniz Cil

Introduction

The United Nations (UN) has been deploying peacekeeping missions since 1948, soon after its founding in the wake of World War II. Over the decades, a total of 69 missions have been conducted in 42 countries around the world.

The missions deployed from 1948–1989, during the Cold War era, mostly consisted of unarmed observers with mandates limited to monitoring ceasefires and investigating claims of violations, following interstate wars. In addition to being smaller in scope, these missions tended to be smaller in scale and uncommon (18 missions in 42 years). The first UN mission, the UN Truce Supervision Organization (UNTSO), was established in order to observe a ceasefire between Israel and the Arab States. The first armed mission, the UN Emergency Force (UNEF I), was deployed in 1956 to address the Suez Crisis.

By contrast, post-Cold War era missions increasingly became more multidimensional and frequent (51 missions in 25 years). The evolution reflects the needs and challenges that arise in addressing different security environments associated with a larger number of internal conflicts, which have progressively shifted the geographical deployment of missions from Europe to Africa and Asia (Figure 16.1). This second generation of peacekeeping missions undertook various new tasks, such as election monitoring; providing support for creating and improving institutions of governance; monitoring

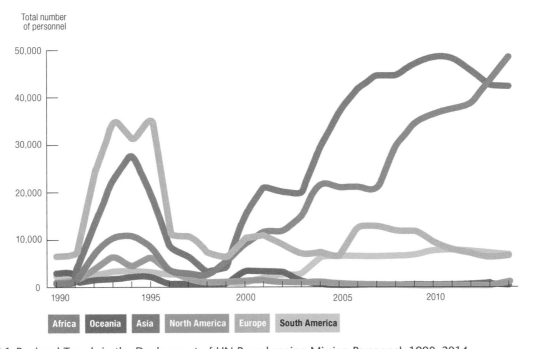

Figure 16.1 Regional Trends in the Deployment of UN Peacekeeping Mission Personnel, 1990–2014

171

programs for the demobilization, disarmament and reintegration (DDR) of ex-combatants; providing training to national police and armed forces as part of security sector reforms and generally to improve the rule of law; and protecting civilians in conflict zones.

Meanwhile, academic research on peacekeeping operations has also evolved. The early work focused on traditional operations during the Cold War, producing mixed results on peacekeeping effectiveness. Studies during the 1990s mostly focused on peacekeeping failures and case studies (Fortna and Howard 2008). Over the last two decades, however, research about peacekeeping missions has shifted to evaluating whether or not they are effective in achieving the various goals, and assessing explanations for the outcomes, in greater breadth and depth. Studies have shown that peacekeeping missions increase the duration of peace following civil wars (Doyle and Sambanis 2006; Fortna 2008), the chances that the conflict will end at the negotiation table (Walter 2002), and the effective protection of civilians (Hultman, Kathman, and Shannon 2013, 2014; Kathman and Wood 2014). Other recent research concentrates on where peacekeepers are deployed (Gilligan and Sergenti 2008; Fortna 2008), contributions of personnel to missions (Gaibulloeu, Sandler, and Shimizu 2009; Gaibulloeu et al. 2015; Uzonyi 2015), and the duration of missions (Wright and Greig 2012). This literature is advancing understanding of how peacekeeping operates in practice and could be altered in design and implementation to achieve better results, using resources more effectively. Continued attention to this subject is essential, as a substantial number of peacekeeping missions – deployed by the UN and other international bodies – currently remain active around the world, carrying out a wide range of tasks in conflict-affected countries.

As of December 2014, 16 UN peacekeeping missions were active (see Table 16.1).[1] Overall, 122 countries were providing a total of 103,798 uniformed personnel (89,607 troops, 12,436 police, and 1,755 observers) to these missions. In

Mission	Mission Name	Location	Start Date
UNTSO	United Nations Truce Supervision Organization	Middle East	May 1948
UNMOGIP	United Nations Military Observer Group in India and Pakistan	India & Pakistan	January 1949
UNFICYP	United Nations Peacekeeping Force in Cyprus	Cyprus	March 1964
UNDOF	United Nations Disengagement Observer Force	Golan	June 1974
UNIFIL	United Nations Interim Force in Lebanon	Lebanon	March 1978
MINURSO	United Nations Mission for the Referendum in Western Sahara	Western Sahara	April 1991
UNMIK	United Nations Interim Administration Mission in Kosovo	Kosovo	June 1999
UNMIL	United Nations Mission in Liberia	Liberia	September 2003
UNOCI	United Nations Operation in Côte d'Ivoire	Côte d'Ivoire	April 2004
MINUSTAH	United Nations Stabilization Mission in Haiti	Haiti	June 2004
UNAMID	African Union-United Nations Hybrid Operation in Darfur	Darfur	July 2007
MONUSCO	United Nations Organization Stabilization Mission in the Democratic Republic of the Congo	Democratic Republic of the Congo	July 2010
UNISFA	United Nations Organization Interim Security Force for Abyei	Abyei	June 2011
UNMISS	United Nations Mission in the Republic of South Sudan	South Sudan	July 2011
MINUSMA	United Nations Multidimensional Integrated Stabilization Mission in Mali	Mali	April 2013
MINUSCA	United Nations Multidimensional Integrated Stabilization Mission in the Central African Republic	Central African Republic	April 2014

Table 16.1 Ongoing UN Peacekeeping Missions as of December 2014

addition, 5,277 international civilian personnel, 11,678 local civilian personnel, and 1,846 UN volunteers were serving in the missions. Across the missions, the approved budget commitment for July 2014–June 2015 was about US$7.06 billion.[2]

The rest of this chapter provides profiles of the 16 active UN peacekeeping missions. The profiles are organized in chronological order based on the dates when they were established. Each profile includes a brief historical overview of the creation, mandate, and operations of the mission, as well as information on the contributor countries and deployment locations. Figures at the outset of the profiles present statistical trends in the number and composition of mission personnel, and the size of the mission budget where data are available. Information on the number of personnel is obtained from the International Peace Institute's Peacekeeping Database, which records total uniformed personnel contributions by type and contributing country for each mission from November 1990–June 2014. The data has been updated to cover remaining months of 2014. In the figures, the average number of personnel for each year are reported. Information on mission budgets is collected from UN General Assembly Resolutions going back to 1990.[3] All budget figures are reported in millions of constant 2014 US dollars, to facilitate appropriate analysis of trends over time.

Profiles of Active UN Peacekeeping Missions

United Nations Truce Supervision Organization (UNTSO)

The first UN peacekeeping operation, the United Nations Truce Supervision Organization (UNTSO), was established in May 1948 and is still in operation. In November 1947, the United Nations General Assembly endorsed a plan for the partition of Palestine into an Arab State and a Jewish State, which was not accepted by the Palestinian Arabs and the Arab States. After the United Kingdom relinquished its mandate over Palestine and the State of Israel was proclaimed, the Arab states reneged on the plan and hostilities broke out. In response, the Security Council decided that the UN Mediator would supervise a truce and be provided with a sufficient number of military observers.[4] Ever since, UNTSO military observers have remained in the area.

In response to the changes in the security situation, especially after the 1956, 1967 and 1973 Arab-Israeli wars, the composition and functions of the mission were periodically adjusted. In 1956, the Chief of Staff of UNTSO became the Commander of the UN Emergency International Force. He was tasked to recruit officers from UNTSO observers and from various UN member-states, excluding the permanent members of the Security Council, to establish the Emergency International Force.[5] In December 1967, the Observation Posts on each side of the Suez Canal increased from 9 to 18 and

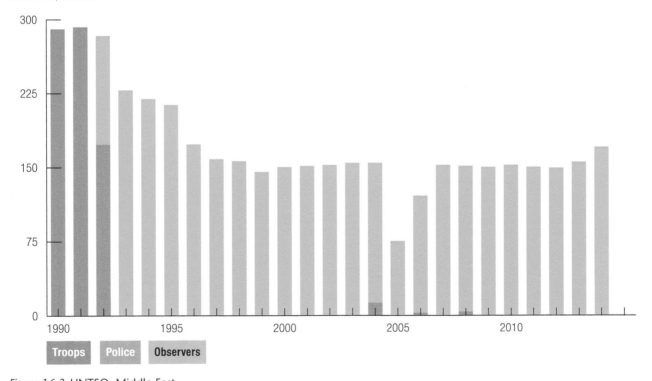

Figure 16.2 UNTSO, Middle East

observer strength increased to 90 in order to monitor the ceasefire.[6] In 1973, several contingents from the UN Peace-keeping Force in Cyprus transferred to Egypt in support of Emergency International Force and the UNTSO Chief of Staff became the interim Commander of Emergency International Force.[7]

The headquarters of UNTSO is located in Jerusalem. In addition, UNTSO currently maintains four observer groups. Observer Group Golan (OGG) supports the United Nations Disengagement Observer Force (UNDOF) in the Golan Heights and is deployed in Teverya (Tiberias). Observer Group Lebanon (OGL) supports the United Nations Interim Force in Lebanon (UNIFIL) in Southern Lebanon. OGL has its headquarters in An Naqurah and maintains two patrol bases in Qiryat Shemona, Northern Israel. Observer Group Egypt (OGE) is deployed in the Sinai Peninsula. Observer Group Golan (OGG-D) is deployed in Damascus, Syria. The UNTSO also has liaison offices in Beirut (Lebanon), Ismailia (Egypt), and Damascus (Syria)

By the late-1990s, the total number of UNTSO personnel had dropped by roughly half from the levels observed in the early 1990s, remaining nearly steady ever since. Between 1991 and 1993, the composition of personnel shifted from exclusively troops to exclusively observers. As of December 2014, UNTSO had 155 observers from 26 countries. The top contributors were Finland (18 observers), Switzerland (14), Netherlands (12), Norway (12), Australia (11), Ireland (11), and Denmark (11). The mission is financed through the UN Regular Budget. Total appropriations for the 2014–2015 budget year were $74,291,900.

United Nations Military Observer Gap in India and Pakistan (UNMOGIP)

Under the scheme of partition provided by the Indian Independence Act of 1947, Kashmir was free to accede to either India or Pakistan. Kashmir's subsequent accession to India initiated a dispute between the two countries, which later turned into an armed conflict. In January 1948, the UN established the United Nations Commission for India and Pakistan (UNCIP), composed of representatives of three UN members (one selected by India, a second selected by Pakistan, and the third chosen by the selected representatives), to investigate and mediate the dispute.[8] In April 1948, the UN Security Council decided to expand the commission and include military observers to stop the fighting.[9]

The first team of observers arrived in the area in January 1949. The observers helped the local authorities in their investigations, while avoiding any direct intervention between the opposing parties until the Karachi Agreement was signed in July 1949. According to the agreement, the UNCIP would deploy units when it deemed necessary in order to help local commanders verify the ceasefire line. Any disagreement over the ceasefire line would be referred to UNCIP. The United Nations Military Observer Group in India and Pakistan (UNMOGIP) replaced the UNCIP in 1951 and continued to observe the ceasefire and investigate reports of violations.

In 1971, hostilities broke out along the border between East Pakistan and India, over the independence movement that led to the creation of Bangladesh. India and Pakistan signed another ceasefire in December 1971 and later an agreement in July 1972 defining the Line of Control (LoC) in Kashmir. India took the position that the UNMOGIP is no longer relevant since its mandate to observe the line established by the Karachi Agreement, had been altered with the new agreement; Pakistan did not accept this position. The mission continued to observe the 1971 ceasefire line. Since 1972, Pakistani officials have filed regular complaints about ceasefire violations to UNMOGIP, while Indian officials stopped filing complaints and restricted the activities of the UN personnel on the Indian side of the LoC.

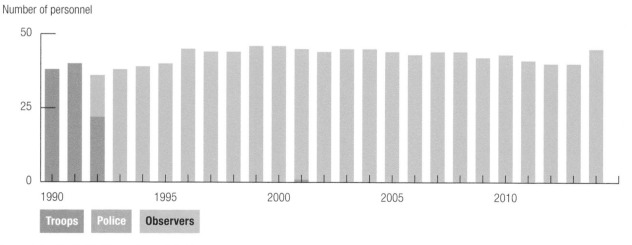

Figure 16.3 UNMOGIP, India and Pakistan

UNMOGIP's headquarters is located in Srinagar and the rear headquarters in Islamabad. In addition, 11 field stations are distributed across the LoC. Since 1993, the mission has been composed exclusively of observers, with the exception of 2001. As of December 2014, the mission had 43 observers, contributed by nine countries. The top contributors were the Republic of Korea (7 observers), Finland (7), Sweden (5), Croatia (5), and Italy (4). The mission is financed through the UN Regular Budget. Total appropriations for the 2014–2015 fiscal year were $19,647,100.

United Nations Peacekeeping Force in Cyprus (UNFICYP)

The United Nations Peacekeeping Force in Cyprus (UNFICYP) was deployed in March 1964, after the outbreak of violence in December 1963 and the failed attempts to solve the constitutional crisis and restore peace.[10] UNFICYP's initial mandate was to prevent the recurrence of fighting and to contribute to the restoration and maintenance of law and order.

The July 1974 coup in Cyprus by Greek Cypriots favoring union with Greece was followed by an intervention of the Turkish military, which occupied the northern part of the island. The UN Security Council called for a ceasefire and requested the withdrawal of Turkish troops.[11] A *de facto* ceasefire came into effect in August 1974. At this point, the new mandate of UNFICYP became to monitor the ceasefire in the buffer zone that separates Cyprus National Guard forces and the Turkish and the Turkish Cypriot forces. This buffer zone extends 180 kilometers (111.8 miles) across the island and varies in width from 7 kilometers (4.3 miles) to 20 kilometers (12.4 miles). UNFICYP troops are deployed along the buffer zone. A police component of the mission was introduced in 2003, after the Turkish Cypriot authorities opened several crossing points for visits.

Under the leadership of the Office of the UN Secretary-General, the parties agreed to a foundation agreement for the Comprehensive Settlement of the Cyprus Problem, which was submitted to simultaneous referenda on April 24, 2004. The plan was approved by the Turkish Cypriots, but rejected by the Greek Cypriot electorate, and therefore did not enter into force.[12] In the subsequent years, the UN Secretary-General's Special Representative continued efforts to solve the

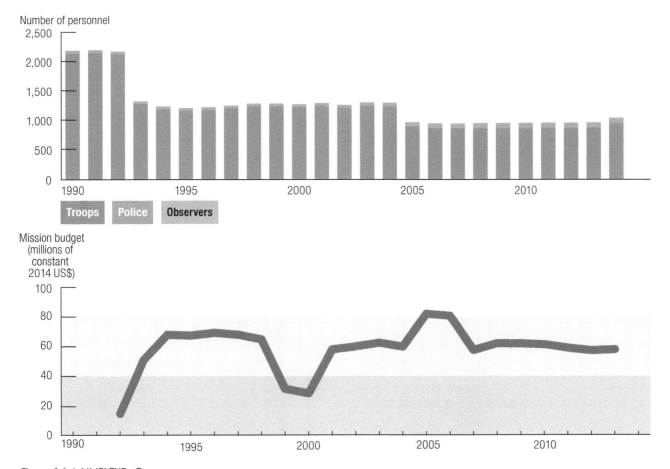

Figure 16.4 UNFICYP, Cyprus

incompatibility. In February 2014, the parties agreed to re-launch high-level negotiations and hold talks in May and June 2014.[13] In October 2014, the talks were suspended due to a disagreement concerning Turkey's attempt to conduct a seismic survey in an exclusive economic zone.[14]

Meanwhile, UNFICYP continues to monitor the ceasefire, clear mines, and help civilians continue daily activities in the buffer zone. The mission and police headquarters are located in Nicosia. Sector headquarters are located in Skouriotissa, Nicosia, and Famagusta. Peacekeepers are deployed throughout the buffer zone in nine locations. As of December 2014, 20 countries were contributing 924 personnel to the mission. The top contributors were the United Kingdom (274 troops), Argentina (268), Slovakia (159), and Hungary (77). Between 1990 and 2004, an average of nine countries contributed personnel, but the number of contributors steadily increased after 2004, even though the total number of personnel decreased by half over the same time frame. The approved budget for the 2014–2015 fiscal year was $59,072,800.

United Nations Disengagement Observer Force (UNDOF)

Following the 1973 outbreak of conflict between Egypt and Israel in the areas of the Suez Canal and the Sinai, as well as between Israel and Syria in the Golan, the UN deployed the United Nations Emergency Force II in October 1974. While the situation was stabilized in the Suez Canal area, the Golan area became increasingly unstable in early 1974. By May 1974, the UN Security Council authorized the United Nations Disengagement Observer Force (UNDOF) to enforce the Agreement on Disengagement between Israeli and Syrian forces.[15]

UNDOF currently maintains a separation area, which is 75 kilometers (46.6 miles) long and 10 kilometers (6.2 miles) wide in the center before narrowing down to 200 meters (0.12 miles) toward the south. In addition to patrolling the area, UNDOF has also supported mine clearance activities and assisted the International Committee of the Red Cross (ICRC) in the passage of mail, goods, and persons through the area of separation.

The situation in the separation area had remained relatively quiet up until the recent outbreak of war in Syria, which started to affect the separation area in 2012. The use of heavy weapons by the Syrian government and opposition groups,

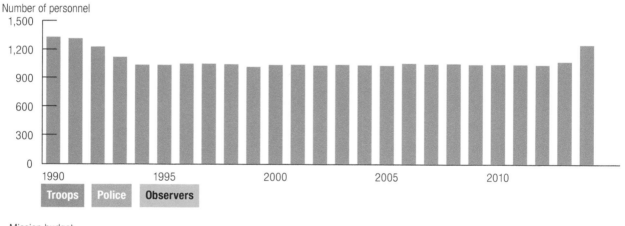

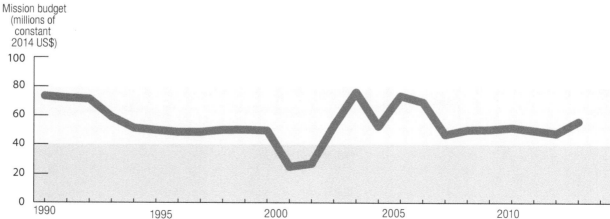

Figure 16.5 UNDOF, Golan

as well as air operations in close proximity to the separation area, continue to undermine the Disengagement Agreement. In August 2014, UNDOF personnel came in direct contact with several armed groups, including the al-Nusra Front, which resulted in the abduction of 45 peacekeepers, as well as the confinement of 72 other peacekeepers to two UN positions. The abducted peacekeepers were released on September 11, 2014. Due to continued heavy fighting, the mission headquarters in Camp Faouar, along with seven positions and two observer posts, were temporarily relocated to the Alpha side in mid-September, limiting the movement of UNDOF personnel on the Syrian side of the UNDOF area.

As of December 2014, the mission had 930 troops, contributed by five countries: Fiji (447 troops), India (189), Nepal (155), Ireland (137), and the Netherlands (2). The average number of contributors has remained the same since the 1990s. The approved budget for the 2014–2015 fiscal year was $64,110,900.

United Nations Interim Force in Lebanon (UNIFIL)

In response to the attacks by Palestine Liberation Organization (PLO), Israeli forces occupied the southern part of Lebanon, except the city of Tyre and its surrounding area, in March 1978. Four days after the invasion, the UN Security Council adopted two resolutions calling for an immediate ceasefire, the withdrawal of Israeli forces, and the establishment of the United Nations Interim Force in Lebanon (UNIFIL), at the request of the Government of Lebanon.[16] The original mandate of UNIFIL was to confirm the withdrawal of Israeli forces, restore international peace, and assist the Government of Lebanon in establishing its authority in the area.

In 1985, Israel withdrew partially from regions of Lebanon occupied in 1982, while retaining control of the southern part, which was manned by the Israeli Defense Force (IDF), De Facto Forces (DFF), and the South Lebanon Army (SLA) until May 2000. In June 2000, UNIFIL confirmed the withdrawal of Israel forces in compliance with UN Security Council Resolution 425 (1978). The Government of Lebanon started to deploy army and police personnel and to re-establish local administration in the occupied areas in August 2000. In July 2006, however, heavy fighting erupted between Israel and Hezbollah, operating from Lebanese territory. In response, the UN Security Council increased the size of UNIFIL to a maximum of 15,000 troops, to monitor the ceasefire and continue to implement its mandate.[17]

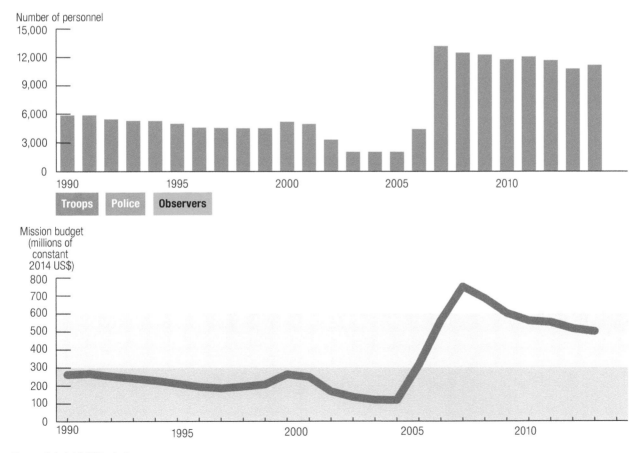

Figure 16.6 UNIFIL, Lebanon

In July and August 2014, the outbreak of the Gaza conflict threatened the stability in the area of UNIFIL operations and along the Blue Line (a border demarcation between Lebanon and Israel, delineated by the UN on June 7, 2000 for the purposes of gauging whether Israel had withdrawn fully from Lebanon). In the wake of rocket attacks launched from Lebanon, UNIFIL continued its close contact with both sides in an effort to de-escalate the situation and restore the cessation of hostilities. A UNIFIL investigation claimed that the attacks were individual initiatives to express solidarity with Gaza during Israel's military operations.[18] UNIFIL conducted on average of 11,000 activities per month, including patrols, checkpoints, and observation tasks, throughout the second half of 2014.

UNIFIL has its headquarters in Naqoura and 51 additional positions throughout southern Lebanon. As of December 2014, UNIFIL had 10,238 troops contributed by 36 countries. The top contributors were Indonesia (1,289 troops), Italy (1,101), India (898), Malaysia (827), and Nepal (869). The average number of contributors was around nine throughout the 1990s and early 2000s, then almost tripled in the second half of the 2000s. The total approved budget for 2014–2015 fiscal year was $427,319,800.

United Nations Mission for the Referendum in Western Sahara (MINURSO)

After the efforts by the Organization of African Unity and the UN Secretary-General during the late 1980s to solve the conflict over Western Sahara between Morocco and Popular Front for the Liberation of Saguia el Hamra and Rio de Oro (POLISARIO)), the UN Security Council established the United Nations Mission for the Referendum in Western Sahara (MINURSO) on April 26, 1991.[19] The initial mandate was extensive: monitoring the ceasefire; verifying the reduction of Moroccan troops; monitoring confinement of Moroccan and POLISARIO troops; taking steps towards ensuring the release of all Western Sahara political prisoners; overseeing the exchange of prisoners; implementing the repatriation; identifying and registering voters; and organizing and ensuring a free and fair referendum.[20] Many aspects of the mandate were successfully implemented, with the notable exception of the referendum.

Identification of voters was finalized in December 1999, after issues about registering the members of the three contested tribes were resolved. Yet differences concerning the repatriation of refugees and the appeals process endured. Two

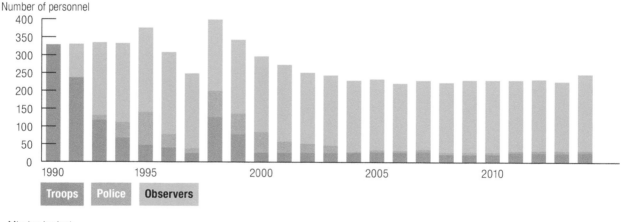

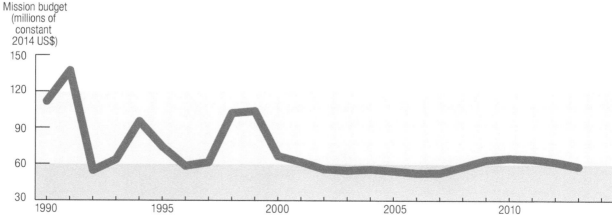

Figure 16.7 MINURSO, Western Sahara

rounds of UN-sponsored talks in June and August 2007, followed by a third round in January 2008 and informal meetings in August 2009 and February 2010, did not lead to substantive progress on resolving core issues. After the failed direct negotiations, the UN Secretary-General's Special Envoy held bilateral talks with the parties and neighboring countries throughout 2013 and 2014, seeking to work towards a solution to self-determination of the Western Sahara.

MINURSO continues to monitor the ceasefire, work to reduce the threat of mines, support confidence-building mechanisms between the parties, assist the UN Refugee Agency (UNHCR) in its activities in the refugee camps near Tindouf, and cooperate with the observer delegation of the African Union (AU) in Laayoune. MINURSO's headquarters is located in Laayoune. Two liaison offices are located in Tindouf and Ad Dakhla. The mission also maintains nine UN team sites on both sides of the berm, a sand wall structure that separates the two sides in the conflict. As of December 2014, 35 countries were contributing 225 uniformed personnel to the mission. The top contributors were Bangladesh (27 personnel), Egypt (21), Pakistan (13), Honduras (11) and Malaysia (10). The number of contributors has stayed relatively stable, around an average of 28 countries, since the establishment of the mission. The total approved budget for July 2014–December 2014 was $55,990,080.

United Nations Interim Administration Mission in Kosovo (UNMIK)

In June 1999, the UN Security Council decided to deploy both a civil and security presence in Kosovo. The civil presence, the United Nations Interim Administration Mission in Kosovo (UNMIK), was tasked with ensuring that the people of Kosovo could enjoy substantial autonomy until a final settlement is reached, including by performing basic civilian administrative functions and facilitating a political process to determine the future status of Kosovo. The security presence, the NATO-led Kosovo Force (KFOR), was tasked with deterring renewed hostilities; maintaining the ceasefire; preventing the return of the Federal and Republic military, police and paramilitary forces; demilitarizing the Kosovo Liberation Army (KLA) forces; and establishing a secure environment for the return of refugees.[21]

UNMIK was the first mission of its kind in two respects. One was assuming a wide range of administrative responsibilities. Another was to have a civil peacekeeping mission under UN leadership that brought together different

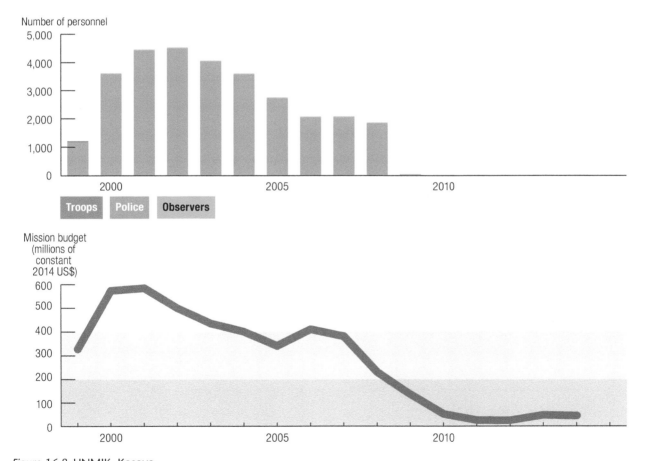

Figure 16.8 UNMIK, Kosovo

intergovernmental organizations, namely the Office of the United Nations High Commissioner for Refugees (UNHCR), the Organization for Security and Co-operation in Europe (OSCE), and the European Union (EU), which were responsible for humanitarian assistance, democratization, and economic development, respectively.

In early 2006, the UN Secretary-General's Special Envoy, Martti Ahtisaari, initiated direct talks between Kosovo's Albanian community and Serbia. In August 2007, a new mediation effort was initiated by the "Troika": the EU, the Russian Federation, and the United States.[22] After the governments of Kosovo and Serbia failed to reach an agreement on the status of Kosovo, the Assembly of Kosovo declared independence in February 2008.[23] In response, the mandate and the size of UNMIK were adjusted accordingly. The mission successfully concluded its gradual reconfiguration and reached the authorized strength of 510 personnel by July 2009, factoring in the deployment of the European Union Rule of Law Mission (EULEX).[24]

UNMIK continues its regular engagement with the governments of Kosovo and Serbia, all communities and relevant stakeholders in Kosovo, and regional and international actors, to promote security, stability, and respect for human rights in Kosovo and across the region. The mission headquarters is located in Pristina and the regional headquarters is located in Kosovska Mitrovica. As of December 2014, 12 countries were contributing 16 personnel to the mission. The only countries contributing multiple personnel were Ukraine (3), the Czech Republic (2), and Turkey (2). The average number of contributors was 49 between 1999 and 2008, but declined sharply thereafter. The total approved budget for 2014–2015 fiscal year was $42,971,600.

United Nations Mission in Liberia (UNMIL)

Liberia's second major civil conflict ended when President Charles Taylor (who played a primary role, as a rebel leader, in initiating the first major civil conflict in 1990) stepped down in August 2003 and the vice-president signed an agreement with the Movement for Democracy in Liberia (MODEL) and the Liberians United for Reconciliation and Democracy (LURD). The National Transitional Government of Liberia (NTGL) was subsequently established in October 2003. On

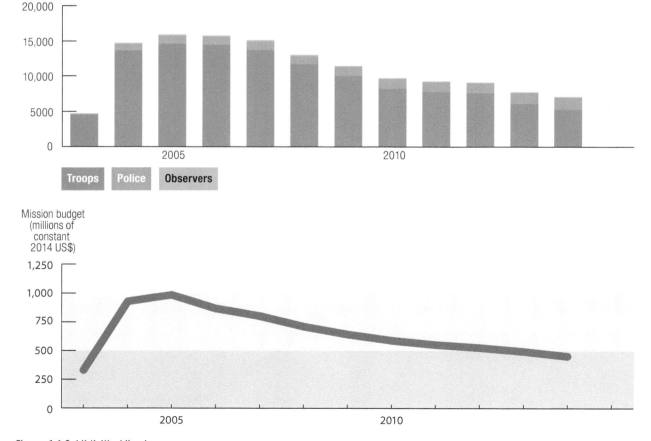

Figure 16.9 UNMIL, Liberia

September 19, 2003, meanwhile, the UN Security Council established the United Nations Mission in Liberia (UNMIL) in order to monitor the implementation of a ceasefire, assist the development of cantonment sites and provide security at these sites, support the work of Joint Monitoring Committee, and provide humanitarian assistance.[25] UNMIL formally assumed responsibilities from the Economic Community of West African States (ECOWAS) Mission in Liberia (ECOMIL) in October 2003, and all troops of ECOMIL were reassigned to UNMIL as UN peacekeepers.[26]

In October 2004, the disarmament of MODEL, LURD, and former government forces was completed. UNMIL assumed a wide range of roles in the demobilization, disarmament and reintegration (DDR) program, including central coordination, mobilization of resources, preparation and security of cantonment sites, and the collection and destruction of weapons.[27] In September 2005, the UN Security Council expanded UNMIL's mandate by deploying 250 UN personnel to neighboring Sierra Leone in order to provide security for the Special Court for Sierra Leone (SCSL), after the mandate of the United Nations Mission in Sierra Leone ended.[28] The SCSL was established in 2002 to address serious crimes against humanity committed during the 1991–2002 civil war in Sierra Leone. This conflict in Sierra Leone had important links to the civil war in Liberia that occurred around the same time. Charles Taylor was eventually arrested and prosecuted by the SCSL (though the trial proceedings occurred at the facilities of the International Criminal Court in the Hague, the Netherlands) for his involvement in the Sierra Leone conflict. UNMIL troops operated only within the premises of the SCSL and provided logistical and security support together with the United Nations Integrated Office in Sierra Leone.

In October 2005, national elections were held in Liberia. UNMIL supported the Liberian National Police at the polling stations on the Election Day and provided logistical support for transporting ballots, while the UNMIL Election Unit assisted the National Elections Committee in planning and organizing the elections.[29] In June 2009, after significant delays, the Liberian Truth and Reconciliation Commission submitted its report to the legislature and the President, in which it recommended that an extraordinary criminal tribunal should be established to prosecute those who committed gross violations of human rights, including the former President Charles Taylor. In May 2012, Taylor was sentenced to 50 years in prison by the SCSL for "aiding and abetting" war crimes and crimes against humanity committed in Sierra Leone. UNMIL later assisted the Liberian National Elections Committee with the 2011 general and 2014 senatorial elections. During the Ebola outbreak in the second half of 2014, UNMIL continued its main activities, such as monitoring human rights violations, but certain activities, including police training, were suspended.[30]

UNMIL's headquarters is located in Monrovia and military and police units are deployed in 21 additional locations. As of December 2014, 53 countries were contributing 5,838 personnel to the mission. The top contributors were Nigeria (1,545 personnel), Pakistan (921), Ghana (748), China (721), and Bangladesh (543). Since the establishment of the mission, the number of contributors has remained relatively stable, with an average of 57 countries between 2003 and 2014. The total approved budget for 2014–2015 period was $427,319,800.

United Nations Operation in Cote d'Ivoire (UNOCI)

In April 2004, the UN Security Council established the United Nations Operation in Côte d'Ivoire (UNOCI), replacing the smaller political mission – the United Nations Mission in Côte d'Ivoire – that had been deployed since May 2003. UNOCI's mandate was extensive: to monitor the ceasefire agreement of May 3, 2003; to help the Government of National Reconciliation in implementing the national DDR program; to protect UN personnel and civilians; to provide assistance, in cooperation with ECOWAS, with the conduct of free and fair elections, as envisioned in Linas-Marcoussis Agreement of January 2003; and to facilitate the delivery of humanitarian assistance.[35]

Over the next four years, the parties signed several peace agreements regulating the different issue areas and/or reaffirming previous agreements. The security situation stayed calm after the Ouagadougou Agreement was signed in March 2007. An integrated command center was established in April 2007. Cantonment of ex-combatants and disarmament were delayed until late-2008, due to disagreements over the reintegration arrangements.[36] The presidential elections, originally planned for November 2008, were postponed several times due to delays in voter registration. In February 2010, reports alleged a fraudulent registration process. In response, the president dissolved both the government and the Electoral Commission. A new government and commission were formed in February 2010.[37]

In the wake of the disputed presidential elections held in October–November 2010, UNOCI and a peacekeeping mission of the French Armed Forces (*Opération Licorne*) undertook military operations to protect their own personnel as well as civilian populations, who came under attack on April 6, 2011. Opposition candidate Alassane Ouattara had been announced as the winner by the Independent Electoral Commission, while the Constitutional Council announced that the winner was incumbent President Gbagbo, who then refused to step down.[38] Fighting between the *Forces Républicaines de Côte d'Ivoire* (FRCI), established by Ouattara, and the pro-Gbagbo forces commenced in mid-March. Gbagbo was arrested on April 11, 2011.[39] As the security situation improved over the next couple of years, the UN Security Council gradually reduced the size of UNOCI, while extending the mission until June 2015.[40]

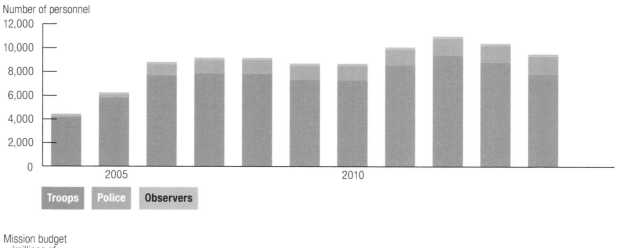

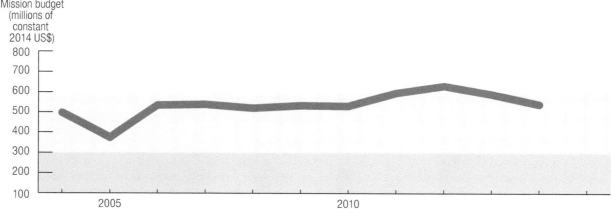

Figure 16.10 UNOCI, Côte d'Ivoire

The headquarters of UNOCI is located in Abidjan. The mission had two sector headquarters, in Daloa (West) and Bouake (East), and 27 additional military and police unit locations. As of December 2014, 58 countries were contributing 7,636 personnel to the mission. The top contributors were Bangladesh (1,860 personnel), Pakistan (1,304), Niger (896), Morocco (717), and Jordan (524). The number of contributing countries has remained stable, with an average of 52 since 2004. The total approved budget for 2014–2015 fiscal year was $493,570,300.

United Nations Stabilization Mission in Haiti (MINUSTAH)

The first UN mission in Haiti, the United Nations Observer Group for the Verification of the Elections in Haiti (ONUVEH), was established to observe the elections of 1990–1991. After the 1991 coup, the situation in Haiti deteriorated, which led the UN Security Council to authorize a multi-national force in July 1994, followed by several missions between 1994 and 2000. Once the conflict restarted in February 2004, the UN Security Council authorized the Multinational Interim Force (MIF) and declared its readiness to deploy a stabilization force.[31] The United Nations Stabilization Mission in Haiti (MINUSTAH) was established in April 2004,[32] then assumed authority from MIF on June 1, 2004. MINUSTAH's mandate included supporting the Transitional Government to ensure security, assisting the National Police with DDR programs, supporting political processes that were underway, and monitoring and reporting on the human rights situation to the United Nations High Commissioner for Human Rights.

In the aftermath of the earthquake in January 2010, the UN Security Council authorized additional troop and police deployments to support the recovery efforts.[33] The capacity of the mission was further increased in June 2010.[34] MINUSTAH also provided technical and logistical support during the 2010–2011 presidential and legislative elections. More recently, MINUSTAH provided transportation for mobile teams, helped to develop the communications plan for the voter registration campaign of the National Identification Office, and held pre-electoral forums for civic education in relation to the October 2014 presidential elections, then aided the Electoral Council and the government with addressing the political impasse that led to the cancellation of the election.

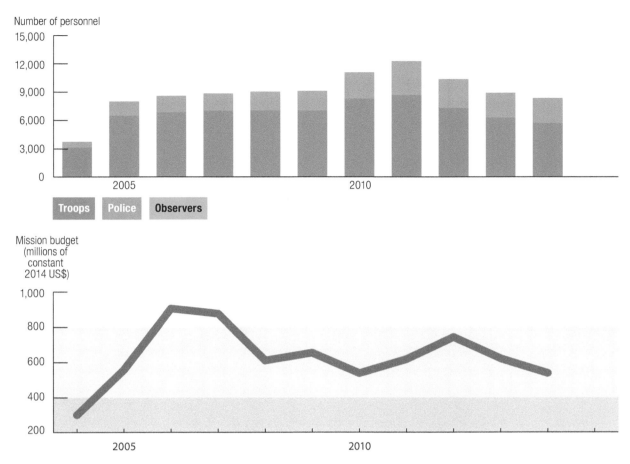

Figure 16.11 MINUSTAH, Haiti

The headquarters of MINUSTAH is located in Port-au-Prince. Peacekeepers are deployed in 10 military unit locations and five police unit locations throughout the country. As of December 2014, 51 countries were contributing 7,213 personnel to the mission. The top contributors were Brazil (1,378 personnel), Sri Lanka (872), Uruguay (595), Argentina (587), India (427), and Chile (422). The number of contributing countries has remained relatively stable, with an average of 46 since 2004. The total approved budget for 2014–2015 fiscal year was $500,080,500.

United Nations–African Union Mission in Darfur (UNAMID)

The conflict in Darfur, Sudan started in 2003, pitting the government of Sudan against the Sudan Liberation Movement/Army (SLM/A) and the Justice and Equality Movement (JEM). In July 2004, the Africa Union Mission in Sudan (AMIS) was deployed with just 60 troops. The capacity of the mission increased quickly to 3,320 personnel in October 2004. AMIS was later replaced by the UN-AU Mission in Darfur (UNAMID) in July 2007.[41]

UNAMID is authorized to take the necessary action, in areas of deployment, to protect its personnel, as well as civilians and humanitarian workers, to support the implementation of the Darfur Peace Agreement (signed on May 5, 2006 by one of the factions of SLM/A), to assist with the restoration of security conditions, and to facilitate the joint UN-AU mediation process. In 2009–2010, several attempts at resolving the conflict were made by the UN-AU mediation team and UNAMID that resulted in the Doha Framework Agreement in February 2010. Negotiations continued throughout 2011 to include the non-signatory groups in the Agreement. The security and humanitarian situations remained significant concerns, with ongoing fighting between government forces and various armed groups during 2012–2013, particularly in Northern Darfur, in addition to ongoing inter-communal conflict over resources (arable land, lucrative minerals, and hydrocarbons). UNAMID facilitated several conferences bringing together civil society representatives and community leaders to address the root causes of resource-based conflict in late-2013. The security crisis in Darfur persisted, despite the direct talks held in November 2014 between the government and non-signatory groups to Doha Framework Agreement. UNAMID continues to provide technical assistance to DDR programs, conduct police and military patrols throughout

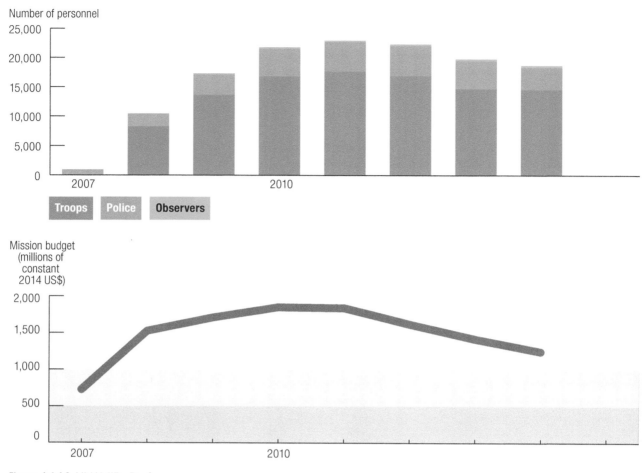

Figure 16.12 UNAMID, Darfur

the region and especially in internally displaced persons camps, engage in training with the national police, and offer technical and logistical support to humanitarian agencies.

UNAMID's headquarters is located in El Fasher, while sector headquarters are located in Zam Zam (North), Nyala and Al Da'ein (North), El Geneina (West) and Zallingei (Central). Peacekeepers are also deployed in 30 other locations throughout Darfur. As of December 2014, 47 countries were contributing 15,869 personnel to the mission. The top contributors were Ethiopia (2,533 personnel), Rwanda (2,526), Egypt (1,148), Senegal (1,106), Pakistan (1,443), Nigeria (999), and Burkina Faso (971). The number of contributors was 27 in the first year of the mission; the average number then increased significantly over subsequent years. The total approved budget for 2014–2015 fiscal year was $1,153,611,300.

United Nations Organization Stabilization Mission in the Democratic Republic of Congo (MONUSCO)

After the July 1999 Lusaka agreement, signed between the Democratic Republic of Congo (DRC) and Angola, Namibia, Rwanda, Uganda, and Zimbabwe, the UN Security Council established the United Nations Organization Mission in the Democratic Republic of the Congo (MONUC). The initial mandate of MONUC was to monitor the ceasefire, facilitate coordination among signatories, and provide technical assistance for the disengagement of forces.[42] Later in 2006, MONUC assisted with the organization of presidential and legislative elections. In 2010, the UN Security Council renamed the mission as the United Nations Organization Stabilization Mission in the Democratic Republic of the Congo (MONUSCO).[43] In conjunction, the updated mandate included the protection of civilians and support for government military operations against the *Forces Democratiques de Liberation du Rwanda* (FDLR) and the Lord's Resistance Army (LRA), demobilization activities, reformation of DRC armed forces and police, and continued efforts to combat the illegal trade of natural resources in North and South Kivu.

In response to renewed conflict in 2012, the UN Security Council decided in March 2013 to introduce an "Intervention Brigade" in order to neutralize armed groups.[44] This measure was also undertaken in furtherance of the Peace,

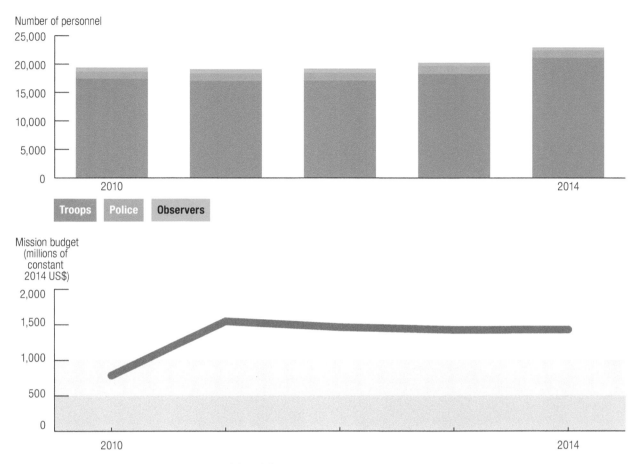

Figure 16.13 MONUSCO, Democratic Republic of the Congo

Security and Cooperation Framework for the DRC, which had been signed by the 11 countries in the region, as well as the AU, the International Conference on the Great Lakes Region, the Southern African Development Community and the UN Secretary-General. The brigade, with headquarters in Goma and acting under the direct command of MONUSCO, was composed of three infantry battalions, an artillery company, and a special forces and reconnaissance company. In November 2013, the rebel group M23 was defeated. Yet FDLR, the Allied Democratic Forces (ADF), and Mayi-Mayi groups remain active in the eastern DRC. MONUSCO continues to engage in joint operations with the DRC's Armed Forces.

MONUSCO's headquarters is located in Kinshasa, with five brigade headquarters distributed across the eastern part of the country. Peacekeepers are deployed to 25 other locations, including seven manned by police units. As of December 2014, 55 countries were contributing 21,036 personnel to the mission. The top contributors were India (4,031 personnel), Pakistan (3,786), Bangladesh (2,697), South Africa (1,341), Tanzania (1,249), and Uruguay (1,192). The average number of contributors has been 57 since the establishment of the mission. The total approved budget for 2014–2015 fiscal year was $1,398,475,300.

United Nations Mission in the Republic of South Sudan (UNMISS)

As a part of the Comprehensive Peace Agreement signed between the Government of Sudan and the Sudan People's Liberation Movement/Army (SPLM/A), a referendum was held in January 2011 to determine the future of South Sudan. Following the vote, South Sudan became independent in July 2011. The United Nations Mission in the Republic of South Sudan (UNMISS) was established to support consolidation of peace, state-building, and economic development, including providing advice to the Government of South Sudan on the political transition, governance, and the establishment of state authority and rule of law.[45]

Throughout much of 2012, a border dispute between South Sudan and Sudan appeared to unify all the political parties in South Sudan in their support for the policies of the government of South Sudan towards Sudan. At the same time, the security situation progressively deteriorated. In addition to inter-communal conflicts in Jonglei, between December 2011

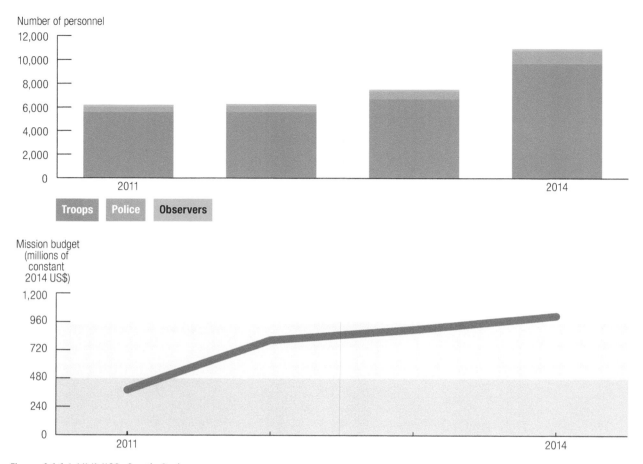

Figure 16.14 UNMISS, South Sudan

and January 2012 two rebel groups emerged: the South Sudan Democratic Movement/Army (SSDM/A) and the South Sudan Liberation Movement/Army (SSLM/A). SSDM/A signed an agreement terminating conflict in February 2012.[46] In April 2013, the president declared amnesty for six leaders of the armed groups. SSLM/A accepted the offer and integrated its force into SPLA. In contrast, the Yau Yau group, which splintered off from SSDM/A, continued fighting. In March and April 2013, UNMISS convoys were ambushed in Jonglei state by unidentified armed elements.[47]

In July 2013, President Salva Kiir dismissed the national cabinet and Vice-President Riek Machar, as well as suspended the Secretary-General of the Sudan People's Liberation Movement (SPLM), who was under investigation for alleged mismanagement of party affairs. In December 2013, fighting broke out in the meeting of the SPLM National Liberation Council. UNMISS could not identify the cause of fighting, while the government announced that there had been a coup attempt. Thereafter, tensions arose between the executive and the legislative branches in 10 state governments and several units defected from the SPLA. Many civilians sought refuge in UNMISS bases as the fighting escalated across South Sudan in late-2013.[48] The security situation has since remained unstable. In response to the crises, the UN Security Council realigned the UNMISS mandate to prioritize the protection of civilians.[49] Meanwhile, negotiations continued under the auspices of the Intergovernmental Authority on Development (IGAD) throughout 2014.

The headquarters of UNMISS is located in Juba. Peacekeepers are deployed throughout South Sudan in 14 locations. As of December 2014, 61 countries were contributing 11,433 personnel to the mission. The top contributors were India (2,317 personnel), Rwanda (1,804), Nepal (1,774), Ethiopia (1,270), Mongolia (863), and Kenya (763). The number of contributing countries was 59 in the first year of mission; since then the average number has since remained stable. The total approved budget for 2014–2015 fiscal year was $1,097,315,100.

United Nations Interim Security Force for Abyei (UNISFA)

The Government of Sudan and the SPLM signed an agreement in June 2011 that called for the demilitarization of the Abyei Area. In July 2011, the UN Security Council authorized the United Nations Interim Security Force for Abyei

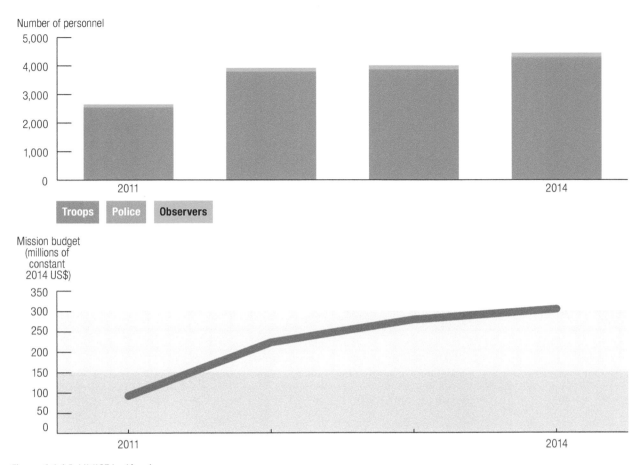

Figure 16.15 UNISFA, Abyei

(UNISFA) to monitor and verify the redeployment of the military forces of both sides, assist with de-mining activities, facilitate the delivery of humanitarian aid, and strengthen the capacity of the Abyei Police Service.[50] The UN Security Council later expanded the mandate of UNISFA to include activities such as assisting the parties in establishing the Demilitarized Border Zone, and supporting operational activities of the Joint Border Verification and Monitoring Mechanism (JBVMM), in order to accommodate demands from parties for help in implementing two additional agreements concerning border security signed on June 29 and July 30, 2011.[51]

In the following years, the mission engaged community leaders to prevent communal conflicts over resources in the area, supported AU attempts to solve the incompatibility, supported the activities of JBVMM, which was operationalized in December 2012 after delays in appointing monitors by both sides, and continued its cooperation with UNMISS and UNAMID on border security and other joint operations. In October 2013, the Ngok Dinka community held a unilateral referendum, which heightened tension in the area due to a large influx of people from South Sudan in advance of the referendum. The Ngok Dinka leadership subsequently announced that 99.99 per cent of eligible voters had opted for the Abyei Area to become part of South Sudan. The Government of Sudan and the Misseriya community called the referendum illegitimate, while the AU condemned the referendum, noting that it would complicate the resolution of the Abyei dispute; the government of South Sudan refrained from making comments.[52] Among the people who arrived in the Abyei area for the referendum, UNISFA observed up to 1,000 SPLA and South Sudan Police personnel, which deteriorated relations between Sudan and South Sudan and caused active fighting between SPLA, the South Sudan police, and the Misseriya militia in the first half of 2014.

The headquarters of UNISFA is located in Abyei, with sector headquarters located in Diffra (North), Dokura (Center), Athony (South). Peacekeepers are deployed to six other locations in the Abyei area. As of December 2014, 29 countries were contributing 4,066 personnel to the mission. Ethiopia was providing most of the personnel (3,988). Since the establishment of the mission, an average of 24 countries have contributed personnel. The total approved budget for 2014–2015 fiscal year was $318,925,200.

Cil

Multidimensional Integrated Stabilization Mission in Mali (MINUSMA)

In early 2012, a conflict commenced in the north of Mali between three sets of actors: government forces, a Tuareg rebel group called the *Mouvement national pour la libération de l'Azawad* (MNLA), and several Islamic armed groups called Ansar Dine, Al-Qaida in the Islamic Maghreb (AQIM) and the *Mouvement pour l'unicité et le jihad en Afrique de l'Ouest* (MUJAO). In response, the UN Security Council deployed the United Nations Office in Mali (UNOM), which was tasked with providing support for the ongoing process of resolving conflict, initiated by ECOWAS, and the planning and organization of the African-led International Support Mission in Mali (AFISMA).[53] As the situation in the northern areas deteriorated in January 2013, France intervened and AFISMA accelerated its deployment. Subsequently, the UN Security Council established the United Nations Multidimensional Integrated Stabilization Mission in Mali (MINUSMA) on April 25, 2013.[54] The mandate of the mission includes the stabilization of population centers, supporting the reestablishment of state authority, the implementation of the transitional road map, provision of humanitarian assistance, protection of civilians and UN personnel, promotion of human rights, and supporting national and international justice.

Four rounds of negotiations were held from July to November 2014, supported by the mediation team that included representatives from the UN/MINUSMA, the AU, ECOWAS, the EU, the Organization of Islamic Cooperation, and the governments of Burkina Faso, Chad, Mauritania, and Niger. These negotiations generated a draft document that includes provisions on greater regionalization, strengthening local governments, and an internationally financed development package for the northern region. The Coordination – comprised of MNLA and two Azawad groups, the *Haut conseil pour l'unité de l'Azawad* (HCUA) and *Mouvement arabe de l'Azawad* (MAA) – and the Government have yet to come to an agreement.

The main headquarters of MINUSMA is located in Bamako. Three regional headquarters are located in Tombouctou (West), Kidal (North) and Gao (East). In addition, peacekeepers are deployed to nine other locations throughout the country. As of December 2014, 46 countries were contributing 9,494 personnel to the mission. The top contributors were Bangladesh (1,718), Chad (1,094), Togo (1,079), Burkina Faso (878), and Senegal (767). In the first year of the mission, 33 countries provided personnel. The total approved budget for 2014–2015 fiscal year was $628,724,400.

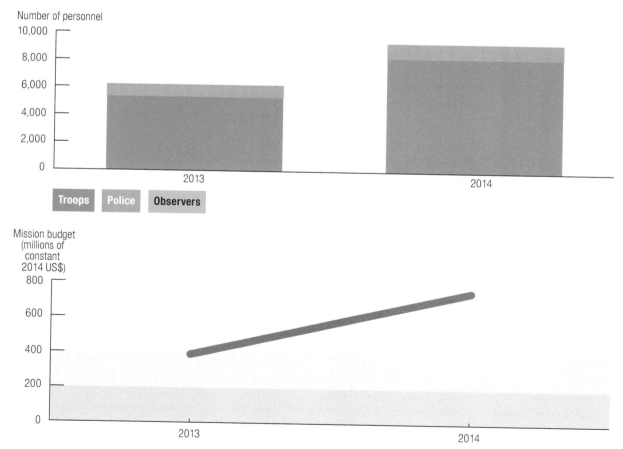

Figure 16.16 MINUSMA, Mali

United Nations Multidimensional Integrated Stabilization Mission in the Central African Republic (MINUSCA)

In December 2012, Séléka – a predominantly Muslim alliance of rebel groups involved in previous conflict in the Central African Republic (CAR) – initiated a series of violent attacks that ultimately led to the fall of President Bozizé's government in March 2013. In August 2013, the leader of Séléka, Michel Djotodia, became the head of the transitional government. As a response to these developments, the UN Security Council changed the mandate of the UN Integrated Peacebuilding Office in the Central African Republic (BINUCA), originally deployed in January 2010, to support the implementation of the transition process.[55] Inter-communal conflict continued, however, when the Christian and animist militias of the anti-Balaka movement immediately took up arms and engaged in an increasing cycle of violence with Séléka militias, which had yet to disband. In December 2013, the UN Security Council authorized the International Support Mission to the CAR (MISCA) and a French-led peacekeeping force (*Opération Sangaris*) to be deployed,[56] as well as commenced the plans for transformation of MISCA into a UN peacekeeping operation. President Djotodia resigned under pressure from regional leaders in January 2014.

In April 2014, the United Nations Multidimensional Integrated Stabilization Mission in the Central African Republic (MINUSCA) was established. The extensive mandate of the mission includes protecting civilians and UN personnel, facilitating the delivery of humanitarian assistance, protecting and promoting human rights, providing support for national and international justice and disarmament, implementing DDR programs, and coordinating international assistance as appropriate. MINUSCA assumed authority from MISCA as planned on September 15, 2014 and continues to implement its mandate. According to the plans, MINUSCA will comprise up to 10,000 military personnel, including 240 military observers and 200 staff officers, and 1,800 police personnel, including 1,400 formed police unit personnel, 400 individual police officers, and 20 corrections officers.[57] As of December 2014, 7,496 troops, 1,125 police officers and 91 observers were deployed, contributed by 41 countries. The top contributors were Cameron (1,301), Burundi (1,141), Rwanda (1,025), Congo (999), and the Democratic Republic of Congo (963). The total budget of the mission for the period of April–December 2014 was $312,976,404.

Notes

1 I opted to omit from this list and the set of profiles the UN political mission in Afghanistan, the United Nations Assistance Mission in Afghanistan (UNAMA), which was established in 2002 in order to support the implementation of the Bonn Agreement. The mission is designed to fulfill the tasks and responsibilities – including those related to human rights, the rule of law, and gender issues – that were entrusted to the UN in the Bonn Agreement, manage all UN humanitarian relief and recovery activities, and promote national reconciliation. As of 2014, two police officers and 20 observers are deployed in Afghanistan, with the personnel contributed by 13 countries. See United Nations Security Council, "The Situation in Afghanistan and Its Implications for International Peace and Security: Report of the Secretary-General," S/2002/278, March 18, 2002, http://www.un.org/en/ga/search/view_doc.asp?symbol=S/2002/278.

2 United Nations Peacekeeping Operations, Fact Sheet: 31 December 2014, http://www.un.org/en/peacekeeping/archive/2014/bnote1214.pdf.

3 One exception is that UNFICYP budget data goes back only to June 1993.

4 United Nations Security Council, Resolution 50, May 29, 1948, http://www.un.org/en/ga/search/view_doc.asp?symbol=S/RES/50(1948).

5 UN General Assembly, Resolution A/RES/1000 (ES-I), "Resolution 1000 (ES-I)," November 5, 1956, http://www.un.org/en/ga/search/view_doc.asp?symbol=A/RES/1000(ES-I).

6 United Nations Security Council, "Report by the Secretary-General on the Observation of the Cease-Fire in the Suez Canal Sector," S/8035/Add.3, October 31, 1967, http://www.un.org/en/ga/search/view_doc.asp?symbol=s/8053/Add.3.

7 United Nations Security Council, Resolution 339, October 25, 1973, http://www.un.org/en/ga/search/view_doc.asp?symbol=S/RES/339(1973).

8 United Nations Security Council, Resolution 39, January 20, 1948, http://www.un.org/en/ga/search/view_doc.asp?symbol=S/RES/39(1948).

9 United Nations Security Council, Resolution 47, April 21, 1948, http://www.un.org/en/ga/search/view_doc.asp?symbol=S/RES/47(1948).

10 United Nations Security Council, Resolution 186, March 4, 1964, http://www.un.org/en/ga/search/view_doc.asp?symbol=S/RES/186(1964).

11 United Nations Security Council, Resolution 353, July 20, 1974, http://www.un.org/en/ga/search/view_doc.asp?symbol=S/RES/353(1974).

12 United Nations Security Council, "Report of the Secretary-General on His Mission of Good Offices in Cyprus," S/2004/437, May 28, 2004, http://www.un.org/en/ga/search/view_doc.asp?symbol=S/2004/437.

13 United Nations Security Council, "Report of the Secretary-General on the United Nations Operation in Cyprus," S/2014/461, July 9, 2014, http://www.un.org/en/ga/search/view_doc.asp?symbol=S/2014/461.

14 United Nations Security Council, "Report of the Secretary-General on the United Nations Operation in Cyprus," S/2015/17, January 9, 2015, http://www.un.org/en/ga/search/view_doc.asp?symbol=S/2015/17.

15 United Nations Security Council, Resolution 350, May 31, 1974, http://www.un.org/en/ga/search/view_doc.asp?symbol=s/res/350(1974).

16 United Nations Security Council, Resolution 425, March 19, 1978, http://www.un.org/en/ga/search/view_doc.asp?symbol=S/RES/425(1978).

17 United Nations Security Council, Resolution 1701, August 11, 2006, http://www.un.org/en/ga/search/view_doc.asp?symbol=S/RES/1701(2006).

18 United Nations Security Council, "Report of the Secretary-General on the Implementation of Security Council Resolution 1701 (2006)," S/2014/784, November 5, 2014, http://www.un.org/en/ga/search/view_doc.asp?symbol=S/2014/784.

19 United Nations Security Council (SC), Resolution 690, "The Situation Concerning Western Sahara," April 29, 1991, http://www.un.org/ga/search/view_doc.asp?symbol=S/RES/690(1991).

20 United Nations Security Council (SC), "The Situation concerning Western Sahara: Report of the Secretary-General," S/21360, June 18, 1990, http://www.un.org/en/ga/search/view_doc.asp?symbol=S/21360.

21 United Nations Security Council, Resolution 1244, June 10, 1999, http://www.un.org/en/ga/search/view_doc.asp?symbol=S/RES/1244(1999).

22 United Nations Security Council, "Report of the Secretary-General on the United Nations Interim Administration Mission in Kosovo," S/2007/582, September 28, 2007, http://www.un.org/en/ga/search/view_doc.asp?symbol=S/2007/582.

23 United Nations Security Council, "Report of the Secretary-General on the United Nations Interim Administration Mission in Kosovo," S/2008/211, March 28, 2008, http://www.un.org/en/ga/search/view_doc.asp?symbol=S/2008/211.

24 United Nations Security Council, "Report of the Secretary-General on the United Nations Interim Administration Mission in Kosovo," S/2009/497, September 30, 2009, http://www.un.org/en/ga/search/view_doc.asp?symbol=S/2009/497.

25 United Nations Security Council, Resolution 1509, September 19, 2003, http://www.un.org/en/ga/search/view_doc.asp?symbol=S/RES/1509%20%282003%29.

26 United Nations Security Council, "First Progress Report of the Secretary-General on the United Nations Mission in Liberia," S/2003/1175, December 15, 2003, http://www.un.org/en/ga/search/view_doc.asp?symbol=S/2003/1175.

27 United Nations Security Council, "Fifth Progress Report of the Secretary-General on the United Nations Mission in Liberia," S/2004/972, December 17, 2004, http://www.un.org/en/ga/search/view_doc.asp?symbol=S/2004/972.

28 United Nations Security Council, Resolution 1629, September 19, 2005, http://www.un.org/en/ga/search/view_doc.asp?symbol=S/RES/1626(2005).

29 United Nations Security Council, "Ninth Progress Report of the Secretary-General on the United Nations Mission in Liberia," S/2005/764, December 7, 2005, http://www.un.org/en/ga/search/view_doc.asp?symbol=S/2005/764.

30 United Nations Security Council, "Twenty-Ninth Progress Report of the Secretary-General on the United Nations Mission in Liberia," S/2015/275, April 23, 2015, http://www.un.org/en/ga/search/view_doc.asp?symbol=S/2015/275.

31 United Nations Security Council, Resolution 1529, February 29, 2004, http://www.un.org/en/ga/search/view_doc.asp?symbol=S/RES/1529(2004).

32 United Nations Security Council, Resolution 1542, April 30, 2004, http://www.un.org/en/ga/search/view_doc.asp?symbol=S/RES/1542(2004).

33 United Nations Security Council, Resolution 1908, January 19, 2010, http://www.un.org/en/ga/search/view_doc.asp?symbol=S/RES/1908(2010).

34 United Nations Security Council, Resolution 1927, June 4, 2010, http://www.un.org/en/ga/search/view_doc.asp?symbol=S/RES/1927(2010).

35 United Nations Security Council, Resolution 1528, February 27, 2004, http://www.un.org/en/ga/search/view_doc.asp?symbol=S/RES/1528%20(2004).

36 United Nations Security Council, "Eighteenth Progress Report of the Secretary-General on the United Nations Operation in Côte d'Ivoire," S/2008/645, October 13, 2008, http://www.un.org/en/ga/search/view_doc.asp?symbol=S/2008/645.

37 United Nations Security Council, "Twenty-Fourth Progress Report of the Secretary-General on the United Nations Operation in Côte d'Ivoire," S/2010/245, May 20, 2010, http://www.un.org/en/ga/search/view_doc.asp?symbol=S/2010/245.

38 United Nations Security Council, "Twenty-Seventh Progress Report of the Secretary-General on the United Nations Operation in Côte d'Ivoire," S/2011/211, March 30, 2011, http://www.un.org/en/ga/search/view_doc.asp?symbol=S/2011/211.

39 United Nations Security Council, "Twenty-Eight Report of the Secretary-General on the United Nations Operation in Côte d'Ivoire," S/2011/387, June 24, 2011, http://www.un.org/en/ga/search/view_doc.asp?symbol=S/2011/387.

40 United Nations Security Council, Resolution 2162, June 25, 2014, http://www.un.org/en/ga/search/view_doc.asp?symbol=S/RES/2162(2014).

41 United Nations Security Council, Resolution 1769, July 31, 2007, http://www.un.org/en/ga/search/view_doc.asp?symbol=S/RES/1769(2007).

42 United Nations Security Council, Resolution 1279, November 30, 1999, http://www.un.org/en/ga/search/view_doc.asp?symbol=S/RES/1279(1999).

43 United Nations Security Council, Resolution 1925, May 28, 2010, http://www.un.org/en/ga/search/view_doc.asp?symbol=S/RES/1925(2010).

44 United Nations Security Council (SC), Resolution 2098, March 28, 2013, http://www.un.org/en/ga/search/view_doc.asp?symbol=S/RES/2098(2013).

45 United Nations Security Council, Resolution 1996, July 8, 2011, http://www.un.org/en/ga/search/view_doc.asp?symbol=S/RES/1996(2011).

46 United Nations Security Council, "Report of the Secretary-General on South Sudan," S/2012/486, June 26, 2012, http://www.un.org/en/ga/search/view_doc.asp?symbol=S/2012/486.

47 United Nations Security Council, "Report of the Secretary-General on South Sudan," S/2013/366, June 20, 2013, http://www.un.org/en/ga/search/view_doc.asp?symbol=S/2013/366.

48 United Nations Security Council, "Report of the Secretary-General on South Sudan," S/2014/158, March 6, 2014, http://www. un.org/en/ga/search/view_doc.asp?symbol=S/2014/158.

49 United Nations Security Council, Resolution 2155, May 27, 2014, http://www.un.org/en/ga/search/view_doc.asp?symbol=S/ RES/2155(2014).

50 United Nations Security Council, Resolution 1990, June 27, 2011, http://www.un.org/en/ga/search/view_doc.asp?symbol=S/ RES/1990(2011).

51 United Nations Security Council, Resolution 2024, December 14, 2011, http://www.un.org/en/ga/search/view_doc.asp?symbol= S/RES/2024(2011).

52 United Nations Security Council, "Report of the Secretary-General on the Situation in Abyei," S/2013/706, November 27, 2013, http://www.un.org/en/ga/search/view_doc.asp?symbol=S/2013/706.

53 United Nations Security Council, Resolution 2085, December 20, 2012, http://www.un.org/en/ga/search/view_doc.asp?symbol= S/RES/2085.

54 United Nations Security Council, Resolution 2100, April 25, 2013, http://www.un.org/en/peacekeeping/missions/minusma/ documents/mali%20_2100_E_.pdf.

55 United Nations Security Council, Resolution 2121, October 10, 2013, http://www.un.org/en/ga/search/view_doc.asp?symbol=S/ RES/2121(2013).

56 United Nations Security Council, Resolution 2721, December 5, 2013, http://www.un.org/en/ga/search/view_doc.asp?symbol= S/RES/2127(2013).

57 United Nations Security Council, Resolution 2129, April 10, 2014, http://www.un.org/en/ga/search/view_doc.asp?symbol=S/ RES/2149(2014).

References

Doyle, Michael W., and Nicholas Sambanis. 2006. *Making War and Building Peace: United Nations Peace Operations*. Princeton, NJ: Princeton University Press.

Fortna, Virginia Page. 2008. *Does Peacekeeping Work? Shaping Belligerents' Choices after Civil War*. Princeton, NJ: Princeton University Press.

Fortna, Virginia Page, and Lise Morjé Howard. 2008. "Pitfalls and Prospects in the Peacekeeping Literature." *Annual Review of Political Science* 11(1): 283–301.

Gaibulloev, Khusrav, Justin George, Todd Sandler, and Hirofumi Shimizu. 2015. "Personnel Contributions to UN and Non-UN Peacekeeping Missions: A Public Goods Approach." *Journal of Peace Research*, June 11. doi:10.1177/0022343315579245.

Gaibulloev, Khusrav, Todd Sandler, and Hirofumi Shimizu. 2009. "Demands for UN and Non-UN Peacekeeping Nonvoluntary versus Voluntary Contributions to a Public Good." *Journal of Conflict Resolution* 53(6): 827–852.

Hultman, Lisa, Jacob Kathman, and Megan Shannon. 2013. "United Nations Peacekeeping and Civilian Protection in Civil War." *American Journal of Political Science* 57(4): 875–891.

Hultman, Lisa, Jacob Kathman, and Megan Shannon 2014. "Beyond Keeping Peace: United Nations Effectiveness in the Midst of Fighting." *American Political Science Review* 108(4): 737–753.

Kathman, Jacob D., and Reed M. Wood. 2014. "Stopping the Killing during the 'Peace': Peacekeeping and the Severity of Postconflict Civilian Victimization." *Foreign Policy Analysis*, April 16. doi:10.1111/fpa.12041.

Uzonyi, Gary. 2015. "Refugee Flows and State Contributions to Post-Cold War UN Peacekeeping Missions." *Journal of Peace Research*, June, 52(6): 743–757.

Wright, Thorin M., and J. Michael Greig. 2012. "Staying the Course: Assessing the Durability of Peacekeeping Operations." *Conflict Management and Peace Science* 29(2): 127–147.

17

Criminal Justice for Conflict-Related Violations

Developments during 2014

Anupma L. Kulkarni

Introduction

In recent decades, criminal investigations and prosecutions for conflict-related violations have increased. Cases have been pursued in international institutional venues such as *ad hoc* war crimes tribunals, hybrid courts and the International Criminal Court (ICC), as well as by ordinary and special national courts, some domestic and others in foreign countries.[1] These cases vary on several key dimensions, including the types of conflicts involved; the length of time that has passed between when violations were allegedly perpetrated and criminal cases are initiated; the status of the individuals being prosecuted; the authorities undertaking the prosecution or investigation of these acts; and the outcomes of the cases.

This chapter profiles legal activity during 2014 in the context of cases involving crimes under international conventions – i.e., war crimes, crimes against humanity, genocide and/or torture – that were ongoing or concluded, plus situations in which such crimes were being investigated by a prosecuting authority.[2] At least 60 state governments are involved in the profiled cases, encompassing countries in which violations occurred and/or with a role in prosecuting accused violators. Based on this global overview, the legal activity exhibits several notable characteristics.

First, impunity continues to weaken due to a growing acceptance of several norms:

- A duty exists for states to investigate and prosecute in cases where the crimes constitute *jus cogens* violations, i.e., acts that run against fundamental, overriding principles of international law, from which derogation is never permitted (Brownlie 1998).
- Such crimes do not have an associated statute of limitations.
- Amnesty provisions for crimes against humanity, war crimes and genocide are not legally valid, thereby creating openings for domestic prosecutions in national courts.

In conjunction, the concept of sovereign immunity is being challenged in multiple legal cases in which former heads-of-state are accused of committing *jus cogens* violations. Also, a number of the active cases have been brought in third-party states on the basis of the concept of universal jurisdiction.

Second, certain of the cases active at the national level deal with violations that were perpetrated 30–40 years ago. This time lag suggests a possible temporal pattern in which a society that has endured crimes of this magnitude may need at least two generations to sufficiently recover and for the political and institutional situation to evolve to a point where it becomes possible to undertake processes that hold criminally accountable individuals responsible for those acts. Yet criminal prosecutions may continue to elicit strong reactions and recriminations, which deeply complicate the legal processes of prosecuting these crimes, as we see in several situations, including Bangladesh, Cambodia and Guatemala.

Third, considerable legal activity pertains to repressive actions taken against protesters, in the course of mobilization against autocratic regimes that resulted in political transition, and election-related violence. This attention serves to reinforce the emergent applications of international criminal law in establishing and reinforcing democratic standards.

These characteristics of the activity are largely consistent with what has been observed in recent years (Olsen, Payne, and Reiter 2010; Sikkink 2011; Sikkink and Kim 2013).

Country Profiles

Box 17.1 Argentina	
Conflict:	Military dictatorship (1976–1983)
Charges:	Torture; crimes against humanity; forced disappearance
Accused:	Members of the military junta, military officers, and collaborating civilians
Prosecuting Authority:	Argentine Courts
Location:	Argentina
Legal Activity during 2014:	Case of abducted babies and the case of La Cacha were completed; *Plan Condor* trial ongoing

From 1976–1983, approximately 30,000 people were killed, disappeared or tortured as the result of the "dirty war" conducted by the Argentine military government. These acts targeted leftists, students, and other perceived members of the opposition. The violence was focused domestically, but also extended internationally with *Plan Condor*, a collaborative initiative with the military regimes of neighboring countries in the region (Bolivia, Brazil, Chile, Paraguay and Uruguay) to eliminate their respective political opponents.

Soon after the Argentine government collapsed in 1983, actions were taken to investigate these atrocities and hold accountable certain of those responsible. A truth commission was organized and completed its work in 1984. In addition, prosecutions were undertaken against the nine members of the military junta, leading to five convictions, between 1984 and 1987. During the years immediately thereafter, under a threat of military backlash, the pursuit of justice was halted and even rolled back by a series of measures: the "full-stop" law (1986), which established a deadline for initiating prosecutions; the "due-obedience" law (1987), which effectively absolved low-ranking members of the military of criminal responsibility, on the basis that they were following orders; and pardons issued by President Menem for those individuals who had been convicted of crimes.

In 2003, President Kirchner had the 1986 and 1987 amnesty laws repealed. In 2005, the Argentine Supreme Court declared the amnesty laws unconstitutional and recognized states' obligation to investigate, prosecute and punish serious violations of human rights conventions.[3] Subsequently, major criminal trials have involved the prosecution of members of the military junta and civilian officials for notorious policies of kidnapping, hiding and changing the identities of the children of political opponents (*Plan Sistemático*); detention, torture and killing in clandestine prison sites, such as La Cacha camp in La Plata and Campo de Mayo; and *Plan Condor*.[4]

As of 2014, 121 trials have been conducted for crimes against humanity, resulting in 503 convictions. In addition, a further 1,611 suspects were reportedly being investigated for their involvement in similar crimes (Human Rights Watch, 2015: 65).[5]

In 2014, several high-profile cases involving numerous military officers and civilians were completed. Among these was the Case of the Abducted Babies, which concerned newborn babies born in the clandestine birthing center of Campo de Mayo who were abducted and hidden by the military dictatorship. The defendants, including two military officers and two civilians, were convicted and sentenced to prison terms. Meanwhile, the trial of two officers for the killing of Bishop Enrique Angelelli also ended in conviction. In addition, 16 military officers and other officials were convicted and sentenced for the murder, detention and torture of 128 people in La Cacha camp. The trial of 25 military personnel accused of conspiracy to kidnap, torture, disappear, and kill political opponents, as part of carrying out *Plan Condor*, was ongoing; a verdict is expected in 2015.

Box 17.2 Bangladesh	
Conflict:	Civil war between West and East Pakistan (1971)
Charges:	Crimes against humanity; war crimes; genocide
Accused:	Members of Pro-Pakistan groups and militias
Prosecuting Authority:	International Crimes Tribunal (ICT)
Location:	Bangladesh
Legal Activity during 2014:	Four trials were completed; several appeals were in progress; investigations are continuing

Kulkarni

In the 1970 elections in Pakistan, which at the time was composed of West Pakistan (now Pakistan) and East Pakistan (now Bangladesh), the Awami League in East Pakistan won nearly all (167 of 169) of the seats in the parliament, concentrating power in the eastern portion of the country for the first time. Unwilling to accept this outcome, General Yahya Khan took repressive military action in East Pakistan. The military campaign caused an estimated 1–3 million deaths; a massive humanitarian crisis, sending approximately 10 million refugees across borders, primarily into India; and an armed insurgency against the repressive actions of West Pakistan.[6] Ultimately, as a consequence of the conflict, two separate sovereign states were formed: Pakistan in the west and Bangladesh in the east.

The ICT were established to prosecute atrocities allegedly perpetrated by 195 Pakistani military officers during the 1971 conflict. None of these officers was remanded to newly independent Bangladesh to face prosecution, and all remain beyond the reach of the Tribunal as currently configured.[7] Though the law creating the ICT was adopted in 1973, soon after the independence of Bangladesh, the tribunal was not actually formed until 2010, following amendment to the original law in 2009. The law was initially written to prosecute members of the Pakistani military, but all of the 27 individuals pursued by the ICT allegedly belonged to groups that were opposed to Bangladesh's secession from Pakistan, including the Razakar and Al Badr [militias] among others, and all are affiliated with the political opposition.[8] They are charged with committing war crimes, crimes against humanity, and genocide, in conjunction with repressive military actions by West Pakistani forces.

As of 2014, the ICT had completed 19 prosecutions (including six *in absentia*). All of these trials have ended in convictions. Fourteen of the convicted individuals have been sentenced to death (one death sentence was commuted to life imprisonment); the remainder received sentences of life imprisonment. In 2014, four trials were prosecuted and judgments in six cases were issued. Eight cases remained ongoing at various stages. In addition, several ongoing appeals processes remained in progress.[9]

The ICT continues its work in a politically contentious and sensitive environment. The Tribunal has come under serious criticism for not conforming to principles and procedures of international law, while simultaneously setting up a separate standard of justice within Bangladesh, most notably by depriving defendants of rights that would be afforded them if they were to be prosecuted according to existing Bangladeshi criminal procedures.[10] The adoption and application of the death penalty by the ICT has also drawn opprobrium from the international human rights community and has been a barrier to working with international institutions, jurists, and legal advisors. Two death sentences issued by the ICT have already been carried out, the first in 2013 and the second in 2015.[11] The executions have been polarizing issues domestically, evoking visible public support and celebrations, as well as public condemnation and protests. Over 500 people have reportedly been killed in the demonstrations, as of the beginning of 2015 (Robertson 2015: 108). The ICT has also been accused of serving the political interests of the Awami League – the current political party in power – and its trials dismissed as a means of eliminating opponents of the ruling party.

Box 17.3 Cambodia	
Conflict:	Khmer Rouge dictatorship (1975–1979)
Charges:	Genocide; crimes against humanity; war crimes
Accused:	Kiang Guek Eav (Duch), Nuon Chea, Khieu Samphan, Ieng Sary and Ieng Thirith, Meas Muth, Ao An and Im Chaem
Prosecuting Authority:	Extraordinary Chambers of the Cambodian Court (ECCC)
Location:	Cambodia
Legal Activity during 2014:	Nuon Chea and Khieu Samphan convicted and sentenced in the first of two cases (002/01) in which they are being tried; cases 002/02, 003 and 004 ongoing

In 1975, the Khmer Rouge, led by Pol Pot, captured control of Phnom Penh, the capital of Cambodia, and established Democratic Kampuchea. The new government undertook a massive campaign of forcible social reorganization. The ensuing reign of terror is estimated to have caused the deaths of 1.2–2.8 million people (Heuveline 1998). The government was toppled in 1978 as the result of an invasion by neighboring Vietnam, which occupied the country until 1989. This period was marked by repression and violent resistance.

Following a 1991 peace agreement, the United Nations Transitional Authority for Cambodia facilitated the transition and restoration of the Cambodian government in 1993. The hurdles to prosecuting the individuals responsible for the massive violence perpetrated by the Khmer Rouge were not overcome until 2005, when the United Nations and the government of Cambodia reached an agreement on establishing and funding a special court for that purpose. In 2007, the ECCC began investigating atrocities committed in Democratic Kampuchea.

As of 2014, the Court has completed the prosecution of two cases (001 and 002/01), involving three individuals. In 2014, the first high-ranking Khmer Rouge officials, Nuon Chea and Khieu Samphan, were found guilty of crimes against humanity and sentenced to life imprisonment. They are also being tried in a second case (002/02) on a different set of charges, including genocide against the Cham and the Vietnamese, forced marriages and rape, and atrocities committed at the notorious S-21 detention center. The original case (002) against Nuon Chea and Khieu Samphan was split; the charges were severed in order to limit the scope of each trial. The proceedings in their second trial are ongoing. Two additional cases, designated 003 and 004, were still in preliminary and investigative stages. In Case 003, Meas Muth was charged (in March 2015), *in absentia*, with homicide, crimes against humanity and war crimes allegedly committed at S-21 and Wat Enta Nhien detention centers, in Kampong Som and Kratie, and against Vietnamese, Thai and other foreigners.[12] The identities of two additional suspects in Case 003 remain under seal.[13] In Case 004, Ao An and Im Chaem are charged, *in absentia*, with homicide and crimes against humanity for their alleged role in the running of a forced labor camp and the deaths of thousands of Cambodians.[14] Cases 003 and 004 have proceeded in an environment of reported political pressure and tension between the Cambodian and international investigative judges, as well as non-cooperation by the judicial police (Open Society Justice Initiative 2015).

Box 17.4 Central African Republic	
Conflict:	Armed conflict following attempted coup d'état (2002–03)
Charges:	War crimes; crimes against humanity; offences against administration of justice
Accused:	Jean-Pierra Bemba Gombo, Aimé Kilolo Musamba, Jean-Jacques Mangenda Kabongo, Fidèle Babala Wandu and Narcisse Arido
Prosecuting Authority:	ICC
Location:	The Hague, the Netherlands
Legal Activity during 2014:	Decision in the Bemba case pending; charges in Bemba et al. case confirmed

In 2004, the Central African Republic (CAR) government referred its own situation to the ICC with respect to war crimes and crimes against humanity perpetrated in a period following a failed coup attempt in 2002. In the ensuing armed conflict, widespread civilian targeting and sexual violence were reported.

In May 2008, the ICC Prosecutor requested an arrest warrant for Jean-Pierre Bemba Gombo, a national of the Democratic Republic of the Congo (DRC) and the President and Commander-in-Chief of the *Mouvement de libération du Congo* (MLC). The MLC allegedly allied with a segment of the CAR national armed forces loyal to President Ange-Félix Patassé, to confront the forces of Francois Bozizé, a former leader of the CAR armed forces who led a rebellion against the Patassé regime. Bemba was charged with three war crimes (murder, rape, and pillaging) and two crimes against humanity (murder and rape) for acts perpetrated during the conflict in 2002–2003. He was apprehended by Belgian authorities and surrendered to the ICC in July 2008. His trial commenced in 2010. In 2014, closing oral statements were concluded. A decision in the case is pending.[15]

In 2013, the ICC Prosecutor initiated a second related case, charging Bemba, along with four others (Aimé Kilolo Musamba, Jean-Jacques Mangenda Kabongo, Fidèle Babala Wandu, Narcisse Arido), of "offences against the administration of justice." This is the first case brought by the ICC Prosecutor for actions related to interfering with witnesses and their testimony. Courts like the ICC face challenges in protecting witnesses, who often remain vulnerable in the aftermath of the conflict. This case can be expected to set an important precedent in signaling the ICC's commitment to ensuring the security of potential witnesses and victims of the serious crimes being prosecuted, as well as the integrity of the evidence presented at trial. The governments of Belgium, the DRC, France and the Netherlands undertook the arrest and surrender of the four additional defendants in this case in 2013. In October 2014, the four defendants were ordered released based on a determination by the Pre-Trial Chamber that their detention prior to the start of trial had continued for an unreasonable length of time. The defendants have been released on an interim basis, pending additional developments in the Prosecution's case that might warrant their re-arrest. The Prosecutor appealed this decision and preparations for the trial continued. In November 2014, the Court confirmed the charges against the defendants. The opening of this trial is anticipated in the fall of 2015.[16]

Kulkarni

Box 17.5 Chad

Conflict:	Dictatorship of Hissène Habré (1982–1990)
Charges:	Crimes against humanity; torture; war crimes
Accused:	Hissène Habré
Prosecuting Authority:	Extraordinary African Chambers
Location:	Senegal
Legal Activity during 2014:	Investigations into Habré's case continue; Defence Office within the Extraordinary African Chambers created

Hissène Habré became the president of Chad through a coup d'état in 1982. During his rule, approximately 40,000 people were reportedly killed and many detained, tortured and disappeared. In 1990, he was likewise ousted in a coup and went into exile in Senegal.

In 2000, the first complaints were filed in Senegal and Belgium accusing Habré of committing crimes against humanity, torture, and genocide. Although calls for his prosecution were persistently put forward by victims of his policies, for a long time there was little movement in that direction in Senegal. The government initially asserted that it could not prosecute Habré for lack of jurisdiction, but simultaneously refused to extradite him to Belgium, which might have prosecuted him under the principle of universal jurisdiction. Belgium then brought the matter to the International Court of Justice (ICJ). In July 2012, the ICJ found that the government of Senegal had not fulfilled its obligations under the Convention against Torture and ordered that it either submit Habré's case to the proper authorities for prosecution or else to extradite him to Belgium.[17] Following this ruling, in August 2012, a formal agreement between the government of Senegal and the African Union (AU) was reached establishing the Extraordinary African Chambers (Chambers) in Senegal to prosecute international crimes committed in Chad from 1982–1990. In February 2013, the Chambers were inaugurated and in July, charges of crimes against humanity, war crimes, and torture were filed against Habré, who was then detained, pending trial. It was announced that Habré's trial would commence in mid-2015. In 2014, an additional agreement between the AU and Senegal established a Defence Office within the Chambers, and investigations in Habré's case continued over the course of the year.[18]

Box 17.6 Chile

Conflict:	Military dictatorship under Augusto Pinochet (1973–1990)
Charges:	Crimes against humanity; torture
Accused:	Pedro Ramón Cáceres Jorquera, Edgar Cevallos Jones, Rosauro Martinez, Sergio Víctor Arellano Stark, Pedro Octavio Espinoza Bravo, and others
Prosecuting Authority:	Chilean National Courts
Location:	Chile
Legal Activity during 2014:	Cáceres Jorquera and Cevallos Jones convicted of torture; Martinez charged and arrested

In 1973, Augusto Pinochet came to power in Chile through a military coup. Repressive actions perpetrated by the military regime resulted in over 3,000 deaths and disappearances and an estimated 30,000 cases of torture. A national referendum in 1988 produced majority opposition to Pinochet's continued rule for another eight years, paving the way for a democratic transition in 1990 following competitive multiparty elections.

A National Commission for Truth and Reconciliation completed work between May 1990 and February 1991, issuing a report that documented human rights abuses resulting in death and disappearance (torture was outside of its mandate). Amnesty decrees adopted by the military leadership remained in effect until 1994, however, precluding the possibility of pursuing prosecutions against the officers and officials of the military dictatorship. Subsequently, the effectiveness and legality of the amnesty provisions began to progressively weaken. Allowances were made for investigations into disappearances, which were considered ongoing crimes. In addition, cases involving the recognition of international law in matters of crimes against humanity and genocide were accepted as binding precedents. Pinochet was arrested in the United Kingdom in 1998 and stripped of his parliamentary immunity by the Chilean Supreme Court in August 2000, after which he and fellow military officers were indicted on a variety of charges. These events opened the door for challenging – and repealing – amnesty protections. Meanwhile, the National Commission on Political Imprisonment and Torture, which operated from August 2003 to November 2004, also documented additional abuses under the military regime.[19]

As of 2014, an estimated 1,086 Chileans have been convicted of and/or charged with human rights violations committed during the Pinochet dictatorship. Approximately 280 individuals have had their trials completed (Human Rights Watch 2015: Chile). In one prominent case, Pedro Ramón Cáceres Jorquera and Edgar Cevallos Jones were convicted in 2014 for the torture leading to the death of General Alberto Bachelet, father of the current President of Chile, Michelle Bachelet.[20] Multiple investigations and trials are ongoing.

Box 17.7 Côte d'Ivoire	
Conflict:	Post-election violence (2010–2011)
Charges:	Crimes against humanity
Accused:	Laurent Gbagbo, Simone Gbagbo and Charles Blé Goudé
Prosecuting Authorities:	ICC; Côte d'Ivoire National Courts
Locations:	The Hague, the Netherlands and Abidjan, Côte d'Ivoire
Legal Activity during 2014:	Charges against Laurent Gbagbo confirmed; Simone Gbagbo on trial in Côte d'Ivoire; Charles Blé Goudé was surrendered to ICC custody and charged

In the aftermath of Côte d'Ivoire's 2010 presidential election, there was contention and confusion regarding the outcome. Opposition candidate Alassane Ouattara was eventually recognized by the Ivoirian election body, the UN, and the AU as the victor. Supporters of incumbent Laurent Gbagbo, claiming he was the rightful winner, carried out violent attacks against individuals and communities supporting Ouattara. The resulting violence, concentrated mostly in the western region of the country, caused approximately 3,000 deaths and 150 reported cases of rape, as well as population displacement that precipitated a humanitarian crisis, which threatened to destabilize Côte d'Ivoire, with potential spillover into bordering Liberia. In 2011, the United Nations created an emergency mission to help bring the situation under control and ensure that Ouattara could form his government and pacify the situation.

In the same year, Côte d'Ivoire recognized the authority of the ICC and referred the matter to the Prosecutor, who requested arrest warrants for the former president and the first lady, Simone Gbagbo. The couple was apprehended by UN and French troops in late-2011. Laurent Gbagbo was arrested and surrendered to the ICC. In 2014, the ICC pre-trial chamber confirmed the charges against Laurent Gbagbo, which consist of multiple counts of crimes against humanity. Simone Gbagbo was taken into custody in Côte d'Ivoire, where she was tried for "undermining state security" and sentenced to a 20-year prison sentence in March 2015. Her trial took place alongside 82 other supporters of Laurent Gbagbo. Many of these trials are continuing.[21] Meanwhile, the ICC arrest warrant for Simone Gbagbo remains active, but has not been acted upon by the Ivoirian government. In addition, Charles Blé Goudé, Minister for Sports and Youth in Gbagbo's government, was arrested and in 2014 charged by the ICC with committing crimes against humanity. He remains in custody. His case will be joined with that of Laurent Gbagbo and proceed concurrently.[22]

Box 17.8 Democratic Republic of the Congo	
Conflict:	Armed conflict between the DRC government and rebel groups (1997–present)
Charges:	War crimes; crimes against humanity
Accused:	Thomas Lubanga Dyilo, Bosco Ntaganda, Germain Katanga, Sylvestre Mudacumura, and Mathieu Ngudjolo Chui
Prosecuting Authority:	ICC
Location:	The Hague, the Netherlands
Legal Activity during 2014:	Lubanga sentenced; Chui acquitted; Ntaganda trial ongoing

The allegations of war crimes and crimes against humanity in the DRC that are being prosecuted by the ICC have roots in the armed conflict for power after the ouster of Mobutu Sese Seko, who was President of what was then Zaire, in 1997. The establishment of the government of Laurent Kabila, via armed takeover, was soon followed by the creation of multiple armed groups. The violent rebellion continued even after Laurent Kabila was assassinated in 2001 and succeeded by his son, Joseph. The civil war, which has involved at least six other nations and cost the country an estimated five million lives, is still being fought in areas, despite peace accords, elections, and a UN mission to help stabilize the country and facilitate a transition to democratic governance.

In 2004, the DRC government referred its own situation to the ICC to investigate and prosecute individuals responsible for war crimes and crimes against humanity committed since 2002. The Prosecutor issued indictments against six senior commanders of four distinct groups involved in the DRC conflicts:

- Lubanga Dyilo, Commander of the *Forces patriotiques pour la libération du Congo* (FPLC);
- Bosco Ntaganda, Deputy Chief of the Staff and Commander of Operations of the FPLC;
- Germain Katanga, Commander of the *Force de résistance patriotique en Ituri* (FRPI);
- Callixte Mbarushimana, Executive Secretary of the *Forces démocratiques pour la libération du Rwanda-Forces combattantes Abacunguzi* (FDLR-FCA);
- Sylvestre Mudacumura, Supreme Commander of the *Forces démocratiques pour la libération du Rwanda* (FDLR); and
- Mathieu Ngudjolo Chui, former leader of the *Front des nationalistes et intégrationnistes* (FNI).

The charges against Mbarushimana were dismissed and he was released from ICC custody in 2011.[23]

Dyilo was found guilty in 2012 of conscripting children to fight; this verdict was upheld after appeal in 2014.[24] He was sentenced and remains in ICC custody. Chui was acquitted and released from ICC custody in 2012, but that verdict was appealed by the Prosecutor. The acquittal was upheld in February 2015.[25] In 2014, Germain Katanga's trial was completed. He was found guilty as an accessory to war crimes and crimes against humanity and has been sentenced; all appeals have been discontinued. He remains in ICC custody.[26] The charges against Ntaganda were confirmed in June 2014 and his trial is ongoing.[27] Meanwhile, the arrest warrant for Mudacumura remains active and he is still at large.[28]

Box 17.9 Former Yugoslavia	
Conflict:	Wars in the Former Yugoslavia (1991–1999)
Charges:	War crimes; crimes against humanity; genocide
Accused:	Political and military leaders, military personnel, and others
Prosecuting Authorities:	International Criminal Tribunal for the Former Yugoslavia (ICTY); national courts in Serbia, Croatia, Bosnia and Herzegovina, and Kosovo
Locations:	The Netherlands, Serbia, Croatia, Bosnia and Herzegovina, and Kosovo
Legal Activity during 2014:	Multiple trials and appeals ongoing

During the 1990s, a set of brutal wars were fought among the republics that emerged out of the breakdown of the former Yugoslavia. In the midst of the wars, the UN established the International Criminal Tribunal for the Former Yugoslavia (ICTY) in 1996. At the time, the prospects for pursuing prosecutions for war crimes and crimes against humanity in the courts of the constituent nations of the Former Yugoslavia were complex and remote. Armed conflict remained ongoing, and suspected war criminals had consolidated power amid the changing political geography of the region. In lieu of domestic legal actions, the ICTY pursued numerous cases. The proceedings concluded as of December 2014 had resulted in 74 convictions, out of 161 total indictments.[29] In addition, the ICTY had acquitted 18 defendants, referred 13 individuals to a national jurisdiction, and withdrew indictments against another 36 individuals. Over the past several years, the work of the ICTY began to wind down and judicial activity in national courts has been increasing.

In 2014, the ICTY had only four active trials and appeals concerning 14 accused in three cases on its dockets.[30] All four of the active trials involved prominent individuals. Radovan Karadžić is charged with genocide, war crimes and crimes against humanity for his role in a joint criminal enterprise (JCE) to permanently remove Bosnian Muslim and Bosnian Croat populations from territory in Bosnia and Herzegovina, as well as the siege of Sarajevo and the Srebrenica massacre. In 2014, his defense team finished presenting its case and closing arguments in the trial were concluded. Trial judgment is expected in December 2015.[31] Ratko Mladić is charged with crimes against humanity and war crimes for his participation in a JCE to permanently remove Bosnian Muslims from the territory of Bosnia and Herzegovina and the siege of Sarajevo. In 2014, the prosecution concluded its case and the defense started to present its case. The judgment is expected in 2017.[32] Goran Hadžić, former President of the Government of the self-proclaimed Serbian Autonomous District Slavonia, Baranja and Western Srem and later President of the Republic of Serbian Krajina (RSK) in Croatia, is charged with crimes against humanity and war crimes for his participation in a JCE whose aim was the forcible removal of the Croat and non-Serb populations from the area in Croatia to create a new Serb-dominated state.[33] Vojislav Šešelj, founder of the Serbian National Renewal Party, is charged with crimes against humanity and war crimes for his role in "forcible removal of a majority of the Croat, Muslim and other non-Serb civilian populations from parts of Croatia, [Bosnia and Herzegovina] and from the province of Vojvodina in the Republic of Serbia." In 2014, the Trial Chamber ordered Šešelj released on grounds of his worsening health.[34] He returned to Serbia in 2014, while awaiting the verdict in his case, expected towards the end of 2015.[35] In March 2015, the ICTY revoked his release, finding that Šešelj had violated its terms.[36] Afterwards, Šešelj publicly declared that he would not return to ICTY custody.[37]

Meanwhile, national-level prosecutions in Bosnia and Herzegovina, Croatia, Kosovo, and Serbia continued during 2014. The greatest activity took place in Bosnia and Herzegovina, where prosecuting authorities aimed to charge as many as 100 individuals for war crimes in 2014. In one prominent example, 15 individuals were charged with war crimes for their alleged role in the Zecovi Massacre.[38] In Kosovo, a case against the Drenica Group, a unit of the Kosovo Liberation Army accused of detainee abuse and torture, is being prosecuted, among others.[39] In Croatia, charges were filed against two Croatian soldiers in two separate cases, relating to war crimes associated with Operation Storm, a Croatian offensive to retake Krajina.[40] Montenegro has been less active in pursuing domestic war crimes prosecutions, but debates about doing so continued in 2014.[41]

In some instances, the pursuit of justice has gone hand-in-hand with continuing political tensions in the region. For instance, Croatia indicted and sought the extradition from Australia of Dragan Vasiljković for crimes committed by him and under his command in the Benkovac and Knin areas of Croatia. Serbia also requested his extradition, on the grounds that he is a national of and fought for the country. The matter has been submitted before the ICJ, which has not yet issued a decision. In May 2015, the Australian High Court approved his extradition to Croatia.[42] These disputes have compounded tensions between Croatia and Serbia, evidenced by their mutual accusations of genocide filed with the ICJ.[43] The tensions were further heightened by the provisional release of Šešelj from the ICTY and his return to Serbia, pending continuation of his trial.[44]

Box 17.10 Guatemala	
Conflict:	Guatemalan civil war (1960–2000)
Charges:	Genocide; crimes against humanity; murder; forced disappearances
Accused:	Efraín Ríos Montt, José Mauricio Rodríguez Sánchez, and Pedro Garcia Arredondo
Prosecuting Authority:	Guatemalan National Courts
Location:	Guatemala
Legal Activity during 2014:	Trial of Ríos Montt and Rodríguez Sánchez remained suspended pending resolution of legal challenges to its resumption; Garcia Arredondo trial commenced

In 1982, Efrain Ríos Montt seized power in a military coup and assumed the presidency of Guatemala. Though armed conflict dated back to 1960, the war entered a new phase of increased intensity and brutality under the 17-month leadership of Ríos Montt. By the time the war ended in 2000, approximately 200,000 people had been killed and 40,000 disappeared. The majority of the victims of this state terror were from the indigenous Maya community.

In 2012, Ríos Montt and his chief of military intelligence, José Mauricio Rodríguez Sánchez, were indicted for the massacre of 1,771 Mayan Ixils, the forcible displacement of 29,000, sexual violations, and torture. Genocide and crimes against humanity were subsequently added to the indictment. The remarkable step of prosecuting these two individuals in Guatemalan courts is rendered even more extraordinary given that Ríos Montt was the sitting President of the Congress at the time charges were brought against him. Moreover, previous efforts to document the casualties of the conflict and seek accountability resulted in a backlash. Among the noteworthy examples of this was the 1998 assassination of Bishop Gerardi, two days after the release of a report on human rights violations in Guatemala, compiled by the non-governmental Recovery of Historical Memory (REHMI) Project that he headed.

In 1999, the UN's Historical Clarification Commission (*Comisión para el Esclarecimiento Histórico*, or CEH) released a separate report about human rights violations during the armed conflict. Though the impact of this investigation was not immediately perceived, it helped to provide a basis for a number of political and judicial decisions that would eventually remove barriers to prosecuting cases of human rights violations. Key steps along this path included the creation of International Commission against Impunity in Guatemala (*Comisión Internacional contra la Impunidad en Guatemala*, or CICIG) in 2007 by the UN and the State of Guatemala; the creation of a special prosecution unit dealing with violations of human rights; a decision by the Constitutional Court that amnesty did not apply in certain cases of grave crimes; and the establishment of a so-called "high-risk" court to try cases of a politically sensitive nature.

On May 10, 2013, Ríos Montt was found guilty of genocide, whereas Rodríguez Sanchez was acquitted (MacLean 2013). This historic judgment was overturned 10 days later by the Constitutional Court, which reasoned that Ríos Montt had been deprived of legal representation when his attorney was temporarily expelled from the courtroom. The court vacated the decision and ordered that the retrial resume from that point in the proceedings. Since then, however, the resumption of the trial has been frustrated by a series of issues. A partial list of the most serious matters causing delays includes:

- A re-consideration by the Constitutional Court of whether the 1986 amnesty could apply in this case.[45]
- Problems experienced by judges facing reprisals.[46]
- A widening corruption scandal that led to the resignation of Guatemala's Vice President and implicated Judge Patricia Flores, the pre-trial judge who originally changed the charges against Ríos Montt from murder to genocide and then ruled that the verdict convicting Ríos Montt and Rodríguez Sanchez of genocide should be annulled and returned to the investigative stage. Flores is now facing calls for her impeachment.[47]
- Most recently, the assassination of Ríos Montt's defense attorney.[48]

In December 2014, the Constitutional Court made it possible for the retrial to go forward in January 2015 by ordering Judge Flores to annul her decision to set the trial back to the investigative stage. Despite this ruling, which attempted to settle one aspect of the question regarding the stage at which the trial should resume, this still appears to be an unresolved issue, effectively suspending trial proceedings indefinitely.[49] The schedule, including when the retrial will resume, remains unclear.

Meanwhile, the trial of Pedro Garcia Arredondo, former head of the National Police Special Investigation Unit "Command Six", began in October 2014.[50] Garcia Arredondo is charged with murder, attempted murder, and crimes against humanity for the killing of 37 people during a siege on the Spanish Embassy compound in Guatemala City in January 1980 carried out by Guatemalan security forces, and the killing of two protesters at the funeral for those killed in the siege.[51] In January 2015, Garcia Arredondo was found guilty of murder and crimes against humanity.[52]

Box 17.11 Haiti	
Conflict:	Duvalier Dictatorship (1971–1986)
Charges:	Torture; crimes against humanity
Accused:	Jean-Claude "Baby Doc" Duvalier
Prosecuting Authority:	Haitian National Courts
Location:	Haiti
Legal Activity during 2014:	Trial proceedings terminated due to Duvalier's death

Jean-Claude "Baby Doc" Duvalier ruled Haiti from 1971–1986, when he was ousted and went into exile. His dictatorship was characterized by widespread abuses, including extrajudicial killings, detention, disappearances and torture. He remained in exile in France until 2011, when he returned to Haiti.

His return made it possible for cases to be brought against him, and he was initially arrested in 2011 and charged with financial corruption. Following his arrest, civil complainants brought charges of human rights violations against him. In May 2011, the Inter-American Commission on Human Rights (IACHR) issued a statement about Haiti's duty to investigate gross human rights violations committed during the Duvalier regime.[53] In January 2012, however, the investigative judge of the Tribunal of First Instance of Port-au-Prince dismissed the human rights violation charges, ruling that Duvalier could only be tried for alleged financial crimes. That decision was appealed by civil parties, with the support of Haitian and international human rights organizations.

In 2013, the Court of Appeals ordered Duvalier to appear before it for the first time to be publicly questioned about the reports of torture, detention, and murder, initiating a process of gathering testimony from witnesses and further investigation. In February 2014, the appellate court paved the way to try him for torture and crimes against humanity when it recognized the acts that Duvalier was accused of qualified as crimes against humanity and affirmed that there is no statute of limitations with respect to such crimes. Consequently, the charges of crimes against humanity were reinstated and preparations for his trial continued through 2014. Duvalier died in October 2014, before his trial commenced.[54]

Box 17.12 Kenya	
Conflict:	Post-election violence (2007–2008)
Charges:	Crimes against humanity
Accused:	Uhuru Muigai Kenyatta, William Samoei Ruto, Joshua Arap Sang, Francis Kirimi Muthaura, Mohammed Hussein Ali, and Walter Osapiri Barasa
Prosecuting Authority:	ICC
Location:	The Hague, the Netherlands
Legal Activity during 2014:	Charges against Kenyatta withdrawn; Ruto and Sang trial ongoing; arrest warrant for Barasa remains active

The 2007 presidential elections in Kenya were followed by a wave of violence, precipitated in part by disputed results and largely involving members of rival political parties, with a significant ethnic dimension. During the violence, an estimated 1,300 people were killed. The Eminent Persons Group, headed by Kofi Annan, brokered a power-sharing accord that helped bring an end to the violence. In the aftermath, several formal inquiries were undertaken.

The Commission of Inquiry into the Post-Election Violence (CIPEV) released a report in October 2008 attributing responsibility to individuals in high levels of government, the security agencies, and political parties – without naming names – for actions and inactions that provoked and fueled the ethnic violence. To address these circumstances, CIPEV proposed measures to hold accountable those complicit in the episode, including creating a special domestic criminal tribunal to try these individuals plus an administrative procedure whereby those who are found guilty can be barred from holding public office, as well as other legislative changes and policy, institutional and sectoral reforms. CIPEV also provided Kofi Annan with a sealed envelope naming key suspects in the violence. Another critical aspect of the report was a binding schedule of implementation, with clear repercussions for inaction. In particular, the Kenyan parliament had until January 31, 2009 to pass legislation to establish the tribunal, which was required to commence operations by March 1, 2009; otherwise, referral to the ICC would ensue. Attempts were made to establish the tribunal, against some resistance by the political leadership, but ultimately failed. In July 2009, Kofi Annan handed over the envelope of suspects to the ICC Prosecutor.

Meanwhile, the Kenyan parliament established a Truth, Justice, and Reconciliation Commission in December 2008 to investigate and recommend appropriate action on human rights abuses committed between December 1963 and February 2008. The mandate of the commission was explicitly envisioned as being complementary to the prosecution – whether by national courts or the ICC – of abuses committed as part of the post-election violence.[55]

In 2010, the ICC Prosecutor initiated an investigation into the situation based on authority granted under Article 15 of the Rome Statute, which allows such investigation even if a case was not referred to the ICC by a State government or the United Nations Security Council. Following these preliminary investigations, the Prosecutor requested that summonses to appear be issued for several individuals:

- Uhuru Muigai Kenyatta, the President of Kenya;
- William Ruto, Deputy President of Kenya;
- Joshua Arap Sang, Head of Operations at Kass FM in Nairobi, Kenya;
- Francis Kirimi Muthaura, Cabinet Secretary and Head of Civil Service; and
- Mohammed Hussein Ali, Member of Parliament.

In 2012, charges of multiple counts of crimes against humanity were confirmed against Kenyatta, Ruto and Sang, but the charges against Ali were not confirmed,[56] while those against Muthaura were eventually withdrawn.[57] In 2013, a new case was initiated, against Walter Osapiri Barasa, charging him with offences against the administration of justice for allegedly attempting to influence ICC witnesses.

In December 2014, following two vacated attempts to start the trial of Uhuru Kenyatta, all charges were withdrawn by the Prosecutor.[58] The cases against Ruto and Sang were ongoing throughout 2014.[59] Meanwhile, there is an active arrest warrant for Barasa, who remains at large.[60]

Box 17.13 Libya	
Conflict:	Repression by Libyan forces against Libyan population and protesters (2011)
Charges:	Crimes against humanity
Accused:	Saif Al-Islam Gaddafi and Abdullah Al-Senussi
Prosecuting Authority:	ICC
Location:	The Hague, the Netherlands
Legal Activity during 2014:	ICC Appeals Chamber confirmed Saif Al-Islam Gaddafi case admissible; ICC declared Al-Senussi case inadmissible; ICC issued a finding of "non-compliance" against the Government of Libya and referred the matter to the UNSC for assistance in removing impediments to Libya's cooperation

In 2011, following uprisings in Tunisia and Egypt, similar movements emerged in Libya to protest the regime of Muammar Gaddafi. In February 2011, the security apparatus of the Libyan government is alleged to have targeted several civilian demonstrators, resulting in deaths, detentions and displacement. Over the subsequent six months, the situation in Libya rapidly deteriorated, as a result of the government's actions, which plunged the country into a civil war. Benefiting from a NATO enforced no-fly zone, Libyan rebel groups succeeded in overtaking the Gaddafi regime in Tripoli and formed an interim National Transitional Council government, which was internationally recognized, in August 2011.

Meanwhile, in early 2011, prior to the fall of the Gaddafi regime, the UN Security Council adopted Resolution 1970, which referred the Libyan situation to the ICC Prosecutor. Following preliminary investigations, the Prosecutor requested arrest warrants for three individuals:

- Muammar Gaddafi;
- Saif Al-Islam Gaddafi, honorary chairman of the Gaddafi International Charity and Development Foundation and *de facto* Prime Minister; and
- Abdullah Al-Senussi, Colonel in the Libyan Armed Forces and Head of Military Intelligence.

The charges against these individuals included multiple counts of crimes against humanity. Muammar Gaddafi was killed by rebel fighters in October 2011. Saif Gaddafi and Al-Senussi were captured in November 2011.

In May 2014, the ICC determined that Libyan authorities would not be able to carry out the requisite proceedings in regards to the charges against Saif Al-Islam Gaddafi and confirmed that his case was therefore admissible.[61] The ICC also ruled that the Government of Libya was in non-compliance for refusal to surrender Saif Gaddafi to ICC custody.[62] In July 2014, the Appeals Chamber of the ICC declared Al-Senussi's case inadmissible before the ICC, accepting he was being subjected to competent proceedings in Libya for the actions that gave rise to the charges by the ICC.[63]

Box 17.14 Rwanda	
Conflict:	Genocide in Rwanda (1994)
Charges:	Genocide; crimes against humanity
Accused:	Multiple across locations
Prosecuting Authorities:	International Criminal Tribunal for Rwanda (ICTR); national courts of Rwanda; foreign country national courts
Locations:	Rwanda, Tanzania, Belgium, Canada, France, Germany, Norway, Sweden
Legal Activity during 2014:	Multiple trials and appeals ongoing

During the 1994 genocide in Rwanda, an estimated 500,000–800,000 people were killed, with a significant segment of the population involved in the perpetration of the violence. Criminal prosecutions related to these atrocities have gone through several stages over the past 20 years and still continue.

Parallel processes in the ICTR, located in Tanzania, and Rwandan national courts began in 1994. The ICTR was established by the UN to try individuals responsible for the most serious offenses, including genocide, war crimes and crimes against humanity. Many of those indicted by the ICTR had fled Rwanda when the Rwandan Patriotic Front defeated the Rwandan army and overtook the government. Among these suspects were those thought to have planned and instigated the genocide, including key figures such as:

- Former Prime Minister Jean Kambanda;
- Former Army Chief of Staff General Augustin Bizimungu; and
- Former Ministry of Defence Chief of Staff Colonel Bagosora.[64]

Individuals accused of involvement in the mass killings were also subject to arrest and prosecution within the national justice system. At one point early in this process, the population of those incarcerated pending trial on genocide charges swelled to 130,000. Recognizing the infeasibility of trying in national courts all those suspected of having participated in the genocide, the Rwandan government established the *gacaca* system of local tribunals in 2000. This system was tasked with expediting the handling of the bulk of those incarcerated for lower-order offenses. More than 40,000 panels headed by *inyangamugayo* (respected person) convened local hearings, through which they gathered information regarding the acts that occurred and rendered judgments in individual cases in a process that combined aspects of a court, alternative dispute resolution, and a truth-seeking process. In just the first five years of the *gacaca* process, starting with the 2002 piloting of the tribunals, the information gathered generated approximately 1 million new case files. In 2012, as the *gacaca* process came to a close, the government reported that nearly 2 million cases were adjudicated via this system.[65]

Those alleged to have planned and instigated the genocide continued to be prosecuted by conventional courts. As of 2014, approximately 10,000 individuals had been tried for genocide in the national court system of Rwanda (Human Rights Watch 2014). During 2014, genocide prosecutions continued in Rwanda, including cases such as that of Charles Bandora, who was the first genocide suspect to be extradited to Rwanda from a European country (Norway). His trial began in Kigali in September 2014. In May 2015, he was convicted of conspiracy, genocide and murders as crimes against humanity.[66] A number of other investigations, indictments, arrest and extradition requests were actively pursued by the Rwandan government in 2014.[67]

As of 2014, the ICTR had indicted 93 individuals of genocide and other serious violations of international humanitarian law. Of these individuals, 61 were convicted and sentenced, 14 were acquitted, 10 were referred to national jurisdictions for trial, and three were fugitives who had been referred to the Mechanism for International Criminal Tribunals (MICT).[68] During 2014, the ICTR was in the process of transferring the remaining cases to the Rwandan government, completing the appeals processes with only one remaining appeals judgment expected in 2015, and setting up the MICT, which will process matters relating to outstanding arrest warrants and administrative needs relating to the work of the ICTR once its trial and appeals chambers are closed.[69]

In addition to prosecutions by the national judicial system of Rwanda and the ICTR, a number of cases have been brought on the basis of universal jurisdiction against accused individuals who reside outside of Rwanda. In 2014, such cases were active in Belgium, Canada, France, Germany, Norway and Sweden (TRIAL, ECCHR, and FIDH 2015).

Box 17.15 Sudan	
Conflict:	Armed insurgency against Sudanese Government (2002–present)
Charges:	War crimes; crimes against humanity; genocide
Accused:	Ahmad Muhammad Harun ("Ahmad Harun"), Ali Muhammad Ali Abd-Al-Rahman ("Ali Kushayb"), Omar Hassan Ahmad Al Bashir, Bahar Idriss Abu Garda, Abdallah Banda Abakaer Nourain, and Abdel Raheem Muhammad Hussein
Prosecuting Authority:	ICC
Location:	The Hague, the Netherlands
Legal Activity during 2014:	Arrest warrants are active and open; ICC Pre-Trial Chamber found that the DRC failed to cooperate with the Court in the execution of the arrest warrant for Al Bashir while he was in their territory and the matter was referred to United Nations Security Council

Following a protracted armed conflict between the northern and southern regions of Sudan dating back to the 1980s, an armed insurgency led by the Sudan Liberation Movement/Army (SLM/A) and the Justice Equality Movement (JEM) against the Sudanese government began in 2002, contemporaneous with the signing of a Comprehensive Peace Agreement. This insurgency was met with force by the Sudanese government, which engaged local groups in the form of the Popular Defense Force (PDF) and *Janjaweed* militias to fight against the rebels. Estimates of the casualties resulting from the conflict are in the vicinity of 400,000 killed and 2.5 million displaced persons.

In 2005, the UN Security Council, acting under Chapter VII of the UN Charter, adopted Resolution 1593, which referred the situation in Darfur to the ICC Prosecutor. Following preliminary investigations, the ICC Prosecutor requested warrants of arrest for seven individuals accused of bearing criminal responsibility for war crimes and crimes against humanity and Genocide in Darfur. These indictments were particularly controversial, as they called for the arrest of the sitting head of state, Omar al-Bashir,[70] along with senior members of his government, including Ahmad Harun, Minister of State for the Interior of the Government of Sudan and Minister of State for Humanitarian Affairs;[71] and, Abdel Raheem Muhammed Hussein, Current Minister of National Defence and former Minister of the Interior and former Sudanese President's Special Representative in Darfur.[72] In addition, charges of war crimes and crimes against humanity were brought against leaders of militarized groups, including Ali Muhammad Ali Abd-Al-Rahman ("Ali Kushayb"), leader of the Janjaweed militia;[73] Abdallah Banda Abakaer Nourain, Commander-in-Chief of JEM, who is now thought to be deceased;[74] and Bahar Idriss Abu Garda, Chairman and General Coordinator of Military Operations of the United Resistance Front. Of those for whom arrest warrants were issued, only Garda appeared before the ICC, whereupon the Pre-Trial Chamber did not confirm the Prosecutor's charges.[75]

As of 2014, the arrest warrants for President al-Bashir, his ministers and Rahman are open and there appears to be no movement on the stalemate between the government of the Sudan and the ICC in this matter. In 2014, Pre-Trial Chamber II of the ICC found that the DRC had failed to cooperate in the arrest and surrender of President al-Bashir during a February 2014 visit.[76] The Pre-Trial Chamber referred the matter to the UN Security Council (UNSC). Subsequently, in March 2015, the ICC Pre-Trial Chamber II issued a finding that the government of Sudan had failed to cooperate with the ICC in its request to arrest President Al-Bashir and surrender him to the Court and referred the matter to the UN Security Council.[77]

Box 17.16 Uganda	
Conflict:	Armed conflict between Lord's Resistance Army (LRA) and the Ugandan Government (1987–present)
Charges:	War crimes; crimes against humanity
Accused:	Joseph Kony, Vincent Otti, Okot Odhiambo, Raska Lukwiya, and Dominic Ongwen
Prosecuting Authority:	ICC
Location:	The Hague, the Netherlands
Legal Activity during 2014:	Arrest warrants for Kony and Otti are active; surrender of Ongwen (January 2015)

The armed rebellion by the Lord's Resistance Army (LRA) against the Ugandan government began in 1987 and is estimated to have caused close to 100,000 deaths, involved nearly 100,000 abductions – nearly half of children – across four countries, and displaced approximately 1.7 million people. The LRA is especially notorious for the abduction of children, who have been used for labor, sex and war fighting. The protracted length and nature of this conflict has taken a profound humanitarian toll. Its resolution and the progress towards recovery are greatly complicated by the coerced involvement in the hostilities of a significant share of the population in northern Uganda.

In 2003, Ugandan President Yoweri Museveni referred the actions of the LRA to the ICC. In 2005, the ICC Office of the Prosecutor issued indictments against five senior figures of the LRA for alleged war crimes and crimes against humanity. Arrest warrants were subsequently issued against Joseph Kony, LRA Commander-in-Chief; Vincent Otti, Vice-Chairman and Second-in-Command; Okot Odhiambo, LRA Army Commander;[78] Raska Lukwiya, LRA Army Commander;[79] and, Dominic Ongwen, Commander of the LRA's Sinia Brigade.[80] In 2011, the United States deployed approximately 100 special-forces troops to aid Uganda and the AU in the search for LRA commanders, who have reportedly moved into areas of the Sudan, the DRC and the CAR. In 2013, the United States offered a monetary reward for information leading to the accused. The US military procured additional air support for the search in 2014.

Of the accused, only Dominic Ongwen has been arrested, surrendering to US troops in the CAR in January 2015 and subsequently remanded to ICC custody. Proceedings in the Ongwen case are pending. Kony and Otti remain at large and the search for them continues. Lukwiya and Odhiambo were never apprehended and are now reportedly deceased.

Other Major ICC Activity

Full Investigations

In addition to the cases profiled above, the ICC's Office of the Prosecutor engaged in full investigations about two countries during 2014. Following a preliminary examination, the Office of the Prosecutor may seek authorization from the Court to pursue a full investigation if the Court determines that the evidence collected at the preliminary stage is sufficient to support a "reasonable basis to believe that a crime within the jurisdiction of the Court has been or is being committed" and therefore proceeding with a full investigation is warranted.[81]

Mali: In January 2012, the Malian armed forces and several non-state armed groups, including the *Mouvement National de Libération de l'Azawad* (MNLA), al Qaeda in the Islamic Maghreb (AQIM), Ansar Dine, and the *Mouvement pour l'Unicité et le Jihad en Afrique de l'Ouest* (MUJAO), clashed over control of the northern territories of Mali. In March 2012, just before the presidential election, the government of President Touré fell in a military coup led by Amadou Haya Sanogo. In April 2012, Malian forces were pushed out of the northern region by rebel groups. The ensuing period was characterized by fighting among various armed actors to establish territorial control. Concurrently, the Economic Community of West African States (ECOWAS), the AU, and the UN sought to establish a transitional government, create a new timeline for elections, and discuss plans for an intervention force to assist the government in quelling the developing violence in northern Mali. In May 2012, the government approached the ICC Prosecutor to request an investigation into the situation in the regions of Kidal, Gao and Timbuktu, which were under the control of rebel groups. In July 2012, the UN Security Council adopted resolution 2056, expressing concern for the destruction of religious and historic cultural monuments, acts that constitute war crimes. Around the same time, ECOWAS requested that the ICC Prosecutor investigate war crimes allegations. As of 2014, the ICC investigation remained ongoing.[82]

Central African Republic II: Following a coup d'état through which Michel Djotodia, leader of the Séléka group, ousted President François Bozizé, ex-Séléka forces continued to pursue an offensive against populations in the north of the country. The targeted areas were associated with support for Bozizé. In response to the armed attacks of ex-Séléka, "anti-balaka" groups emerged to resist the assaults. Though Djotodia ostensibly disbanded Séléka, its fighters have reportedly continued an armed campaign. In December 2013, as the AU was deploying its peacekeeping mission, with support of French troops, anti-balaka forces attacked the position of ex-Séléka forces in Bangui. In the ensuing conflict, anti-balaka and ex-Séléka forces reportedly targeted geographic areas with large Muslim populations, in a campaign of ethnic cleansing. In May 2014, CAR authorities referred the situation to the ICC Prosecutor, who has determined that there is reasonable basis to believe that both ex-Séléka and anti-balaka forces committed crimes against humanity and war crimes. Accordingly, the Prosecutor's second investigation into the CAR situation was undertaken and is ongoing.[83]

Preliminary Examination Initiated or Continued

The ICC Office of the Prosecutor engaged in preliminary examinations about nine countries during 2014. The preliminary examination stage focuses on whether the allegations presented constitute crimes within the jurisdiction of the ICC, such as war crimes, crimes against humanity or genocide; whether the matter is admissible; and whether the interests of justice would be served by pursuing further investigation and prosecution of any cases that might arise.[84]

Afghanistan: This examination focuses on alleged war crimes and crimes against humanity by both anti-government groups (targeting of specific types of civilians, including women, children, and aid workers) and pro-government groups (torture of detainees) from 2003–2013.

Colombia: This examination focuses on alleged crimes against humanity and war crimes perpetrated by the government and paramilitary groups since 2002, in the context of a 50-year armed conflict. Crimes under investigation include murder, abduction, forced displacement, torture, sexual violence, conscription of children, and assaults on civilian populations.

Georgia: This examination focuses on alleged war crimes and crimes against humanity perpetrated during the armed conflict between South Ossetia and Georgia in 2008. Allegations under investigation include forcible transfer of ethnic Georgians, attacks on Georgian civilians by South Ossetian forces, and an attack on Russian peacekeepers.

Guinea: This examination focuses on alleged crimes against humanity during a violent military action against a gathering of the political opposition in September 2009 at Conakry Stadium. Allegations under investigation include the killing of nearly 160 protesters, sexual violence and rape, disappearances, and torture of detainees.

Honduras: This examination focuses on alleged crimes against humanity following the 2009 coup d'état that removed President José Manuel Zelaya from office.

Iraq: This examination focuses on alleged war crimes, including mistreatment, torture, and killings of Iraqi detainees and civilians by UK officials in Iraq from 2003–2008.

Nigeria: This examination focuses on alleged crimes against humanity and war crimes perpetrated in the armed conflict between Boko Haram and Nigerian security forces. Allegations under investigation include armed attacks against civilians and abductions by Boko Haram and torture and mass civilian executions by the Nigerian military.

Ukraine: This examination focuses on the alleged injury and killing of protestors, disappearances, and torture during the Maidan protest events of 2013–2014.

Preliminary Examinations Closed

In 2014, the ICC also closed two preliminary examinations. The Office of the Prosecutor determined that there is not a basis to seek authorization to proceed with full investigation of these cases.[85]

Koreas: This examination concerned the sinking of a South Korean warship, the *Cheonan*, and the shelling of South Korea's Yeonpyeong Island by North Korea in 2010. The ICC Prosecutor determined there was not a reasonable basis to find that either of these two incidents constituted a crime within the jurisdiction of the court.

Vessels of Comoros, Greece and Cambodia: This examination concerned an incident in which the Israeli Defense Force intercepted a humanitarian aid flotilla and boarded one of the vessels, in the course of which 10 persons were killed. The ICC Prosecutor concluded that while there is a reasonable basis to believe that war crimes were committed, the cases potentially arising from this incident were not of sufficient gravity, as well as being beyond the limitations of jurisdiction.

Universal Jurisdiction Cases

Below is a list of countries where legal activity occurred in 2014 to pursue or undertake prosecutions of third-party nationals for violations committed outside the territory of the national prosecuting authority and involving victims who are not nationals of that country. The basis for bringing these legal actions is the concept of universal jurisdiction for *jus cogens* violations, such as crimes against humanity, war crimes, and genocide. The countries where the legal actions occurred are listed first, followed in parentheses by the countries whose conflicts were the subject of such legal activity (TRIAL, ECCHR, and FIDH 2015).

Argentina (Paraguay, Spain)
Belgium (Liberia, Rwanda)
Canada (Rwanda)
France (Algeria, Congo, Libya, Morocco, Rwanda, Syria)
Germany (DRC, Rwanda, Syria)
Norway (Rwanda)
Senegal (Chad, DRC)
South Africa (Madagascar, Zimbabwe)
Spain (China, Cuba, El Salvador, Guatemala, Iraq)
Sweden (Rwanda)
Switzerland (Algeria, Liberia, Guatemala)
United Kingdom (Nepal)
United States (Somalia)[86]

Notes

1 Additional cases have been pursued for civil violations, through courts and human rights commissions. These cases are outside the scope of this chapter.
2 This chapter focuses on cases in which violations of international criminal conventions are alleged. Each of these legal categories of crimes incorporates numerous types of possible violations. Particular situations and cases often involve allegations of multiple types of violations and may include specific charges, such as rape, enslavement, deportation, killing, forced disappearances, kidnapping, use of children as combatants, and so forth. For brevity, the charges referred to in these profiles designate the broad categories of crimes. When possible, references to full case summaries are made where specific charges are completely and precisely elaborated.
3 See TRIAL, http://www.trial-ch.org/en/resources/trial-watch/trial-watch/profiles/profile/844/action/show/controller/Profile/tab/context.html.
4 See the National Security Archive's declassified documents, briefs and books on *Operation Condor*, at http://nsarchive.gwu.edu/NSAEBB/NSAEBB514/.
5 Human Rights Watch's source for this number was the Centro de Estudios Legales y Sociales (CELS).
6 See Sajit Gandhi (ed.), "The Tilt: The U.S. and the South Asian Crisis of 1971," National Security Archives Electronic Briefing Book no. 79, December 16, 2002, as well as accompanying declassified documents pertaining to the 1971 crisis, available at http://nsarchive.gwu.edu/NSAEBB/NSAEBB79/#docs.

7 See International Crimes Tribunal Bangladesh, http://www.ict-bd.org. Charges against the 195 Pakistani officers were dropped and they were repatriated to Pakistan as part of a 1974 Tripartite Agreement. For discussion, see Robertson (2015: 50).

8 This figure is derived from multiple sources, including trial monitoring by TRIAL and judgments and decisions handed down from the ICT.

9 While the website for the ICT makes available documents relating to judgments and decisions, it does not yet provide specific case information.

10 See Robertson (2015). The Robertson report provides a methodical analysis of the 1973 law creating the original Tribunal, as well as subsequent legal adaptations when it was implemented starting in 2009. His analysis finds the ICT, in its present form, in breach of a number of legal standards now accepted and developed through the experiences of international criminal tribunals, including those for Rwanda, the former Yugoslavia, Sierra Leone and the International Criminal Court (2002).

11 "Islamist Opposition Leader Executed for War Crimes in Bangladesh," *The Guardian*, April 11, 2015, http://www.theguardian.com/world/2015/apr/11/islamist-opposition-leader-executed-for-war-crimes-bangladesh-muhammad-kamaruzzaman.

12 For a full description of charges and case status, see ECCC, http://www.eccc.gov.kh/en/case/topic/286. The charges against Muth were brought *in absentia* reportedly due to a lack of cooperation by the Cambodian judicial police (TRIAL, http://www.trial-ch.org/en/resources/trial-watch/trial-watch/profiles/profile/4269/action/show/controller/Profile/tab/legal-procedure.html).

13 See ECCC, http://www.eccc.gov.kh/en.

14 For a full description of charges and case status, see ECCC, http://www.eccc.gov.kh/en/case/topic/98.

15 *The Prosecutor v. Jean-Pierre Bemba Gombo*, "Case Information Sheet," ICC-PIDS-CIS-CAR-01–010/14_Eng, updated November 14, 2014.

16 *The Prosecutor v. Jean-Pierre Bemba Gombo, Aimé Kilolo Musamba, Jean-Jacques Mangenda Kabongo, Fidèle Babala Wandu and Narcisse Arido*, "Case Information Sheet," ICC-PIDS-CIS-CAR-02–009/15_Eng, updated May 29, 2015.

17 International Court of Justice, "Questions Relating to the Obligation to Prosecute or Extradite (Belgium v. Senegal)," Judgment of July 20, 2012, http://www.icj-cij.org/docket/files/144/17064.pdf.

18 See also, Chambres Africaines Extraordinaire, http://www.chambresafricaines.org.

19 See United States Institute of Peace, http://www.usip.org/publications/truth-commission-chile-90.

20 Case of Pedro Ramón Cáceres Jorquera and Edgar Cevallos Jones, as reported by TRIAL, http://www.trial-ch.org/en/resources/trial-watch/trial-watch/profiles/profile/4581/action/show/controller/Profile.html.

21 Case of Simone Gbagbo, as reported by TRIAL, http://www.trial-ch.org/en/resources/trial-watch/trial-watch/profiles/profile/3875/action/show/controller/Profile.html

22 *The Prosecutor v. Laurent Gbagbo and Charles Blé Goudé*, ICC-PIDS-CIS-CI-04–02/15_Eng, updated March 31, 2015; *The Prosecutor v. Simone Gbagbo*, "Case Information Sheet", ICC-PIDS-CIS-CI-02–004/15_Eng, updated March 23, 2015.

23 *The Prosecutor v. Callixte Mbarushimana,* "Case Information Sheet," ICC-PIDS-CIS-DRC-04–003/11_Eng, updated March 27, 2012.

24 *The Prosecutor v. Thomas Lubanga Dyilo*, "Case Information Sheet," ICC-PIDS-CIS-DRC-01–012/15_Eng, updated March 25, 2015.

25 *The Prosecutor v. Mathieu Ngudjolo Chui*, "Case Information Sheet," ICC-PIDS-CIS-DRC2–06–006/15_Eng, updated February 27, 2015.

26 *The Prosecutor v. Germain Katanga*, "Case Information Sheet," ICC-PIDS-CIS-DRC-03–011/15_Eng, updated March 25, 2015.

27 *The Prosecutor v. Bosco Ntaganda*, "Case Information Sheet," ICC-PIDS-CIS-DRC-02–008/15_Eng. updated April 22, 2015.

28 *The Prosecutor v. Sylvestre Mudacumura*, "Case Information Sheet," ICC-PIDS-CIS-DRC-05–003/15_Eng, updated March 25, 2015.

29 For summary, see http://www.icty.org/sections/TheCases/KeyFiguresoftheCases.

30 For details and documents related to ICTY trials and appeals cases, see http://www.icty.org/action/cases/4.

31 *Prosecutor v. Radovan Karadžić*, IT-95–5/18, http://www.icty.org/case/karadzic/4.

32 *Prosecutor v. Ratko Mladić*, IT-09–92, http://www.icty.org/x/cases/mladic/cis/en/cis_mladic_en.pdf.

33 *Prosecutor v. Goran Hadžić*, IT-04–75, http://www.icty.org/x/cases/hadzic/cis/en/cis_hadzic_en.pdf.

34 Milka Domanovic and Marija Ristic, "Vojislav Seselj Returns to Serbia after 11 Years," *Balkan Insight*, November 12, 2014, http://www.balkaninsight.com/en/article/vojislav-seselj-arrives-to-serbia-after-11-years.

35 *Prosecutor v. Vojislav Šešelj*, IT-03–67, http://www.icty.org/x/cases/seselj/cis/en/cis_seselj_en.pdf.

36 Thomas Escritt and Matt Robinson, "War Crimes Court Revokes Serb Nationalist Seselj's Compassionate Release," Reuters, March 30, 2015.

37 "Serbian Nationalist Rebuffs Order to Return to War Crimes Court," *Reuters*, March 30, 2015.

38 Denis Dzidic, "Bosnia Charges 15 Serbs for Zecovi Massacre," *Balkan Insight*, December 12, 2014, http://www.balkaninsight.com/en/article/zecovi-massacre-indictment-raised.

39 Marija Ristic, "The Troubled Trial of Kosovo's 'Drenica Group'," *Balkan Insight*, May 27, 2015, http://www.balkaninsight.com/en/article/kosovo-awaits-kla-guerilla-verdict.

40 Sven Milekic, "Croatia Indicts Soldier for Operation Storm Killings," *Balkan Insight*, November 26, 2014, http://www.balkaninsight.com/en/article/indictment-for-operation-storm-killings-1.

41 Dusica Tomovic, "Montenegro Must Tackle War Crimes, Chief Prosecutor Says," *Balkan Insight*, May 20, 2015, http://www.balkaninsight.com/en/article/montenegro-needs-to-tackle-war-crimes-chief-prosecutor-says.

42 Rick Wallace, "'Captain Dragan' Looks Set to Be Extradited to Croatia," *The Australian*, May 15, 2015, http://www.theaustralian.com.au/news/nation/captain-dragan-looks-set-to-be-extradited-to-croatia/story-e6frg6nf-1227356356814.

43 International Court of Justice, "Application of the Convention on the Prevention and Punishment of the Crime of Genocide (Croatia v. Serbia)," Judgment, February 3, 2015.

44 International Criminal Tribunal for the Former Yugoslavia (ICTY), http://www.icty.org; Marija Ristic, "Serb Paramilitary 'Captain Dragan' Pleads for Release," *Balkan Insight*, May 16, 2014, http://www.balkaninsight.com/en/article/captain-dragan-asks-for-his-release.

45 Emi MacLean, "Renewed Amnesty Threat to Rios Montt Prosecution," *International Justice Monitor*, December 28, 2014.

46 Emi MacLean and Sophie Beaudoin, "Guatemalan Judges Reportedly Facing Retaliation for Judicial Independence," *International Justice Monitor*, March 6, 2015.

47 Sophie Beaudoin, "Impeachment Request Filed against Judge Carol Patricia Flores," *International Justice Monitor*, May 4, 2015, http://www.ijmonitor.org/2015/05/impeachment-request-filed-against-judge-carol-patricia-flores/.

48 Emi MacLean and Sophie Beaudoin, "Rios Montt's Defense Attorney Killed by Hitmen in Guatemala City," *International Justice Monitor*, June 4, 2015.

49 Emi MacLean and Sophie Beaudoin, "Guatemala Court May Block Resumption of Rios Montt Genocide Trial," *International Justice Monitor* December 12, 2014.

50 Emi MacLean and Sophie Beaudoin, "More Than 30 Years Later, Guatemala's Deadly Spanish Embassy Siege is on Trial in a Guatemalan Courtroom," *International Justice Monitor*, November 25, 2014.

51 Sophie Beaudoin, "In Closing Arguments, Prosecution Seeks Life in Prison for Former Guatemalan National Police Official for Spanish Embassy Fire," *International Justice Monitor*, January 15, 2015.

52 Emi MacLean and Sophie Beaudoin, "Guatemalan Police Official Found Guilty of Homicide and Crimes against Humanity," *International Justice Monitor*, January 20, 2015.

53 Inter-American Commission for Human Rights, "Statement on the Duty of the Haitian State to Investigate the Gross Violations of Human rights Committed during the Regime of Jean-Claude Duvalier," Washington, DC, May 17, 2011.

54 "Case of Jean-Claude Duvalier: Decision of the Court of Appeals of Port-au-Prince, February 20, 2014," unofficial English language translation from French, Center for Justice and Accountability, http://www.cja.org/section.php?id=552; Bureau des Avocats Internationaux and Institute for Justice and Democracy in Haiti, "Human Rights Organizations Applaud Court's Decision to Reinstate Human Rights Crimes against Jean-Claude Duvalier," Port-au-Prince, February 21, 2014, http://www.ijdh.org/2014/02/topics/law-justice/human-rights-organizations-applaud-courts-decision-to-reinstate-human-rights-crimes-against-jean-claude-duvalier/#.Uwu1NPldUgU.

55 See United States Institute of Peace, http://www.usip.org/publications/truth-commission-kenya.

56 See ICC, http://www.icc-cpi.int/iccdocs/doc/doc1314543.pdf#search=confirmation%20of%20charges%20Ali.

57 See ICC, http://www.icc-cpi.int/iccdocs/doc/doc1568411.pdf#search=confirmation%20of%20charges%20Muthaura.

58 *The Prosecutor v. Uhuru Muigai Kenyatta*, "Case Information Sheet," ICC-PIDS-CIS-KEN-02–014/15_Eng, updated March 13, 2015.

59 *The Prosecutor v. Uhuru Muigai Kenyatta*, "Case Information Sheet," ICC-PIDS-CIS-KEN-02–014/15_Eng, updated March 13, 2015.

60 *The Prosecutor v. Walter Osapiri Barasa*, "Warrant of Arrest," ICC-01/09–01/13–1-Red2, August 2, 2013.

61 *The Prosecutor v. Saif Al-Islam Gaddafi*, "Case Information Sheet," ICC-PIDS-CIS-LIB-01–011/15_Eng, March 26, 2015.

62 ICC Pre-Trial Chamber I, "Decision on the Non-compliance by Libya with Requests for Cooperation by the Court and Referring the Matter to the United Nations Security Council," ICC-01/11–01/11, December 10, 2014.

63 ICC Appeals Chamber, "Judgment on the Appeal of Mr Abdullah Al-Senussi against the Decision of Pre-Trial Chamber I of 11 October 2013 Entitled 'Decision on the Admissibility of the Case against Abdullah Al-Senussi'," ICC-01/11–01/11OA6, July 24, 2014.

64 For a complete list of indictees, see ICTR, http://www.unictr.org/sites/unictr.org/files/publications/ictr-key-figures-en.pdf.

65 Ibid.

66 Charles Bandora case, as reported by TRIAL, http://www.trial-ch.org/en/resources/trial-watch/trial-watch/profiles/profile/905/action/show/controller/Profile/tab/fact.html.

67 See TRIAL, http://www.trial-ch.org/en/resources/trial-watch/search/action/search/controller/Profile.html?jf=61&tx_wetwdb_profile%5BjudgementPlace%5D=61&cHash=85f7cf1fa8c3e38acb3448a57b4f029d.

68 See ICTR, http://www.unictr.org/en/tribunal.

69 See ICTR, "Report on the Completion Strategy of the International Criminal Tribunal for Rwanda as at 5 May 2015", S/2015/340. See also, MICT, "Assessment and Progress Report of the President of the International Residual Mechanism for Criminal Tribunals, Judge Theodor Meron, for the Period from 16 November 2014 to 15 May 2015", S/2015/341, and ICTR, "Nineteenth Annual Report of the International Criminal Tribunal for the Prosecution of Persons Responsible for Genocide and Other Serious Violations of International Humanitarian Law Committed in the Territory of Rwanda and Rwandan Citizens Responsible for Genocide and Other Such Violations Committed in the Territory of Neighbouring States between 1 January and 31 December 1994," A/69/206; S/2014/546.

70 *The Prosecutor v. Omar Hassan Ahmad Al Bashir*, "Case Information Sheet," ICC-PIDS-CIS-SUD-02–004/15_Eng, updated March 26, 2015.

71 *The Prosecutor v. Ahmad Muhammad Harun ("Ahmad Harun") and Ali Muhammad Ali Abd-Al-Rahman ("Ali Kushayb")*, "Case Information Sheet," ICC-PIDS-CIS-SUD-001–004/15_Eng, updated March 25, 2015.

72 *The Prosecutor v. Abdel Raheem Muhammad Hussein*, "Case Information Sheet," ICC-PIDS-CIS-SUD-05–003/15_Eng, updated March 25, 2015.

73 *The Prosecutor v. Ahmad Muhammad Harun ("Ahmad Harun") and Ali Muhammad Ali Abd-Al-Rahman ("Ali Kushayb")*, "Case Information Sheet," ICC-PIDS-CIS-SUD-001–004/15_Eng, updated March 25, 2015.

74 *The Prosecutor v. Abdallah Banda Abakaer Nourain*, "Case Information Sheet," ICC-PIDS-CIS-SUD-04–006/15_Eng, updated March 23, 2015.

75 *The Prosecutor v. Bahar Idriss Abu Garda*, "Case Information Sheet," ICC-PIDS-CIS-SUD-03–002/11_Eng, updated June 15, 2012.

76 ICC Pre-Trial Chamber II, "Decision on the Cooperation of the Democratic Republic of the Congo regarding Omar Al Bashir's Arrest and Surrender to the Court," ICC-02/05–01/09–195, April 9, 2014, http://www.icc-cpi.int/iccdocs/doc/doc1759849.pdf.

77 ICC Pre-Trial Chamber II, "Decision on the Prosecutor's Request for a Finding of Non-Compliance against the Republic of the Sudan," ICC-02/05–01/09, March 9, 2015, http://www.icc-cpi.int/iccdocs/doc/doc1919142.pdf.

78 *The Prosecutor v. Joseph Kony, Vincent Otti and Okot Odhiambo*, "Case Information Sheet," ICC-PIDS-CIS-UGA-001–004/15_Eng, updated March 26, 2015.

79 ICC Pre-Trial Chamber II, "Decision to Terminate Proceedings against Raska Lukwiya," ICC-02/04–01/05, July 11, 2007, http://www.icc-cpi.int/iccdocs/doc/doc297945.pdf.

80 *The Prosecutor v. Dominic Ongwen*, "Case Information Sheet," ICC-PIDS-CIS-UGA-02–003/15_Eng, updated March 26, 2015.

81 Article 53(1)(a)-(c) of the Rome Statute, http://www.icc-cpi.int/NR/rdonlyres/ADD16852-AEE9-4757-ABE7-9CDC7CF02886/283503/RomeStatutEng1.pdf.

82 The Office of the Prosecutor, ICC, "Situation in Mali: Article 53.1 Report," January 16, 2013.

83 ICC, "Situation in the Central African Republic II: Article 53(1) Report: Executive Summary," September 24, 2014, http://www.icc-cpi.int/iccdocs/otp/SAS-CARII-Art53-1-Executive-Summary-24Sept2014-Eng.pdf.

84 The Office of the Prosecutor, ICC, "Report on Preliminary Examination Activities 2014," December 2, 2014.

85 Ibid.

86 Case of Samantar Mohammed Ali (former General in the Somali National Army (SNA), Minister of Defence, First Vice President and Prime Minister of Somalia) facing allegations of torture brought in US courts; see case report by TRIAL, http://www.trial-ch.org/en/resources/trial-watch/trial-watch/profiles/profile/1067/action/show/controller/Profile/tab/legal-procedure.html.

References

Brownlie, Ian. 1998. *Principles of Public International Law*. 5th edn. Oxford: Oxford University Press.

Heuveline, Patrick. 1998. "'Between One and Three Million': Towards the Demographic Reconstruction of a Decade of Cambodian History (1970–1979)." *Population Studies* 52(1): 49–65.

Human Rights Watch. 2014. "Rwanda: Justice after Genocide, 20 Years on." http://www.hrw.org/sites/default/files/related_material/2014_March_Rwanda_0.pdf.

Human Rights Watch. 2015. *World Report 2015: Events of 2014*. New York: Seven Stories Press.

MacLean, Emi. 2013. *Judging a Dictator: The Trial of Guatemala's Ríos Montt*. London: Open Society Foundations.

Olsen, Tricia, Leigh Payne, and Andrew Reiter. 2010. *Transitional Justice in Balance: Comparing Processes, Weighing Efficacy*. Washington, DC: United States Institute of Peace Press.

Open Society Justice Initiative. 2015. "Recent Developments at the Extraordinary Chambers in the Courts of Cambodia: March 2015." Briefing Paper. Open Society Foundations.

Robertson, Geoffrey. 2015. "Report on the International Crimes Tribunal of Bangladesh." International Forum for Democracy and Human Rights.

Sikkink, Kathryn. 2011. *The Justice Cascade: How Human Rights Violations Are Changing World Politics*. New York: W.W. Norton & Company, Inc.

Sikkink, Kathryn, and Hun Joon Kim. 2013. "The Justice Cascade: The Origins and Effectiveness of Prosecutions of Human Rights Violations." *Annual Review of Law and Social Science* 9: 269–285.

TRIAL, ECCHR (European Center for Constitutional and Human Rights), and FIDH. 2015. "Universal Jurisdiction Annual Review 2015."

Index